Spiritually Speaking

~ A Metaphysical Interpretation of Spiritual, Religious, and Modern Day Secular Terms for those who are more spiritual than religious ~

Rev. Dr. Bil Holton
Rev. Dr. Cher Holton

Prosperity Publishing House
Durham, NC 27712

Spiritually Speaking

First edition 2014

© 2014 Bil & Cher Holton

Thank you for respecting the hard work of these authors.

Discover other titles by Bil & Cher Holton at
http://www.YourSpiritualPractice.com/products

All Rights reserved

The *Spiritually Speaking* text may be quoted in any form (written, visual, electronic, or audio) up to and inclusive of one hundred twenty five (125) words without the express written permission of the publisher, providing notice of copyright appears on the title or copyright page of the work as follows:

> The quotation(s) contained herein are from Spiritually Speaking: *A Metaphysical Interpretation of Spiritual, Religious, and Modern Day Secular Terms For Those Who Are More Spiritual Than Religious*. Copyright 2014 by Rev. Dr. Bil Holton and Rev. Dr. Cher Holton, and published by Prosperity Publishing House. Used by permission. All rights reserved.

Quotations and/or reprints in excess of one hundred twenty five (125) words, as well as other permission requests, including commercial use, must be approved in writing by the Permissions Office, Prosperity Publishing House, 1405 Autumn Ridge Drive, Durham, NC 27712.

Cover design by: Cher Holton

Library of Congress Control Number: 2014910727

ISBN: 978-1-89-309509-0

Dedication

This book is dedicated to humankind and offered for humankind's spiritual growth, illumination, and enlightenment. It is for those who want to stop "no-ing" themselves and start "knowing" themselves.

~ Spiritually Speaking ~

Introduction

This glossary is written for New Thought truth seekers AND "*Church Alumni, Unfulfilled Church Attenders, and Church Avoiders*" to use as a higher consciousness resource as they continue their spiritual growth 'plugged into' and/or outside of the limitations of mainstream religion.

It is written with the knowledge that there are a growing number of people involved in New Thought spiritual communities who have outgrown their religious roots, and it is written with the understanding that there are more *church alumni* and *church avoiders* in America and throughout the world than there are church goers.

What's more, it should come as no surprise that there are tens of millions of *unfulfilled church attenders* who are not having their emotional, intellectual, and spiritual needs met within mainstream religion.

This worldwide demographic is much more than a simple trend. It is the result of a fantastic shift in global consciousness which is changing the way we see ourselves in relation to, well, everything!

And this stunning shift in human consciousness is literally transforming the way we see and experience spirituality and religion. The shift is absolutely monumental and enduring. It is a testament to humankind's perennial search for who we are, why we are, where we've come from, and where we're going.

New Thought truth seekers, church alumni, unfulfilled church attenders, and *church avoiders* are people at the leading edge of this consciousness shift. They are people who are more spiritual than religious, They are seeking deeper meaning, higher purpose, and transcendent spiritual experiences outside the bounds of mainstream, dogmatic religions that are characterized by empty ritual, blind adherence to religious teachings that are out of step with our time, belief in the authority of an external deity, placing undue emphasis on monetary commitments, and demanding an unquestioned belief in a literally-interpreted inerrancy of scripture that has been proven to be filled with mistranslations and errors.

This glossary moves beyond those "mistranslations and errors." It stays outside of dogmatic blinders and the underbelly of religion. It offers a grander, more spiritual perspective on important concepts, events, human qualities, and relationships that either dampen our spiritual growth or foster our collective enlightenment.

That being said, we must add that there is no exoteric, spiritual, religious, esoteric, theosophical, anthroposophical, allegorical, metaphorical, literal interpretation of sacred scripture, and/or secular writing that is definitive by itself, including this glossary. Interpretations are just that – interpretations!

~ Spiritually Speaking ~

While interpretations and translations are offered to shed more light on the path of Self-discovery, they can occasionally miss the mark, no matter how well intended, because ultimate truths aren't known. Spiritual teachers, including myself, are still trying to connect the dots when it comes to ultimate knowledge. So, it's not rocket science to suggest that even the best thinking is only an approximation of Ultimate Reality.

This glossary, this well-thought-out approximation, is written for people who are forward thinking and open-minded. We combine ancient truth traditions, spiritual and esoteric knowledge, and cutting edge science in order to offer the clearest, most sane, and 21st Century relevant content to assist you in your spiritual growth.

Picking up this glossary will require you to keep an open mind as you expand your awareness, and broaden and deepen your knowledge of the esoteric meanings associated with even the most mundane things. People, animals, plants, places, and events are interpreted as aspects within our own consciousness (thoughts, emotions, tendencies, inclinations, habits, talents, skills, and behaviors, etc.).

A Note About the Semi-colon:

This glossary is presented to you, the reader, as a work in progress. You will notice that each reference ends with a semi-colon instead of a period to reinforce the notion that there is more room for growth when it comes to understanding a particular reference.

However, in its present form, this version of *Spiritually Speaking* offers substantive interpretations of spiritual, religious, and secular terms as well as whimsical definitions of modern terms that will be of tremendous value to students of truth who are pursuing a more enlightened perspective of thinking, being, and doing.

Acknowledging Our Sources:

Great care has been taken – and continues to be taken for any updates – in the compilation, editing, revelatory inspiration, esoteric deduction, and wordsmithing to do justice to the myriad authorities, dictionaries, glossaries, lexicons, and metaphysical literature consulted for this monumental work.

We have drawn from the esoteric knowledge and teachings of a wide variety of faith traditions as well as my own thoughtful study, meditation, and revelatory experiences. We are privileged to have learned and continue to learn from the following esoteric perspectives: Amazonian, American, Arabic, Assyrian, Australian, Aztec, Babylonian, Baha'i, Brazilian, Buddhist, Celtic, Chaldean, Chinese, Cuban, Egyptian, Gaelic, Germanic, Greek, Hawaiian, Hebrew, Hindu, Inca, Islamic, Jamaican, Japanese, Latin, Mayan, Mexican, Norse, Pali, Palestinian, Persian, Phoenician, Roman, Russian, Scandinavian, Sumerian, Swahili, Tibetan.

~ Spiritually Speaking ~

We also consulted sources like: Anthroposophy, Burmese, Confucianism, Christian Science, Free Masonry, Gnosticism, Hellenism, Jainism, Judaism, Kabbalism, Metaphysics, Mohism, Native American, Religious Science, Rosicrucian, Sikhism, Shintoism, Sufism, Taoism, Theosophy, and Zoroastrianism.

We hope you will find this glossary interesting, easy to navigate, validating your own inner wisdom, stimulating, riveting at times, fun, edutaining, and most of all enlightening.

* * * * * * *

Aaron's Rod: the spinal cord:

Abacusic Intellect: primitive intelligence; basic computation; outdated thinking;

Abaddon, Apollyon: a hellish thought; the implosive nature of error; (The name given to the angel of the bottomless pit);

Abandon: fear; failure to appreciate current opportunities, abilities, and contributions; disillusionment; seeking redefinition;

Abandonment Rate: the rate at which we drop spiritually-oriented thoughts for worldly-oriented thoughts, whims and desires; (In online marketing lingo, the abandonment rate refers to the patterns of use of virtual shopping carts. Brick and mortar shoppers rarely abandon their carts, but online shoppers abandon virtual shopping carts quite frequently.);

Abba: the Eternal Presence; the One Reality;

Abbey(s): peace of mind; religious contentment; religious dedication;

Abbot-like: conventional religious thinking; religious discipline;

Abbreviation(s): thinking there are shortcuts to enlightenment;

Abdomen-like: stomaching hardships; digesting life experiences; intuitive instincts;

Abduction: manipulation by ultra-strict doctrinal biases; feeling a lack of control; a sense of coercion or unwanted compliance; a sense of loss of control;

Aberration: deviation from our norm or what we think is right and acceptable; atypical; an error in judgment; a subtle body that appears unexpected;

Abhayan Resolve: our fearlessness and courageousness; (In Gnostic terms, abhayan refers to one who does not cause fear in others);

Abhiseka: bathing in sacred water; cleansing our mind, body, and soul; (Abhiseka is a Sanskrit term for devotional, prayer, or religious rite);

Abhorrence: uncongeniality; a divinity-denying thought or inclination;

Abiding: dwelling mentally in sacred thoughts, words, and actions;

Abiogenesis: the process in which our ideas come into conscious awareness; (See Spontaneous Generation);

Abnormalities: thoughts, feelings, and actions that are out of sync with our divine nature;

Abominable Ailments (Stench): longstanding error orientations that we have not decided to outgrow;

Aborigine: primordial, natural instincts;

Abortion: refusing to apply, or outright rejecting, a newly formed idea or insight that we believe is too premature or has produced too much cognitive dissonance for us to handle; getting rid of thoughts and/or concepts we believe are too transformative for our neophyte sensitivities; a miscarriage of higher knowledge;

About-Face Beeper: our conscience; moral scruples; the still small voice;

Above: high ideas; lofty ideas; ambitious pursuits; transpersonal experiences;

Ab Ovo (From the Egg) Unfoldment: our unfoldment as conscious beings from the Multiverse to the universes of which we become a part of as we add to the story of our spiritual enlightenment;

Abracadabra-ing: employing mindfulness meditation, affirmative prayer, and positive affirmations as the open sesames to healing and enlightenment;

Abroad: our propensity for seeking sensory experiences; our desire for more expansive perspectives; experiencing astral projection, out-of-body experiences, and hypnogogic visions;

Abscess: an old, underlying resentment, doubt, or negative emotion that needs to be expressed; inflammatory thoughts; fermenting thoughts over hurts and slights;

Absent Healing: healing that occurs when healers are not in direct physical contact with the people being healed; (See Remote Healing);

Ab-Sooian Space: the openness and expansiveness we create in our consciousness when we delve into the greater mysteries of esoteric knowledge; (Ab-Soo is a mystic name for space, the waters of the universe);

Absolute, the: the Eternal Perfect Presence; Supreme Consciousness; the Infinite Isness; Brahma; the All-pervading Presence; Divine Mind; Ultimate Reality; the Unloosed and Freed;

Abstinence: the ability to abstain from sense appetites that limit and/or block our spiritual growth;

Abundance: living at the speed of our Christ (Buddha, Krishna, Allah, Great Spirit) Consciousness;

Abundance Kiosk: We are pre-wired for abundance. Abundance is part of our spiritual DNA. It is in a "supply booth" that never runs on empty. (If we are having less than perfect experiences in our finances, our relationships, our work, our health, our attitude, our life ~ just know that it is simply an outer manifestation of what is going on in our subconscious. And we have the power to make changes! As a matter of spiritual fact, our greater good is never more than a thought away! It's closer than the objects that appear in our rearview mirror. It's as close as our next breath. It's as close as our next thought, intention, word, choice, or action. (It's as close as the glossary you are holding. We can SAY we believe we live in an abundant universe, that we always have everything we need at the point of need, that there is plenty to share and plenty to spare ... but if our choices don't support and feed those beliefs, we will not see them manifest in our life! In order to experience the highest, most elevated manifestation of our spiritual laws of prosperity and abundance, we need to make conscious choices, with serious intention);

Abuse: chronically thinking error thoughts, making error-prone choices, and taking error-ridden actions; being 'molested' by our error-proneness;

Abysmal Asphyxiation: the appalling feeling of suffocation we experience just after we know we've done something terribly wrong that most likely cannot be repaired; deep anxiety caused by the denial of our innate divinity;

Abyss-like: the denial of our divinity; our repressed emotional depths; low spirits; depression; deep disappointment; no basis in reality; (Psychologists tell us that depression is associated with a particular gene, called the 5-HTTLPR, which comes in two forms, the long and short. The short allele is undesirable to have because it rids the brain of the neurotransmitter serotonin needed to mitigate depressive symptoms. The good allele gene protects us from depression by making us resilient. Denying our innate divinity is associated with the 5-HTTLPR gene);

Academy: religious, spiritual, mental, emotional, and physical discipline;

Academy Awards: mastering skin school (the academy) lessons (awards) through superior religious, spiritual, mental, emotional, and physical discipline;

Acadia Quality: the epitome of innocence; gentleness;

Accelerator: personal drive toward achievement; pushing ourselves; ambitious progress;

Accelerant(s): inflammatory thoughts that produce intense emotions which ignite robust actions; (In firefighting terms, an accelerant is a flammable fuel (often liquid) used by arsonists to increase size or intensity of a premeditated fire.);

Accent(s): employing esoteric language to deepen and expand literal conceptions of spiritual truths;

Accessories: multiple interpretive meanings of religious and spiritual terms;

Accident: the belief in discontinuity and disconnections; being out-of-sync with the flow of life; a karmic wake-up call; a series of contributing factors that mature into an incident;

Accomplice(s): corroborating error thoughts, words, choices, and actions;

Accumulated Consciousness: the sum total of all we have ever thought, seen, intuited, visualized, said, or done during all of our incarnational and pre-incarnational experiences;

Ace: power and authority; hidden qualities and resources that are powerful and peerless; heralded achievement;

Aceldama: the price of error;

Acheron: the pain and discomfort caused by our sense-oriented five senses; (In Greek mythology, Acheron was known as the river of woe, and was one of the five rivers of the underworld);

Aches and Pains: disharmony and dis-ease in soul growth; error thoughts and choices that limit our spiritual growth; opportunities to realign our mind, body, and soul; the consequences of error thoughts;

Achit Stain: the absence of an intellectual understanding of secret esoteric knowledge; (A Sanskrit term for unknowing);

Acid: extreme negativity; unconscionable hatred, rage, or anger; vengeful motives; sharp and biting sarcasm; caustic relationships; untrustworthiness; betrayal; a concern that something is, or may, 'eat at us' and is cause for caution; anxiety; worrisome thoughts;

Acmeistic Steps: our tendency to react negatively against higher spiritual thought and settle for literal thinking when it comes to scriptural interpretation;

Acne, Dermatitis, Eczema: feeling awkward with the image we're projecting; embarrassment on the verge of erupting; error thoughts; feeling as if we're imperfect manifesting as blemishes;

Acorn(s): potentialities; possibilities becoming probabilities; spiritual and religious terms, concepts, tenets;

Acosmistic Cosmology: believing the universe is not real, but simply maya;

Acoustics of Amnesty: the feelings of relief, joy, and bliss we receive when our errors are pardoned by our next Christcentric choice;

Acoustics of Experience: Spirit is concerned with the vernacular of the heart of an experience, not the ego-burdened event itself. The acoustics of experience, any experience, tweaks us, prunes us, even prods us to honor the truth of who we really are. It is the tone of our responses that determines the quality of our lives. We have an opportunity to learn from each experience. Each experience is a catalyst for growth. Experiences, then, are a very real form of compulsory education. (We all receive *in*formation at the rate of 500 billion bits per second. What really matters is the *out*formation – what we *do* with the *in*formation. Will we use it to express our Godness through our goodness, or our godlessness through fear, greed, or selfishness?);

Acrobat(s): flexible ideas; agile inclinations; being able to juggle religious and spiritual concepts and paradigms;

Actor, Actress: our small 's' self (the large 'S' Self is our Divine Nature, the Extraordinary Us); pretending our materialistic ambitions are spiritual aspirations;

Acupoint: an instance in our awareness when we are receptive to a poignant esoteric teaching; a point on our body treated by acupressure and/or acupuncture;

Acupuncture: aligning our worldly form with our spiritual essence; restfulness; a mini Sabbath;

Acupressure: a form of healing that uses the fingers to apply manual pressure to specific bodily pressure points; applying positive affirmations and denials along with physical therapeutic touch in treating physical ailments;

Acute Malnutrition: listening to a fundamental message in a mainstream religious service on any given Sunday; (In nutrition industry terms, acute malnutrition means rapid deterioration in our nutritional status over a short period of time.);

Acutomancy: divining by tossing pins and needles on a flat surface and then interpreting the meaning of the patterns they form;

Adam: the inverted *ashvattha* tree (its roots are in heaven and its branches on earth);

Adamant Thingamajigging: casting off a part of us that doesn't work anymore - things like lack of confidence, bad habits, debilitating addictions, recurring doubts, chronic fears, and negative attitudes – you know, things that minus us;

Adamic Amnesia: forgetting that we are spiritual beings who have chosen a human experience; (Tahmurath is the Iranian Adam, That Esmun is the Egyptian Adam);

Adamic Arsenic: the unenlightened ego is poisonous (arsenic) to our spiritual growth;

Adamic Consciousness: sense consciousness;

Adam Kadmon, Original Man: our ability to potentialize thoughts and generate their offspring (subsequent thoughts) at will; (In the Kabbalah, Adam Kadmon is the first of the highly complex 'Five Spiritual Worlds' in creation which spawns the divine will and plan for all subsequent creations, cosmic and quantum. The Adam, Adam Ha-Rishon, in the Bible prototyped all future humans on earth only.);

Adder: sly and/or cunning inclinations;

Addict(s): surrendering our power to our warped egocentric nature; denying our responsibility to become the best Christ (Buddha, Krishna, Allah, Great Spirit) we can be;

Addiction(s): our obsession to reincarnate causing us to suffer through another unnecessary skin school experience; (According to mythologist Joseph Campbell, the existential dilemma is that in the beginning we were united with the Eternal Presence, but separated from the Source, and now must find a way to return);

Addictiondom: trying to accelerate ourselves out of our melancholy, but only managing to accelerate our addictions;

Additive Monster(s): a divinity-denying error thought that adds monstrous choices and actions as its consequences;

Address: our *home address* is our spiritual address; our *biological address* is our incarnational address;

Adept-like Attributes: attaining Christ (Buddhic, Vishnuic, Allahic, Krishnic) Consciousness; mastering incarnational living; skilled in esoteric knowledge and wisdom; attaining illumination and mastery in applying spiritual teachings and principles;

Adhyatmic Address: our spiritual home which is our Christ Consciousness or the Kingdom of God; (Adhyatm is a Sanskrit term for inner self);

Adi-Buddha: the highest essence of the One Presence, the Wondrous Being, the Infinite Isness;

Adonai: a prayerful appeal for psychic communion;

Adrasteia Susceptibility: karma caused by our own thoughts, words, and actions:

Adultery: Choosing error thoughts, words, and actions over spiritual thoughts, words, and actions; rickets of disharmony within our thoughts;

Advent: the coming of (preparation for) enlightenment: the reiteration (coming again, repetition) of spiritual thoughts into conscious awareness:

Adventure Novel: any of our particular skin school experiences;

Adversary, the: the unenlightened, sense-soaked ego bent on denying its divine origins;

Advertisement: the way we show up in the world; the actions we take – or don't take;

Aeonic Endowment: having a highly transformative spiritual thought that has a lasting effect on our awareness and is so potent that it lays the groundwork for the next highly transformative spiritual idea:

Aerial Fire: the level of excitation when a spiritual idea comes into contact with an egocentric thought and transforms it into its higher spiritual essence:

Aeromancy, Chaomancy: divination using shapes seen in the sky;

Aesopic Immunity: our penchant for using simple stories, fables, and analogies about basic animal instincts to understand how we can improve ourselves;

Aether: the cosmic aspect of Supreme Consciousness (Adi-buddha) expressing Itself as physicality; the expansiveness of the transcendent aspect of our super-consciousness;

Affirmations: positive statements (autosuggestions) declaring the efficacy of truth; (Never make an assertion, no matter how true it may look on the surface, that you do not want to see manifest in your life. Think about this phrase. It forces you to be really aware of what you are saying. Even something as simple as "I am so tired." Or "I'm broke." You don't want to see those things manifest, so don't say them! And by becoming aware of what you are saying, you are also becoming aware of what you are thinking! Affirmations launch a powerful vocal vibration that holds the key to unbelievable spiritual growth that leads to your ability to divinely order your experience); [R. Spencer, T. Verstynen, M. Brett, and R. Ivry share their findings in "Cerebellar activation during discrete and not continuous timed movements: An fMRI study," *Neuroimage*, 2007, June, 36 (2): 378-87: "The mere repetition of a sound or phase over a period of time significantly reduces symptoms of stress, anxiety, depression, and anger, while improving the practitioner's perception of the quality of life and spiritual well-being."];

Afflictions: error thoughts, attitudes, choices, and actions: (In Buddhist philosophy, ten general forms of afflictions are described: attachment, hostility, pride, ignorance, doubt, seeing the false 'I' as real, seeing the false 'I' as lasting or wrongly believing self to end with death, beliefs in wrong views, beliefs that certain behaviors lead to liberation, and wrong views in general. In Christianity, the seven deadly sins are our worst afflictions.); the consequences of error judgment;

Afterlife: the continuation of existence after our earthly transition;

Afternoon: our waking consciousness; the time just after a revelatory experience [dawn] when we find ourselves processing the esoteric teachings we have just learned and before we reach a state of confusion [darkness] because we've learned just enough to have more questions; middle age;

Agama: acquiring spiritual knowledge;

Agapae, Agape: charity; loving kindness; harmonizing and synthesizing spiritual and material thoughts; unconditional love; universal love;

Agathodaimon: benevolent genius; (Agathodaimon was believed to be a Hellenistic hybrid god who was a beneficent spirit and protector of Alexandria);

Agathon: the Universal Presence; the Eternal God Essence; Plato's Supreme Deity;

Age: cycle; stage; aeon; epoch; level of spiritual maturation;

Ageless Wisdom: the accumulated total of the esoteric teachings shared by the world's great spiritual teachers throughout time immemorial; (In *Nicholas of Cusa: In Search of God and Wisdom: Essays in Honor of Morimichi Watanabe by the American Cusanus Society*, editors Gerald Christianson and Thomas M. Izbicki quote Cusa: If anyone held that all things are in created in wisdom, and if another person held that all created things are in the Logos, would they not be saying the same thing? Even though there seems to be a difference in expression, yet they express the same idea, for the Logos of creation in whom all things were created can be nothing other than divine wisdom." Pg. 112);

Ageratum Quality: steadfastness; commitment; devotion;

Agnostic Tendencies: the strong assumption that we cannot possibly know or understand all higher truths;

Agon Shū: believing we can achieve enlightenment in our current incarnation; (Agon Shū is a Neo-Buddhist religious society that sees its teachings as the teachings of Buddha);

Ahankaric Tendencies: our egotistical, self-aggrandizing proclivities;

Ah-hi Capacity: cosmically-oriented, universal spiritual thoughts:

Ahi Anomoly: an error thought that attempts to strangle a newly-formed spiritual insight;

Ahimsa: causing no harm or discomfort; (A Pali term meaning 'do not injure');

Ahura Mazda: the Universal Presence; (In the Zoroastrian tradition Ahura Mazda is God or Ormazd);

AIDS: feelings of defenselessness and vulnerability that negatively affect the immune system;

Aikido-like Redirection: focusing on the 'way of the harmonious spirit' in order to reframe and/or redirect the energies of error thoughts to their highest spiritual essences; a kind of jujutsuing of error to establish harmony;

Ain Soph: (See Eyn Soph);

Air: abstract thoughts; transcendental intuitiveness; superior comprehension;

Airbag: the ready availability of a support system; optimistic thinking; a *deployed air bag* implies protection being administered; (See White Light Technique);

~ *Spiritually Speaking* ~

Airborne Glyphs: symbolize ascension into higher states of consciousness; the morphing of an insight in consciousness to a completely formed thought and/or concept; the enthronement of a spiritual urge into a transformational spiritual practice; the attainment of adeptship;

Airbrushing: describing events (painting a picture) in glowing terms during a guided meditation: (In the nail care industry, airbrushing is the art of applying nail decorations with an airbrush gun.);

Air Conditioning: yawning; (It's easy to be offended when someone yawns while you're talking. But that yawn may not mean what you think. A growing number of researchers believe the purpose of this little-understood behavior is to cool the brain, says a research review published in *Frontiers in Evolutionary Neuroscience*. Changes in climate affect how often people yawn. People are nearly twice as likely to yawn when they are surveyed during the winter, when they could inhale cool air to reduce the temperature of the brain, says a follow-up study, published in 2011 in *Frontiers in Evolutionary Neuroscience*. Participants yawned less when surveyed in the early summer, when temperatures outdoors were about the same as the human body. For centuries, yawning was thought to remove "bad air" from the lungs and increase oxygen circulation in the brain. Recent studies have discredited this old belief);

Aircraft: desiring to have or actually experiencing, highly spiritual perspectives; *being hijacked* suggests we have allowed a corrosive thought or belief to derail our spiritual progress; a *plane crash* represents the sudden decision to abandon a line of thought we consider to be potentially disastrous; moving through higher dream realms;

Air Freshener: enjoying life's simple pleasures; over-powering fresheners suggest over-consumptive sensory appetites; tact; diplomacy;

Airport(s): our waking consciousness; our ability to generate new insights (departures) and field incoming insights (arrivals);

Air Raid: feeling threatened by highly intellectual thoughts and concepts;

Aisa: karma; reincarnational residue;

Aisle(s): conventional thinking; traditional perspectives;

Ajaic Thoughts: unborn and/or unexpressed thoughts;

Ajna: clear vision; the Eternal Present; (See Third Eye);

Aka Cords: the mystical 'super strings' that connect our consciousness with everything else in the universe;

Akashic Records: an *'aetheric library'* imprinted on an omnipresent *akasha* (a soniferous ether) so we can mentally 'Google' all of the past, present, and future knowledge of the universe anytime we want when we are in certain states of heightened consciousness; depending on our psychic sensitivity and Akashic interests we can even 'bookmark' various knowledge banks so the information is available to us instantly; the memory of the hum of physicality;

Akicita Parameters: our conscience; (In Lakota Sioux terms, akicita are village police chosen among the worthiest members of the warriors);

Alabadoic Mind Action: the act of praying: (In Inca Shamanistic terms, *alabado* means prayer);

Alabaster Jar: denotes receiving incredible purity and great wisdom and pouring both out on humankind; (White alabaster is associated with the Egyptian Goddess Bast [hence alaBASTer] and Sophia [Divine Wisdom];

Al-Aitic Thoughts: fiery thoughts and/or tendencies;

Alarm: our conscience; an illness and/or injury; potential risk;

Alarm Clock: being acutely aware of wake-up calls; gaining victory over darkness; being constantly vigilant; choosing movement over inertia; anxiety or nervousness;

Albatross: our incarnational burden; physicality itself;

Album: a collection of nostalgic memories; remembrances; the record of our composite incarnations; (See Quantum Self);

Alchemical Birth: going from darkness into the light; elevating our Adamic consciousness to Christ Consciousness; moving from coma consciousness (egocentric awareness) to super-consciousness;

Alchemical Quincunx: denotes the whole being more, much more, than the sum of its parts; able to ascend from human consciousness to higher spiritual consciousness;

Alchemy: the transmutation process of our spiritual unfoldment; seeking unity between the many and the One; creating unity beyond diversity; turning base thoughts into spiritual thoughts; purging alloys (error thoughts) from pure metal (spiritual thoughts);

Alcoholism: liquid lunacy; the denial of our ability to master the human experience; *Self* denial through *self* diminishment; self-rejection and Self-rejection;

Algorithm(s): spiritual and religious teachings designed as life instructions;

Alibi Management: excuse-ology; pretense camouflage; false acquittals;

Alice in Wonderland: the story of our incarnational journey;

Alien(s): sensory appetites that we allow to kill our spiritual aspirations; foreign concept; an uncharacteristic thought;

Alien Abduction: anytime we mindlessly allow a self-defeating habit or action to resurface that we thought we had outgrown;

Alignment, Attunement: the process of our human self becoming indivisibly attuned with our Divine Self; the unimpeded relationship and establishment of a direct connection between our human awareness and our super-conscious awareness; consciously joining our human self with the Extraordinary Us (the Christ Us, Buddha Us, Allah Us, Krishna Us, Great Spirit Us, Vishnu Us) so that our human essence is raised to its higher vibratory level which is Cosmic Consciousness;

Alignment Antipathy: disharmony between our worldly ego and our divine Self;

Alimony: karma;

Alkahestic Consciousness: Christ Consciousness; an illuminated consciousness; (Coined by Paracelsus, alkahest was believed to be the Philosopher's Stone);

Alkahestic Thoughts: highly spiritual thoughts that can dissolve the most encrusted and rigid error thoughts;

All, the: the Boundless; Limitless; Infinitely Macro and Infinitely Micro; God; Universal Presence; the One; the emptiness of inner space and the fullness of inner space;

Allah: the Infinite Isness that underwrites the universe; the Supreme Being of Islam;

Alley-like: chancy shortcuts; risky peripheral lines of thought; narrow points of view and/or interests;

Alligator Aptitude: clarity in the midst of ambiguity and chaos; fluidity; fearlessness; protecting vulnerabilities; precise and poised; well-developed sense of timing; strength and stealth;

Allopathic Perspective: represents mainstream religion as opposed to nontraditional religion and New Thought spirituality; (In medicine, allopathy refers to the difference between Western medicine and homeopathy);

All Seeing Eye, Frontal Eye, Central Eye, Third Eye, Eye of Immortality: living in the eternal present; (From the point of view of the Third Eye in relation to the two eyes that flank it, the left eye [moon] relates to the past; the right eye [sun] corresponds to the future; and the Third Eye alludes to the eternal present);

Almond Aspect: purity; virgin birth;

Almanac: our infatuation with trends and predictions; stereotyped attitudes; our desire for certainty;

Alms: a receptive state of affairs; spiritual food;

Aloe: a healing disposition;

Alogon: irrational thoughts;

Alpha: our divine Self before our descent (fall) into matter; the first emanation of our cosmic beingness; (See Omega);

Alphabet: conceptualizing the universe and our relationship to it in writing;

Alphabiotic Thinking: the belief that faith is a necessary condition in the healing process and that all dis-ease is the result of an imbalance and/or blockage in energies essential to health and well-being; (Alphabiotics is the brainchild of Dr. V. B. Chrane who started practicing it in the 1920's);

Alphatizing: being able to establish the perfect beginning, inauguration, starting point, origin, commencement; inducing an outflowing energy; creating an initial *out*picturing;

~ Spiritually Speaking ~

Altar(s): physical body which enshrines our innate divinity; open heart; cusp in consciousness where one level of awareness is sacrificed for another; an *altar call* is devoting ourselves to live at the speed of our Christ Consciousness;

Altered States of Awareness: dogmatic thinking; the repression of women; negative emotions; religious fundamentalism's unwavering attachment to the inerrancy of and the literal interpretation of Biblical scripture;

Alternative Medicine: In today's limited understanding of medicine, any healing therapy or practice that falls outside of what is considered to be conventional medicine; [One day, traditional medicine will be considered alternative medicine and nontraditional medicine will be seen as mainstream medicine]; (Sharon Begley, senior health and science correspondent at Reuters, says depression and other mental illnesses can be treated by rewiring the neural pathways in the brain instead of flooding the brain with problematic drugs.);

Aluminum: corrosion-resistant attitude; thinly disguised strength;

Alzheimer's Dis-ease: our refusal to deal with the world by isolating ourselves; our fear turned inward; a cutting off of the vital force that runs through our brain;

Amaranth-like: timelessness; immortality;

Amber: magnetic attraction; harnessing the flow of life; electromagnetism;

Ambitious Carding: the psychosomatic process where a particular truth principle surfaces into our conscious awareness to help center us when we face life challenges, disappointments, setbacks, etc.; (In magic terms, an ambitious card is a card effect where a selected card continually rises to the top of the deck after being placed into the middle of the deck.)

Ambrosia: immortality; intellectual nectar; the upward arc of an intellectual evolutionary cycle;

Ambulance: feeling a sense of panic or uneasiness about a health concern; putting off a health issue until the last possible moment; a spiritual thought replacing an error thought; a healthy habit replacing a bad habit; our white blood cells responding to a physical wound;

Ambush: subconscious material surfacing; ulterior motives expressed;

Amen: permanency; what is true; a spiritual certainty; it is so; Om-ness objectified; (Its use in Judaism dates back to its earliest texts. In Islam amen is the standard close to supplications. In Christianity, it usually ends prayers and hymns, but is also used to denote strong agreement as in "amen to that" or "Do I hear an amen?"

Amethyst-ness: humility; piety; spiritual discernment; transformation; dream recall;

Ammonia: quarrelsome disposition; repulsiveness; breathlessness;

Ammunition: having an arsenal of thoughts, words, and actions to defend our point of view; explosive potential; *running out of ammunition* suggests having only a basic knowledge about a New Thought subject and feeling we can't hold our end of the conversation;

Amnesia: denying, avoiding, and/or repressing our innate divinity and any thought of our being a spiritual being having a human experience; an incarnational experience;

Amphisbaenian Mistake: denotes our misguided belief that we can open our Third Eye (the tickling of the ant) by trying to be more spiritual and material at the same time; (Amphisbaenas are ant-eating lizards with a head on both ends, and their name literally means 'goes both ways.');

Amphitheater: the physical world; consciousness itself (Universal Mind); the universe; the Multiverse;

Amputation, Pruning: cutting a bad habit, materialistic perspective, outdated belief, profanity, troublesome inclination, self-deprecating tendency out of our lives;

Amritan Sustenance: the ambrosial drink (esoteric knowledge) that brings us immortality and enlightenment;

Amulets: any stone, gem, piece of jewelry, token, or charm believed to protect us against harm, injury, disease, or negative influences;

Amusement Parks: relishing playfulness and levity; *run down or vacant parks* mean we need to consider having more fun and merriment;

Amygdala's Freight: fear, doubt, anger, anxiety, depression, hopelessness, psychosis, learned helplessness, insecurity, panic, paranoia;

Analogetic Ability: the ability to interpret analogies, symbolic legends, and myths;

Ananda Moments: moments of joy, happiness, and bliss when we connect with our SuperSelf (Higher Self, Christ Self);

Anathemas: corrosive, toxic, carnal thoughts that must be dropped (banished) from our consciousness;

Ancestor(s): preceding thoughts (attitudes, emotions, choices, habits, perceptions, concepts, inclinations, intentions, belief systems); previous incarnations and/or reincarnations; the 'sins of the fathers' (preceding incarnations or thoughts) 'upon the children' (later incarnations or later thoughts and beliefs);

Ancestor Veneration: preceding thoughts, inclinations, habits, and actions that are 'worshipped' to the extent that we repeat them mindlessly, making them lifestyle habits;

Ancestral Wounds: previous errant thoughts, concepts, and beliefs that have laid the groundwork for our current woes;

Anchor(s): a feeling of stability and security; truth principles; faith; our Divine Nature; a favorite positive affirmation; meditation and affirmative prayer; groundedness and emotional stability;

Anchorless: the instability we feel when we refuse to acknowledge our Divine Core; the plight of an unenlightened ego;

Ancient Astronauts: fossilized religious beliefs; the sacred cow that jumped on the moon;

Ancient of Days: the Eternal Presence; Cosmic Christ; our Extraordinary Self in physicality; (*Atik Yomin* in Aramaic, *Palaios Hemeron* in the Greek Septuagint, and *Antiquus Dierum* in the Vulgate);

Androgynous Thoughts: positive and negative thoughts; spiritual and materialistic perspectives;

Anesthesia: conscious unconsciousness; freeing our astral inclinations from bodily restraints; feeling numbed by or unconnected with a particular situation or life event; (The term *anesthesia* was suggested by Oliver Wendell Holmes, Sr. in 1846);

Angelolatry: worshipping the power of higher thoughts to perform miracles;

Angelophany: the visible – and tangible – manifestation of an angel (believed to be guardian angels) to guide and/or protect us;

Angel(s): highest spiritual insights and intuitions; Spirit's mRNA; intermediary connective energies between spiritual thoughts and worldly thoughts; *descending angels* denote receiving spiritual insights; *ascending angels* represent elevating spiritual ideas as catalysts for further enrichment;

Angel of the Bottomless Pit: the destructive nature of suppressed negative impulses;

Angels of Darkness: formative thoughts that do not become creative thoughts; black holes in our thinking; (According to forward thinking quantum physicists, given enough energy and resources, it is within our power as spiritual beings in human form to accumulate enough gravitating material to make a black hole. At the center of the black hole, at the so-called singularity, space and time are destroyed. So even *we* can destroy space time); [In *The God Theory*, Bernard Haisch asserts that "esoteric traditions attribute primacy to light rather than matter. Arguably, matter cannot exist apart from space and time, and is dependent upon them. Einstein's relativity theory suggests that space and time are defined by the propagation of light. I argue that light propagation may actually create space and time. The zero point field inertial hypothesis implies that the most fundamental property of matter, namely mass, is also created by light." Pg. 119];

Animal Nature: base desires, instincts, and passions that remained with us when we entered our higher evolutionary level of human beingness; *taming animals* represents the mastery over our lower nature; *a herd of wild animals* indicates group instincts, prejudices, and strong biases; *young animals and pets* indicate undisciplined or under-developed qualities; *domesticated animals and pets* generally represent higher order base instincts; *branding animals* implies how we can brand ourselves through certain instinctional behaviors; *grooming animals* suggests that we are encouraging those aspects and attributes in others; *shearing or trimming animals* implies a need to curtail or better control our own base instincts;

Anima Mundi: the entire life-consciousness essence of the cosmos from the divine to the denser state of being we call physicality; the world soul; The idea of a world soul originated with Plato);

Ankh-ish: moving toward a spiritual consciousness and out of a limited egocentric state of awareness; timelessness; foreverness; (An ankh is an Egyptian cross with a looped handle denoting eternal life);

Ankle: spiritual poise; unyielding determination and self-assurance; Mercurious wings on ankles indicate psychic and astral freedom; *injury to ankles* suggests lack of understanding in regards to the relationship between spiritual principles and life itself and/or rough emotional roads that leave us feeling alone and unsupported; *broken ankles* denote martyrdom;

Annihilation: the continual unfoldment in consciousness of our spiritual dimension so that previous thoughts are transmuted and transformed into the next versions of their growing edges;

Anniversary: two or more completed cycles of skin school experience;

Anoiaic Consciousness: an unenlightened consciousness; (*Anoia* is a Greek word for lack of understanding);

Anointing: receiving spiritual illumination and wisdom; consecrating thoughts and emotions; anointing head with oil means illumination;

Anomalous Phenomenon: observed apparitions for which there is no scientific explanation;

Anorexia: a literal-only interpretation of sacred scripture; extreme fear of rejection and loss of control;

Antagonist(s): recalcitrant, combative, argumentative thoughts;

Antahkarana: the link between the middle and higher mind, the reincarnating expression of the mind; (In Hindu philosophy, antahkarana refers to the totality of two levels of mind, the higher level [Buddhi] and the middle [manas]. It is the reincarnating part of the mind);

Antelope Proclivities: grace; speed; mercurial thinking;

Antenna: heightened spiritual awareness; our conscience; our authentegrity; our morals; our sense of fair play;

Anthropocentric Arrogance: believing that human beings are the central, chosen, and most significant species on the planet; (Its critics consider this view to be the root cause of problems created by human interaction with the environment); [In The *Coming of the Cosmic Christ*, Matthew Fox posits that "the Cosmic Christ liberates us all, and like Moses of old, leads a new exodus from the bondage and pessimistic news of a Newtonian, mechanistic universe so ripe with competition, winners and losers, dualisms, anthropocentrism, and the boredom that comes when our exciting universe is pictured as a machine bereft of mystery and mysticism." Pg. 135];

Anthropomorphic Stain: (Mainstream religions are plagued by a recurrent anthropomorphic stain that soils the garment of a more enlightened awareness. Unfortunately, these religious fiefdoms seem content with the dogmatic spot and continue to sell a punitive, vengeful, goodie God 'out there' and a devilish satan personage. Although a more enlightened "spot remover" is available, mainstream religious traditions prefer the hissing sounds of religious exclusivity and separateness to vocalize their blindness. The anthropomorphic stain of blinding dogma can be cleared-up by using the world's #1 religious "stain remover" – an open mind calibrated for expanded spiritual awareness and growth);

Anthropomorphism: the ascription of human traits, qualities, attributes, and even possibly human form to divine and/or devilish beings; thinking that deities and divinities must be copies of humans; (Anthropomorphism comes from '*anthropos*' which means man. I'm going to suggest that the punitive, revengeful, anthropomorphic God of the *Hebrew Testament* and the anthropomorphic satanic devil are limbic stains, stains of our primitive reptilian brain. People who still believe in such a deity and/or its adversary are stuck in the darkness of the amygdala. It is my hope that they will venture out of their self-imposed cave of darkness into the light of their frontal lobe);

Anthroposophical Thinking: believing that we humans have been reborn many times but have reached the point where we have forgotten our spiritual origins and have become lost in the material world;

Antibiotics: affirmative prayer; meditation; truth principles; hugs; loving touch; kind words; compassion; nurturing presence;

Anti-Christ: an error-filled thought elevated to a discordant belief system that refuses to acknowledge our oneness with the Christ of us; an anti-

Christ mentality sees separation, breeds separation, and leads to a life of unnecessary isolation from Spirit; a propensity toward darkness; our divinity-denying unenlightened ego;

Antidisestablishmentarianism Antics: our propensity for not wanting to withdraw the unenlightened ego's rulership over our human personality;

Antidote: truths expressed; antibiotics applied; (See Antibiotics);

Antifreeze: any empathic courtesy that protects us from cold shoulders; an open mind to cold hard facts;

Antique(s): traditional and conventional ideas and beliefs; dogmatic principles;

Antinomianist Perspective: believing that the Gospel frees us from obedience to any particular law (scriptural, civil, or moral), and salvation is attained solely through faith and the gift of divine grace rather than through obedience to any established laws and/or rules;

Antipathy: the disharmony between our human consciousness and our super-consciousness;

Antiperspirant(s): affirmative prayer; positive affirmations and resolute denials; devotion to truth principles; integrity; being in alignment with our Authentic Self; standing in our truth; right actions;

Antiseptic Disinfectants: healing thoughts;

Ant-like Abilities: the constructive power of the Vital Force (the Eternal Presence) bringing things harmoniously and orderly into physicality; the atom-forming process between Spirit and matter; well-grounded spiritual thoughts and intentions preparing future thoughts for divine husbandry; (See Tickling of the Ant);

Anvil: the power of choice; the focused and direct application of truth principles; our ability to shape thoughts and forge new relationships;

Anxiety Disorder: the persistent belief in original sin, incurable dis-eases, and the devil; (See Persecution Bias);

Apartheid: separating our thoughts from our emotions; refusing to honor our spiritual nature so we can immerse ourselves in material pursuits;

Apartments: a series of connected thoughts;

Apavargaic Clarity: emancipating ourselves from repeated error thoughts and behaviors; refraining from repeated incarnations; (In Sanskrit, apavarga is the path of liberation);

Ape, Gorilla Tendencies: nobility; regality; strength; temperance;

Apepic Desire: the fire of passion; (Psychologists like Csikszentmihalyi encourage us to live with passion. We must give ourselves permission to play and find activities that uniquely allow us to enter into a flow state. Flow states, says Csikszentmihalyi, are those peak moments in which we become fully absorbed in an activity, when the challenges that the activity poses are high and well-matched by our talents and skills. Our every choice, action, and movement flows naturally from the last. We are passionately engaged with life); (According to Gnostic traditions *apep* is the symbol of the tempting serpent);

Apocalypse: the end of an egocentric level of awareness which has been raised to its super-conscious expression as Christ Consciousness; the end of a stale belief system; our true spiritual nature is revealed by going through a dark night of the soul;

Apocalypse Unsealed: the process of unfolding into our enlightenment; the initiatory process into the greater mysteries;

Apocalyptic Universe: is humankind in the process of unveiling our innate divinity;

Apocatastasis: restoration; a return to wholeness;

Apocrypha: dubious, questionable assumptions; debatable premises; secret, hidden knowledge;

Apocryphon: a hidden teaching;

Apodictic Affirmations: incontrovertibly true; demonstrably true and correct;

Apogee Choices: choices we make that are in direct opposition to our morals, beliefs, values and best intentions. (They're the choices that seem contradictory to our nature. They are the choices our family and friends would describe as being totally uncharacteristic of us);

Apollyon, Abaddon: the shadow side of human nature; destructive thoughts; dark thoughts; the angel of the bottomless pit [our divinity-denying nature];

Apologist: what we are when we attempt to defend our limited awareness of greater truths;

Apostasy: the willful disregard of cultivating a spiritually-oriented consciousness by choosing a materialistic world view;

Apostle-like: having divine ideas, inclinations, intentions, pious moments;

Aporrtheta: the hesitance to share mystical knowledge and eternal truths with the unenlightened; the psychic rub between a spiritual thought and a worldly thought;

Apotropaic Indignation: our susceptibility to lose our temper and assume an uncharacteristic belligerent and angry countenance when we witness an inhumane act of some kind directed at humans, animals, and even nature; (Apotropaic images are used in many cultures to ward off evil influences or malevolent spirits. Fierce Fu dogs are carved outside the entrances to Tibetan temples, gargoyles and grotesques adorn medieval cathedrals to keep evil spirits away from holy ground, hideous apotropaic figures are carved on the front of ships to protect sailors from evil spirits.)

Apparition(s): an anthropomorphic god; original sin; (See Ghost(s));

Appendix: our capacity for collecting astral seepage and/or psychic overflow caused by misuse of our higher essences;

Apperception: higher self-conscious thoughts and intuitive understandings of a higher nature;

Applause: acclaim; recognition; the feeling we get when we realize we've gotten a life-changing spiritual insight; the heightened awareness we receive when we attend to our spiritual studies;

Apple Blossom Quality: encouragement; sensuality;

Apple Proneness: experiencing bliss; love; marriage; fertility; inner peace; inner knowledge;

Appliance(s): the words we use and the gestures we make to communicate persuasively and clearly;

Apport: the dematerialization and/or rematerialization of objects from one location to another location; the sudden appearance of an object out of nowhere;

Apportation: the projecting of a thought through our conscious awareness;

Apprentice: a spiritual idea that is a follow-up to an originating spiritual idea;

Apron Features: the physical body we don when we incarnate; when a thought becomes a choice; will; a *triangle apron* represents the protective action of the will;

Aquarium: compartmentalized subconscious life patterns that have not quite surfaced but are viewed as possible contributors to our continued unfoldment;

Arbutus-like: freshness; newness; beginningness;

Arc: a spiritual insight;

Arcana: hidden wisdom;

Arch: a well-defined portal (entry and/or exit point, transition point) for spiritual growth;

Archaeology: digging into our subconscious;

Archaeologist(s): introspective thoughts and intentions;

Archangel Nature: experiencing the highest forms of spiritual thought; a most ancient and perennially powerful Universal Truth Principle;

Archebiosis: pre-existent life before an incarnation; pre-existent thoughts before they materialize into intentions;

Archery: intense focus on a well-defined goal; laser-like focus;

Archetypal Energies: recurring patterns of mental energies that pervade our collective consciousness: (In Mayan terms, recurring fields of consciousness that permeate the universe and the soul);

Archetype Dispositions: enjoying the prototype of an expanding spiritual idea;

Architecture: our pre-incarnational pattern of beingness; our inter-dimensional qualities and traits that migrate with us into our various incarnations;

Arduous Piety: refusing to reduce our religious and/or spiritual experience to flat materialism;

Argonaut Whimsicalness: our adventurous, risk-taking traits and qualities;

Argumentum ad Verecundiam: claiming we ought to accept the validity of what is said by a 'guru' just because the 'guru' said it;

Argyle: methodical thinking;

Ark-like: cradle; womb; our causal body; our quantum self (see Quantum Self); *soma pseuchicon* (soul body); the vehicle for our super-conscious, subconscious, and conscious attributes in each particular incarnation and/or reincarnation; a consciousness that has risen (floats) above base sensual appetites; the Earth; the universe; the Multiverse;

Ark of the Covenant: consciousness housed in our mind with its lower aspect called our brain in context with the limitations of physicality;

Arm(s): strength and mobility; expansiveness and reach;

Armadillo-like: protecting and/or shielding ourselves by applying the spiritual principles we know; retreatest tendencies when our basic human needs are threatened;

Armageddon: the battle between our ears (between our egocentric consciousness and our super-consciousness) when we finally overcome the world and our illumined soul rises to union with our Indwelling Spiritual Self, the Authentic Us; the eschatological battle between error thoughts and materialistic tendencies that characterize an egocentric consciousness and the immanent unfolding of a spiritually-attuned consciousness filled with Christed (Buddhic, Vishnuic, Allahic, Krishnic) thoughts and inclinations; (In the famous allegory, the forces of evil under the Persian Ahriman battled against the forces of good under Ahura-Mazda); Armageddon signifies the 'weighing' of our soul and the concept is borrowed from the Mysteries of Osiris; (The rising of the dead from their graves and from the sea of illusion represents the consummation of the process of human regeneration. The sea of fire into which those are cast who fail in the ordeal of initiation signifies the fiery sphere of our base animal instincts.

Arminian Viewpoint: believing that humankind doesn't inherit a sinful nature and is inherently good;

Armor: meditation and prayer; positive affirmations; spiritual laws; also denotes defense mechanisms;

Armored Car: feeling the need to protect our investments; our defense mechanisms; (The Motor Scout was designed and built by British inventor F.R. Simms in 1898. It was the first armed petrol engine powered vehicle ever built);

Aromatherapy: heightened sensory awareness; literally, using essential oils and other aromatic compounds for the purpose of altering our mind, mood, cognition or health;

Arranged Marriage: the union between spiritual and/or religious thoughts, concepts, and inclinations; the Cosmic Christ animating our physical forms as we enter into reincarnational and/or incarnational experiences; the alignment (marriage) between our human self and our Divine Nature;

Arrested Development: a literal-only, dogmatically-stained knowledge and understanding of sacred scripture;

Arrow-like: the fiery thrust of spiritual energies; the force of will; the driving energy toward accomplishments and achievements; a laser-like spiritual insight; male energy;

Arsenic Sulfur: denotes poisonous, satanic thoughts and desires; (In Gnostic terms, it is the 'tail' of satan);

Arson: incendiary rage that seeks destructive outlets; highly combustible emotions that intentionally target long-standing resentments and vulnerabilities;

Arteriosclerosis: our unfortunate penchant for being narrow-minded and short-sighted;

Arthritis: repressive thoughts; resistance toward or resentment of authority; rigidity toward change – planned or unplanned; rigid reaction to criticism;

Artifact(s): prior thoughts, words, choices, and actions that we value and on which we place great emphasis;

Arupic Essence: an energetic sheath (spiritual body) that is more etheralized than our gross physical bodies;

Ascension: every time a worldly thought or inclination rises to its spiritual octave we experience an ascension in consciousness; when our consciousness is filled with Christed (Buddhic, Krishnic, Vishnuic, Allahic) thoughts the degree of our ascension will be based on the quality of those thoughts;

Asceticism: refraining from unnecessary worldly appetites; (Ascetics practice asceticism not as a rejection of the enjoyment of life, or because the practices themselves are virtuous, but as an aid in the pursuit of physical, psychological, and spiritual health);

Ascribed Status: our divine status as spiritual beings in human form (clothing);

Ashes: humility; penance; the end of an era; dashed hopes and/or resolute and willing release;

Ash Wednesdayized: walking around everyday as if you are the sinner of sinners who needs to fast from the good things in life;

Ashiqic Bliss: being filled with divine love; (In *Why God Won't Go Away*, Andrew Newberg and Eugene D'Aquili report that "mystical union, rapture, ecstasy, and sexual bliss all use similar neural pathways." Pg. 125);

Ashram: a spiritual hermitage; a locus of spiritual activity devoted to religious education, music, yoga, residential religious schools for children; physiologically, the 49 spiritual energy centers (chakras) in our body – 7 major centers and 42 minor centers;

Ash Tree Mannerisms: expansiveness; mystical connection;

Asomatic: bodiless beingness;

Asparagus: persistent forging ahead; delayed gratification;

Asp-like: self-destructive thoughts and tendencies;

Aspen Urges: transformation; awareness of transcendental truths that lead to blissfulness; precognition; (Mystical union, rapture, ecstasy, and sexual bliss all use similar neural pathways according to neuroscientists);

Aspidic Intentions: viperous thoughts;

Ass (mule, donkey) Temperaments: our stubbornness, especially as it relates to trumping our spirituality with materialism; our base willful instincts;

Assassins: thoughts that are the products of hashish consumption; undue criticism; harsh feedback; emotional saboteurs;

Assemblage Point: an incarnational and/or reincarnational experience; concepts as collections of ideas;

Asters-like: generosity; a giving consciousness; (Generosity, it seems, brings more happiness than selfish indulgence. Giving just a few dollars or a few minutes to someone else may help you live longer, be happier, and be healthier. It really is better to give than receive. No longer just a mother's admonition, but a guide to happiness according to research findings by psychologists Aknin and Dunn);

Astral Aeronautics: astral travel;

Astral Body, Eidolon, Ka, Doppelganger, Chhaya: our ethereal beingness that is not limited by physical form;

Astral Plane: the next, higher vibratory, cosmic plane above the dense physical plane in which we find ourselves;

Astral Projection: the process whereby our fully conscious etheric being separates from the physical body and travels on the astral plane; (See Astral Travel);

Astral Travel: experiencing being able to move freely through different planes (dimensions) of being without the encumbrances and limitations of our physical body;

Astral Wanderlust: our intense desire to astral travel;

Asvattha: the tree of the knowledge of good and error; (See Tree of the Knowledge of Good and Error);

Asylum: retreat from life;

Ataraxia Moments: tranquil, calm, composed states of mind; (Research by neuroscientists Andrew Newberg and Eugene D'Aquili supports the possibility that mind can exist without ego, and that awareness can exist without self);

Atheistic Whims: cultivating a mental attitude that denies the existence of the One Presence;

Atlantis: a continent now submerged in the Atlantic ocean, according to esoteric teachings;

ATM Machine: borrowing from ourselves; accessing our energetic resources;

Atma: our universal, divine spirit;

Atma Jnana: experiential knowledge of our True Self; (In Pali, atma jnana means knowledge that is inseparable from the total experience of reality);

Atom Bomb: the complete dissolution of our current way of thinking, being, and doing by an incredibly explosive spiritual insight; the total annihilation of an error thought by the laser-like application of a highly potent truth principle;

At-One-Ment: every time we 'entrain' ourselves toward the vibrational power of the Christ *indivisibilized* as us; each spiritual thought, every Christ-centered intention, each step into our super-conscious awareness moves us into at-one-ment with our divine nature;

Attachments: Humankind's attachment to material wealth, status, money, power, and prestige has enslaved millions of people to the lure of outer appearances. Our tendency toward gold fever has left us with lead feet when it comes to choosing spirituality over materiality. (The truth is, says psychologist Dan Gilbert, money and material things *do* make us happy. But our misunderstanding is that we think they will bring lots of happiness for a long time, and actually they bring a little happiness for a short time.);

Attack Marketing, Ambush Marketing, Guerrilla Marketing: religious proselytizing; (In marketing lingo, attack marketing uses a series of influential social interaction techniques to build and maintain public awareness of products and services to ensure adequate buzz.);

Attendance Hibernation: becoming dissatisfied with a particular faith tradition and deciding to remain dormant for awhile before looking for another church to attend;

Attic: our multi-storied super-conscious; a *cluttered attic* denotes the accumulation of unused spiritual thoughts and insights that are lying dormant in our consciousness; a tidy and organized attic suggests an orderly progression of spiritual thoughts leading eventually to our enlightenment;

Audience: the cells and atoms of our physical bodies reacting to our thought processes;

Augury Readings: divining by interpreting signs and omens found in natural outdoor settings;

Aunic Attributes: virility; our infatuation (attachment) to physicality; In Japanese folklore, *aun* means ' the beginning and end of all things');

Aura Visibility: a biopsychic emanation from quantum beings, including us, that contains our vital energies; this personal spiritual atmosphere contains colorful spiritual energies that permeate the egg-shaped luminous auric envelope (sheath) that surrounds our physical body;

Authentegrity: allowing our soul to sing its song; the degree to which we are true to our own Essential Nature (our Authentic Self), core values and beliefs, and character, despite external pressures. It is seen as coming to terms with being in a material world and how we encounter external forces, pressures, and influences presented to us by the external world. People with a high degree of authentegrity respond to their intrinsic motives. They exercise autonomy. They dismiss the illusion of outer appearances. They make a conscious effort to choose among the extrinsic motives available to them. Their thoughts, beliefs, words, and actions originate deep from within and they are true and secure enough in their own integrity to resist self-defeating and destructive external pressures. It is one of the seven core abilities that characterizes the Extraordinary Us, our Christ Self. (See the Extraordinary You); [In *In Search of Authenticity*, Michael Kernis and Brian Goldman define authenticity as "the unimpeded operation of one's true or core self in one's daily enterprise."];

Authentegrity Leakage: the incongruence of our actions with our stated beliefs and values; (In *Born to Believe*, neuroscientist Andrew Newberg says that the "human brain has the propensity to reject any belief that is not in accord with one's own authenticity. However each person also has the biological power to interrupt detrimental, derogatory beliefs and generate new ideas. These ideas can alter the neural circuitry that governs how we behave and what we believe.");

Authentegrity Peekaboo: taking a good, hard, long introspective look in the mirror;

Autobiography: our quantum record; (See Quantum Self);

Autograph: our demonstrated behavior; our professed faith complemented by our faithful actions;

Automatic Writing: divining that involves the act of spontaneous trance writing and/or drawing pictures without knowing beforehand what is to be recorded;

Automation Addiction: depending too much on the world of outer appearances for answers instead of our own inner guidance; (According to the FAA, automation addiction is the term applied when commercial airline pilots rely too much on automation in the cockpit, thus becoming deficient in basic flying skills);

Automobile-like: refers to the human body and its mobility;

Autopoiesis: our ability to repot ourselves and, at the same time, continue to recognize ourselves; (Contemporary science has its own version of resurrection and reincarnation, known as autopoiesis. Introduced by Humberto Maturana in the early 1970's, autopoiesis refers to the ability of living systems to renew themselves continuously and to regulate this process in such a way that the integrity of their structure is maintained and enhanced);

Autopsy, Postmortem: an introspective look at the 'old' us to uncover any stale and/or pathological life patterns that we don't want to interfere with our continued spiritual growth; past life regressions; life review;

Autoscopic Perspective: seeing a double (original copy) of ourselves by looking at our body in an out-of-body experience;

Autumn: the maturing (harvesting) of our current level of spiritual knowledge and understanding with the realization that there is much more that we don't know (growing darkness);

Avalanche: feeling overwhelmed (snowed under) by a host of negative thoughts that want to crush our intention to have a mountaintop (highly spiritual) experience; the sudden weight of unexpected circumstances;

Avatar Attributes: a powerful enlightened thought (savior) that transforms our consciousness; it is a Christed thought, a Vishnu thought, an Allahic thought, a Buddha thought, a Krishna thought;

Avichian Repetition: the recurrence of gross error thoughts that 'die' and are 'reborn' without interruption, making it difficult for us to redeem ourselves from past error mindsets and habits; (In Buddhism, avichi is the lowest level of the Naraka or 'hell', into which the dead who have committed grave misdeeds may be reborn);

Avidya: the unawareness of our Spirit/matter connection;

Awahelic Spirit: the spirit of the eagle, according to Native Americans; a very elevated spiritual perspective;

Awesome Four-Letter Words: love; hope; give; pray; good; pure; true; heal; life; zeal; kind; calm; glad; safe; grow; rest; real; rich; wise; play; sing; like; neat; etc.;

Awfulizing Scripture: total dependence on dogma; misinterpretations and mistranslations;

Axe, Hatchet: our ability to clear obstacles and separate ideologies; our ability to cut through contentiousness; (In antiquity, axes were called 'thunder stones' or 'lightning stones' and symbolizes lightning bolts. The stone axe of Parashu-Rama and the stone hammer of Thor are identical.);

Axiom: a self-evident truth;

Axis Mundi: generally symbolized by the World Tree, a ladder, rope, or pole, it refers to the point where three worlds converge – heaven, earth, and hell; another interpretation is that it represents our consciousness (earth) where both heaven and hell exist as merely states of consciousness and not places we go after we die;

Ayre's Rock (Uluru): a high state of consciousness defined by the Aborigines as including dream-like states;

Ba: the immortal soul;

Babies: newly formed esoteric thoughts; newly expressed emotions; innocence; new beginnings; the start of a new incarnational experience;

Babuin(s): small, sometimes leering oftentimes silly, irritating inclinations that lie at the edge of our spiritual growth that remind us we still have work to do to rid ourselves of materialistic tendencies;

Baby's Breath Quality: innocence; transparency;

Baby Carriage: our desire to nurture new ideas and insights;

Baby Clothes: a neophyte's conception of esoteric truths;

Baby Food: literal translations of holy scripture;

Babylon: our incarnate experience with its unbridled sensory (carnal) addictions and passions;

Babymoon: the period of time when neophytes enjoy basic esoteric teachings before they are introduced to more advanced teachings; (In social networking, a relaxing or romantic holiday taken by parents-to-be before their baby is born);

Baby Shower: preparing to work on our inner child; recognizing the need for a new start;

Babysitter(s): our desire to nurture and protect new spiritual ideas;

Bachelor: the intellect without wisdom;

Bach Flower Therapy: using specific flower fragrances to alleviate certain types of emotional illnesses;

Backbone: chief organizing principle; center of stability;

Backdoor: trying to find shortcuts to enlightenment;

Backdraft: the emotional combustion that happens when repressed subconscious material bursts to the surface causing our emotions to ignite; (In firefighting terms, a backdraft occurs when heat and heavy smoke (unburned fuel particles) accumulate inside a room, depleting the available air, and then, when oxygen/air is re-introduced, the *fire triangle* is completed and leads to rapid combustion.);

Backpack, Knapsack, Rucksack: material support;

Backpedaling: retreating to the safety of the embedded theology we grew up with whenever we feel threatened by spiritual concepts;

Back Problems: *lower back* (financial worries and concerns); *middle back* (letting irritations and guilt get the best of us); *upper back* (feeling lack of emotional support);

Backsliding: the ouiji-ing around of error thoughts in our mind;

Backstage: inner work;

Backyard: proprietary thoughts; front yard, public sentiments expressed;

Bacteria: invasive error thoughts that can become viral and weaken our sense of well-being; *bacterial infections* suggest our having been undermined by our own negativity;

Bad Breath, Halitosis, Morning Breath: mortal tendencies; worldly disposition;

Badware: error thoughts that surface in our consciousness and catch us by surprise; (In IT language, software that has been installed on a computer without the user's knowledge, consent, or control);

Baggage: inherited karma; the consequences of poor choices; the after effects of embedded theology;

Baggage Claim: admitting our mistakes and error tendencies; (In the airline industry, baggage claim is the area in the airport where we can pick up our checked luggage before we take ground transportation home);

Bahiric Attainment: achieving enlightenment: (Bahir is the Kabbalistic term for illumination);

Bailiff: karmic debt;

Bait: denotes our manipulative nature;

Balance Beam: disciplined focus; concentration; a balancing act;

Balcony: bridled freedom; public aspirations mediated by private concerns;

Ballad, Ditty, Folk Song: our nostalgic inclination to honor the past;

Ballet: grace; poise; balance; harmony;

Balloon(s): ideas that we want to test;

Ballroom Dancing: the harmonious synchrony between our masculine and feminine qualities;

Bamboo Traits: longevity; resilience; happiness; truthfulness;

Bandage: offering a literal interpretation of scripture; a quick fix;

Bandhaic Incarceration: incarnational experiences; being held in bondage by sense thoughts and actions; unawareness of our divine nature; (In Sanskrit, bandha means bondage);

Bandwidth: our capacity for understanding the total spectrum of sacred writing – from a literal interpretation to a spiritual interpretation;

Bank(s): prosperity ponds; images of Universal Substance; our brains with their immense mental capacity; financial security; asset management;

Bankable Deposits: spiritual ideas and beliefs; skin school experiences where respectable spiritual growth occurs; the donations and tithes we give to worthy causes that bring us prosperous returns from many channels;

Bankruptcy: spiritual depletion; spiritual famine; physical exhaustion; losing all of our spiritual determination and drive;

Banner(s): recognizing noteworthy accomplishments; prideful moments;

Banner Ad(s): familiar religious and spiritual axioms and trite expressions voiced during conversations to defend our current thinking and sell listeners on our brand of theology;

Banquet, Feast: Universal Substance;

Baphometic Insight: superior wisdom; growing (being baptized) into higher thought;

Baptism: cleansing our consciousness of error thoughts and inclinations; pulling ourselves out of the illusion of our separation from Spirit; raising a worldly thought to its spiritual essence; lifting ourselves out of the negativity of the moment;

Baptismal Bildungsroman: a coming-of-age journey of enlightened growth;

Barbarians: savage instincts; brash drives and motivations;

Barcode: commercial interests;

Bardo: the afterlife; the interval between an ending thought and the next thought; (In the Tibetan tradition bardo refers to a state of existence intermediate between two lives on earth);

Barefoot Shiatsu: macrobiotic massage; down-to-earth understanding; basic understanding unfettered by the need for conventional parameters; our penchant for treading lightly over difficulties;

Barge: slow moving progress; going slow to go fast;

Barrenness: spiritual unawareness, unresponsiveness, unfruitfulness; uninitiated consciousness;

Bartender: an attitude we've cultivated for addiction dispensing to help us forget our troubles;

Basement, Cellar: our subconscious; our tendency to store old, repressed life patterns, belief systems, and warped perspectives that can weigh us down if we continue to allow them to inhibit us and squelch our potential; a cluttered and messy basement symbolizes our need to rid ourselves of stagnant and debilitating emotions, habits, and false assumptions that keep our potential buried and our waking life burdened with defense mechanisms;

Basket(s): womb; receptivity; a temperament for collection;

Bat-like: the ability to see past the world of illusion and duality; sensitivity; rebirth;

Bath, Bathing: cleansing; purifying; restoring; clarifying;

Bath Mat: a reminder not to slip into old habits;

Bathrobe: needing a sense of privacy;

Bathroom, Washroom, Toilet, Restroom: cleansing; elimination and release; preparation;

Battles, Brutality, Wars: conflict between egocentric thoughts, attitudes, impulses, and actions and spiritual thoughts, aspirations, ideals, and actions;

Bat(s): resurfaced fears and concerns;

Beaches: our subconscious impulses surfacing into our waking consciousness requiring us to yearn for clarity, introspection, and even rest; the state of mind that reminds us to spend some time alone to heal and incubate ourselves from the pressures of the daily grind;

Beach House: a conscious comfortability with change, transition, and the need for relaxation;

Beard-ish: authority; vitality; authoritative thoughts; robust nature;

Bear Virtues: temporal power; strength; resurrection; power; sovereignty;

Beast: anti-Christed thinking; *beast that rises out of the sea* denotes warped self-will; *beast that ascends out of the bottomless pit* represents the emergence of repressed negativity; *beasts of the earth* symbolize negative forces; (See **666**);

Beatitude #1: in its literal interpretation says: *"Blessed are the poor in spirit: for theirs is the kingdom of heaven."* The root word that is translated "spirit" comes from the word *ruach* which is more accurately translated "pride, or narcissistic pride." The second half of the 1st Be-Attitude says: *"for theirs is the Kingdom of Heaven."* Now keep in mind that 'heaven' is not a *place we go to* but a *state we grow to!* Heaven is our super-consciousness – which we are only beginning to understand. The root word for *heaven*, which is the Aramaic word Jesus would have used, means "expanding spiritual potential." So, this is what I believe Jesus is saying in this 1st Beatitude: *"We are enriched when we lack narcissistic pride, when we are teachable, when we are open and receptive to eternal truths, when we practice humility – and it is from that level of consciousness that we shall expand our understanding so we can fulfill our divine potential."*

Beatitude #2: in its literal translation says: *"Blessed are they that mourn; for they shall be comforted."* This has usually been interpreted to mean that sorrow and sadness are virtues and that we will be comforted when we get to heaven. Sorrow and sadness are not virtues. They are mournful states of being. We are not put here to be sorrowful. The Christ as Jesus said he (the Christ within) came (incarnated) that we might have life and have it more abundantly. When we take a closer look at the 2nd Beatitude it reveals this truth: *"Blessed, enriched, are those who yearn for a closer relationship with their Christ Self for they are guaranteed unlimited opportunities for soul growth."*

Beatitude #3: as it is generally written says: *"Blessed are the meek; for they shall inherit the earth."* As it is normally understood, *meek* means *modest, resigned, submissive, self-abasing*. It suggests a willingness to 'be seen and not heard.' To willingly submit to authority. To be compliant and silent. It promises us that we will be blessed if we are submissive and self-abased! It implies that submissive, withdrawn people will inherit the earth. We think not! We're fair students of history and current events and I can tell you *meek, submissive, withdrawn people*, no matter how nice they are, seem to be followers and not leaders. They don't run for President. They aren't world leaders or CEO's of mega-corporations. They don't coach sports teams or stand out in a crowd. They aren't top-selling salespeople. The word *meek* is a mistranslation. It is a categorical boo boo! The more accurate translation of the word *praeis* has an undeniable connotation of '*nonresistance*' or *unrestrained receptivity.*' And *earth*, as it is used in this Beatitude means our '*waking consciousness.*' So, 'inherit the earth' has nothing to do with world conquest and the wars and politics that go with it! So, I believe this Beatitude means: *Blessed are those who are nonresistant, who are unrestrained in their receptivity to their divinity; for they shall inherit a waking consciousness grounded in Truth principles."*

Beatitude #4: as it is generally written says: *"Blessed are they that hunger and thirst after righteousness; for they shall be filled."* Righteousness, spiritually interpreted, means 'right thinking.' It means spiritually-attuned thinking. It implies keeping our thoughts at a spiritual octave instead of at a religious pitch. So, I believe the 4th Beatitude says: *"Blessed are those who dedicate themselves to Christed thinking, being, and doing' for they shall unfold their divine potential."*

Beatitude $5: as it is usually stated it reads: *"Blessed are the merciful; for they shall obtain mercy."* To have mercy is a wonderful human trait. Mercy, in all of its forms: kindness, tenderness, empathy, leniency, and clemency is a soulful thing to offer anyone. However, the word mistranslated as *'merciful'* from the original Aramaic is *rakhma* which means *unconditional love*. It means loving people the way they are regardless of who they are, how they are, where they are, and why they are. I believe the 5th Beatitude, correctly interpreted says: *"Blessed are those who offer unconditional love; for they shall receive unconditional love."*

Beatitude #6: in its traditional interpretation the is a heart-centered message. As it is commonly understood it reads: *"Blessed are the pure in heart; for they shall see God."* This translation implies that if we are good, decent, moral, and virtuous human beings, we will see God when we stand before the Pearly Gates. Devoting ourselves to 'pure living' is certainly a good thing to do. However, the implication that we will stand in the presence of an anthropomorphic god in the sky one day misses the central teaching point of this Beatitude. In the original Aramaic the correct translation for *dadcean* is not "pure in heart" per se. It's more correctly translated as 'spiritual perspective.' It's referring to an enlightened mind. A mind centered in super-conscious awareness. A mind that values the spiritual over the material. The word 'see' as it is used in the standard interpretation of the 6th Beatitude is a mistranslation of the word *mikhazoun* which means 'comprehend.' So, the 'seeing' implied here is not physical sight, but an internal 'seeing.' So, I believe a more correct interpretation of the 6th Beatitude is: *"Blessed are those who see things from a Christ perspective; for they shall comprehend their innate divinity."*

Beatitude #7: A literal interpretation of the 7th Beatitude says: *"Blessed are the peacemakers, for they shall be called the children of God."* 'Peacemakers' is a mistranslation of the Aramaic expression *abdey shlama* which means "through service, work conscientiously to find inner peace." Spiritually, *children* represent divine ideas, and childhood symbolizes our Christ potential. So, being true to the original Aramaic meaning and adding a pinch of spiritual interpretation, I believe the 7th Beatitude says: "Blessed are those who conscientiously follow a spiritual practice for they shall experience inner peace and actualize their Christ potential."

Beatitude #8: As it is traditionally translated says: *"Blessed are they that have been persecuted for righteousness' sake; for theirs is the kingdom of heaven."* Unfortunately, this mistranslation has led hundreds of millions of people through the ages to accept martyrdom and to wear victimization and poverty as badges of honor. Essentially it has been interpreted to mean that we are blessed when we are persecuted for being Christian. The key word that is mistranslated as '*persecuted*' actually comes from the Aramaic word *dea-tredepo* which means 'to *restrain from temptation.*' The only *persecution* this Beatitude is talking about takes place between our ears. And our persecutors are errant thoughts, stale belief systems, and self-defeating habits which are the chief characteristics of a selfish, materialistic, egocentric consciousness. The word *righteousness* means '*right thinking.*' The '*kingdom of heaven*' is a spiritual idiom that stands for '*our innate divinity.*' It is this innate divinity that is the altar of our *spiritually-attuned consciousness*. It's a spiritual Petri dish that grows divine ideas. The 8th Beatitude, reinterpreted and brushed off says: "*Blessed are those who do not allow worldly temptations to deter them from right thinking; for they shall horror their innate divinity.*"

Beatitude #9: In its mistranslated traditional version says: "*Blessed are you when people insult you, persecute you and falsely say all kinds of evil against you because of me. Rejoice and be glad, because great is your reward in heaven, for in the same way they persecuted the prophets who were before you.*" This mistranslation asks us to wear reproach and persecution like badges of honor and promises us our suffering will be rewarded when we step through the Pearly Gates. And the justification for taking this abuse is that our loved ones, and friends, and Biblical prophets all went through the same *gauntlet of misery* for their faithfulness. So, be tough like they were it instructs us! The truth is the reproaches, persecutions, and false accusations mentioned in this Beatitude are all *mental hiccups* that take place in here (I'm pointing to my head). I believe the 9th Beatitude says: "*Blessed are those who press on, who do not allow the inertia of past programming and embedded theology to dampen their spirituality. Their devotion to right thinking will pay off.*"

Beauty Pageant: showing an appreciation for the harmonious alignment of our mind, body, and soul; a parade of various acts of kindness and altruism; a flower garden; breath-taking landscapes;

Beaver(s): industriousness; conscientiousness;

Bed, Berth: our physical incarnation;

Bedbugs: the error thoughts, words, choices, actions, and unhealthy consequences that disturb our rest;

Bedeviling Beasts: thoughts and statements that deny our innate divinity;

Bedroom: the need for insuring privacy and rest; the desire for intimate, romantic companionship; a collection of highly private thoughts, tendencies, and inclinations;

Bedtime Prayer(s): not taking yesterday's troubles or today's concerns to bed with us;

Bee Fancies: rulership; diligence and indefatigable effort; industriousness; *honey bees* denote immortality and resurrection;

Beehive(s): our physical body with its cells and atoms as microcosms of our continuous and uninterrupted skin school busyness, industry, and organization;

Beer: our desire for an altered state of consciousness; a liquid escape; the whim to flirt with oblivion;

Beggar(s): a consciousness of lack, entitlement, and unworthiness;

Begonia-like: dependent; a willingness to be herded; conforming;

Beheading: putting ego aside; going beyond merely intellectual knowledge into a higher spiritual understanding: surrendering one's human personality to one's spiritual individuality; restricting the analytical mind from interfering with higher spiritual perception; 'dying within ourselves' by removing the influence of the unenlightened ego once and for all (decapitation); losing the power of rationality; succumbing to irrational thought; (Beheading refers to 'mystical death,' symbolized in all great religions by decapitation (John the Baptist was beheaded). It the process through which all that is false [the unenlightened ego] is removed, leaving only the purity of the free consciousness. Beheading is called 'annihilation' in the Buddhist tradition.);

Behemoth Impulses: self-imposed muteness when it comes to assigning blame to anyone else other than ourselves for our uncontrolled battery of base instincts in this particular incarnation; our impure thoughts and unpurified actions that we have to control and eliminate in order to align ourselves with our divine nature;

Beige-ing: valuing neutrality, compromise, and detachment; displaying an unbiased viewpoint and/or position; simplicity;

Being: Godness actualized and unactualized; relative absoluteness;

Being Bamboozled: purchasing the wares and believing in the promises of 'snake oil' salespeople; choosing error thoughts over spiritual thoughts;

Beliefs: ego filters that color our experience. (We manufacture them to make sense out of our human dramas. Sometimes we hide behind them. Sometimes we change them when we find the courage to look beyond the obvious. Our spiritual growth depends on our being able to look beyond the obvious. In order to grow spiritually we must leave formaldehyde beliefs and atrophied dogmas behind. We must be ready for a thought triage, a new calculus of belief. We must also understand that spiritual growth needs landing gears as well as wings);

Believers in Exile: spiritual thoughts that have been elevated above their religious limitations; (I borrowed this phrase from a concept coined by John Shelby Spong, a retired bishop of the Episcopal Church. It refers to Christians for "whom the God experience is still real, but most of the religious forms used to interpret that reality have lost all meaning." These 'exiled believers' have outgrown the embedded theology of their childhood and are searching for a new path).

Bell(s) Qualities: the act of drawing attention to (proclaiming, broadcasting, voicing) something important;

Belly Button, Navel, Tummy Button, Umbilical Dip: our somatic metaphor for choosing another incarnation; elemental spiritual fire; birth; renewal; sexuality; fertility; cosmic altar; (Nearly 72,000 subtle nerves [nadis] converge at the navel); [Here's a question for you: Did Adam and Eve have belly buttons? ☺];

Belomancy: divining by drawing marked arrows from a bag;

Beloved City: Christ Consciousness; the New Jerusalem;

Below: carnality; our subconscious; base instincts; depression;

Bench, Seat, Pew: rest; pacing ourselves;

Benign Burlesque: poking harmless fun by satirically spoofing someone else's faith tradition;

Benooic Passage: the return to light (higher thought) from darkness (unenlightened thought); resurrection;

Berasitic Insight: having the kind of superior wisdom that leads to the creation of magnificent *out*picturings of Divine Substance;

Bereitschafts Potential: making wise choices; literally, the narrow neural time line between deciding to act and actually acting; (In neurology, the Bereitschafts potential (German, *readiness potential*), also called the pre-motor potential, is a measure of activity in the motor cortex area of the brain indicating voluntary muscle movement. The Bereitschafts potential is a manifestation of cortical contribution to the pre-motor planning of volitional movement. It was first recorded and reported in 1964 by Hans Helmut Kornhuber and Luder Deecke at the University of Freiburg in Germany. In a series of experiments in the 1980's, Benjamin Libet studied the relationship between conscious experience of volition and Bereitschafts potential and found that the Bereitschafts potential started about 0.35 sec *earlier* than people reported conscious awareness that they felt the desire to take some kind of action. He found that people were able to prevent an intended action at the last moment by consciously vetoing these actions);

Bere'shith: elemental wisdom that transcends context or bias;

Bermuda Triangle, Devil's Triangle: represents our penchant for 'losing ourselves' in altered states of drug-induced consciousness (Mescaline, psilocybin, and lysergic acid diethylamide [LSD] triangulated are three psychoactive drugs that send us into a Bermuda-like triangle of warped consciousness); (There's also an area of sea 100km south of Tokyo, Japan called the Devil's Sea that has a history similar to the Bermuda Triangle);

Be Still and Know: the psycho-emotional process of eradicating gusts of sense-soaked thoughts and emotions that dampen our spirituality by focusing our attention fully upon our innate divinity;

Beth Elohim: having a godly, enlightened consciousness (house of the gods);

Betyles: magical stones; magical affirmations; magical thoughts;

Bezzie, Bestie: spiritual and/or religious thoughts and concepts that usually go together – like Father and Son, discernment and judgment, faith and hope; (In social media, denotes a person's best or closest friend);

Bhagavad-Gita: the 'Song of the Lord' comprising eighteen chapters of the *Bhisma Parva* of the *Mahabharata*;

Bhaktic Devotion: our aptitude for unselfish, unconditional love; (In Sanskrit terms, it means to be attached or devoted to religious life and the path of spiritual growth);

Bhakti Yoga: the path of devotion;

Bhrantidarsanatahic Impressions: conceiving or attempting to comprehend something based on false doctrines or dogmatic assumptions; (In Sanskrit means perplexity or confusion in our attempts to describe the illusions arising out of the egotistical, imperfect human mind in its attempts to understand reality);

Bible: one of the most complete, unadulterated, uncensored, absolutely telling, uncannily relevant, and highly revealing stories of our evolving spiritual consciousness; (There are many translations and interpretations of the Bible – which is to be expected. After all, it chronicles our spiritual unfoldment. As we grow, our understanding of sacred scripture grows. Those who fixate on merely a literal interpretation of sacred scripture generally find it difficult to connect all of the theological dots. That could explain why they end up with a linear, dogmatically superficial religious perspective. A more metaphorical, esoteric, or metaphysical perspective would help them take off the parochial blinders and deepen their theology. Any true Bible scholar has to admit that hundreds of legitimate manuscripts were deleted by a panel of Constantine groupies in 325 C.E. The council tossed divinely inspired texts that would have benefitted humankind immensely, texts like the Book of Thomas, The Gospel of Mary, the Book of Levi, the original Apostle's Creed, the Book of Enoch. Current Christian Bibles will continue to be incomplete until and unless other divinely inspired and deserving sacred writings are included).

Bible Belt: the region in the south-eastern and south-central United States which practices extreme religious fundamentalism and mainstream Christianity;

Biblical Ballast: mistranslations and misinterpretations;

Biblical Handcuffs: carrying a Bible in both hands at the same time – usually a religious fundamentalist practice;

Biblical Literalism: belief in the inerrancy of scripture;

Bibliomancy: Divining by reading the first words on a page of a book that is opened at random in reply to a question;

Big Bang: the creation of a thought or idea in mind. Once an idea has exploded into conscious awareness it creates energy as an expression of that explosive cognitive moment. The energy it creates leads to other explosive moments (the formation of thoughts). These super-heated moments (the formation of thoughts) expand into ideas that expand (cosmic inflation) into beliefs (galaxies), which expand into choices that lead to physical actions. Each thought (Big Bang) is the outgrowth of our psycho-emotional make-up with its clusters and super-clusters of past experiences, patterns of behavior and habits, hang-ups, memories, and personal beliefs and prejudices. (Mainstream quantum physicists today believe the universe began 13 to 20 billion years ago with a massive explosion, or multiple explosions. Astronomer Fred Hoyle coined the term "Big Bang" in 1951. Computer models suggest that a mass the size of a green pea was so compressed that its temperature was guesstimated to be in the neighborhood of 18 billion million million million degrees Fahrenheit. Temperatures that super heated are many times hotter than the sun. It is important to know that the Big Bang did not occur somewhere or sometime in space. It created space. That there was no space *before* the Big Bang is just one of the counterintuitive ideas of modern cosmology); [The earth is still so radioactive from the initial Big Bang that its core is kept hot by continuing nuclear reactions, and trillions of atoms all over its surface – in rocks and trees, even in our own bodies – are still exploding. In our own bodies there are more than three million potassium atoms exploding every minute];

Bigoted Intolerance, Bigamy: running into ourselves; professing our love for, and commitment to, spirituality while expressing the same two sentiments for worldliness; (Our intolerance for certain actions of others is an indication that there is an aspect of that same behavior in our make-up that annoys us. When we strongly object to someone else's behavior and feel repulsed by it, we are usually confronting something in ourselves that we find objectionable—something with which we are struggling to change which offers opportunities for our own soul growth);

Biijic Healing: a Native American ceremony that features singing that reverses our way of thinking to shift from giving the body wrong information to knowing how to inform the body of correct information for wellness restoration by reawakening to spiritually-attuned thinking;

Bija: life's perennial urge to express itself; the impulse toward wholeness and expansion;

Bike(s), Bicycle(s): accomplishment; drive; balance;

Billboard(s): commercial proselytizing;

Binary Star System(s): we humans are binary beings. We are simultaneously spiritual beings and human beings. The 'Primary Sun' of the spiritual us is our Christ Self and the 'secondary sun' of our human self is the ego. Just as a solar system with two or more suns would not be friendly to human life, a human life that tries to express its Godness and hold onto materialism at the same time would not be having a good hair day. (A binary star system is a star system consisting of two suns orbiting around a common center of mass. The brighter sun is called the primary sun and the second sun is its companion sun or secondary star. About half of all known star systems are part of either binary star systems or star systems with more than two stars, called multiple star systems. A solar system with two or more suns would not be favorable to human life);

Binge Watching, Binge Viewing: binging on guided visualizations; binging on metaphysical YouTubes and/or spiritually-oriented TV movies; (In online media language, binge watching is the practice of watching TV for longer time spans than usual, usually for binging on a single TV show queued-up on Netflix or Amazon Prime);

Binoculars: the desire to see spiritual, allegorical, figurative, metaphorical, theosophical, and anthroposophical perspectives more clearly; discernment;

Biochemical Engineering: healthy eating;

Biodegradable Waste: mental manure; error thoughts;

Bioenergetics: a bodywork therapy that employs difficult body postures, muscle manipulations, and breathing techniques. (It requires releasing our emotions by screaming, crying, and even kicking and punching combined with psychoanalysis to achieve mental and emotional health); [Focused breathing enhances self-awareness by increasing activity in the *precuneus*, an important circuit that regulates consciousness];

Bioenergy: the Universal Life Force that animates our physical bodies;

Biogenesis: all life springs from the One Life;

Bioluminescence: Invisible rays that surround people or things that can be seen by Kirlian photography;

Bioresonance: the unique frequency at which all living things that have mass resonate;

Bipartisan, Bilateral, Dual: our thinking and feeling natures characterized by their cooperativeness, agreement, compromise, and complementariness; our aligned human self and Divine Self;

Birch Peculiarities: being highly adaptive and resilient; having mental toughness; renewal; igniting our energies and passions;

Bird Bath: the emotional cleansing that takes place when we allow a spiritual insight (bird) to enter our waking consciousness (birdbath);

Bird Cage: capturing a spiritual insight, but turning it into dogma;

Birdhouse(s): collections of down-to-earth spiritually-attuned ideas and insights;

Bird-like: working toward higher spiritual aspirations and a deified consciousness; a *caged bird* denotes feeling stuck or even imprisoned in a lower, more egocentric way of thinking; a *wounded bird* represents letting an old doctrinal belief or religious bias interfere with a newly gained spiritual insight; (The glyph of the pelican tearing open its own breast to feed its seven young symbolizes the pouring out of the inexhaustible aspirations to activate all seven chakras);

Bird of Paradise Quality: unity; exalted vision;

Birdseed: basic ideas that lead to higher spiritual aspirations;

Bird's Eye View: being, doing, and having from an elevated spiritual perspective;

Birth Control, Contraception: preventing a new spiritual insight from further expression; aborting an incarnational experience;

Birthdays: every time we awaken (give birth) to new spiritual insights and illumined thoughts; each new incarnational experience;

Birthmark(s): karmic tattoos; (More appropriately should be called 'rebirth marks' since they are visible reminders of injury sites we may have had in a past life); the visible consequences of our poor choices;

Birthright: our divine Core Essence, our innate divinity; our Christ-centric individuality;

~ *Spiritually Speaking* ~

Bishop's Miter: religious intellectualism;

Bison Disposition: experiencing abundance; having tremendous strength;

Bitmap: keeping an open-minded, big picture perspective (grasp) of certain esoteric teachings so we can more easily connect the proverbial dots;

Blackbird Tendencies: realizing our potential; being secretive;

Black Box, Flight Recorder: our brain which records and stores everything about our human experience;

Black Comedy, Dark Comedy, Gallows Humor: making statements like, "Go to hell" – "You are worthless" – "I'll never forgive you"; (Black comedy is comic work that satirizes, mocks, and attempts to make trivial serious subject matter in cynical, and oftentimes disrespectful ways.);

Black Fire: a Kabbalistic term for Absolute Wisdom (*Bodha-Bodhi*) and Light which are incomprehensible to our finite human intellects;

Black Hole: a consciousness filled with the gravity of engrained error thoughts and tendencies that deny our divine nature (light);

Black-ish: realizing that our unenlightened egocentric self must be annihilated (become totally selfless and accepting) by being absorbed into our Deeper Self called our Christ individuality if we are to become illuminated beings; [What is very interesting about the color black is that all three of the basic primary colors (red, yellow, and blue) when mixed together produce the color black. So, black is not the absence of color, it simply selfishly absorbs colors and doesn't radiate them outward)]; also, black implies intellectually 'extinguishing' ourselves as a separate ego and instead seeing ourselves as indivisibly linked to the One Presence; power; sophistication; formality; elegance; anonymity; mourning and death;

Black Lodge: an egocentric consciousness; (In the Gnostic tradition a black lodge is an organization or intelligence that seeks to pull souls into attachments to desire-sensations and trap them in a consciousness characterized by lust, anger, pride, envy, doubt, guilt, prejudice, etc.);

Black Magic: negating positivity for negativity;(Black magic is the   of the impure priesthood);

Blackout: completely succumbing to our warped egocentric nature; choosing and/or allowing ignorance over enlightenment;

- 51 -

Black Widow: domineering feminine energies that devour (limit, cut off) any masculine tendencies from expression; possessiveness; parasitical and malicious nature;

Blamestorming: thinking of all of the reasons of our unworthiness because we think are sinners since we believe in original sin; (See Original Sin; Tourniquet);

Blasphemy: denying our divinity;

Blazing Star: the Divine Presence within as us; (In Hebrew tradition it is seen as the star the astrologers followed to the place where the Christ Child laid;

Bleeding Heart Quality: sacrifice; martyrdom; bulimic with bulimic empathy;

Blender: walking the spiritual path on practical feet; integrating worldly and spiritual tendencies to create balance and a harmonious wholesomeness;

Bless, Blessing: to confer prosperity on; (So, we must always bless, confer prosperity upon, what we want to manifest. We have the incredible power to confer prosperity upon everything, everyone, and every circumstance that comes to us — and in so doing, we create an unending ripple effect of prosperity and abundance.

Blessing Fallout: If you have ever said things like or agree with someone else saying things like "*the cancer blessed me*," or "*lime disease blessed me*," or "*a broken nose blessed me*," or "*this heart attack was the best thing that ever happened to me*," or "*getting fired blessed me*," you are giving your power away and assigning a blessing on something that doesn't deserve to be blessed! What blessed you was not what happened to you but how you responded to what happened to you.

Blindness: unreceptivity to inner light; failing to see our innate divinity; choosing adulterous thoughts over enlightened thoughts; choosing not to see beyond the world of outer appearances;

Blind Date: our willingness to accept unknown aspects and qualities within us as we strive for self-definition;

Blindfold: seeing the world through a warped egocentric lens;

Blinkered: not being open to new ideas, especially esoteric and spiritual concepts; (Horses wear blinkers to keep them from being startled by peripheral movements);

Bloatware: needing to give an inordinate amount of courseware, training materials, and one-on-one coaching so truth students can understand the New Thought material just presented;

Blog, Blogcast: publicizing our thoughts; thinking out loud; standing on the platform of words; moving thoughts into words and feelings into print;

Bloggables: thoughts, insights, and spiritual concepts that are perfect content for blogs, sermons, workshops, and study groups; (In IT parlance, information that is suitable or sufficiently interesting as a topic for a blog);

Bloggy: represents the nature of thinking, being, and doing spiritual and/or religious things; (In IT circles, having the characteristics and features of a blog or blogs);

Blood: the vitalized Consciousness of the Eternal Presence reduced to Its material essence, blood coursing through our veins symbolizes truth coursing through our consciousness; life force; *spilled blood* is our outpoured divine activity and/or spiritual essence; *drinking blood* represents a conscious realization of our unity and indivisibleness with the Eternal Presence; *drinking the blood of Christ* symbolizes the attainment of Christ Consciousness, immortality; (Jesus raised the level of purity in his blood by becoming consciously one with his Christ Nature. His neurology was also cleansed and quickened when his human self aligned completely with his Christ Self. The potency of his spilled blood is a gift to all of us. It opens the door to our transfusion in consciousness);

Bloodstone-like: the ability to ground the energies of the solar plexus; our ability to detoxify;

Bloodthirsty Mobs, Crowds: anti-spiritual thoughts, intentions, and inclinations that contemptuously murder divine ideas and aspirations;

Blossom: new beginnings; freshness;

Blueprint(s), Map(s), Template(s): sacred teachings from spiritual and religious texts;

Blown Chakra: a chakra damaged, impaired, and/or disabled by unwise use of drugs;

Bluebell-ish: belief in invisible helpers; belief in spirits;

Blue-Chip Discernment: putting our common sense, better judgment, innate wisdom, and patience in gear before we put our mouth in motion;

Blue-Collar Ideas, Commoners: normal, concrete operational, everyday thoughts and ideas;

Blue-ness: denotes our penchant for contemplativeness, meditativeness, and intellectual astuteness; tranquility and harmony; loyalty and calmness; (Physiologically, the color blue slows down the metabolic processes of our biology and soothes the 'noise' in the nervous system, making it conducive for us to center ourselves and calm ourselves); [Blue is the color of the throat chakra];

Boa: paralyzing tendencies;

Boastful Baseness: discrediting the innate divinity in others while boasting of our own divine connection;

Bodha Bailiwick: this area of expertise is the same for all of us because it refers to what is ours to do, which is to say, we are all responsible for attaining self-knowledge;

Bodhichittic Attainment: an enlightened mind; illumined mind; aspiring to become enlightened in order to relieve humankind of its suffering;

Bodhisattva Essence: the essence of deep abiding wisdom; (Buddhists believe Buddhisattvas need only one more incarnation to become perfect Buddhas);

Bodhi Tree, Bo Tree, Bodhi Druma: awakening; enlightenment; illumination; longevity; bliss; tranquility; peace and calmness; Buddhic (Christ) Consciousness; attaining Buddhahood, Christhood; (Buddhism tells of Sakyamuni's birth accompanied by a flash of light that traveled around the world that sparked the first growth of the Tree of Perfection – a sacred fig tree that it is said to have been 400 feet high that bloomed with glowing flowers and glistening fruit. It is also said that the Buddha was born, attained his enlightenment, taught his first sermon, and made his earthly transition all under the Bodhi tree. Some say he sat under the tree for six years protected by the tree during his enlightenment.

Bodies of Sin: perpetuated error thoughts;

Body English: the condition of our bodies as the consequence of our thoughts, eating habits, and actions; (In sports terms, body English refers to the common practice of contorting our body while a shot, hit, stroke, or swing is in play, usually in the direction we wish a ball to travel, as if in the vain hope that this will influence the balls' trajectory.);

Bodyguard(s): our intentional decisions as to what types of information and experiences to allow into our conscious awareness;

Bog: dim view or outlook; unseen possibilities; negative outlook;

Bogatyric Abilities: our latent supernatural strength and psychic abilities; (These abilities appear in Russian folk-epics and songs);

Bondage: incarnational and reincarnational experiences; an egocentric consciousness;

Bone-ish: intuiting an organic crystallization of thoughts that create the spiritual scaffolding for our actions;

Bonsai Contemplation: concentrating only on a single word, thought, concept, spiritual experience, or item;

Booby Prize, Susceptibility-like Endowment: understanding without experience;

Book, Tome, Volume, Text: our incarnational history; deposits from our consciousness;

Book of Life, Book of the Living: the *out*picturing of the Godhead in both the manifest and unmanifest universes; the Multiverse which unfolds into universes which unfold into consciousness which unfolds into us as spiritual beings in human form;

Boomerang: karma; the consequences of our thoughts, words, and actions;

Boom Town: our consciousness [town] expanding as a result of being introduced to new and compelling spiritual teachings; (In cowboy terms, a boom town is a town that experiences rapid growth due to a mining frenzy and/or a cattle trail meeting a railroad.);

Boot Camp: each human incarnation and reincarnation; each level of an initiation;

Boot Ready: a religious fundamentalist's Sunday sermon that's getting so deep with you know what that protecting ourselves by keeping our feet dry (higher spiritual understanding) is necessary;

Born Again: *spiritual obstetrics*; to transcend sense attachments; moving beyond material appetites; adopting a consciousness that is not tied to the world of appearances; realizing that there is no separation between us and Spirit;

Botched Journey: not applying the teachings;

Bottom Feeders: repressed negative life scripts and self-negating emotional patterns that are warehoused as sediments in our subconscious;

Bottomless Pit: our insatiable, over-consumptive, sense-addicted nature that is the outgrowth of our egocentric bias for skin school experiences;

Bounce Rate: the percentage of people who walk into a church on Sunday or on a Wednesday night and stay for only a few minutes before realizing they are in the "wrong" place; (In IT language, the percentage of visitors to a particular website who leave the site after viewing only one page);

Bow Attributes: recognizing our innate spiritual power and latent divine energies; exercising spiritual discipline; respecting the combination of power and force; being ready and able to store up our energies; being able to handle dynamic tension; the *bow drawn with string taut* represents the dynamic tension between positive power (the bow) and negation (the string); *broken bow* symbolizes mastery over sense desires and passions; (The bow is the our mind, the string is the brain, the arrow is the product of the mind and brain's interaction: a piercing thought);

Bowderized Bible Treatment: spiritually interpreting traditional translations to expurgate (censor, remove) distorted passages that retail an anthropomorphic God or Devil, the subjugation of women, denial of our innate divinity, etc.;

Bowl(s): receptivity;

Bowl of Saki: a compendium of 366 brief quotations, one for each day of the year, selected from the teachings of Hazrat Inayat Khan;

Bow-Wow Nature: the base instinct part of our nature that is still cultivated by our materialistic urges; (In linguistics, the idea that language began when we imitated animal noises or other natural sounds.);

Boy Scout(s): personal development thoughts and inclinations;

Brahma: the third aspect of the Hindu trinity – Brahma (mother/intelligence), Krishna (son/love), and Siva (father/will);

Brahman: the One Reality; the Eternal Presence;

Braille: nonverbal knowledge and instruction acquisition using our fingertips as the sensing medium; feeling our way around the human experience;

Brain Candy: spiritual, metaphysical, and esoteric teachings;

Brain Cramp(s): dogma; literal-only interpretations of scripture;

Brain Spin: what we get when we are introduced to highly spiritual concepts for the first time;

Brainteasers: allegorical, figurative, spiritual, metaphorical, metaphysical, theosophical, anthroposophical thoughts and teachings;

Brainwashing: seeing the world of sensory experience as our only connection to what we perceive as real; (In *Born to Believe,* Andrew Newberg asserts that the "belief that we only use 10% of the brain is a myth. Some have tried to substantiate this misconception by citing excess or silent neurons, or that 90% of the brain is composed of glial cells. The fact is we may lose half of our brain cells by age thirty, but not because they are unused. They simply are not needed." Pg. 117);

Brand Loyalty: remaining a follower of a particular faith tradition and/or New Thought thought rather than seeking other avenues of spiritual and/or religious fulfillment; (In marketing terms brand loyalty refers to people who buy products and services from the same manufacturer repeatedly without shopping around for other suppliers.);

Brazen Serpent Proclivities: our sense-shellacked mind which is tempted by material things;

Bread Qualities: universal substance; potentiality; *unleavened bread* represents our being able to transcend our concept of individuality by seeing only the One Life of which we are an indivisible expression; *eating consecrated bread* represents applying esoteric wisdom;

Breakfast: basic esoteric knowledge;

Breastfeeding: being in sync with femininity and the nurturing principle; demonstrating the essence of motherly love and tenderness;

Breath: the expansion and contraction of cosmic life energies at all levels of being; *ruach*; *pneuma*;

Breatharianism: believing that we can live without food and drink by subsisting only on pranic light (channeled information) and that our nourishment can be directly gained by sun-gazing the sun's energy;

Breath of Life: denotes the coupling of the Vital Life Force and Universal Consciousness (Cosmic Consciousness) in physicality;

Breathwork: achieving psychosomatic health and well-being through establishing disciplined patterns of inhalation and exhalation;

Briar(s): trials; hindrances; off the beaten path troubles;

Briareos Complex: the monstrous consequences of our unbridled carnality that can result in a hundred forms of misery; (In Greek mythology, Briareos was one of the Hekatonkheires, three ancient storm giants with a hundred hands and fifty heads apiece);

Bribery, Hush Money: soaking-up the world of outer appearances;

Bridal Chamber: the union of soul and spirit within us; (Valentinian Gnosticism expands this myth to say that the Christ is the masculine spirit from above which descends to Sophia, the feminine soul below, in order to redeem her and ascend together to the Upper Aeons, where they will unite in the Bridal Chamber. Their meeting [union of the bride and bridegroom in the Bridal Chamber] restores the unity which Adam and Eve lost when they were divided);

Bridge(s): transitional thoughts and experiences; psychic connectivity;

Bridle(s): religious tenets that focus on strict conformity instead of spiritual growth;

Briefcase, Attaché: preparedness; readiness;

Brimstone Quirks: the destructive nature of gross sense appetites; the burning of our own guilty conscience;

Brimstone Banshee: the wailing and crying we do when we suffer the unsettling consequences of our gross sense appetites; suffering and tribulation; (See also Chemicalization);

Bronchitis: inflamed thoughts and the strained communications that are the result; concern about not accomplishing what we want to do in life which affects the passion and enthusiasm we want to feel, but fail to express;

Brook-ish: stream of consciousness;

Broom-like: the capacity for removing impediments to our spiritual, mental, emotional, and physical health; domesticity;

Bropocalypse: filling our mind with so many error thoughts (bros) from our base nature that the choices we make and actions we take are destined to be degradative and self-defeating; (In social media parlance, this practice involves a gathering of bros on a mission to accomplish one thing and one thing only: to get bombed [tanked, wasted] and end up with a hangover.);

Brothers and Sisters of Jesus: similar thoughts (brothers) and complementary emotions (sisters) that characterize a consciousness that realizes its divine nature (our Jesus-like awareness);

Brothers of the Shadow: error thoughts that characterize the 'left-hand' path, the sense addicted path;

Brown-ness: represents our down-to-earth-ness; denotes an internal locus of control and self-sufficiency; implies our practicality and conservative nature; reliability; endurance; comfort;

Bubble(s): ephemeral ideas; passing inclinations; superficial intentions;

Bubble Bath: emotional catharsis; a few moments of joyful relaxation;

Bubble Gum Theology: chewing on old, stale religious beliefs and worshipping dogma (bubble gum) that usually bursts when it's filled with enough hot air;

Bucking Chute: a conventional belief system when it is challenged by new information that causes a high degree of cognitive dissonance; (In rodeo terms, a bucking chutes are the stock pens in a rodeo arena where the wild horses and bulls are placed just before they are ridden.); (See Chemicalization);

Buck *It* List: a list of the self-defeating habits, negative thoughts, false beliefs, and groundless assumptions that keep us from being as happy as we can be *while we are still living*; (It's not a *to die for* list, it's a *to live for* list! It's a list to help us lighten our load. It's a list of habits, beliefs, attitudes, and assumptions that are burdens we want to get rid of);

Buddha: one who is enlightened; the world teacher who historically manifested through Gautama;

Buddhi: the Universal Soul;

Buddhic Plane: the hyperplane (world) in which the soul exists; divine intuition;

Bug(s), Insect(s): pesky thoughts; bothersome idiosyncrasies;

Bug Spray, Insecticide: powerful positive affirmations and denials;

Bulimia, Bulimarexia: sensory overload; stuffing our consciousness with trivialities;

Bulletproof Vest(s): affirmative prayer and meditation;

Bull-ishness: male ardor; powerful masculine energy; robust and vigorous thoughts;

Bull's Eye: telescopic vision; a well-defined goal;

Bummer Experiences: curriculum;

Bumper Sticker Theology: walking our talks; (The most powerful and effective bumper sticker is, and always will be, the one we wear on our sleeves, on the tip of our tongues, and from the bottom of our hearts. It's a bumper sticker we wear 24 – 7 – 365. It doesn't come with fluorescent ink or pressure sensitive adhesive. It comes with skin, and a personality, and a spiritual perspective. These bumper stickers are one of a kind. They come in different shapes, and sizes, and colors, and temperaments. These bumper stickers either adhere to truth principles or stick to false surfaces. These bumper stickers are you and me. They are the image we project to the world through our Christ-centered words, choices, and actions.);

Bum Rush: eliminating a bad habit, poor choices, and/or negative language as fast as we can from our life; (In boxing terms, a bum rush means trying as fast as you can to hustle the opponent out of the ring, and thus, out of the fight.);

Bundle Theory: believing nothing exists outside of our consciousness; the objects we perceive can be described and understood simply as "bundles" or properties. (Thus, there is no underlying 'substance' or 'essence' which exists independent of its superficial qualities, properties, and/or supposed dimensions);

Bungee Jumping: going from one incarnational experience to another using the Silver Cord as our suspension rod: (See Silver Cord);

Bunk Bed(s): the manifest and unmanifest worlds; our higher mind and lower mind;

Bunyipic Balistics: spiritually, denotes volatile and destructive emotions; (In Australia, is a terrifying creature that haunts waterways);

Burglar(s): unfulfilling activities that steal our energy and swipe our happiness;

Burning Bowl: the alchemical process of burning off the dross of error; (Ritualistically, a ceremony in which we symbolically purge negative influences from our consciousness and our lives by writing on a piece of flash paper whatever habits, attitudes, behaviors, and relationships are limiting our good and the good we can do for others. The negative influences written on the flash paper are placed in a bowl and burned. The very act of releasing them establishes in our consciousness thought currents that reinforce the alchemical process of letting go of error. Just as the fire transforms the energy contained in the flash paper into heat energy and light, the symbolic act of burning what we want to release in the Burning Bowl symbolically purges those negative influences from our consciousness.);

Burning Bush: an extremely powerful transformation in consciousness; the fiery rise of the serpentine energies within us that burn off the dross of error; (We will experience our own 'burning bush' when our consciousness is purified of all error thoughts and inclinations. We will have reached a high state of enlightenment. But like Moses, we still have a lot of work to do. Even mystics pay taxes and occasionally need to de-friend someone off their Facebook account. From a 'burning bush' state of awareness we can free our thoughts (Israelites) from the darkness of duality and separation (Egypt);

Burnt Offerings: self-purification; renouncing base desires; sublimating one's lower egocentric nature to one's higher spiritual nature; renouncing error; transmuting error thoughts into their spiritual equivalents;

Burping: the misapplication of sharing spiritual truths; inconsequential thoughts;

Burr(s): the consequences of poor judgments that cling to us;

Bushido: disciplined restraint and action; (In the Japanese tradition *bushido* is the samurai code);

Business Card: the work itself that we do that helps define our calling; our everyday language; the tone of our voice;

Bus Station: a consciousness that is filled with conventional routes and outlets of moving from one line of thought to another;

But Rebuttal: kissing our 'buts,' 'ought tos,' and 'should haves' goodbye;

Buttercup-like: childlike innocence; malleable;

Butterfly Qualities: experiencing transformation; having angelic thoughts and tendencies; going through the ephemeral nature of incarnational existence; having a psyche;

Buttery Principles: truth principles that work in both spiritual terms and mainstream religious terms [i.e. divine order, salvation, resurrection]; (Buttery is a snowboarding term that describes snowboards with good flex);

Button(s): decisions we make to seal our choices;

Buzurgic Intentions: venerable, noble, holy intentions;

Buzzard-like: wanting to use archaic, outmoded, useless resources; (See Vulture-like Tendencies);

Cable Modem: symbolizes our ability to enjoy a speedy and continuous connection with our Divine Self without going through the interference created by a recalcitrant ego;

Cable Tow: our umbilical cord; (See Umbilical Cord); (In Masonic esoterism is a symbol of a First Degree Mason. The length of the Cable Tow is the sacrifice we are willing to make on behalf of our brethren. It is in our heart, not to be measured by miles. It is not gauged by distances, but by deeds.);

Cactus Flowers: forgiveness; repentance;

Caduceus Virtues: activating our helixed serpentine energies that are harnessed to bring us into enlightenment; mastering incarnational dualities;

Café: surface knowledge;

Cafeteria(s): sensory experience; books (texts, courses) containing religious and/or spiritual teachings;

Cafeteria Christianity: being able to choose which religious doctrines we will follow and ignoring those we see as limiting, unfulfilling, and/or irrelevant;

Cage(s): any thought that limits our spiritual growth; a well-entrenched negativity bias; repressed emotions; an unwillingness to let our inner child out; any of the 'isms'; dogmatic thinking; chronic fear, shame, and doubt; inhibitions; shyness; self-imposed restraint; sense of entrapment and restriction; loss of freedom and mobility;

Calcite-like: our ability to refresh and revitalize our spiritual energy centers (chakras);

Calculator: the computation power of our mental faculties;

Calendar(s): our penchant for keeping tract of linear beingness;

Calf-like Tendencies: *Fatted calf* symbolizes the richness of intuitive wisdom and mature spiritual faculties; the *molten calf* symbolizes backsliding into gross materialism and forgetting to honor spiritual knowledge by adopting a limited literal interpretation of sacred scripture, subservience to embedded theological beliefs;

Calling: the urge to be the Authentic Us, the Divine Us, the Extraordinary Us; the soul urge, inner prompting to be alignment with our True Self; (Exoterically, a perceived 'calling' refers to being called by an anthropomorphic god for a specific purpose);

Calorie-Free Opium: compelling and transformative truth principles and riveting spiritual teachings; an out-of-body experience; beautiful music beautifully played and/or sung; a spiritual truth realized for the first time – and the second time, and the twentieth time, and the thousandth time; loving touch; a mystical experience; a child's laughter; an illness-free diagnosis; runner's high; a riveting meditation and/or prayer experience; an astral travel experience; an encounter with an apparition; mental, emotional, and physical intimacy; a cathartic experience; a past lives regression experience; an 'ah ha' experience; a wonderful massage;

Camellia-like: psychic abilities;

Camel Penchants: patience; lengthy endurance; conservative;

Camera(s): our penchant for capturing and then committing things to memory;

Camouflage: our physical form; our human self as opposed to our Divine Self; our personality which covers our individuality;

Camp(s): temporary perspectives, points of view, and/or beliefs that we consider along our way toward enlightenment;

Campus: the material world; the universe; unitive consciousness;

Canal(s): our desire for shortcuts toward enlightenment;

Cancer: caustic thoughts that eat away at us; self-directed resentment and anger; stifling happiness and joy; a belief in the proliferation of ills; deep hurts that metastasize;

Candles: intelligent potential; predictive awareness; *golden candles* denote immanent enlightenment;

Candy; desiring the sweet things in life; enjoying the pleasantries that bring palatable delights; also represents the enjoyment we get from receiving new spiritual insights that are like 'soul' sweets; esoteric principles; life-changing 'A ha's';

Cannibalism: getting information as fast as we can from someone; draining other people's energy; depleting someone's resources with no intent of giving back;

Can of Worms: discussions between New Thought people and religious fundamentalists;

Canonical Intellectualizing: doctrinal grandstanding;

Canvas: each new day; the present;

Canyon(s): the subconscious;

Cap(s) Capacity: denotes our penchant for exposing intellectual, theoretical, playful preferences; *conical caps* refer to our wizardry and psychic powers; dunce caps symbolize the ignorance of our innate divinity; *jester's caps* remind us of our ability to mock convention and tradition, or just being able to be silly;

Capnomancy: divining that uses the rise and fall of smoke from a candle, incense, or small fire as the source of interpretation;

Capital Punishment: self-imposed pain and suffering caused by our complete disregard for our innate divinity;

Captivity: an egocentric perspective;

Carcass, Corpse, Remains: an idea or opportunity that is allowed to rot;

Cardinal-like Virtues: enduring love and compatibility; warmth;

Carnation-like: our penchant for valuing social correctness, connectivity, and schmoozing; festivity;

Carnelian-like: our tendency for analytical prowess;

Carnivalesque Captivity: the error-prone state we find ourselves in when we put traditional spiritual principles and truths aside and elect instead to spend our time in cavalier worldly pursuits; the default state of a paranoid ego;

Carnivorous Collapse: the decision to stop eating meat;

Carousel of Dysfunction: fixating on the Bible's supposed inerrancy, an anthropomorphic goodie God in the sky or a malevolent devil, and women occupying subordinate roles blinds the "faithful" into believing that the illusions they have spun are real and credible;

Carpet: softening (cushioning) our presence, especially when it comes to sharing spiritual principles in religious settings; comfortable footing;

Car Sickness: not being able to move about in a healthy way; feeling our speed and/or momentum is out of sync with what we believe we are here to do;

Cartomancy: a form of divination using a standard deck of playing cards;

Cartoon(s): perceiving certain aspects of our lives in a comedic and lighthearted way; an appreciation for fun and joviality;

Casino(s): searching for Universal Substance thinking it comes *to* us instead of *through* us;

Castor Oiling: the flushing out of error when truth and error collide; (See Chemicalization);

Cat(s): our psychic nature; independence personified;

Cataclysms: the gradual beginning, progressive intensification, culmination, and gradual diminution of an encrusted belief system that no longer serves our greater good;

Catacombs: repressed pockets of hard-to-release life patterns and the neuro-pathways that lead to them which need to be outgrown;

Cataract: an egocentric lens (perspective, world view);

Catastrophe: searching for spiritual ends by using material means; denying our innate divinity by choosing to worship – and fear – an anthropomorphic god in the sky or an evil, horned, red devil with a tail;

Catharsis: the release of negativity, doubt, and fear; a *psyche* cleansing;

Cathedral: Christ Consciousness (Buddhic, Krishnic, Allahic, Vishnuic Consciousness);

Cathedral of Enlightenment: Cosmic Consciousness;

Cat-ishness: independence; playfulness; resourcefulness; aloofness; psychic propensities;

Cat Nap Fraud: pretending to sleep during a religious or political discussion so we don't have to say anything;

Cattle, Livestock: contentment; denotes our herd instinct; the status quo;

Cattle Drive: a herd of thoughts that runs through our mind making it difficult to sleep; (In cowboy terms, a cattle drive is the movement of a herd of cattle from a ranch to a railroad line for shipment.);

Caves: birth, burial, and rebirth into higher spiritual understanding; womb; portals into enlightenment;

Caviar: expensive sense appetites;

CD-ROM (Compact Disc-Read Only Memory): the belief by religious fundamentalists in the inerrancy of the Bible (Compact Disc) and that it 'should not be altered or erased';

Ceke Connections: In Inca shamanism, *ceke* lines are sacred energy lines that connect people, places, and things);

Celebrities: well-known spiritual laws and principles;

Celestial Dew: the spilled blood of an illumined one;

Celestial Hierarchy: the assembly of enlightened, illuminated, ascended beings not constrained by physicality who are arranged by their level of enlightened development; cosmic beings who assist, guide, and mediate incarnated and/or reincarnated beings;

Celestite-like: mental acuity:

Celibacy: a consciousness that is not filled with spiritual thoughts and inclinations; a life that is devoid of generosity, kindness, compassion, joy, unconditional love, etc.;

Cell-ebrate: honoring, revering, and rejoicing in the marvelous intelligence and transformative power of our oldest ancestors – the 100 trillion cells in our body.

Cell Phone Salute: symbolizes our intent to summon the help of an anthropomorphic god in the sky; (In social media language, represents our attempt to increase the chances of receiving a text and/or add smart phone bars since there is little to no reception by raising our phone up in the air thinking that we will miraculously gain more bars);

Cell Phone Tower: a reminder that there is no geography in spirit; a World Axis energy point; (See World Axis);

Cellular Anthropology: the belief that our cellular architecture is a path to uncover hidden messages of life itself that support us and allow us to build our spirituality.

Cellular Consciousness: every cell in our bodies is a conscious, intelligent being;

Cellular Theology: Each cell, every molecule, each atom is a sacred tabernacle of Spirit. These sacred tabernacles are connected. There is no denominational sparing. Their biology is their theology. (When we realize the significance of this invisible connection we will honor the human soul's relationship to Spirit. When we acknowledge this connection, from soul to cell, our body becomes the highly-charged sacred ground of our being. When we achieve this perfect synchrony we experience the inner peace, joy, health, and wholeness which are the truth of us);

Cemeteries: severely repressed emotions; spent thoughts and ideas that were never used; a materialistic consciousness; aspects of ourselves that have been laid to rest;

Cenobite Witnessing: demonstrating our profession of faith in the world rather than sequestering ourselves within a monastic setting;

Census: A time when all of the beliefs, values, and assumptions gained from sense consciousness are called into account;

Center of the World, Seat of Intelligence, Radiating Heart, Flaming Heart, Preserver of Thought: the vitalizing psychic elements of our individuality beyond our physical beingness: the Sun; the Primordial Principle; the Word of God; a singularity; our Quantum Self which provides the umbilical [silver cord] for us to experience a multiplicity of dimensional incarnations and/or reincarnations; (The Center exists before all else. It is the Point of departure of all things, the principle point that is without form and dimensions. Everything issues from it and must finally return to it.);

Central Sun: the Christ Self, Buddha Self, Krishna Self, Allah Self, etc.;

Centrifugal Comeuppances: the disastrous consequences of our chronic error thoughts, words, and actions that cause us to spiral into a merry-go-round of woeful experiences;

Cerebral Census: polling our intellectual nature to make sure our braininess is giving equal time to our heartfeltness;

Cereology: seeing or sensing unusual shapes in natural settings; (See Crop Circles);

Cesspool(s), Quagmire: impure feelings; base emotions; impious attitudes;

Cha-Ching: the sound of materialism;

Chaff: error; dogma; feelings of unworthiness; fear; doubt;

Chain of Being: believing that existing things can be hierarchically ordered, from least to greatest, in an unbroken line from inanimate particles of matter to the deity who created them; (This elaborate cosmological model of the universe originated in the Middle Ages and the Renaissance.);

Chain of Union, Chain of Alliance: uniting heaven and earth; [The symbolism of the chain of union alludes to knots at intervals along the chain and these knots usually number twelve in all alluding to the zodiac]; (See Rainbow);

Chain of the Worlds, Garland of Being: having the awareness of the interconnectedness between the manifest and the unmanifest; (In the Bhagavad-Gita it says, "On me all things are threaded, as rows of pearls on a string. All things [*sarvam idam*) – that is, the totality of all manifestation which includes all visible and invisible worlds.); [A rosary and string of beads allude to this extended cosmic relationship];

Chaitanyan Clearing: the clarity gained by an awakened consciousness; (Chaitanya Mahaprabhu was an Indian saint thought to be an avatar of Krishna);

Chakras, Lotuses: seven main super-physical (subtle body) consciousness centers within our physical body (spinal cord) that are activated by the serpentine energies; an exteriorization, an outward affirmation of the Tree of Life; (According to Hindu metaphysical and tantric/yogic spiritual traditions, the chakras are vortexes in the subtle body – and not our physical body. They are located at the physical counterparts of our major plexuses of arteries, veins, and nerves. Every thought, inclination, and experience we have ever had at the quantum level of consciousness is filtered through these chakra "databases" and is recorded in the 100 trillion cells that constitute our physical being. "Our biography," says Caroline Myss, "is our biology." In addition to our seven major chakras there are 42 more minor chakras that start below the Root Chakra and extend down our legs to our feet. These correspond to our lower, more base instincts and include our repressed subconscious material: Ken Wilber, in J. White (ed.), Kundalini, Evolution and Enlightenment, pg. 127, outlines how we experience the chakras when they are open: Different feelings and cognitions are 'located,' or best contained in, certain well-defined segments of the body. (We) feel stability and groundedness in the legs and feet...; orgasmic ecstasy in the genitals; joy-vitality-laughter in the gut; openness-affirmation-love in the chest; intellection-insight in the eyes and head; and spirituality at the crown… This, then, is the basis of the chakra system as presented in terms of feelings, vibrations, or energetics." The seven major chakras are: Base Chakra (Muladhara) – located at the coccyx bone, Sacral (Navel) Chakra (Swadhistana) – located at the prostate, Solar Plexus Chakra (Manipura) – located in the navel area, Heart Chakra (Anahata) – located in the heart center, Throat Chakra (Vishuddha) – located at the throat and neck area, Brow (Third Eye) Chakra (Ajna) – located between the eyebrows, and Crown Chakra (Sahasrara) – located at the top of the head; (Also called lataif-e-sittas);

Chalice-like: absorption of spiritual knowledge and potential illumination; redemption; immortality;

Chalkolibanonic Junction: the place in consciousness where 'heaven meets earth,' which is to say *chalkos* (a hollowed out vessel – our human consciousness) becomes aware, *libanos* (incense, frankincense), of our divine nature; (a fine metal, or yellowish frankincense);

Chameleon-ish: adapting to change; being able to blend in and intermingle in conversations involving higher thought; over-accommodative;

Chameleon Silks: changing our spiritual and/or religious beliefs and values to suit our materialistic whims and wants; (In magic circles, chameleon silks refers to color-changing handkerchiefs. For example, when a magician places a red handkerchief in h/her hand, and when it's pushed out the other side, it emerges a different color.);

Champagne-ness: the desire to celebrate and feel a little highbrow and wealthy;

Chandelier: grandeur; elegance; prosperity, abundance; wealth;

Changchub Sempa: Tibetan equivalent to Buddhahood, Christhood, Krishnahood;

Change Rate: the amount of time it takes to vacillate between a worldly consciousness and a spiritually-attuned consciousness;

Chaos: whirled order; excited order; a pre-spiritualized state of consciousness; egocentric dominance of one's personality; attachment to materiality; a consciousness void of spiritual inclinations;

Chapel: a spiritually-attuned consciousness;

Charachara: the aggregate of all of our thoughts, newly formulated as well as seasoned;

Charades: skin school experiences characterized by a materialistic consciousness;

Charger Challenged: failing to take advantage of reading an inspirational quote or meditation to get charged-up and rejuvenated when we're having a bad day; (In social media language, it is the inability to remember to recharge our smart phone, iPad, laptop, etc., or decide which of our *e*paraphernalia gets recharged because we only have one battery charger between them to prevent a dead battery);

Chariot-like: our physical body or ordinary consciousness (human personality); the unenlightened intellect striving for illumination is the charioteer; the mind and the physical senses are the reins; the wheels represent our capacity to move from one level of awareness to another; the pole connecting the chariot to the horses symbolizes the spinal cord endowed with the serpentine energies; the horses are our senses that must be reined in if they are sense-bound and given free-rein if they are quickened;

Chariots of Fire: sensing the rise of *kundalini, parakletos, speiremic* (serpentine) energies; feeling the activity of the Holy Spirit; recognizing our mastery and authority over our physical senses; our charioteer-ness helps us master the art of living [the charioteer represents our super-consciousness that holds the reins (our willpower, intellect, and knowledge) to direct the steeds (the chi, dynamic life force) that pull the chariot (our ordinary consciousness);

Charlatan: the unenlightened, sense-addicted, paranoid ego;

Chasing Money: our attachment to materiality; (In gambling and billiard terms, our inability to stop gambling once we have lost money because we 'have' to get our money back.);

Chassidic Discipleship: devoted study of Kabbalistic teachings;

Chastity: abstaining from error;

Chastity Belt: spiritual teachings and principles that we've wrapped around our conscious behavior; (Prejudicially, religious indoctrination that encourages followers to criticize, but not associate with the 'unchurched'); (See Unchurched);

Chatbot: a typical 'conversation' between a New Thought truth student and a religious fundamentalist who 'simulate' interest in each other's thoughts but find it difficult to really pay attention; (In IT language, a computer program designed to simulate conversation with human users, especially over the Internet);

Chatter Bomb: an intrusive thought that enters, and possibly spoils, a meditative experience;

Chauffeur(s): our incarnational physical bodies;

Chayot Hakodesh: pious thoughts; holy inclinations; (In Kabbalistic terms, a group of angels);

Cheat the Pocket: seeing probabilities in possibilities; (In billiard terms, cheating the pocket means to aim at an object ball such that it will enter one side of the pocket or the other, rather than the center, of a pocket. This allows the cue ball to strike the object ball at a different contact point than the most obvious one. Cheating the pocket is used to improve a given position and to prevent scratches on head-on shots.);

Cheerleader(s): inspiring spiritual thoughts and riveting esoteric principles; positive affirmations;

Cheesy Connivances: highly subversive and conspiratory inclinations;

Chela(s), Lanoo(s): disciples, truth students, one who receives instruction in esoteric teachings; heuristic thoughts that are the outgrowth of an original, compelling spiritual thought;

Chemicalization: *spiritual floss*; loosening the crust of old tapes, conventional assumptions, and subconscious thought patterns; cleaning up our act; the dissonance between the *spiritual us* and the *material us* causes us to experience a depth charge of inner transformative energies that intensify and lead to what can be a rather volatile process of interior cleansing and purification; the fusion of enlightened thought and stale belief systems causes an internal combustion that sends specks and flecks of our ego's insecurities to the surface; the interior transformation that occurs penetrates all levels of our being, purging us from error; receiving a new piece of life-changing information that blows our mind, our old programming resists the new information and we experience an internal upheaval that leads to spiritual growth; 'spiritual Alka Seltzer' which settles the rough and tumble growth curve new spiritual insights force on our old life patterns; new spiritual insights create cognitive dissonance which upsets old patterns of thinking, being, and doing - sending us into inner turmoil (turbulence), a time of questioning, soul searching, and finally into an enlightened perspective;

Chemicalized Co-morbidity: experiencing more than one insecurity at a time;

Chenresic Compassion: a highly developed sense of humility, love, and caring for others; (Chenresi is the patron deity of Tibet. Most commonly depicted as standing with one-thousand arms reaching out to aid suffering beings in all the worlds.); [A Stanford University study found that compassion activates our brain's limbic system [our brain's emotional network] so that just four minutes of kindness and compassion result in increased feelings of social connectedness and positivity toward others);

Cherub Proneness: having spiritual intentions;

Cherubim Proclivities: a number of extremely elevated spiritual intentions; the cerebral cortex which protects the cerebrum (It covers the cerebrum, and is divided into two cortices, covering the left and right hemispheres);

Chess, Checkers: our ability to manage polarities, contradictions, and contrariness; our aptitude for governing both our higher spiritual nature and our egocentric nature; the belief in competitive solutions; (The juxtaposition of the white and black or black and red squares on these board games represents polarities, the manifest and unmanifest, me and my True Self, mortal and immortal, the initiated and the uninitiated, heaven and hell, yin and yang, etc.);

Chewing Gum: attempting to assimilate indigestible, recalcitrant thoughts that we find difficult to stomach because we realize they have no 'nutritional' value; being initially pleased to tackle a sticky subject, but then tiring of it because it loses its appeal;

Chi: vital life force; (Also known as Ki (Japan), Prana (India) Ha or Mana (Polynesian cultures), Qi (Taoists), Chi (China), Ka (Ancient Egypt);

Chiahic Reshuffling: revitalizing our thinking to move beyond disappointments, setbacks, and tragedies;

Chieftains: exalted thoughts; consummate skills, talents, and abilities; (In the Zohar, chieftains are celestial guardians);

Children: newly formed divine ideas, intentions, and inclinations;

Chillaxing: taking a mini sabbatical by 'chilling out and relaxing' from worldly concerns;

Ching Tso: quieting the flow of thoughts with the intent to connect with our original godness; (Ching Tso is a Chinese form of quiet meditation that focuses on relaxation and attaining the goodness of our original divine nature);

Chisel(s): I am statements repeated with resolve;

Chit Mastery: highly developed abstract thought; absolute intelligence;

Chlorinated Texting: mainstream religious practice of identifying the words of an original autograph copy and then eliminating later forgeries, spelling errors, etc.;

Chocmah: divine wisdom; highest feminine intuition; (In *The Science of Religion*, Paramahansa Yogananda explains: "(We) have the power of intuition, as we have the power of thought. In intuition we are in tune with Reality – with the world of bliss, with the unity in diversity." Pg. 96.);

Chohanic Sight: the clearest, most pure and elevated enlightened vision of an illumined consciousness;

Choice Management: our choices propel us towards collisions of experience and each collision is a new point of contact with our cumulative self, for better or worse.

Choice*ectomies*: eating the proverbial menu instead of the meal when it comes to seeing the absence of choice as no choice; (The truth is, we can't *not* make choices. Everything we do involves choice. Every choice we make constitutes everything we are and have been up to the point of each choice we make. Each choice signifies the cumulative us, the prosperity conscious us or the negative self-defeating us, the spiritual us or the materialistic us);

Choir: harmony in mind, body, and soul;

Choreographer: will; our ability to choose, decide, direct, and determine;

Chorten: exoterically, Tibetan for a container of holy relics; spiritually our super-consciousness as a container for divine ideas;

Chosen of God: divine ideas;

Christ: the Eternal Presence we call God in physicality; the cosmic and planetary expression of the Godhead; the Only Begotten Son of God; our True Self; the incarnated Word of God; the physical embodiment of the One Eternal Presence; [In *Breakthrough: Meister Eckhart's Creation Spirituality in New Translation*, editor Matthew Fox quotes Eckhart: "What good is it to me if the Son of God was born to Mary 1400 years ago but is not born in my person and in my culture and in my time?" pg. 336]; (See Deeper Self);

Christ Consciousness: enlightenment; illumination; errorless consciousness; super-consciousness; the highest state of awareness; absolute, universal knowing; supreme awareness; (In *Mysticism*, Evelyn Underhill says that the "incarnation, which is for popular Christianity synonymous with the historical birth and earthly life of Christ, is for the mystic not only this but also a perpetual cosmic and personal process. It is an everlasting bringing forth, in the universe and also in the individual ascending soul, of the divine and perfect Life, the pure character of God." pg. 118];

Christcentric: living truth from the inside out;

Christendom: a collective and united mind, body, and soul that is Christed; (Unfortunately, that's not where mainstream Christianity is. In *The Coming of the Cosmic Christ*, Matthew Fox says: "The coming together of the historical Christ and the Cosmic Christ will make Christianity whole at last. Christianity has been out of touch with its 'core,' its center, its sense of mystical practice and cosmic awareness. It has succumbed to a patriarchal mindset that has eroded its worship, message, and identity rendering them flat and lifeless." Pg. 7);

Christening: an affirmation of the Christ within; bestowing prosperity upon our spiritual undertakings;

Christhood: the conscious attainment and continued fulfillment of Christ Consciousness;

Christing Up: seeing ourselves as the best Christs we can be; (I invite you to *Christ up*! View your life from your Christ perspective. Imagine how fulfilling and thrilling your life will be when you live at the speed of your Christ Consciousness!);

Christmas: recognizing and celebrating that we are the Christ Presence expressing Itself as us in human form; the dawning of our awareness that we are the Christ at the point of us; the birth of the Christ Idea in us; the second coming of Christ (the first being the Christ Presence incarnating as us when we are born into human form);

Christmas Tree: spiritual enlightenment;

Christology: the theoretical psychologies, anthropologies, mythologies, liturgies, theologies, and philosophies of the meaning of the Christ Presence;

Christophanies: denotes the appearances of the Christ as Jesus after his resurrection as the enlightened being Jesus of Nazareth;

Christos: the Anointed One; fully enlightened; the stainless, deathless Individuality of the Christ Principle;

Christotokos: exoterically, the One who gave birth to the Christ'; spiritually, the Christ Principle is the cosmic aspect of the Eternal Presence in physicality, so the Eternal Presence (God) 'gave birth to' Its quantum expression, the Cosmic Christ that becomes a Planetary Christ to animate us;

Christ Principle: God *indivisibilized* as the Perfect Idea of Godness in physicality; the presence of God actualized through the Christ at the point of us as quantum beings;

Christ Self: the individualized and indivisibilized Cosmic Christ expressing as us in human form through Its planetary aspect;

Chromotheraphy: using color and light to balance the energies in our body, mind, and soul;

Chronic Fatigue Syndrome: our inability to feel a sense of purpose or believe we are going to find a clear sense of purpose; feeling weighted down by life circumstances and find ourselves looking through negative lenses;

Chronic Malnutrition, Stunting: depending entirely on a literal interpretation of scripture; (In nutrition industry terms, chronic malnutrition means a form of growth failure that develops over a long period of time);

Chronic Pejorism: being habitually pessimistic; having a Ph. D. in a negativity bias; (Pessimism, according to positive psychologist Martin Seligman, promotes depression; it produces inertia rather than activity in the face of setbacks; pessimism is self-fulfilling and is associated with poorer physical and mental health; and even when they are right and things turn out badly, they feel worse);

Chrysanthemums: our impulse for expressing joyfulness; our need for tranquility; our innate capacity for longevity; conventional beliefs;

Chrysocolla-like: our capacity for balanced self-expression, stability, and communicativeness;

Churchianity: filling one's consciousness with religious dogma, biases, and judgments; seeing one's religious views as the only legitimate religious views;

Church: cultivating a religious orientation toward spiritual growth; a collection of religious thoughts;

Church Alumni: people whose spiritual journey no longer includes going to church; a consciousness filled with more spiritual, than religious, thoughts and aspirations; (There are more church alumni in America and throughout the world than there are church goers. This worldwide demographic is much more than a simple trend. It is the result of a fantastic shift in global consciousness which is changing the way we see ourselves in relation to, well, everything! And this stunning shift in human consciousness is literally transforming the way we see and experience spirituality and religion. Make no mistake about it, the shift is absolutely monumental and enduring. It is a testament to humankind's perennial search for who we are, why we are, where we've come from, and where we are going);

Church Climatology: the spiritual consciousness of the members;

Churching: the habitual practice of regularly going to church; church hopping;

Cigarette(s), Cigar(s): foolish pursuits; false security; portals to oblivion;

Cimmerians: highly materialistic ideas and propensities;

Cinema: mental pictures; visualization;

Cinnamon-like: having purity in thought and right-thinking;

Ciphertext: glossolalia; (In IT language, ciphertext is the encrypted form of the message being sent.); (See Speaking in Tongues);

Circadian Synergy: the continuous, rhythmic, internal dialogue between the nervous, immune, and endocrine systems that governs our waking-sleeping cycle, glandular secretions, and highs and lows in body temperature; (Despite all external manipulations of "sensory nutrition" no organism, including human beings, can ever be completely entrained away from its true inner rhythm. For example, using circadian rhythms, animals gauge the angle of the sun above the horizon and combine it with the timing of light and darkness to get an accurate sense of their position. Oysters open their shells when the moon is high. Seasonal winds carry a low-frequency pulsation audible to migrating birds, allowing them to find their way back home. We humans are blessed with these inner circadian rhythms that prompt us to make circadian choices, choices that are consistent with our inner nature, our Indwelling Christ Nature);

Circle-like: experiencing eternal universality; boundless being; infinitude of oneness; spirit and matter are indivisible; the full spectrum of traits and qualities associated with zodiacal temperaments; the eternal now;

Circulations of the Multiverse: the primordial paths, channels, and/or pathways migrating we follow as etheralized spiritual beings as we travel from one universe, dimension of being, to another on our quest for Christhood;

Circumcision: the cutting off of error tendencies;

Circumambulating Around: mindfully and respectfully walking around a sacred object (altar, monument, pole, statue) to ritualistically honor and sanctify the place as holy;

Circus Daredevils: thoughts that push the limits of our current thinking;

Circuit Board: esoterically, the electro-chemical processes in our brain;

Circuit Breaker: metaphorically, denotes the need to take a 'break,' to shut our activities down when we're feeling over-worked and/or overwhelmed;

Circuit Training: engaging in a wide variety of New Thought disciplines to further our spiritual growth; (In the health and fitness industry, circuit training is going quickly from one exercise apparatus to another.);

Citizenship: the feeling of oneness and kinship with all living things; (The common division of the world into subject and object, inner world and outer world, body and soul is no longer adequate, said physicist Werner Heisenberg);

City, Town, Village: consciousness; major belief system; our body and its constituent parts; our brain and its neural real estate; a concept and the thoughts and ideas that characterize it;

City Hall: the mayoral ego, with its elected officials (worldly thoughts), as the seat of our personality;

City That Lieth Foursquare: our heart with its four chambers which is the throne of God within us;

Clairalience: clear smelling; (Psychic perception accomplished by smelling without a physical cause for the smell);

Clairaudience: clear hearing;

Claircognizance: clear knowing without observable evidence of how the knowing is accomplished;

Clairgustance: clear tasting without touching anything to our tongue;

Clairsentience: clear feeling evidenced by superior intuitive knowing; hunches; gut feelings;

Clairvoyance: superior spiritual vision; clear seeing; discerning reality beyond the veil of illusion and duality;

Clamorous Consequences: the results of error thinking and poor choices; (Consequences do not enter our lives by accident. They are the "reap-what-we-sow' result of poor choices. Some consequences enter our lives as major memos. Others are only footnotes, warning us to seek more balance and joy. All consequences, regardless of their derailment potential, teach us about ourselves);

Clapperboard: the motivation to take action; a prompting to express ourselves;

Class: intellectual direction; cognitive opportunity;

Classical Conditioning: repeating incarnational and/or reincarnational experiences; [It is said that a great world teacher laughed when he found himself in another human incarnation. Like many spiritual teachings this one reminds us that no matter how enlightened we may think we are, we are still prone to classical conditioning. Consciousness, as soon as it expresses itself in human form, finds itself in a dilemma: at the super-conscious level it knows it is one with the One Reality and at a human (egotistical) level it discovers how laughable its choice has been to subject itself to another classically conditioned 'skin school' experience]; (Classical conditioning, also called Pavlovian reinforcement, or respondent conditioning, is associative learning that was first demonstrated by Ivan Pavlov in 1927. The process for inducing classical conditioning involves presenting a neutral stimulus along with a high value stimulus. The neutral stimulus could be any event that doesn't result in an overt behavioral response from the test subject. Pavlov referred to this as a conditioned stimulus [CS]. Presentation of the high value stimulus, on the other hand, elicits an innate, often reflexive, response. Pavlov called these the *unconditional stimulus* [US] and *unconditioned response* [UR], respectively. If the CS and the US are paired repeatedly, the two stimuli become associated and the subject begins to produce a behavioral response to the CS. Pavlov referred to this as the *conditioned response* [CR]);

Classmate(s): focused thoughts and inclinations; emotions that complement specified intellectual interests; the group of souls that generally reincarnate with us time and time again;

Classroom: each incarnational experience and the various circumstances associated with that experience;

Claustrophobia: the closed in feelings we get when we feel the pressure of the consequences of our poor choices;

Clay Mannerisms: having our comprehension underwritten by human experience;

Clean Install: denotes religious fundamentalist and/or New Age brainwashing;

Clergy: mostly religious, sometimes spiritual, thoughts and aspirations;

Clickjacking: symbolizes putting someone into a trance state or hypnotic state for malicious purposes; (In the IT world, clickjacking is the malicious practice of manipulating a website user's activity by concealing hyperlinks beneath legitimate clickable content, which causes the user to perform actions which h/she didn't intend);

Cliff: an important decision point; the end, or turning point, of a particular direction;

Climacteric Point: a critical period in our spiritual unfoldment;

Climate: our emotional atmosphere;

Clinic: mind, body, and soul repair;

Cloak-ish: our ability to conceal thoughts and intentions, as well as our physical form; our penchant for intrigue, trickery, and contrivances;

Clock(s): our sense of temporality; our belief in the necessity of linearness;

Clone(s): the identical mistake repeated twice, three times, again and again;

Closet Apologists: religious fundamentalists;

Clothes Hanger: the supporting framework for our favorite perspectives;

Clothesline(s): the stream of consciousness linking our various perspectives;

Clothespin(s): the felt need for 'pinning down' a particular perspective;

Cloud, the (Cloud Computing): the electronic version of the Akashic Records;

Cloud Attributes: On the one hand, clouds represent a veiling (clouding) of the lower mind from illumination, and on the other hand, the conveyance of a divinely inspired revelation; a *white cloud* denotes an unobscured or descending Christ consciousness, spiritual intuitiveness and wisdom revealed; full realization of unity; unable to grasp (a clouding) higher spiritual truths; veiling of understanding;

Cloud of Knowing: All truth seekers, whether their journey to higher consciousness takes them through Mecca, Jerusalem, Allahabad, Amristar, CERN, Mir, or Fermilab are in good company as they search for the One which is present in All. Fortunately, the most seasoned – and enlightened – seekers of the Light are not bound exclusively by the sacred texts of their upbringing: the Bible for Christians; the Torah for Jews; the Koran for Muslims; the Guru Granth Sahib for Sikhs; the Vedas, Upanishads, and Epics for Hindus. The monumentally fortuitous thing about courageous truth seekers – the thing they have in common – is their election to expand their thinking past the literal interpretations of their particular faith tradition and soar into the esoteric and spiritual "cloud of knowing" that will someday revolutionize human thought and raise our collective human consciousness to its highest spiritual octave;

Cloud Music: spiritual truths in the cloud of knowing are music to our ears; (In Internet circles, personal digital music collections stored on secure remote servers so that they can be accessed anytime and anywhere);

Cloud of Virtue: the realization that when we eliminate the false idea that in order to be happy we need material things, a centering calm envelopes us;

Clover, Shamrock Nature: *three leaves* denote divine order (mind, idea, expression), the Trinity, humankind's three aspects (body, mind, soul), (See the Number Three symbolism); *four leaves* represent luck and prosperity, the four aspects of being (spiritual, mental, emotional, and physical), (See the Number Four symbolism); five leaves symbolize humankind, the five senses, (See the Number Five symbolism);

Clown(s): silly, lighthearted, jovial emotions that characterize our inner child; our uninhibited nature;

Clumsy Chit-Chat: a conversation between a religious fundamentalist and a metaphysician;

Coach: our conscience;

Coat of Arms: denotes our pride in our familial roots; our genealogical identity;

Coat of Many Colors: the One becomes many; the Multiverse produces many universes; unity in duality and duality in unity; spiritual gifts; outward expression (the colors that are enfolded in the white light) of our dynamic spiritual powers (white light); *losing the coat* represents losing the visible shades of our aura when we assume human form, neglecting our spiritual gifts;

Cobra: dangerous psychic powers;

Cobweb Feeling: experiencing a sensation of what feels like a phantom cobweb on our face and arms which can indicate brushing against the veil (boundary) of another dimension;

Cobwebs: neglecting our responsibilities and aspirations; unused mental powers; lingering karmic attachments;

Cockamamie Curfew: putting a limit on someone's quest for spiritual knowledge;

Cockeyed Choices: changing our principles to suit our choices instead of making choices based on our principles; (The siren call of principle-centered choices has to lift its music above the noise of expediency, the serenades of instant gratification, and the catcalls of ambition. Squeezed out of most people's lives because of the their reactions to demands of the moment, principled choices usually take a back seat to expedience, compromise, and cowardice);

Cocoon, Envelop, Cloak: our physical body; our aura; our earth experience; our mind;

Coffee-ness: desiring intellectual stimulation; enjoying a time of sociability and warmth; creating a climate of rest and serenity;

Coffee Maker: our ability to engineer intellectual stimulation; our aptitude for creating enriching social experiences;

Coffice, Cofficing: an office away from our office – with plenty of coffee; using a coffee shop as an ashram, chapel, mini spiritual center,

Cognitive Cliff: the sudden drop in attention span and buy-in caused by too much cognitive dissonance when being introduced to a mind-bending religious and/or esoteric concept; (See Abortion; Chemicalization);

Coins: thoughts about money, opportunities, consumption, spending;

Cold Boot, Hard Boot: sharing highly esoteric teachings with someone who has never taken a New Thought course before; an episode of drastic cognitive dissonance;

Cold Calling: praying to an anthropomorphic goodie god in the sky for something we want;

Cold Storage: the place we put all of those unopened CD's, books, DVD's, albums, and other church-related material we buy from speakers and workshop leaders;

Collapse Zone: our body is a collapse zone when we fill it with self-negating, base, worldly thoughts that weaken it and lead to dis-ease; (In firefighting terminology, a collapse zone is the area around a burning and/or burned structure that could be filled with debris if the building were to collapse.);

Collapsing the Wave: The One (God, El Shaddai, Ahura Mazda, Omitofo, Yehovah, Allah, Brahman, EK Onkar, Yahweh, Aigonz, Ishvara, Dadar, Mino-satihgar, Japa, Elohim, Infinite Invisibleness, Kane, Siebog, Odin) becoming the *many* (matter in all of its forms: human beings, intergalactic beings, cosmic beings, invisible beings, planets, suns, galaxies, universes) is an ancient dictum. And, so, we propose, in a quantumly spiritual sense, the One expresses Itself as a wave and becomes the many (particle) when consciousness assumes separation and duality [collapsed wave]. We are the activity of God (the One by many names) expressing Itself into visibility at the point of us. Most of the esoteric wisdom traditions allude to this truth. Collapsed waves are particles expressing *isness* in limited, parametered forms. As collapsed "spiritual waves" we humans have chosen a "particulate existence" (an incarnation) in order to understand who we really are. (It appears that when a light photon is not being observed, it exists in its wave form, but at the moment it is observed, the wave collapses and becomes a particle. The act of observation collapses potentiality into reality. Prior to being observed, the wave exists in a state of potentiality. That potential becomes *manifest* into a particularity when we look at it.);

Collateral Household: the thoughts and ideas that make up a particular belief system; (In anthropological terms collateral household refers to the extended family including siblings and their spouses and children.);

Collective Apparition: an apparition seen simultaneously by more than one person;

Collective Unconscious: the pool of our individual unconscious archetypes, universal mental predispositions, and quantum life patterns that we carry from one incarnation and/or reincarnation to another; (In psychology, the collective unconscious is a Jungian term that describes the archetypes [atavistic and universal images, cultural symbols, and recurring themes present the fundamental experiences of human life] passed along to each generation to the next in folklore and stories, dreams, art, myths, and spiritual and religious icons.); our collective psychological, primordial (pre-human), and psychic inheritance;

Colleges, Universities: incarnational experiences that follow our initial skin school experience;

Coloring Book(s): childhood experiences; the intersection between conformity and creativity; (In *The Progress Principle: Using Small Wins to Ignite Joy, Engagement, and Creativity at Work*, Teresa Amabile says that "creativity is positively associated with joy and love and negatively associated with anger, fear, and anxiety. People are happiest when they come up with a creative idea, but they're more likely to have a breakthrough if they were happy the day before. There's a kind of virtuous cycle. When people are excited, there's a better chance that they'll make a cognitive association that incubates overnight and shows up as a creative idea the next day. One day's happiness often predicts the next day's creativity");

Coma Consciousness: our ego-driven, sense-oriented consciousness which is wrapped up in the illusions spun by the world of outer appearances; a consciousness that dwells on sickness, lack, fear, guilt, and greed; being ordered around by disorder; a state of gross unawareness that keeps us comatose and clueless as to our divine origins; a 'walled in' consciousness that needs to be resuscitated; the worship of outer appearances that consistently gives dominion to material things; a consciousness that perpetually denies our innate divinity; a dogmatic consciousness based on a literal-only interpretation of sacred scripture;

Comb(s): reminders to focus and direct our inner strength and vitality;

Comedians: metaphorically, lighthearted life experiences that make us laugh and bring us joy and comfort; 'full circle' experiences that remind us not to take life too seriously;

Comedy of Errors, Comedy of the Absurd: repeated incarnational and reincarnational experiences; the mindless parade of error thoughts, words, choices, and actions;

Comedy of Innocence: the loss of memory of our previous incarnations and/or reincarnations to spare us any sense of guilt or shame of choosing another unnecessary skin school experience; (In anthropological terms, a comedy of innocence is a ritualized symbolic behavior designed to alleviate individual or communal guilt about an execution, sacrifice, or to hide the collective blame for such an action. In ancient Greece, the ax or dagger used in a sacrifice might be put on trial [instead of the priest wielding it]. A sacrificial animal might be required to 'volunteer' by shaking its head or by walking up to the altar to eat the grain sitting on it. A sacrificial victim might be 'condemned' *after* being released where it could go a forbidden holy grove or tabooed sacred mountain [Exodus 19:12-13; Judges 11:30-40]. Remnants of the comedy of innocence include the hangman's black mask [to erase the executioner's identity], the custom of granting a condemned prisoner's last request or final the meal (to alleviate any sense of cruelty on the jailer's part);

Comet(s): highly evolved spiritual A ha's;

Comic Book(s): the record of humankind's incredibly naïve journey toward enlightenment;

Coming-of-Age-Stories: Bible, Torah, Koran, etc.;

Common Denominators: things common to all faith traditions: prayer, meditation, rituals, hymns, sacred texts, doctrine, beliefs, sacraments, etc.;

Common Grace: general, everyday opportunities we have to expiate error from our consciousness by choosing reverence and goodness;

Compass Traits: spiritual laws; personal integrity;

Competition, Rivalry, Contest: a monument to a consciousness of lack;

Compost: spent ideas, aptitudes, capacities, inclinations, quirks, mannerisms, endowments, and whims that can eventually be used in different ways with a little nourishment;

Computer Traits: the need for cultivating the rational, linear, unemotional aspects of ourselves; this technology also denotes our capacity for storing memories, retrieving them, and categorizing them; our sense of having unexplored potential is also indicated; computers also imply our inclination for searching the Akashic Records for knowledge; *hackers* denote any thought or emotion that characterizes our attempts to sabotage our spiritual growth and human happiness; computers can also suggest our logical thinking processes; *computer games* contribute to our need for play in any medium; (See Akashic Records and the Internet);

Conceptual Pareidolia: seeing an illusionary, but familiar image, or hearing a recognizable sound that is not consistent with what we are looking at or listening to. (seeing the image of Mother Mary outlined on a screen door; seeing the face of Jesus in a cloud formation; hearing a manipulative message on a record being played backwards; interpreting a Rorschach ink blot test);

Concupiscence Contamination: the natural tendency of error thoughts to produce harmful consequences;

Concurrent Sentence: a particular reincarnation experience where we get to burn off the dross of a number of karmic errors; (In the legal system, concurrent sentences are prison terms that require two or more offenses to be served at the same time, rather than one after the other.);

Concussion: what we get with the absence of heart-to-head resuscitation;

Concussion Management: spiritual, religious, psychological, cosmological, philosophical, and anthropological triage rendered to help correct our proverbial 'fall from grace';

Confessing on the Run: recognizing (confessing) an error thought, word, and/or action on our journey toward enlightenment and correcting the mistake by choosing a more spiritual thought, word, and/or action in its place;

Confetti: joyful, happy, optimistic thoughts; an air of celebration; (Studies show that optimists are more likely to report a sense of mastery and high self-regard and less likely to show depression and anxiety);

Confidential Phishing: sharing confidential personal information with someone we trust who uses that information against us; (In IT security language, phishing is the use of e-mails that appear to originate from a trusted source in order to trick a user into entering h/her valid credentials at a fake website.);

Confirmation Bias: tending to look for what confirms to our current beliefs, and to ignore or undervalue what contradicts those beliefs;

Conflict of Interest: studying spiritual teachings and truth principles, but engaging in highly materialistic undertakings;

Conglomerate(s): ruling spiritual and/or religious concepts;

Congregational Cussedness: an unfortunate phenomenon that occurs quite frequently when members of an organized church abandon their religious training and become an angry mob of childish contrarians;

Conking Out: zoning out from spiritual discussions; choosing to be more religious than spiritual;

Conopas: denote good luck, prosperity, and protection: (Conopas are devotional Inca stone figurines that bring protection and prosperity);

Consciousness: a Universal and Cosmic energy that is the ground of all being; the Source of Mind which is the source of our brain; (This is a partial but concise summary of 2,600 years of philosophical, psychological, theological, and scientific speculation on the nature of human consciousness, according to neurobiologists J. Neisser: Awareness. Attentiveness. Alertness. Wakefulness. Intelligence. Self-arousal. Self-reflection. Mental representation. Self-recognition. Symbolic association. Active thinking. Learned behavior. Linguistic understanding. Cognizance. Experience. Imagination. Internal testimony. Comprehension. Introspection. Personal identity. Remembering. Predicting. Imitation. Mind. Free will. Moral conscience. Inner speech. Explicit memory. Temporality. Subjective imagination. Analogy formation. Intentionality. Endogenous feedback. Rational control. Mental time travel. Emergent creativity. Qualia. Universal being. God);

Consciousness Omega Point: the end of one conscious level of development and the beginning of another; (In *Observer Mechanics*, Donald Hoffman says that "consciousness and its contents are all that exists. Space-time, matter and fields never were the fundamental denizens of the universe, but have always been, from their beginning, among the humbler contents of consciousness, dependent on it for their very being.");

Consecutive Sentences: a series of reincarnational experiences; (In legal circles, consecutive sentences refer to prison terms that require two or more offenses to be served one after the other.);

Conspicuous Consumption: the particular way some people dress, act, and communicate that displays their brand of religion and theology;

Consumption Audience: worldly and/or spiritual thoughts that create their respective choices and actions; (In marketing terms, a consumption audience is simply a target audience of both prospects and potential buyers);

Cookie Cutter Outlook: dogmatic perspective;

Cosmic Cosmology: recognizing that we are all expressions of the Universal Eternal Presence and therefore come from the same cosmological dust;

Consecutive-Moments-Of-Nowness: being a permanent resident of the present;

Constellation Proclivities: fixed belief systems;

Contacts, Glasses: the desire to see the phenomenal world more clearly with the recognition that we must be able to function successfully in skin school; *3D glasses* suggest that Universal substance is closer than we think;

Contortionist(s): twisted, distorted, lopsided, asymmetrical thoughts and inclinations that characterize our warped belief that we can achieve spiritual ends through gross material means;

Controlled Circulation: applying truth principles to everything we do, knowing that every situation in which we find ourselves is 'qualified' to receive a spiritual treatment; (In advertising terms, controlled circulation is circulation that is limited to people who qualify to receive a particular publication);

Conversational Chiggers: snide remarks and hurtful innuendoes that 'get under our skin';

Conversion Experience: adopting a spiritual perspective as our default perspective:

Convict, Prisoner, Criminal: imprisoned potential; misdirected aims and ambitions;

Cookie(s): I am statements; sweet words to self; soul treats;

Copenhagen Interpretation: Out of all of the infinite possibilities in our thought universe (our consciousness) whenever we formulate a particular thought (a collapsed wave) we have just given a location to a thought form. From a spiritual standpoint, thoughts are things. And if they are things they are collapsed wave functions. Our consciousness is filled with thought potential. Once a thought form rises from the infinite sea of thought possibilities it becomes a concretized vibration that has slowed down long enough to become an actual thought in the midst of an infinite number of thought possibilities. [Sounds a little Copenhagen, don't you think?]; (The Copenhagen interpretation holds that a key feature of quantum mechanics is that the state of every *particle* is described by a *wave function*, which is a mathematical representation used to calculate the probability for it to be found in a location or a state of motion. That's quite a sentence. Let's see if we can make it more intelligible. According to the Copenhagen interpretation, the act of measurement causes a calculated set of probabilities to "collapse" to the value defined by a particular measurement. This feature of the mathematical representations is known as *wave function collapse*.);

Cop-Out Cop: spiritual discernment; superior intuition;

Copper Temperament: intellectual acumen; ability to reason;

Copycat(s): similar thoughts and emotions;

Copyright: our quantum (incarnational) and spiritual identity; (We are copyrighted. We are one of a kind – and, we are not our genes. Psychologist Sonja Lyubomirsky says our genes do not determine our life experiences and behaviors. Our hard-wiring can be dramatically influenced by our experience and behavior.);

Corn-ishness: the multi-storied human ego; a grain of corn represents one of many belief systems; the *husk* is the egocentric consciousness (unenlightened human personality) that must be discarded if we are to become enlightened; *harvested corn* represents the spiritual capacities attained at the end of one's current level of spiritual unfoldment;

Cornerstone, Keystone, Mainstay, Linchpin: our innate divinity, especially as an expression of the Christ Presence; the Only Begotten Son which has become the Only Forgotten Son; (The cornerstone analogy is an ancient one and is generally based on the cornerstone symbolism of Biblical texts (Psalm 118:22, Matthew 21:42, Mark 12:10, and Luke 20:17) which confuse the foundation stone with the cornerstone. A foundation stone is placed at the very outset of construction and is referred to as the first stone. It is at ground level. If it is "rejected" the building will not take place. The 'real' stone these passages are referring to is more likely an 'arch stone' or keystone [capstone] which is not only unique and one of a kind, but critical for holding up an arch 'from above,' bringing the perfection and stability the structure needs.)

Cornucopia: eternal life; each skin school experience; consciousness itself; Universal Substance; potentiality; the worlds of possibility and probability;

Corpse(s): spent ideas; unrealized dreams;

Corridor(s): seeking conventional routes to enlightenment; choosing traditional lines of thinking to move between newly formed concepts and ideas; the birth canal;

Corroboree: transformational thinking: (In Australian Aboriginal terms means a place ceremony and creative expression that leads to transformation);

Cosmetics: anything and everything outside of us in the phenomenal world;

Cosmetic Catechism: introspectively reminding ourselves, through informal question and answer sessions, about our stated religious and/or spiritual beliefs when we begin to doubt how well we've applied them;

Cosmic: Universal and Multiversal harmony, regulation, and order which inter-permeates everything in the manifest and unmanifest, finite and infinite, visible and invisible realms of being; the totality of Eternal Beingness;

Cosmic Christ: the universal *indivisibleness* of God expressing Itself in space time; realized eschatology; (In *The Cosmic Christ*, Hans-Werner Schroeder writes. "From the very beginning Christ holds cosmic position: he is before the world, before all 'creation.' Pg.); [In *Quantum Theology*, Mairmuid O'Murchu asserts, "The Cosmic Christ is the God of universal life and love, whose revelation unfolds over 18 billion years of (known) evolution, to be the originating mystery from which we devise all our divine personages and images. All the god-figures of the different religion, including Christianity, emanate from this cosmic originating source." Pg. 190.]; (In *The Coming of the Cosmic Christ*, Matthew Fox explains: "The Cosmic Christ ushers in an era of coherence, of ending the separations, divisions, dualisms, piecemealness that characterize a world without mysticism, a society without a living cosmology." Pg. 135);

Cosmic Consciousness: the Universal, Unifying, Limitless Essence that radiates from the Eternal Presence that pervades everythingness and nothingness; the Foundation of all that is and isn't in universes and multiverses; It's definable aspects are universal omniscience, omnipresence, omnipotence, and omni-activity;

Cosmic Cube: the consciousness we possess when we are incarnated (unfolding a cube turns it into a cross, which represents our human form with outstretched arms, forming the cross – our crucified material form);

Cosmic Diving Board: our decision to plunge into another skin school experience;

Cosmic Eye, Solar Hub, Exit From the Cosmos: the opening of the Crown Chakra;

Cosmic Inflation: We have access to the spiritual realms through the activity of our 'inflated' thinking. Our thoughts are *particles* within our consciousness, which will expand according to the quality of our expanded spiritual awareness. We can move to different levels of awareness, which will take us to higher levels of consciousness, one of which is Cosmic Consciousness; (The Quantum perspective of cosmic inflation holds that a nanosecond before the Big Bang that created our universe – less time than it would take to return someone's smile who just smiled at you – the 'space' that would become our universe expanded exponentially (10^{78} in volume, driven by a negative-pressure vacuum energy density). That is, in each consecutive-moment-of-now the universe expanded to twice the size it was a nanosecond before. The original theory of 'cosmic inflation' was proposed by Alan Guth in the 1980's. During cosmic inflation, space repels space continuously, so that the more space there is, the more space there is going to be because space is repelling space exponentially.);

Cosmic Law(s): the *out*picturing of the Eternal Presence in physicality measured mathematically and quantumly by our limited awareness of the nature of the universe and universal principles;

Cosmic Life: our sojourn in physicality;

Cosmic Net: In Matthew 13:47-50 Jesus' disciples cast a net into the sea, and bring up a whole bunch of stuff in it. It's chock full – but not everything is "gold." So they pull the net to shore and separate the good fish from the bad fish and other junk caught up in the net. (The good fish are put in a basket, and the outcast stuff is thrown away. There's a final verse here that says, *"This is how it will be at the end of the age. The angels will come and separate the wicked from the righteous and throw them into the fiery furnace, where there will be weeping and gnashing of teeth."* What this is saying from a spiritual perspective is that a higher spiritual perspective is like a "cosmic net" which catches all of our thoughts, intentions, ideas. At some point, we review these and are able, with divine wisdom and understanding, to keep the ones that serve our higher good, and discard the ones that could limit our spiritual growth. The 'weeping and gnashing of teeth' reference means that sometimes it isn't easy, because we get attached to our habits, our thoughts, our embedded theology. It is difficult to release them, and we sometimes complain, or make excuses, or resist. But when we are able to let them go, we are able to move to a whole new level of awareness of our Oneness with Spirit!);

Cosmic Play: any and all emanations of the Supreme Consciousness (God) in the manifest and unmanifest realms of being;

Cosmic 2x4: a self-denigrating assumption I invite you to compost! (The belief in a cosmic 2x4 – that there is some celestial being or something 'out there' trying to get our attention to teach us an important lesson. There is no cosmic 2x4! The 'whack of clarity' between our eyes comes from our Third Eye, the inner spiritual eye, the mystical gate or portal that represents the seer in us. The 'whack' doesn't come from 'out there.' "I've been hit by a cosmic 2 x 4" is the phrase we tend to use when we run smack into an experience that feels bad, that is so sudden and shocking that it wakes us up.

It could be a serious illness, or a job challenge, or something whacky with our relationships. Or maybe it's something showing up that we thought we had long since handled! Whatever it is, it feels uncomfortable — so we use the cosmic 2x4 expression to justify it, implying that some being outside of us is trying to get our attention to teach us some important lesson! And if we don't get it the first time, look out! The whack is going to get progressively worse till we finally pay attention. We've got to get over that kind of rationalization. There is no cosmic 2x4);

Cosmogenesis: the birth of enlightened thoughts and belief systems;

Cosmogony: the branch of cosmology that seeks to explain the origin of the universe and its quantum parts;

Cosmology: the science of the structure, laws, and operations of the universe; (Serious students of Truth must be willing to legitimize a shared cosmology with quantum physics and the sciences. A cosmology which holds that the origin and nature of the universe is inextricably linked with the origin and nature of our relationship with the One Reality we call by many names. That shared cosmology will be criticized. It will be misunderstood. It may even be ridiculed. But the marriage between science and spirituality, between quantum physics and prayer, between the neocortex and forgiveness, between the Hayflick limit and the sky's the limit must take place); (See Hour Glass for description of Hayflick limit);

Cosmos: the space-time, quantum expression of the Eternal Presence within the galactic nature of Super-Consciousness;

Cosmos Connection: achieving the farther reaches of our collective super-conscious potential;

Cosmotheism: believing that there is an intentional purpose in life and in the cosmos, and that there is an essential unity (universal consciousness) that binds all living beings in, and including, the inorganic cosmos, as one;

Cost Per Impression: the effect our personal image, language, and behavior have on whether or not people see us as credible advocates of our professed spiritual and/or religious tradition; (In online marketing terms, the cost per impression refers to the costs associated with internet advertising where advertisers pay each time an ad is displayed and viewed by potential buyers);

Costs: the mental, emotional, and physical consequences of denying our innate divinity;

Costume(s): deliberate attempts to disguise our intentions or conceal our motives; playful expressions of our libido, historical and future interests, creativity, and childlike merriment; our corporeal bodies; our emotional facades; (In *A Treatise on White Magic*, Alice Bailey writes that "mixed motives are universal. Pure motive are rare and where they exist there is success and achievement. Singleness of purpose may occasionally be realized in high moments, but it does not abide with us always." Pg. 558-559);

Costume Party: the collective denial of our innate divinity;

Cotahuasi Valley: denotes the deepest, unknown region of our subconscious; (In Inca ecological terms it is the deepest valley in the world – 11,600 feet);

Coto-Máchacuy: the presumably unknown parts of us that lie deep within our psyche; (In Amazon mythology, a giant serpent with two heads which inhabits the bottom of large lakes); (See Sasquatch, Big Foot);

Couch Potato: someone who doesn't apply the truth teachings h/she knows;

Cough(s): nervousness; reticence; coughing up phlegm suggests our desire to eliminate past non-productive experiences such as unresolved resentments and compulsions;

Cough Drops: the self-talk we employ to keep us from saying (coughing up) something we know we'll regret later; healing thoughts;

Country Club: our earth experience;

Coup d'état: the small group of conspiratory ideas that lead to the concept of original sin and an external, anthropomorphic god in the sky and/or a evil, horned, red devil with a tail that take over our thinking;

Coupons: positive affirmations;

Coup Stick: used by Lakota warriors for counting coup on the enemy; truth (coup stick) cancelling out error (enemy);

Courthouse, Courtroom: feeling judged or tried in some way; experiencing a stressful period in our lives that suggests our being caught up in possible legal issues or dealing with authority; Universal Spiritual Laws;

Covenant Qualities: mastering the skin school experience; a *new covenant* denotes aspiring toward illumination;

Covered Dish Weight: the amount of pounds (3 to 8) we put on at a typical church's covered dish get-together;

Cover-Up(s): intentional mistranslations of scripture; unintentional mistranslations of scripture that are found and then left uncorrected and unammended;

Covetousness: desiring spiritual rewards while relishing material attachments;

Cow Attributes: acknowledging the feminine principle; honoring the nourishing, sustaining, vital, and life-giving principle in nature;

Cow Horse: a minister and/or congregant who seems to have a sense for when people are honoring the sacred cows of their religious denomination; (In cowboy circles, a cow horse is a horse who has an uncanny ability to anticipate the behavior of cattle. ☺);

CPR: applying spiritual laws and principles;

Crab Peculiarities: sensing the need for contingency management; opting for indirectness and unorthodox movement; preferring the path of least resistance; could also simply suggest a 'pinch' of crabbiness;

Crackerjack Choices: divinely-inspired, hallowed, spiritually-attuned decisions;

Crackpot(s), Lunatic(s), Wacho(s): divinity-denying thoughts;

Crackpot Fallacy: seeing ourselves as merely human beings;

Cradle(s): represents our tendencies for beginning anew and seeking fresh starts; also suggests the origin and/or epicenter of new ideas; (See Manger);

Crank Call(s): false assurances from our warped ego;

Cranky Congregation: a collection of unruly inclinations, unscrupulous thoughts, or unsettling intentions;

Crapware: spiritual and/or religious teachings that are created solely for their monetary value without any thought given for their transformational value;

Crash: the consequences of neglecting our spiritual growth; the collision of powerful thoughts and ideas;

Crater(s): our subconscious; (Much of what we see 'out there' is actually manufactured 'in here' by our brain, much like photo software shades in the red areas of people looking toward a flash. According to radiologist Zhang Raichle, only a small fraction of the inputs to our occipital lobe comes directly from the external; world; the rest comes from internal memory stores and perceptual-processing modules);

Crawling: implies struggle and laborious movement;

Crawl Space: our subconscious;

Cray Perspective: an insane (crazy) belief in the inerrancy of scripture, an anthropomorphic god or devil in the sky, and holding onto fossilized dogma;

Creation: the boundless Be-ness of the One Presence; the coming forth of something out of something else;

Credit Cards: the choices we make;

Creditor(s): karmic debts that we carry from one incarnation into another;

Creed Seepage: the poorer our religious conviction, the richer the excuses are to justify it;

Creepypasta: a thought that seems so uncharacteristic of us surfaces unexpectedly and catches us off guard, because it's not something we believe we would even think about or come from our consciousness; (In literary circles, creepypasta is a short story posted online designed to shock, frighten, or disconcert readers.);

Cremation: fiery truth incinerating error;

Crepe Myrtle-like: traditional and conventional propensities; domesticity;

~ Spiritually Speaking ~

Crib: each skin school experience; pediatric theology;

Crime Scene: each error thought, word, and action;

Criminal(s): error thoughts, inclinations, tendencies, dispositions, impulses, penchants, preferences, proclivities, temperaments, fancies, urges, whims, peculiarities, mannerisms, traits, choices, beliefs, and actions;

Criminalize: letting one error thought, word, or action lead to another;

Cringe-Worthy Slips: thoughts we have that are totally uncharacteristic of us and are thoughts we have not shared with anyone else because we feel embarrassed to have had them; blasphemous statements, expletives, and obscenities that belittle our divine connection;

Cripple(s): thoughts that stifle emotions from being expressed; emotions that censor reason; dogmatic thoughts that characterize our refusal to accept legitimate scientific proofs;

Crisis Apparition: an apparition in which a person is seen within a few hours of an unexpected tragedy such as an accident, sudden illness, or death;

Christ: God in physicality; our True Essence;

Critter Control: Critters are false assumptions, engrained beliefs based on those false assumptions, self-defeating habits, feelings of unworthiness, fears, doubts in our ability to prosper, negative thinking, and a host of other wild and untamed thought and feeling critters. (These are all critters that keep us flat out or up a tree instead of living confidently and happily at the speed of our Christ Consciousness. A bear of a doubt or a grizzly of a false assumption can keep us immobilized or up a tree for years);

Crocodile Disposition: gaining inner clarity; intuitive fluidity; fearlessness; being creative and innovative; having physical power and fierce determination; using patient stealth; depending on our physical strength;

Crocus-like: growth-oriented; embrace new beginnings; welcome change;

Crop Circles: sizable, mysterious, uniform patterns created outdoors by the flattening of crops such as corn, wheat, barley, and rye;

Cross-Dressing: donning our physical bodies when we choose another incarnational experience;

Cross-Fertilization: making it a practice to study the tenets and teachings of a number of faith traditions and then integrating the teachings into our daily lives;

Cross-like Qualities: physicality itself; our human experience; our incarnational and reincarnational experiences; our skin school matriculation; (the cross bar, our cruciform nature, represents human consciousness, coma consciousness - the vertical bar represents Spirit's descent into human consciousness); (From a dogmatic fundamentalist perspective the cross is a gruesome religious symbol which retails guilt, sin, shame, blood, suffering, and condemnation. From a spiritual perspective, the mud, blood, and burden of the cross misses the most important point of the Easter experience! A more esoteric view of the crucifixion takes it out of a mainstream religious guilt trip and lifts the Easter story to its spiritual significance. The crucifixion represents the crossing out of error from our consciousness);

Crossing Over: the moment when we, animals, and plants leave our dense physical bodies and enter the astral world; making our transition;

Crossroads: the intersection of spirit and matter; opting for the spiritual over the material; choosing light over darkness; choosing spiritual perspectives over the embedded theology of our childhoods;

Crowd Funding, Equity Crowd Funding, Crowd Equity: using both brain hemispheres, life experiences, our three levels of consciousness (subconscious, conscious, and super-conscious) to 'fund' our current thinking, being and doing; [In finance and relief terms, the practice of funding a project or venture by raising small amounts of money from large numbers of people, typically via the Internet (Televangelists, musicians, filmmakers, and artists have successfully used crowd funding to garner money from the masses)];

Crowdsourcing: using a variety of esoteric perspectives to interpret scripture;

Crown Properties: illumined intellect; superior knowing; the summit of enlightenment;

Crown of Thorns: Sovereignty over a materialistic consciousness and the path to enlightenment are attained through subordinating the intellect;

thorns are prickly biases and assumptions, misjudgments, barbs caused by uncontrolled sense appetites, and drawing wrong conclusions;

Crucifixion: the crossing out of error; involution and evolution; the process biologically where cruciform DNA recombinates and repairs itself in the cells is similar to our personal cosmology where our cruciform nature recombinates with our cosmic divine essence; (We actually experience two crucifixions: the first being our descent into physicality when the physical body is the cross and the five senses are our five 'wounds'; and the second crucifixion is our ascent toward a perfected spiritual beingness which takes place in the place called Golgotha 'the skull.');

Crucifixion Eclipse: a period of darkness (indecision) just before error is crossed out; (See Readiness Potential Isthmus, Bereitschafts Potential);

Crufting: poorly crafted religious language and/or spiritual courseware that confuses congregants with its complicated imagery and scholarship; (In IT lingo, badly designed, unnecessarily complicated, or unwanted code or software);

Crutches: aids not only for our physical mobility but can also denote conventional thoughts we cling to when highly transformative spiritual concepts shake our conventional foundations; conventional dogma; literal interpretations of sacred scripture; excuses;

Crypt(s), Mausoleum(s), Sepulcher(s): our subconscious; subterranean vaults used for initiations and/or burials; (Actually, the entire cosmos is a sepulcher from which we must come forth into our regenerated spiritual bodies);

Cryptomnesic Recall: trying to explain the origin of experiences that we believe to be original but which are actually based on memories or recollections of events we've forgotten;

Cryptozoology: researching creatures such as the Abominable Snowman, Yeren, Yowie, werewolf, the Loch Ness Monster, Zeuglodonts, and the unicorn whose existences have not been verified; our search for our hidden animal nature;

Crystal Ball: our natal chart coupled with our power of choice; when we are fully aligned with our Divine Nature and connect with our inner wisdom we receive the guidance and direction we need;

Crystal Cord: the laser-like Light Essence of the Eternal Presence that animates and sustains us as physical beings; (See Silver Cord);

Crystallomancy: divining that uses a crystal ball as the medium for interpretation;

Cube Farm: the place (our head) where we cross out error (the cube is a collapsed cross); (In business terms, a cube farm is an office filled with cubicles);

Cuckoo-ish: harboring deviousness and deceitfulness; dealing with feelings of unreciprocated affections and unrequited romantic love;

Cue Power: using a well-known spiritual and/or religious tenet to inspire followership; (In billiards terminology, cue power describes the amount of control a player can manufacture when playing shots with heavy spin and great pace.);

Cul-de-Sac(s): circular thinking; spiritual communities cuddling next to mainstream religious 'highways';

Cult-like Propensities: materialistic thoughts that spring from a highly narcissistic ego that demands mindless followership;

Cultural Lag: gaining spiritual knowledge and then not applying the learning; (Sociologically, a dysfunction in the sociocultural system that occurs when a change occurs in one part of the system without a complementary adjustment in another part of the system);

Culture Shock: the surprise and disorientation, accompanied with awe and wonder we experience when we go from one cusp of consciousness into another, more enlightened perspective;

Cum Laude Vegetarianism: veganism; (See Vegan);

Cupid-like Impulses: the desire for union, oneness; loving thoughts;

Cupping, Meyboom, Baguan: a form of alternative Oriental healing that involves placing glass cups on specific meridians to cleanse, detoxify, and mobilize blood flow;

Cuppy Lie: spending our day in a depressed mood; (In golf terms, a cuppy lie is when the ball is sitting down slightly, usually in a small depression, making it difficult to play.);

Curfew: the temporal lifespan of each human incarnation;

Curing Agent(s): positive words and affirmations; meditation and affirmative prayer; right actions; (In the nail care industry, curing agents are substances - catalysts or accelerators - used to "harden" [cure] a product.);

Curses: an unenlightened ego's antics;

Curtain(s): points of unawareness; obscured vision; the extent of our knowledge in a particular area; a mental block;

Cusp Threshold: the narrow consciousness veil between one level of awareness and another;

Customer Lifetime Value, User Lifetime Value: the value placed on a church volunteer who offers h/her time, talents, tithes and treasures; (In marketing language, the customer lifetime value is defined as the dollar value of a customer relationship);

Cyberbaiting: setting up a spiritual and/or religious teacher who is leading a workshop so that h/she gets upset at your behavior and loses self-control in the heat of the moment. A video of the awkward moment is recorded and posted on social media sites.

Cyberbullying, Physical Bullying, Denominational Bullying: harassing, threatening, embarrassing, and/or humiliating behaviors leveled at someone who is different than we are; prejudicial exclusion of people whose life preferences are not mainstream preferences;

Cyberchondriac: believing that all of the religious and spiritual information we find on the Internet not only applies to us, but is reliable and factual; (In IT language, the penchant for compulsively searching the Internet for information about real or imagined symptoms of illnesses we believe we have;

Cyberspace, Electronic Superhighway: virtual reality; etherality; the astral plane;

Cybersquatting: denotes claiming the rights to something simply by occupying it; some religious and spiritual "teachers" claim the rights to a certain story, terminology, and/or practice as their own thinking that if it's private domain they can use it and prevent others from using it; (In the mid-1800's in America, squatters claimed rights to land they didn't own simply by occupying the land in question. In the early 1990's squatters saw the potential value of high profile domain names and registered as many as they could for investment purposes. Then companies who wanted domain names for their own company names had to buy them from squatters);

Cyclopeaic Circumference: the pervasiveness and omnipresence of the Eternal Presence throughout physicality;

Cyst(s): error thoughts and attitudes that we allow to fester;

Cytonaut(s): those of us who see human, animal, and plant cells as centers of spiritual and biological intelligence that can teach us how to bridge the cellular us and the spiritual us.

Daathology: our inborn need for and pursuit of knowledge, and from a spiritual standpoint – esoteric knowledge; (Daath is a Gnostic term for knowledge);

Daffodil Flexibility: the trumpeting of newness and change; our propensity for cheerfulness, positivity, joy, and optimism;

Dagger, Knife, Switchblade: a cutting remark leveled at us that we see as threatening; a sharp barb or poignant thought that cuts us to the quick;

Dahlia-like: spiritual; esoteric interests;

Daimonic Possession: our Divine Nature; (Daimon is a Greek term not to be confused with demon. It is our inner instructor, the Divine Spirit, the Extraordinary Us, who guides our soul to perfection. In the original Hermetic works daimon means 'god,' 'angel,' or 'genius.');

Daisy-ness: innocence; chastity; purity; freshness; love and its hopefulness; humanitarian instincts; goodwill orientation;

Dakinic Pedigree: superior wisdom and discernment; (In Tibetan mythology, dakinis were a race of awakened female entities who were renowned for their great wisdom and power.);

Damnable Defunding: If our mental energy is not used to elevate our worldly thoughts to spiritual thoughts, the mental energy degenerates into a stagnant pool of mentation that produces malignant vibrations which perpetuate chronic degenerative thinking;

Danburite-like: our aptitude for traveling the spiritual path with ease and grace;

Dance Floor: a skin school experience;

Dancing: enjoying the thrill of harmonious partnering; desiring celebratory movement and happy relationships; also denotes harmonious liaisons and the union of masculine and feminine qualities;

Dance Recital: our Quantum Self's reintegration process that prepares us for our next incarnation;

Dandelion-ish: gypsy-like; wanderer; explorer;

Dandruff: the consequences of error; the fall-out from poor choices;

Daredevil: a spiritual idea entering an egocentric consciousness;

Dark Forces: our error-prone impulses, inclinations, actions, and habits;

Dark Matter: dark matter is the harmonic aspect of Cosmic Consciousness because cosmic connectivity, unity, and equilibrium unite everything. Believe it or not Cosmic Consciousness has gravitational pull, yet an eternal expansive quality that keeps it perennially active and vibrant; (According to quantum physicists, dark matter is matter that is inferred to exist from gravitational effects on visible matter and gravitational lensing of background radiation, but that neither emits nor scatters light or other electromagnetic radiation, and so cannot be directly detected via optical or radio astronomy. Ninety-five percent of the density of the universe is comprised of dark matter and dark energy: 25 percent dark matter and 70 percent dark energy. Although dark matter is invisible, it has mass, and so it causes space to curve, which means it bends light. Dark matter is referred to as 'dark' because it is invisible and has as its background 'color' space. Observations of the speeds at which galaxies rotate and the speed at which they move in clusters have led most astronomers to conclude that galaxies are embedded in an envelope of dark matter consisting of five to ten times the amount of visible matter they contain);

Darkness, Pawl: unawareness of or refusal to believe in our innate divinity; using an enlightened spiritual perspective as the basis for material appetites and misdeeds; ignorance of spiritual principles and laws; a purely materialistic world view; non-manifested light; unactualized illumination; neglected enlightenment;

Darkroom: a carnal concept; a grossly materialistic consciousness; a thought that denies our innate divinity;

Darkslide: following errant thoughts with errant actions; (In photography terms, a darkslide refers to placing an opaque sheet over the front of a sheet film holder to protect the film from exposure to light);

Data Processing: processing information between our ears; (In information technology, data processing typically refers to the processing of information by machines);

Daughter-likeness: maturing emotions; ripening emotions; blossoming feelings;

Dawn Disposition: the initial realization of a spiritual insight; renewal of our spiritual journey;

Day-like Qualities: intellectual clarity; higher understanding; spiritual illumination;

Day of the Lord: the moment of illumination (day) when we move beyond our egocentric consciousness (coma Consciousness) into our Christed Consciousness;

Days and Nights of Creation: represent the back and forth flow of divine activity (day) and the dormancy of unspiritualized thought (night);

Dazzling Detox: recognizing that worry, shame, guilt, anger, and fear are the self-vetoing equipment in the emotional darkroom where negatives develop;

Dead, the: carnal thoughts; error thoughts;

Deadbeat Whims: cursing words; using impure thoughts;

Dead End: experiencing the need for an about face; our susceptibility to back ourselves into a corner; feeling forced to make a different decision and/or taking another course of action; religious dogma;

Dead Language: dogmatic rhetoric;

Deadline, Time Limit, Zero Hour: a preset bifurcation point;

Dead Sea: being cut off from our higher nature;

Dead Sea Scrolls: repressed religious material that we allow to surface in bits and pieces;

Deafness: refusal to listen to the truth; shutting out guidance;

Death, Departure, Deceased, Expiration, Euthanasia: a spiritually bankrupt consciousness; a completely materialistic, sense-soaked consciousness that limits our spiritual growth; denying our innate divinity; liberation from incarnational and reincarnational experiences; total spiritual unawareness; [In Esoteric Astrology, Alice Bailey asserts that "death and limitation are synonymous." Pg. 615.]; (Physical death is liberation from a human experience not the end of our conscious beingness. It reminds us that our physical body is too dense to travel to our next assignment);

Death Bed Visions, Visitations: experiences by people who are close to their physical transitions whereby they see relatives and/or friends who have pre-deceased them and who appear to help them 'cross over to the other side';

Death Sentence: the mindless and deliberate decision to deny our innate divinity;

Debt-ishness: the accumulation of error thoughts and actions; negative memories that keep surfacing and self-defeating habits that continue to erode our chances for enjoying a more prosperous and fulfilling life;

Debtor's Plan: seizing every opportunity we can to align our human self with our Christ Self so we can be the best Christ we can be; (In legal lingo, a debtor's plan is a debtor's detailed description of how h/she intends to pay creditors' claims over a specified period of time.);

Deceleration: choosing another physical incarnation over an illumined cosmic unfoldment; stifling the rise of the kundalini fire within us by seeking material attachments and addictions; not believing there is a direct connection between the mystical and the religious;

Decentered Self: our unenlightened ego which is not the ultimate source of knowing;

Decoy, Lure, Pretense: tossing out a religious and/or spiritual perspective to see what reaction we get before continuing the conversation; matter enticing us into another skin school experience;

Deeper Self: our Authentic Self; our True Self; our Christ Self; the Extraordinary You; the Wise You; the Spectacular You; the Phenomenal You; the Peerless You; the Exceptional You; the Unparalleled You; the Legendary You; the Marvelous You; the One-of-a-Kind You; the Remarkable You; the Awesome You; the Astounding You; the Stunning You; the Electrifying You; the Sensational You; the Mesmerizing You; the Amazing You; the Spellbinding You; the Hypnotic You; the Fascinating You; the Fantabulous You; the Stupendous You; the Jaw-Dropping You; the Mind-Boggling You; the Dazzling You; the Brilliant You; the Adept You; the Enlightened You; the Illumined You; the Cosmic You; (According to neuroscientists, the occipital cortex, which is at the back of our brain, helps us envision an anthropomorphic [Deeper Self], while the temporal lobes allow some people to hear that [Deeper Self's] voice); (From a neurological perspective, images of our Deeper Self are unavoidable, but from many theological perspectives, there is no true image of that Deeper Self. Thus, if we cling to our childhood perceptions, we will limit our perception of the nature of our Deeper Self. This is the drawback to any belief system that insists upon a literal image of the Deeper Self. If we limit our vision, we will probably feel threatened by those who have more expanded visions of their Deeper Self); (See Christ;

Deer Capabilities: benevolence; striving for prosperity; peaceful;

Defacement: thinking, saying, or doing something that compromises our stated spiritual and/or religious values; (In IT terms, defacement refers to the method of modifying the content of a website in such a way that it becomes 'vandalized' or embarrassing to the website owner);

Defects: error thoughts and actions;

Defenders of the Faith: religious and spiritual thoughts, inclinations, beliefs, and attitudes;

Defense Mechanisms: the not-so-cute, accusatory retorts we use to defend our own faith tradition by saying such things like: "You're nothing but a cult," or "We teach the FULL gospel of (whoever our chief god or founder is)," or "If you believe that you're going to hell," etc.;

Defibrillator: a well-placed, highly-emotional statement that jumpstarts our religious and/or spiritual growth;

Deforestation: complete disregard for devoting ourselves to actualizing the serpentine energies of the Tree of Life; (See Tree of Life);

Deformities: having crippling thoughts that make it difficult, if not impossible, to feel good about ourselves; perverted and depraved inclinations that 'disfigure' our truth walk by ruining any good we can do;

Defriending: dropping error thoughts, words, and actions from our life experience;

Degradation, Decomposition: refusing to be born again, that is allowing our egocentric consciousness to be our ruling consciousness;

Dehydrated Theology: theology that adheres only to a literal interpretation of scripture;

Deity Virtues: transcendent and immanent super-consciousness;

Déjà entendu: the distinct feeling that we have heard certain sounds and/or voices before; (In French *déjà entendu* literally means 'already heard');

Déjà lu: reading something entirely new, but having the distinct impression of having read the book (article, newspaper, letter, magazine) before. In other words, the illusion of having already read something that is actually being read for the first time;

Déjà vu: feeling strongly that a present moment, situation or event is extraordinarily familiar, as if it was experienced prior to that moment; (See Jamais Vu);

Delaminate: losing traction in our spiritual and/or religious practice because we're not applying the truths we know; (In snowboarding terms, delaminate describes what happens when the top sheet of a snowboard begins to chip or peel off as a result of a crash, long term use, a board defect, or poor snowboard maintenance);

Delayed Broadcast: deliberately hesitating to share our particular religious and/or spiritual views publically; (In advertising terms, a local station broadcasting a scheduled network program at a time other than its regularly scheduled time.);

Deligious Experience: enjoying soul food (religious and/or spiritual teachings), actual food and drink, or a highly substantive experience that is like a mountaintop religious experience;

Delinquency: choosing gross materialism over spiritual growth; settling for darkness over enlightenment;

Delphinium-like: community interests; relationship oriented; (Evolutionary psychologists Baumeister and Leary remind us that our innate need to affiliate and form social bonds is literally wired into our biology. When we make a positive social connection, the pleasure-inducing hormone oxytocin is released into our bloodstream, immediately reducing anxiety and improving concentration, focus, and our immune system);

Deluge, Torrent, Downpour: pent-up emotions; an emotional out-pouring;

Delusion Trafficking: perpetuating the belief in original sin; evil; an anthropomorphic God and a satanic personage called the devil; incurable illnesses; duality; separation between Spirit and matter;

Dementia, Alzheimer's Dis-ease: feeling a tremendous sense of uncertainty, anger, and insecurity about our future and what we will do for the rest of our lives, while at the same time feeling resigned to our fate;

Demerited Thinking: error thinking; anti-Christed thinking;

Demiurge: the collective belief in the world of appearances as real;

Demon(s), Fiend(s), Ogre(s), Brute(s): chronic, negative, error thoughts and feelings like – envy, anger, greed, narcissistic pride, lust, gluttony, etc.;

Demon est Deus Inversus: a Kabbalistic axiom meaning "the devil is god reversed" (the forces that create good can also create error, depending on our level of consciousness);

Denialdom: the refusal to give power to outer appearances, whether those appearances take the form of health challenges, lack or limitation, financial challenges, natural disasters, disappointments, work issues, relationship issues, etc.; the conscious erasure of the apparent invincibility of the world of outer appearances that keeps us centered on the truth that we can choose wholeness instead of negation, faith instead of fear, confidence instead of confusion, victory instead of victimhood, health instead of illness;

Denim Disposition: denotes a certain ruggedness and durability when it comes to walking our talk;

Denisovan Beliefs: beliefs and values that are extremely extinct, but once served a worthwhile purpose; (In anthropological circles Denisovans were an enigmatic lineage of humans dating back over 400,000 years ago whose remains were found in the Sima de los Huesos cave in Spain with a Siberian linkage. The Denisovans were ancestors of the Neanderthals.);

Denomination(s): church sects; religious cliques and/or colloquiums; religious or spiritual concepts; spiritual and religious perspectives; (The world doesn't need another religious denomination. However, a sassy, in your face, forward thinking, truth-focused spiritual 'denomination' could be just the right perspective we need to elevate humankind's collective consciousness to a truly enlightened level of awareness);

Denominational Calumny: spreading inaccurate and generally unfavorable information about another religious denomination as a one-up-manship tactic;

Denominational Dandruff: the criticism leveled at faith traditions other than our own;

Denominational Quarantine: the systematic and perpetual separation of religious and spiritual faith traditions from each other;

Denominational Salad: adopting various religious beliefs, practices, rituals, and sayings as ingredients in our own religious practice;

Denominational Sparing: (See Ultimate Attribution Error);

Dense Body: our physical body; our materialistic consciousness;

Dense World, Temporal World, World of Illusion: matter; the physical universe;

Density: the quantity and compactness of material thoughts in our consciousness;

Dentist: exercising our resolve to protect essential logical and pragmatic thoughts that help us digest our human experience; correcting any difficulty in understanding new information; our aptitude for polishing novel information so others are enamored by it;

Dentures: renovating outdated thoughts that need updating and improved relevance;

Department Store: Universal Substance;

Depth Perception: the ability to understand spiritual laws and principles;

Derelict(s), Vagrant(s), Tramp(s): error thoughts;

Descent Into the Underworld: experiencing repressed urges, patterns, and life scripts in the subconscious; (The descent into hell (the underworld) motif has been around since time immemorial. For example, in the early apocryphal books of the Bible, such as the *Gospel of Nicodemus*, the Christ as Jesus descends into hell during the three days after his crucifixion and frees the souls there, which is an apocryphal belief that appears in the Apostle's Creed even though most religious fundamentalists reject apocryphal texts in favor of those books considered canonical.);

Desert-like: spiritual aridity and dehydration; a consciousness devoid of spiritual thoughts and inclinations;

Designated Community: our ability to compile a collection of associated thoughts that form a concept which we can wrap our heads around; (In IT language, the particular constituency for which archived information is relevant, reliable, and useable);

Desk: the intellect;

Deskilling: eliminating old, self-defeating materialistic attitudes, habits, and tendencies when we move into a more spiritually-oriented mindset;

Destiny: going from coma consciousness to Christ Consciousness;

Detour(s): material appetites; religious exclusivism; guru worship; fossilized dogma; cursing God; perpetuating hunger, violence, and racism; unforgiveness; the seven deadly sins; misinterpretations and mistranslations of holy scripture;

Detoxification: cleansing our consciousness of error thoughts, inclinations, and intentions; (In SPA industry terms, detoxification refers to cleansing our body of accumulated poisons.);

Devas: spiritual thoughts; (In Hindu mythology, devas are gods and angels);

Devata(s): spiritual thoughts; divine beings; angels;

Developmental Problems: adherence to strictly a literal interpretation of sacred scripture; belief in an anthropomorphic God or devil; defending dogma;

Deviant Subculture(s): repressed subconscious material; carnal thoughts; purely selfish thoughts; divinity-denying thoughts; violent thoughts;

Devic Instincts: natural propensities;

Devil, Iblīs, Shayṭān: the shadow side of human nature; the state of collective conscious that denies our innate divinity;

Devilish Thoughts: anti-Christed thoughts built up through eons of human incarnations that refuse to acknowledge our authentic spiritual nature;

Devout Fussiness: criticizing the unconventional religious practices of others;

Dhammapadaic Ethics: using Buddhistic ethics to live a morally sound life;

Dhikrian Devotion: maintaining a sacred awareness of our relationship with God by using devotional acts like the repetition of divine names, supplications, and aphorisms; (Dhikri is Swahili for God);

Dharma Wheel: the process of liberation;

Diabetes: having an intense preoccupation with what we consider to be the seriousness of life to the neglect of the joy we could feel if we allowed ourselves to loosen up and feel the success we deserve;

Diamond Eye: our Third Eye; (See Third Eye; Tickling of the Ant);

Diamond Qualities: immortality; our disciplined journey toward enlightenment culminating in the attainment of enlightenment; ascension;

Diamond Scepter: supernatural power;

Diapason Harmony: the numerical perspective of universal harmony;

Diarrhea: not being able to stomach what we believe to be hardships by mindlessly letting go of any support we could get;

Diasporaian Meltdown: the scattering (forgetting) of our twelve spiritual powers as we begin each new incarnational experience;

Dice-like Attributes: opting for an external locus of control; feeling that chance and/or luck determines our success; our tendency to abdicate responsibility by giving circumstances jurisdiction over our power of choice;

Dictator: our recalcitrant, unenlightened ego;

Dictionary Attack, Glossary Attack: a detractor attempts poke holes in our spiritual and/or belief system by questioning all of our tenets, laws, teachings, and principles; (In IT security language, a dictionary attack tries all of the phrases or words in a dictionary, trying to crack a password or key.);

Diddlysquat Order: the opposite of divinely ordering our experience; error ordering; the cause of abnormal fluctuations, disturbances, and disorder – which are all ghosts of our poor choices; (See Divine Order);

Dieting, Fasting: abstaining from toxic error thoughts, beliefs, and attitudes; (See Fasting);

Diehard Drivel: argumentatively defending our religious point of view without open-mindedly listening to someone else's perspective; (Open-mindedness is the willingness to search actively for evidence against our favored beliefs, plans, or goals, and to weigh such evidence fairly when it is available. Being open-minded does not imply that we are indecisive, wishy-washy, or incapable of thinking for ourselves. After considering various alternatives, an open-minded person can take a firm stand on a position and act accordingly. (The opposite of open-mindedness is what positive psychologist Martin Seligman calls the *myside bias*. The *myside* bias refers to the pervasive tendency to search for evidence and evaluate evidence in a way that favors our initial beliefs. Unfortunately, most people show a *myside* bias);

Digital Detox: going on a spiritual retreat and/or sabbatical to decompress and revitalize; (In IT circles, a period of time during which a person refrains from using electronic devices such as smartphones, iPads, or computers, in order to reduce stress and/or focus on social interaction in the 'real' world);

Dillydallying Around: going from one mainstream religious institution to another expecting to find the spiritual depth and transformative knowledge you believe you need to attain enlightenment;

Dinosaur(s): many mainstream and fundamentalist religious beliefs and practices; dogmatic perspectives; racism; sexism; same sex couple prejudice; most of the "isms"; embedded theology; war and violence; religion's fear of scientific proofs; belief in an anthropomorphic god or evil, malevolent devil; (See Detours);

Diploma: enlightenment; illumination; adeptship;

Diplomat(s): non-combative thoughts; tactful tendencies;

Dirah Be Tachtonim: our novential understanding of the purpose of creation; (Quoted from the **Midrash**, "God desired to have a dwelling place in the lower worlds.");

Directionally Challenged: pursuing the path of materialism, base instincts, and self-aggrandizement;

Disabled: dependence on dogma; belief in a literal-only interpretation of sacred scripture; belief in the inerrancy of holy scripture; belief in an anthropomorphic god in the sky or satanic devil; (See Super-Abled);

Disaster: destructive consequences; (See Disability; Detours);

Disciplined Dieting: watching what we eat so we don't live beyond our seams;

Disciplined Druthers: realizing that disciplined choices are our handrails when the fatigues of life assault our body, mind, and spirit;

Discombobulated Adjustment: (See Chemicalization);

Discomgoogolation: the emotional state we find ourselves in when we realize we aren't allowing ourselves to move beyond material addictions;

Discordant Energy: unresolved patterns of energy that continue to express themselves in our repeated incarnations unless we clear them (soul clearing);

Dis-ease Proneness: the misalignment between our human self and our Christ Self; the perpetuation of erroneous beliefs in the necessity of duality, separation, dogma, wars, violence, hunger, racism, same sex discrimination, subjugation of women, religious upmanship, ruining our environment, etc.;

Disgraceful Disguise: a grossly materialistic demeanor;

Disheveled Sermons: stream of consciousness deliveries characterized by lack of preparation;

Disinfectant(s): truth principles; denials; (See Denialdom);

Disingenuously Defriending: the pejorative censorship of a budding relationship with another person whose religious views are different from our own;

Disjecta Membra: esoteric truths that have been pulled apart and disassociated by 'literal only' interpretations of sacred scripture; disjointed or scattered fragments of a formerly whole body of knowledge which has been dispersed into hard to recognize bits and pieces by the process of transmission or deliberate obfuscation, thus obscuring the original meanings and context;

Disneyland, Disney World: daycares (outlets) for our inner child;

Disneyfication: watering down a Sunday truth talk or sermon to create an inoffensive, benign, neutral product;

Dispassion: the attainment of that state of consciousness where neither pleasure nor pain rules;

Disputed Diploma: experiential spiritual growth through revelatory episodes and meditational practices verses merely academic credentialing and scientific reductionism; (Self-knowledge cannot be attained by studying the world's religious texts to gain intellectual understanding and book knowledge. There is no use of studying sacred books and other scriptures in order to acquire the non-dual wisdom. That is why Buddha rejected the scriptures, because he knew that ultimate truth lies beyond religion. And that is why the Dalai Lama believes that the innate need to affiliate and form social bonds is literally wired into our biology. When we make a positive social connection, the pleasure-inducing hormone oxytocin is released into our bloodstream, immediately reducing anxiety and improving concentration, focus, and our immune system);

Dissociative Church-Going Identity Disorder: an all too common disorder where people display a church personality at church and quite another personality during the week;

Ditches: rigid unchallenged thinking (ruts); well-entrenched beliefs, attitudes, and habits;

Divided Kingdom: an egocentric consciousness unaware of its higher aspect, our Super-Consciousness;

Divination Urges: traditionally, it is the practice of using external tools and instruments to understand the nature of things; esoterically, it means obtaining hidden knowledge and/or access to that knowledge by connecting telepathically with our deeper selves;

Divine City: Christ Consciousness; the heart of Christ; pure consciousness; (*Purusha* is the cosmic man and/or the 'Self' that pervades the universe, in Hinduism);

Divine Comedy: our unconscious, although oftentimes comedic, attempts to align our human self with our Christ Self; our incarnational and/or reincarnational experiences; (As an initiate in the greater mysteries Dante wrote the Divine Comedy as an outline of the complete path of the Bodhisattva, a path traveled by very few beings of this humanity. It is our trek through our incarnational and/or reincarnational experiences. The Divine Comedy reflects, according to Dante himself, a previous work called the *Aenied*, written by the Roman poet Virgil, who in Dante's era was universally regarded as the wisest man in history.);

Divine Concierge: a spiritual insight that opens the door to greater spiritual insights;

Divine Geometry: the phenomenal world, including us, the planets, and the solar system; (Pythagoras' statement, "All things are in numbers, the world is a living arithmetic in its development--a realized geometry in its repose" sums up the sacred mathematics in all of its forms and functions);

Divine Good: thoughts, intentions, words, choices, and actions that spring from a Christed consciousness;

Divine Guidance: divine pitch and resonance from within us;

Divine Holograms: Quantum physicists describe the holographic nature of the universe as "holomovement" – with every part containing the whole. Suppose the 'whole-in-each-part' applies to us when it comes to our relationship with the One Presence? You could say that makes us divine holograms in human form. As holograms, we are God stuff becoming conscious of our God stuffness. We are the total spiritual package who doesn't know we are the total spiritual package. (To extend the analogy, those who realize they are the Presence of God expressing as them can sense their 'holomovement' status. Those who are oblivious to their divine 'hologramness' are running around as 'hollowmovements' without any real appreciation of their oneness with Spirit);

Divine Mind, Universal Mind, Cosmic Mind, Supreme Mind: the Eternal Presence; the Infinite Isness; God; the Consciousness that created consciousness; Potential and Realized Potential; the Universal Groundedness of the Eternal Presence; the Ground of all being; etc.;

Divine Mother: the omni-activity of the Eternal Presence within us and as us; the kundalini fire within us that animates us and powers us; the power of nature; the container we call physicality; the superior wisdom and intuitive power of the universe itself; (Among the Aztecs, she is known as Tonantzin; among the Greeks, Diana; in Egypt she is Isis);

Divine Order: the creative process of Mind, Idea, and Expression that occurs within us; working all things together for good; turning millstones into milestones; (Divine Order is not an external God-generated fiat or something a celestial deity imposes upon us. Divine Order is not an event. It is a process. It is not a noun. It is a verb. It is not a pre-determined outcome. It is a pre-emptive course of action on our part, as Christed beings in human form, to manifest something visible from the invisible); (Because Divine Order is the creative process of Mind – Idea – Expression it is an intentional act of creation. We can *divinely order* good or we can misapply Divine Order and create error expressions. A Divine Idea can be expressed spiritually or selfishly. Spiritually expressed it is a capital "D" Divine Idea. Selfishly expressed it is 'diddlysquat order' since a Divine Idea has been misapplied. Divine Order is when we divinely order our experience from the consciousness of our oneness with Spirit. *Diddlysquat order* is a millstone perspective. It means allowing our fractured and frightened egos to tempt us into believing that we are separated from Spirit, that we are not divine beings, and that all good things must come to an end. What we need to remember most is that we are always divinely ordering our human experience. There is always an order to what we are doing! We just don't always use it at its highest, most elevated level of consciousness. Sometimes we are Divinely Ordering our lives, and other times we are manifesting what I love to call "diddlysquat order!" – See Diddlysquat Order);

Divine Principle, Akasha, Avir, Ether in the Heart: the center of our spirituality; the primordial hidden essence that becomes manifest in, as, and through us, leading to our eventual enlightenment;

Divine Substance: the future waiting to be born; God Essence potentialized;

Divine Viewpoint: a Christed perspective;

Diving: evolution; entry into a skin school experience;

Divining Board: our Quantum Self;

Divorce: our masculinity rejecting our femininity and/or the opposite; our thoughts disengaged from our emotions and/or the opposite; the absolute denial of our Divine Nature;

DNA: our biological scaffolding; God stuff manifesting in a material matrix;

Docetae-ness: an illusionist; ability to see through the murkiness of dogma;

Doctor, Physician: our enlightened mind;

Doctrinal Chewing Gum: religious creeds, canons, tenets, articles of faith;

Doctrinal Endogamy: an unwillingness to "wed" religious and spiritual teachings;

Doctrinal Loafing: getting stuck in dogma;

Doctrinal Quibbling: disputing almost everything someone from another faith tradition says about their spiritual beliefs in order to retail your own beliefs;

~ *Spiritually Speaking* ~

Doctrinal Wheezing: purposefully mistranslating sacred scriptures;

Documents: feeling a strong sense of commitment and responsibility; *tearing up a document* suggests our desire to be free from an obligation and/or from entering into a commitment in the first place; *burning a document* represents achieving closure on a lengthy obligation or the cessation of a contractual agreement;

Dog Features: loyalty and fidelity; obedience; protectiveness of spiritual truths; safe passage into and out of the psychic realm; natural instincts;

Dog Fight: our natural instincts warring with each other;

Dog House: a consciousness characterized by its dog features: (See Dog Features);

Dogma: a spiritual lobotomy; theological fog; awfulizing scriptural interpretation; spiritual inertia; missing the forest for the trees; conviction that resembles the purr of a dog and the bark of a cat; a religious fiasco; spiritual sterility; religious thoughts that ossify into empty formulas; Jurassic theology, asphyxiating on its own lack of depth; a "walled" religious perspective that is filled with smidgeons of false assumptions, pinches of inaccuracies, and light touches of misconceptions concerning the nature of things; fear-based religious indoctrination; (The light of the dogmatic lamppost keeps many people in the dark);

Dogmageddon: filling our personal theology with so much dogma that we become overwhelmed with a walled-in religious myopia;

Dogma Reversed: The spiritual view of dogma is in reverse order. Dogma spelled backwards is 'am god.' Wasn't it the Christ as Jesus who said, "*Ye are gods?*"; (In *The Complete Works of Meister Eckhart*, the mystic is quoted as asserting that "God is *novissimus* (the newest thing there is). He championed "celebrating an ancient tradition of the childlikeness of divinity – a divinity that is not old and tired, controlling and judgmental, but spontaneous, playful, erotic, full of surprises."); [Also, *In Why Christianity Must Change or Die*, Bishop John Shelby Spong sounds a rousing call for "a Christianity based on critical thought rather than blind faith."];

Dogmatic Dystopia: the horrible fear and distress caused by an entrenched dogmatic perspective; (In *The Coming of the Cosmic Christ*, Matthew Fox asserts that "Fundamentalism is patriarchy gone berserk." Pg. 27);

Dogwood-like: believing in resurrection and new beginnings;

Dolphin Attributes: playfulness; astute intellect; courageous; pure of heart; compatible with both yin and yang energies; fierce protector and guardian; generosity; a high degree of curiosity; hidden power that can be suddenly and forcefully released; the guides of sanctified souls;

Doll(s): childhood memories;

Domain Name(s): Buddhism; Hinduism; Christianity; Sufism; Judaism; etc.;

Domestic Violence: mistreating our mind, body, and soul;

Dominoes: a sequence of actions that usually lead to a predetermined outcome;

Dondam-Pai-Den-Paic Piety: attaining the highest level of spiritual illumination and divine perception resulting in an appreciable understanding of absolute Truth; (*Dondam-Pai-Den-Pa* is Tibetan for absolute truth);

Donkey, Mule, Ass: denotes our lower, base nature; (The rider on a donkey theme in esoteric literature is a common spiritual symbol. The rider represents our Higher Self, our Christ Self, an enlightened us, our Authentic Self, in spiritual terms. The donkey is our lower self, the unquickened spiritual us, our human personality - characterized by stubbornness, material addictions, and an unwillingness to surrender to Spirit);

Dome(s): the sense that heaven and earth are joined; our head (dome) sits on our body (the quaternary);

Domesticated Animal Tendencies: compliant attitudes; governable actions; easily influenced perspectives; acquiescent emotions;

Doodling: expecting literal-only interpretations of scripture to reveal hidden spiritual truths;

Doohickey: a religious and/or spiritual tenet, ritual, basic belief, service, workshop, ceremony, etc.;

Doorbell(s): sensory antennae;

Door(s), Gate(s), Gateway(s): the entrance/exit from one cusp of consciousness to another; a decision point; mental filter or lens; the still point leading to illumination; the portals between our subconscious,

conscious, and super-conscious states of being; gateways to new opportunities; entryways into other dimensions of being; embracing the unknown; vital passages connecting our body, mind, and soul; *doors opening outward* suggest our willingness to explore the unknown, welcome change, and face what life has to offer us; *doors opening inward* denote our hesitance to embrace change and/or explore opportunities; *locked doors* imply our lack of readiness or insufficient training to proceed with an endeavor; *door into heaven* means the path of initiation, meditation, and/or serious spiritual study;

Door of the Gods: the Crown Chakra;

Door of Initiation: the Root Chakra;

Door to Heaven: our quickened spinal column energetically stimulated by the kundalini's rise;

Doormat Theology: the belief that the meek will inherit the earth;

Doppelganger Effect: a powerful spiritual idea that can be felt and/or intuited by us that emanates from other inter-dimensional versions of ourselves;

Dormitory: a collection of educated guesses;

Double Date: complementary thoughts and feelings; integrating spiritual practices with religious rituals;

Double-Dealing: selling fear, guilt, doubt, and shame and then expecting the faithful to believe in a loving god;

Double-Edged Sword: the Word of God with Its twofold power as Creator and Destroyer;

Double Jeopardy: an errant thought followed by an errant choice or action;

Double Negative(s): error thoughts, words, choices, and actions that accompany each other;

Double Standard: not seeing the harm in having base, degenerative, worldly thoughts fill our consciousness and define our behavior along with more spiritually-oriented thoughts and actions;

Doubting Thomas Effect: 'spiritual recoils' which can catapult us into our next growth curve; (Self-doubt can lure us into Self-denial – that's denial of our capital 'S' Self, our Christ Self. We need to doubt our doubts about not being spiritual beings who have chosen a human experience. Our doubts can be walls or speed bumps when it comes to our spiritual awakening);

Dove-like Inclinations: peacefulness; devotion; ascension; the soul; pure wisdom and spiritual knowledge; spiritual intuition; the archetypal principle of the innocent neophyte who seeks to know the greater mysteries; *selling doves* symbolizes debasing sacred knowledge for personal gain, gaining then misusing higher spiritual laws;

Downloading: our ability to receive information from another person as a result of spoken communication, visual observation, and/or telepathy; using dreams to capture our day's experiences; (In IT parlance, to download files by electronically requesting them from a Webpage on another computer);

Downstairs Cubbyholes: ingrained subconscious thought patterns;

Dowsing: our search for spiritual enlightenment by using a variety of external tools (I-Ching, Tarot cards, personal assessment tests, coaches, classes, etc.) to discover hidden potentials; (Literally, searching for water, minerals, gemstones or other naturally occurring objects that are underground by holding and interpreting the movement of a y-shaped divining rod);

Doxa: the Divine radiance (zero point field) that fills the entire universe and every inch of our consciousness;

Dragonfly-ness: denotes immortality and the continuity of consciousness even after our physical transition;

Dragon-like Endowments: seeking to balance the polarities of superior and initiatory wisdom that must be united and harmonized; (The *victories of heroes and knights over dragons* symbolize the harmonization of wisdom's opposites so equilibrium and right thinking can be established. Victory also represents the conquest over immortality, which is represented by some object to which the dragon bars approach.);

Drawbridge: receptivity and/or unreceptivity;

Dream(s): faxes from our Quantum Self; (See Quantum Self);

Dressing Room: each incarnational experience;

Drive-By Theology: diverting our attention away from a breath-takingly beautiful spiritual truth and giving in to the first worldly temptation that comes our way; unused and/or neglected spiritual knowledge; affirming our good a hundred times a day but doubting if those very affirmations will work; not living a prayer-conditioned or meditation-active life;

Driver's License: free will subject to karmic restrictions;

Driver's Test: matriculation through skin school;

Drought, Famine: spiritual aridity and/or barrenness;

Drought Tolerance: the amount of time we can go without engaging in an act of kindness or compassion, thinking spiritual thoughts, feeling happy and content, etc.; (In landscaping terms, drought tolerance refers to ability of plants to thrive without much water.);

Drowning: being overwhelmed by our emotions; sinking into negativity; allowing our subconscious patterns and self-defeating life scripts to take over;

Drugstore, Pharmacy: our physical body;

Drunkedness: being intoxicated with error thoughts;

Dry Cleaners: cleaning up and/or straightening a soiled perspective;

Dual Ego: our Higher Self and our human self;

Duality, Dualism: seeing a separation between matter and Spirit;

Duck Tape: affirmative prayer; meditation; positive affirmations; denials;

Duet: our human self working in concert with our Divine Self (Extraordinary Self);

Duhology: spiritual and religious truths that are self-evident and clearly obvious;

Dukkhaian Pestilence: overwhelming sorrow of having missed the mark (sinned); deeply felt pain caused by our intentional errors; (In Buddhism *dukkha* means suffering or unsatisfactoriness);

Dumb Phone: symbolizes religious perspectives that refuse to take into account the findings of current – and relevant and credible – scientific research; (In IT language, dumb phones are basic mobile phones that lack the advanced functionality characteristic of smartphones);

Dungeon, Oubliette, Cell: feeling confined, constrained, or restricted in our thinking, being, and doing;

Durood: a benedictive blessing;

Dustable: a seldom used spiritual principle, affirmation, or meditation that needs "dusting off" for our continued growth;

Dust-like Disposition: having the sense that our thinking has been too static or lethargic; having sluggish thoughts; repressed thoughts and emotions that are 'collecting dust' in our subconsciousness; unappreciated abilities;

Dust of the Ground: materialistic, self-aggrandizing, and carnal thoughts (dust) that come from an egocentric consciousness (ground);

Dvekutic Piety: adhering to a disciplined devotion to our spiritual and/or religious practice: (Dvekut is a Kabbalistic term for devotion);

Dvoyeverie Peculiarities: our propensity for mixing pagan, religious, and spiritual elements in our desire for illumination; (Dvoyeverie is Slavic for double faith);

DVD's: mental pictures; (See Cimema);

Dwarf-like: our penchant for starting to develop a talent, skill, ability, or body of knowledge and then bailing out on it before it's fully developed or refined; a diminutive thought;

Dweller on the Threshold: as we near the 'threshold' of our enlightenment our recalcitrant ego will remind us of all of our failings and shortcomings which disqualify us for spiritual advancement;

Dybbukian-Choked Thoughts: maniacal, diabolical, hellish thoughts meant to cause harm and pain; (In Jewish mythology, a *dybbuk* is a malicious possessing spirit believed to be the dislocated soul of a dead person);

Dying: spiritual inertia; repressing higher truths; neglecting to apply higher spiritual principles; (There is a growing amount of research on the dying process. As people move closer towards their transition there may be a surge of energy as they get nearer. Oftentimes they may want to get out of bed and talk to loved ones, or ask for food after days of no appetite. This surge of energy may be less noticeable, but is usually used as a dying person's final physical expression before moving on. The surge of energy is usually short, and the previous signs become more pronounced as death approaches. As the last breath is taken there is a sense that the life energy leaves the loved one's physical body);

Dynamite, Bombs, Mines: represent our compulsion toward exploding angrily by blowing up at someone or something that upsets us;

Dystheistic Thinking: believing God exists but is not good;

Dystopia: an egocentric consciousness;

Dzogchenic Teachings: the highest spiritual teachings; (In Tibetan Buddhism, dzogchen is the natural, primordial state and the particular teachings that help us realize that state of illumination);

Dzynic Potpourri: a pool of divine knowledge; (Dzyn is Tibetan for higher knowledge);

Each-consecutive-moment-of-now: the future becoming the present at the speed of consciousness; (Most people see it as a consecutive sequence of seconds or minutes of time. However, it is more like instantaneous shifts in consciousness);

Eagle Perspective: feeling the divine self grasping our lower nature to transmute it into its higher spiritual essence; gaining incredible perception; having a sense of guardianship; cultivating elevated psychic vision and authority; having a sense of protectiveness; enjoying intellectual acuity; attaining the all-piercing Eye of the seer; demonstrating cosmic strength;

Earache: listening to hell fire and brimstone sermons; hearing things which are against our nature;

Ear Infection, Deafness: strong resentment in hearing what we don't want to hear; unreceptivity to new information that we find annoying and/or ridiculous; resistance to being open to spiritual truths;

Ear Plugs, Ear Wax: refusal to listen; protection from unwanted noise;

Earth: egocentric consciousness or our physical body;

Earthbound: the propensity for preferring an egocentric consciousness instead of a Christed perspective; choosing another physical incarnation;

Earthquakes: experiencing the instability and impermanence associated with sense consciousness; self-defeating subconscious patterns surfacing; having our materialistic foundations shaken to the core;

Earthplane: human consciousness; temporal awareness; material existence;

Earthshaking Downpour: transformative spiritual thoughts that enter (pour into) our egocentric consciousness (earth) and cause a reformation in our thinking; (See Chemicalization);

East: spiritual illumination; higher consciousness;

Easter: the complete alignment of our human self with our Christ Self; attaining enlightenment; becoming a fully illumined spiritual being – again; (Spiritually, Pontius Pilate stands for the carnal will. [Piletos - dense or muddy - in Greek, and in Latin means Pontius Pilate [muddy water]. So, the Christ as Jesus, symbolized as a fish, suffered under muddy water. Muddy water represents the murkiness of the sense appetites of a carnal mind. So Spirit suffers, is limited by, Its descent into matter and our ego's material appetites);

Eating: absorbing esoteric wisdom; eating consecrated bread implies applying esoteric knowledge; eating the flesh of Christ symbolically denotes becoming illumined, understanding divine truths, comprehending the highest spiritual laws;

Eating Utensils: psychological, sociological, spiritual, religious, scientific, philosophical, etc., methodologies that help us get the 'soul' food we need;

Eavesdropping: petitioning prayer to an anthropomorphic god;

Eccedentesiast Facade: hiding hardships or sorrows behind our smiles;

Ecclesia: a collection of spiritual thoughts;

Ecclesiology: the study of the dogmatic religious doctrines propagated by mainstream and fundamental churchianity;

Echoes: experiencing (hearing) the consequences of our errant thoughts, words, and actions; actions are the feedback on our choices, choices are the feedback on our beliefs, beliefs are the feedback on our thoughts, thoughts are the feedback of our state of consciousness; repeated errors; (Echoes can also be positive – see Retweet Forward);

Eckankaric Disposition: desiring to make a personal connection with God;

Eclectic Aversion: the tendency to avoid studying, practicing, and/or honoring the stated principles of faith traditions other than our own;

Eclectic Tendencies: Refusing to be poked, prodded, or "cattled" into accepting any one particular faith tradition's doctrines and religious biases;

Eclipses: milestones in spiritual development; guideposts along the initiatory path;

Ectenic Force: the operative force behind psychic abilities; In parapsychological terms, ectenic force involves moving objects without contact by the medium or very light contact by the medium which would not be enough contact to move the object in question. The existence of such a force was coined by Count Agenor de Gasparin, to explain the phenomena of table turning and tapping);

Edgy Down Payment: investing emotionally in a new theological concept that we see as a possible foundational concept, but anticipating its 'heaviness' causes us to hesitate adopting it too quickly;

eDosing: extrinsic, materialistic over-consumption of worldly things;

Efficacious Grace: our immediate and spontaneous awareness of choosing a spiritual thought, word, and action over a worldly thought, word, or action;

Egg: eternity; the primordial matrix; birth and rebirth; renewal; immortality; fertility; incubated potential;

Ego: the aspect of our divine individuality that has become imprisoned in materiality as the self of human experience; our conscious identification with physical form (It is a form of 'soul sleep' that we have created to help us cope with our decision to become physical beings); urbanized thought; the center of egocentric I-am-ology; our impermanent self;

Egocentric Eschatophobia: the fear of the imminent end of our current state of unenlightened awareness and its sense-soaked attachment to material appetites as we sense a more spiritually-oriented consciousness on the horizon;

Egocentricism: It's all about me-ness; pathological narcissism; mistaking facsimile for reality;

Egoic Secularization: the process by which our unenlightened ego becomes increasingly secular rather than spiritual;

Ego Surfing: being so narcissistic that we find ourselves listening in conversations at spiritual and/or religious retreats and meetings for our name being used and praised by others without paying much attention to anything else being said; (In the IT world, ego-surfing is habitually searching the Internet for examples of our own name or links to our own website);

Egotistical Bents: easing growth out; (Believe it or not, an over-sized ego does not have our best interests in mind. That may sound a little Freudian, but it's true. All egos, regardless of breed or upbringing, have a tendency toward self-preservation and self-aggrandizement and prefer to keep the more spiritual parts of us in check);

Egyptian Book of the Dead: the postmortem transformation of worldly thoughts into their high spiritual essences after they leave our waking consciousness and travel into our super-consciousness;

Ehozinic Thinking: holy thinking to establish balance and harmony; (Native American term for holy thinking for balance and harmony within the natural order of things);

Eiffel Tower: masculine and feminine equality; love and romance; the need for an elevated perspective; evolutionary desire to return to our spiritual roots; (See Skyscrapers, Towers);

Eight Ball: to be 'behind the eight ball' represents the belief in a god "out there" who watches every move we make and punishes free thinkers and favors those who follow out of fear, guilt, and unworthiness;

Eightfold Path: According to the Buddha, the only way to achieve nirvana is through the eight fold path: Right understanding, right thoughts, right speech, right action, right livelihood, right effort, right mindfulness, and right concentration;

Elder Abuse: showing disrespect and distain for conventional and traditional ideas and beliefs (elders);

Elect, the: spiritual thoughts and ideas;

Elect Angels: the higher, more spiritually-attuned thoughts and propensities we enter into each incarnational experience with that become the foundation for our continued spiritual growth;

Electricity: vital force; cosmic vitality; atomic intellect;

Elephant-like Tendencies: employing a large measure of prudence, dignity, and intelligence to everything we do; achieving an abundance of spiritual knowledge; perseverance over seemingly insurmountable obstacles; a *white elephant* denotes bountifulness and fertility;

Eleusinian Mysteries: mythological thinking; things that will be revealed; (The Eleusinian Mysteries were Greek initiation ceremonies held every year for the cult of Demeter and Persephone. The mysteries represented the myth of Persephone's abduction from her mother Demeter by the king of the underworld and her reunion with her mother. The mysteries were founded by Eumolpos about 1,400 years before the birth of the Christ as Jesus. Initiates of the Eleusinian School were famous for the beauty of their philosophic concepts and the high standards of morality that they demonstrated in their daily lives.);

Elevator(s): denote our trips into our three levels of human beingness (subconscious, conscious, super-conscious); a *malfunctioning elevator* suggests our lack of progress toward a particular area, a problematic issue that has gotten us stuck or out-of-touch, or feeling stymied in some way; the reincarnational process;

Eleventh Hour: the latest possible time to act; a short time remaining; last minute decision-making; the 'last minute' narrow neural waiting between deciding to act and actually acting so there is absolute congruency between our thoughts and our actions; (See Bereitschafts Potential);

Eli, Eli, Lemana, Shabakthani: At the ninth hour, Jesus' words from the cross interpreted mean: "My God, my God. for this purpose I have come." (The traditional, commonly quoted expression, *"Eloi, Eloi, l'mana Sabachtani,"* which means, *"My God, My God, Why hast Thou forsaken me?"* is a mistranslation. It does not square with the life and teachings of Jesus Christ. Unfortunately it appears in almost all standard Bible translations. This errant translation intentionally tries to put distance between Jesus and His God Nature. And it's implication is if God forsook Jesus God will forsake us too! What Jesus really said, in the original Aramaic was *"Eli, Eli, l'mana Shabakthani"* which means: *"My God, My God, It is for this purpose I have come"* or *"this is my destiny."*);

Elixir: the immortal energy that comes from our extraordinary spiritual nature, the Authentic Us, our Christ Nature;

Elohim: Androgynous manifestations (emanations, essences, attributes) of the One Presence expressing Itself in physicality (in the universe as well as within our consciousness); a mixture of religious and spiritual thoughts;

Elocut Urge: our desire to align ourselves completely with our divine nature; (In Kabbalistic terms, godliness);

El-Shaddai: the Holy Spirit; the Eternal Presence;

Email(s): although our thoughts register anytime day or night we can choose to transform (send) our thoughts immediately into actions or allow them to remain in our heads longer until we choose to share them or translate them into choices and then actions; also denotes thoughts we have that we'd rather not say face-to-face because we would feel uncomfortable sharing them out loud;

Emanationism: believing that a Supreme Being did not directly create the physical universe, but instead accomplished it through lower spiritual beings;

Emancipation: What we call 'death' refers to the discontinuation (emancipation) of our flesh and blood physical bodies from physicality. It is the passage of a limited human form into one or another of its higher vibratory essences. (It is the exiting [release] from our incarnational humanness into a more expanded cosmic existence – an existence that has become accustomed to many iterations as we unfold into the next version of us. Each emancipation (physical death) takes us closer to the ultimate freedom we all desire – full and complete enlightenment. Our earth life is but one school of unfoldment. It is 'skin school.' It is a somatic apprenticeship. For some, leaving skin school is a graduation – it signals the end of a limited state of awareness into a higher, more profound, level of consciousness, making the earth experience no longer necessary for soul progression. For others, transitioning out of a 'skin school' experience means there will be more – many more – 'skin school' experiences based on the quality of awareness the particular soul possesses. In each dimension of our being we are held there by the gravity of our spiritual awareness. Our earth experience is but one of the stops along the way toward enlightenment. How long we stay and how often we return depend on our level of awareness of eternal truths and on the application of those truths. Our next dimension of being will be consistent with our level of spiritual ripening. Each 'death' experience is a lifting of the veil of illusion. Whether we reincarnate into a human form again or incarnate into a new dimension of higher beingness, our life task will be to become consciously aware of who we really are – the One Presence expressing Itself as us.);

Embedded Theology: dogmatic religious thoughts and biases that have been with us since childhood; literal interpretations and misinterpretations of religious scripture that limit our thinking; (In *Born to Believe,* Andrew Newberg asserts that "from a neurological perspective, images of our (Deeper Self) are unavoidable, but from many theological perspectives, there is no true image of that (Deeper Self). Thus, if you cling to your childhood perceptions, you will limit your perception of the nature of your (Deeper Self). This is the drawback to any (belief system) that insists upon a literal image of the (Deeper Self). If you limit your vision, you will probably feel threatened by those who have more expanded visions of their (Deeper Self);

Emerald-ishness: promotes discernment; regeneration and recovery; faithfulness; hopefulness; healing promotion;

Emerald Tablet, Tabula Smaragdina: a sense of knowing that encapsulates that which is above and what is below, the absolute as well as the relative, the celestial order and the terrestrial order, the first and the last, the manifest and the unmanifest; (The Tablet is a cryptic writing of Hermetica that is believed to contain the prima material and its transmutation, with associations to things like the Philosopher's Stone, alchemy, and both microcosmic and macrocosmic realities);

Emergency Room: mind, body, and soul triage;

Emigration: going from one skin school experience to another;

Emoticon(s): images of our spiritual awareness (i.e., a cross with Jesus nailed to it; pictures with Jesus bleeding from the crown of thorns; a dove; the winged globe; etc.); (Electronically emoticons are text-based faces and objects that give the reader a sense of the texter's feelings behind the message. For example, the classic ☺ represents happiness; @->--> ---- stands for a long stemmed rose to show affection);

Emotional Flypaper: regrets – they keep us stuck in the past; (Doubts, fears, and regrets - like any narcotic - weaken our ability to take control of our life. They are the self-induced sedatives all of us use, from time to time, to numb ourselves to the trials of life);

Emperor: our worldly ego;

Employee(s), Staffer(s): thoughts and emotions;

Empress: our cold, queen beeish, egotistically-based heart which is the consort of a worldly ego;

Encapsulation: the One expressing Itself as the many;

Encyclopedia: our long and short-term memory; accumulated knowledge;

End of the World: the culmination of a particular state of awareness; the maturation of one level of knowing into a greater level of understanding;

Enduements: special mystical and psychic powers and abilities that are latent within us;

Enemies, Foe(s), Antagonist(s): error thoughts, intentions, and inclinations; the worship of a material existence;

Enlarged Prostate: unnecessarily disappointed and/or fearful about our masculinity and about our ability to make a living;

Endless Punishment: conceptualizing error thought after error thought and experiencing the consequences; (See Everlasting Hell);

Enlightened Ones: refers to us and our spiritually attuned thoughts;

Enlightenment: crossed out error; achieving a Christed consciousness; spiritual illumination;

Enoichion (Enoch): the initiatory unfoldment (narrow path) toward our illumination; the disciplined, concentrated effort to become more spiritually attuned; the Third Eye;

Entelechy, Energeia: the belief that everything's *thinghood* is a kind of work in itself; our 'thinghood' is our divine nature which is expressed in our particular human personality in any given incarnation; (the terms were coined by Aristotle to explain our tendency towards 'being-at-work' in a particular way that is our proper and 'complete' way of doing things);

Entheogen(s): Any substance, such as a plant or drug, taken to elicit extra-sensory experiences;

Entrainment: our human nature becoming one with our Christ Nature; living, moving, and being in at-one-ment with our extraordinary Christ Self; God's Godness enthroned in our human physicality; transcending the illusion of any separation between our human beingness and our true I-Am-ness; recognizing our indivisibleness as God expressing Godness at the point of us; (In *The Coming of the Cosmic Christ*, Matthew Fox reminds us that "a theology of the Cosmic Christ is not embarrassed by the deification of humans." Pg. 109);

Entrée(s): spiritual and religious teachings; metaphysical principles;

Entropy: the gravity of error; divine, spiritual, mental, emotional, psychic, and astral dishevelment;

Envelope, Wrapping, Packaging: our aura;

Epiclesius: prayerfully invoking the Holy Spirit; (Epiclesius is Greek for Eucharistic prayer);

Epidemics: uncontrolled sense addictions and contagious dysfunctions; infectious or contagious beliefs and attitudes that are usually negative in nature;

Epidermic Reading: a literal-only scriptural reading and interpretation;

Epinoia: exceptional intuitive perception; divinely revealed knowledge not easily accessible to the uninitiated; (In Gnosticism means awakening and/or preserving hidden knowledge as the means of correcting ignorance and unknowing);

Epiphany: experiencing a revelation of such power and insight that our world view is changed to such an extent that we are changed at depth;

Episode(s): having thoughts; making choices; doing things; experiencing another incarnation and/or reincarnation;

Epopteia: full alignment with our divine self; our initiation into seership; (The final initiation rite in the Eleusinian Mysteries);

Epunamunian Temperament: mercenary thoughts; (Epunamun is the Inca god of mercenary war);

Equator: the veil between our waking conscious and subconscious;

Eraser(s): denials; (See Denialdom);

Eremitic Tradition: our desire to seek spiritual enlightenment in isolation; (See Monastic Thinking);

Ergonic Insightfulness: our soulful looking at our capacity to tap into the infinite universal rhythms that are mirrored in our own psyches;

Eros: universal harmony; love; union;

Erosion, Attrition, Abrasion: becoming more materialistic than spiritual;

Error Arrogance: trying to build castles out of outhouse material;

Error Etiology: the study of the causes and remedies of error thinking:

Error Euthanasia: error removal; (See Crucifixion);

Error Extinction: (See Crucifixion);

Errornami: cultivating such an error-prone consciousness that we seem to make errors in epidemic proportions;

Errorpocalypse: a catastrophic series of errors that oftentimes results in our earthly transition; (See Errornami; Evil);

Error Thinking: materialistic, egocentric thoughts, inclinations, beliefs, and assumptions that limit and/or block our spiritual growth; mental indigestion; mental arrhythmias; rational and/or irrational lies; debilitating mental antics; mental kudzu;

Error Thought Poltergeists: racism; sexism; mental, emotional, and physical dis-ease; also the Twelve Poisons;

Escalator: the initiatory process; (See Jacob's Ladder); travel between the three states of human consciousness;

Eschatology: the study of the end times;

Esoteric Christianity: the inner, more spiritual and mystical roots of Christianity founded on the ancient wisdom traditions;

Esoteric Knowledge: highly mystical and sacred spiritual teachings that require higher thought, intellectual depth, and superior intuitive insights to comprehend what goes far beyond the literal interpretation of exoteric writings; secret wisdom; perennial super-knowledge;

ESP: extra-sensory perception;

Essential Oils: healers and psychics use these oils that are extracted from plants and other botanical sources and preserved in a pure form. They are used in aromatherapy by being diluted in water or with other, more gentile oils;

Etheric Plane: the highest quantum expression of matter; (When we reach that level of being we will operate as etherized beings who will continue to have spiritual work to do and enlightenment to seek);

Eternal Life: a life of endless possibility, vitality, expanded awareness, higher consciousness, invigoration, vibrant beingness; a life without restriction, worry, or limitation; a life of unbridled joy and happiness; a life without the need for constant error triage; a life of passport-free travel around the Milky Way Galaxy and beyond; a life that is available to us wherever we are, whenever we are, however we are, and whatever we are; (we are going through the human phase of our eternal life which has many states of being); [According to a Scott Pierce article entitled "Yes, It's a Big Bang," in the September 22, 2007 issue of *Deseret Morning News*," Galaxies are not believed to be moving apart from one another through space, but space itself is said to be expanding, so that the gaps between the galaxies are stretched like a rubber sheet. Cosmologists frequently cite the analogy of a balloon with spots spread evenly over its surface; as the balloon expands, the spots "move" further apart. The spots act like clusters of galaxies and the balloon like the structure of space time."];

Eternal Presence: (See God);

Eternity: an indefinite, indescribable past and an indefinite, indescribable future;

Ether: spiritual substance; the 'field';

Ethernet: telepathy;

Ethereality: the refined and much less dense form of matter than the matter we are accustomed to experiencing; super-conscious thought that comes from rarified spiritual pathways;

Ethical Hacker: intentionally testing the extent of the esoteric knowledge of someone in order to help h/her grasp the teachings; (In IT lingo, a cybercop who hacks into a computer network in order to test or evaluate its security, rather than with malicious or criminal intent);

Eucastrophe: the Apocalypse and/or Armageddon; knowing there is a happy ending in store for us when we go from an egocentric perspective to a Christed perspective; (See Apocalypse; Second Coming);

Eucharist: the manifestation – mental, emotional, and psychic – of our extraordinary, spiritually vitalized core essence;

Eunuch: the intellect without wisdom; knowledge without understanding; logic without compassion;

Euthanasia: putting a 'terminally ill' idea, belief, or habitual habit to *rest*; the ability to willingly discard our physical body when we have mastered the human experience; sacrificing a spiritually potent idea by sharing it with someone who is not ready to hear higher spiritual truths;

Eutheistic Thinking: believing an external God exists and is good;

Everlasting Hell: remaining in a hellish state of consciousness by refusing to acknowledge our innate divinity; (See Endless Punishment);

Ever-Living Self: the Christ as us;

Evil: divisive error thoughts, words, and actions that we allow to undermine our spiritual nature; humankind's answer for self-punishment; error-pocalypse;

Evil Eye: using our advanced spiritual knowledge for selfish and/or destructive purposes;

Evolution: mindfully moving toward our pre-human state of consciousness from our incarnational state of consciousness; spiritual reclamation; dissipated, watered down, differentiated wholeness returning to its original state; the physical form of Spirit on its way 'back up' to its original spiritual essence; matter becoming wave again;

Excess Baggage: an inordinate amount of karma that is either generated in our current lifetime and/or carried over from a previous lifetime; (In airline industry terms, excess baggage is checked luggage that exceeds the weight of the baggage allowance);

Exclusivity Bias: believing a particular faith tradition is the only way to salvation; (Unfortunately, religion's exclusivity bias derails it from its mystical roots, and thus, its enlightenment value. Until and unless it gets back on track religion's derailment will prevent it from reaching the station and status it deserves);

Excommunicating Gossip: letting our ethics work faster than a gossiper's tongue;

Excuseology: the path of least insistence; (Excuses aren't dead-ends. They're circles of doubt, fear, or disinterest. Excuses are only prophylactic fixes to shuffle blame or responsibility onto something or someone else);

Excuse Smurfing: coming up with a wide variety of reasons to justify not doing something;

Exfoliation: pruning bad habits, negative points of view, false assumptions, and people who are crazymakers out of our life; (In SPA industry language, exfoliation refers to skin treatment where the upper layers of dead skin cells are sloughed off by a loofah sponge, sea salt, brush, etc.);

Exile, Deportation, Expatriate: skin school experiences; the repressed regions in our subconscious;

Existence: beingness and non-beingness; manifest and unmanifest; the phenomenal form of reality;

Exit Strategy: preparing for our next incarnational experience by being the best Christ (Buddha, Vishnu, Allah, Great Spirit, Krishna) we can be;

Exorcist Capabilities: casting out devilish and/or demonic thoughts that possess us from time to time; our being able to cast out error thoughts; using the truth to cast out error;

Exoteric: hidden wisdom (esoteric knowing) clothed in literal, dogmatic concrete thinking; egocentric knowledge, comprehension, and understanding;

Extension Cord: the umbilical connection between spirit and matter; our navel; (See Silver Cord);

Extraordinary You: our Christ Self; Philosophers and spiritual leaders have referred to it by many names. But so have psychologists and sociologists. Psychologist D. W. Winnicott coined the term "True Self" in 1960 to describe a "sense of self based on spontaneous authentic experience, a sense of all-out personal aliveness" or "feeling real. Psychologist Alice Miller agrees and says that when the 'true self' is liberated it "emerges like a butterfly liberated from its chrysalis and an unexpected wealth of vitality is released." Carl Rogers also referred to it as the true self. Psychologist Daniel Stern calls it the Core Self and Eric Fromm called it the Original Self. I call it our Core Essence but also refer to It as the *Extraordinary You*, the *Wise You*, the *Spectacular You*, the *Authentic You*, *your Deeper Self*, *your Extraordinary Self, the Phenomenal You, the Peerless You, the Exceptional You, the Unparalleled You, the Legendary You, the Marvelous You, etc.*; (A neurological approach suggests that the Extraordinary Us is not the product of a cognitive, deductive process, but is instead "discovered" in a mystical or spiritual encounter made known to our human consciousness through the transcendent machinery of the cosmic mind); (See Deeper Self);

Extra-Sensory Perception: obtaining information by psychic means beyond the five senses; anomalous cognition; (See ESP);

Extraterrestrial: a spiritual thought that surfaces in an egocentric consciousness and/or a worldly thought that intrudes in a spiritually-attuned consciousness; an incarnating spiritual being who comes from another dimension of being;

Extreme Gumption: unyielding conviction and discipline when it comes to our religious beliefs; standing firmly in our convictions no matter what;

Eye(s): windows to our soul – and beyond; *flaming eyes* denote superior discernment and spiritual knowledge;

Eye Drops: spiritual insights;

Eye Infections: looking outside ourselves for answers instead of trusting our innate wisdom;

Eye of the Needle: our psychic vision; our superior intuitive ability; (See the Third Eye; the Narrow Door); [The crow's nest, eye of the sun, and summit of the dome all allude to the crow's nest perspective];

Eye of the Purified Soul: our 'opened eye' which is the spiritual eye of our seerness (the Third Eye); (See Third Eye);

Eyn Soph: beingness above humankind's current level of understanding; universal comprehension that has not been stepped-down enough for us to grasp; mysticalness which is still mysterious; the mystic White Fire;

Fable(s): an anthropomorphic god in the sky or an anthropomorphic devil; the inerrancy of scripture; not going to heaven or hell until we die; the creation stories;

Face-to-Face: direct perception;

Facebook, P'interest, MySpace: our preference for social networking on a global scale; oneness; interconnectedness; community; the 'projected' us;

Facelift, Facials: an outer way to reveal the inner us; our Sagittarius drive;

Face Paint: a type of façade;

Fairground(s): our complete 'menagerie' of egocentric thoughts, attitudes, basic instincts, and subconscious patterns that are enlivened and stimulated by our five physical senses;

Facsimile(s): our human consciousness and physical form; the material universe; matter; the facades we wear;

Fad, Craze, Trend, Whim: trying out new religions, mainstream or non-traditional, just for the sake of trying out new religions;

Failure: listening to a warped ego; denying our innate divinity;

Fairness Fantasy: Assuming the world will treat us fairly because we are a good person is like expecting a tiger not to eat us because we are vegetarian. (Just because we are highly spiritual and/or religious doesn't mean we will have immunity from trials and tribulations during our skin school experience);

Fairy Originality: creating magical ideas;

Fairy Tale(s): the anthropomorphic god or devil 'out there' fabrication; (See Fables);

Faith: heart-to-head resuscitation spiritual trust and knowing; believing with confidence – to have conviction – to know that you know that you know; a deep abiding trust in our divine connection; a spiritual night light in hallways of darkness; *blind faith* denotes a more religious perspective that places its trust in a higher power outside of us; (In Sanskrit, the word for faith is *shraddha,* which is akin to *cor,* "the heart," in Latin. Faith is more a quality of the heart than of the mind. It is the knowing of the heart that transcends the intellect);

Faith Communities: collections of spiritual and religious thoughts and belief systems;

Faith Healing: harnessing the incredible power of the placebo effect; (In *Placebo: Mind Over Matter in Modern Medicine,* Dylan Evan says humorously that "sometimes a doctor who uses placebos, says that the 'fake' medicine is 'Obecalp,' which is "placebo" spelled backwards, or Feileb which is belief spelled backwards." Pg. 67);

Faith-Lifts: times when we are being faith-full (trust-full) in our connection as Spirit in human form; reminders to ourselves to stay true to our beliefs;

Fake: our manipulative, self-aggrandizing, paranoid ego;

Falcon Features: attaining superior vision and focus; achieving one-pointedness; growing in intensity; gaining superiority in an expanded perceptiveness; ruthless pursuit;

Fall, the: incarnation and/or reincarnation; the descent from an elevated consciousness into an egocentric perspective; our willing romp into corporeality; (The 'Fall' happens every time we purposefully choose to excel in *selfology*, *errorology*, and *greedology*);

Fallen Angels: spiritual ideas used for purely self-aggrandizing material aims; (Essentially, we are fallen angels, beings whose consciousness has 'fallen' to a lower level of awareness that believes in separation and duality);

Fallen Star: our debased psychic mind that rules the abysmal depths of our egocentric nature; human desire, the bottomless pit of our selfish passionate nature in each incarnational experience;

Fallout: the consequences of error consciousness;

Falsa Cabeza(s): façade; (Spanish for false head. They are large mummy bundles covered with wigs);

False Awakening: believing we are fully enlightened when we become illumined for the first time; (In dream psychology, false awakenings occur when the dreamer believes h/she has awakened to the physical world but is actually still dreaming);

False God: the unenlightened ego;

False Prophets: egocentric thoughts that retail the benefits of materialism and sense appetites over spiritual thoughts, words, and actions;

False Self: the unenlightened ego; the sense-coated ego; the divinity-denying ego;

False Teeth, Dentures: improving our ability to digest and absorb spiritual truths;

~ Spiritually Speaking ~

Family: a collection (household) of thoughts on a related topic; pedigreed thoughts and concepts; our brood of repressed and suppressed subconscious material; the thoughts and feelings associated with our waking consciousness; the gloriously divine thoughts and insights 'born' in our super-consciousness; our body, mind, and soul as closely-knit siblings; humankind;

Family Feud: disconnects between our mind, body, and soul;

Famine: spiritual barrenness; spiritual bankruptcy; spiritual neglect; the absence of illuminated thoughts;

Famous People: noteworthy ideas; illustrious insights; prominent thoughts; distinguished personal traits;

Fantasy: anything that suggests our separateness from the Eternal Presence; (See Fables, Fairy Tales);

Far Country: materialistic consciousness; sense consciousness;

Farce(s): materialism, racism, sexism, egoism, communism, fatalism, nihilism, perfectionism, etc.;

Fare: the experiences associated with each incarnation; the actions (and their consequences) resulting from our choices;

Farm: our ordinary consciousness; the world;

Far Memories: recalling memories of prior incarnations and/or reincarnations;

Farmer's Market: a smorgasbord of choices; sensory experiences;

Far-Out Philosophy: an out-of-the-box view that makes us realize that nonsense can make perfect sense;

Farsighted: having a grasp of esoteric truths;

Fast Food: religious doctrines and basic spiritual principles;

Fasting: refraining from toxic error thoughts, beliefs, and attitudes that create an illusion of separation between us and our innate divinity; abstaining from egocentrism, dogma, judgmentalness, and prejudice; dieting from doubts in our self-worth and fear of eternal damnation; eliminating the thinking that we are sinful by nature; (I believe that when we fast from anything that interferes with our conscious oneness with Spirit, we are filled with joy! In fact, we base our perspective on Matthew 6:16-18, when Jesus instructed: *"When you fast, don't look all gloomy, so everyone knows you're fasting."* In other words, if it's just a façade, the fasting means nothing! And there's no lasting impact from it. *"But when you fast,"* Jesus said, *"put oil on your head and wash your face, so that it will not be obvious to others that you are fasting."* In other words, when we allow ourselves to experience the absolute joy of oneness, and allow our light to shine as a result of fasting from error thinking, we will be rewarded with the growing consciousness of Divine flow in our lives);

Fast Lens: being able to frame our human experience quickly in terms of our spiritual perspective; (In photography language, a fast lens has an aperture that opens wide, making it possible to get more light than a slower lens at its widest aperture.);

Fate: our next choice; (The assertion that '*nothing happens by accident*' implies that everything happens as it is supposed to happen. And what is supposed to happen is determined by fate, or karma, or God, or cosmic beings 'out there' who are in charge of micro-managing our earth experience. Cher and I invite you to '*get over*' that way of thinking as soon as possible. It places your power, and self-determination, and your ability to be the captain of your fate outside of you. We are NOT here to be the products of an 'outside in' fear-based mythology. We are here to be the architects of an inside-out spiritual practice. The expression – *what will be will be* - is another cop out expression. It is based on the perception of a God in the sky who orchestrates what happens to us without our knowledge or consent. It is a phrase which suggests that outcomes are determined by something outside of us no matter what we do. The truth is what *will be* is what we *will to be*. The point of power is our will power);

Fat Fingering: the accidental mistranslation of scripture; (In IT language, refers to clumsy or inaccurate typing and texting, typically resulting from one finger striking two keys at the same time); (See Gene Doping);

Father: a previous thought and/or concept that precedes a current thought;

Father-in-Law: a thought that gives rise to an emotion that causes us to rethink our position or point of view;

Faxes: subconscious messages that surface in our waking consciousness; dreams;

FBI, CIA: our amygdala wiring; our concern for security and protection;

Fear: the amygdala's answer to a paranoid ego; (Someone once said that fear is 'false evidence appearing real.' From a spiritual point of view the 'false evidence' appearing as real comes from our unenlightened ego which is grounded in materiality. When we subordinate our human ego to our higher spiritual nature the acronym for fear changes to 'facing every appearance realistically);

Feast of Fools: choosing carnal, base, impure, and crude actions, tastes, and habits over spiritual behaviors;

Feast of Wise Ones: choosing to enjoy spiritual principles and teachings, offering loving kindness and generosity, and demonstrating compassion and humility;

Feedback Loop: the reactivity of the body to the activity of the mind; the consequences of our choices; the answers to our prayers;

Feet: understanding; *bare feet* represent receptiveness in understanding, humility; *shoed feet* symbolize protecting one's current understanding and/or one's understanding being limited by intellectual restraints; *washing feet* symbolizes cleansing of one's consciousness; purifying one's understanding, clarifying one's understanding of truth principles; two feet represent justice and righteousness; *burnished bronze or brass feet* denote stability and understanding; feet of clay represent materiality and dependence on outer appearances;

Feldspar: our ability to detach ourselves from materialism;

Felony, Felonies: error choices and actions that are the result of errant thoughts; (In the legal system, felonies are serious crimes, usually punishable by at least one year in prison.);

Fences: defense mechanisms; boundary management issues; conceptual enclosures;

Ferhoic Endowment: incredible creative power and innovative expertise;

Fern-like: protectiveness; quietude; serenity;

Ferris Wheel: our conscious movement around the full range of our thoughts and emotions; moving through the twelve divisions (signs) of the zodiac;

~ Spiritually Speaking ~

Ferry-like Aptitude: denotes our movement from one cusp of consciousness to another; the ferryman represents our Higher Self;

Festivals: celebrations; jovial atmosphere; joyfulness; coming across a collection of spiritual truths;

Fib(s), Fiction: original sin; heaven and hell as places we go to after we die; the sun standing still; the earth created in six calendar days; women being subservient to men; the sun rising every morning and setting every evening; the Bible as the inerrant word of god; Jesus, the man, as the Only Begotten Son; incurable dis-eases; Armageddon as a cataclysmic event in our future; at the end of this age, there will follow a 1,000 years of peace, after which Jesus will return to defeat satan at last, and set up his kingdom; animals came aboard Noah's ark two-by-two; Shadrach, Meshach, and Abednego (three Jewish lads who were defriended by the king) being tossed in a fiery furnace, but surviving without being roasted; etc.;

Fickled Allegiance: The endless fronts fair-weather friends have;

Fictional Characters: an anthropomorphic god or devil;

Fideistic Fence: to believe what we think we're supposed to believe without asking if the belief 'holds water';

Field Trip: an incarnational or reincarnational experience; astral travel; visualization; exploring new intellectual and/or emotional territory;

Fiend(s): error thoughts; belief in the world of appearance;

Fig Tree-like: achieving the wholesomeness of illumination; attaining the positiveness of enlightenment; a *barren fig tree* represents a sterile or unproductive state of mind and/or the negation of our True Nature (Christ Individuality;

Figurehead: our unenlightened ego;

Fikr: contemplative thoughts; meditation; (In Sufi terms, means concentration on God);

File Cabinet: our subconscious; our memory bank;

Filigreed Spirit: humankind; the physical forms we embody in our myriad dimensions of spiritual beingness;

Fill Light, Fill-in Light: a spiritually-attuned intellect that grasps a metaphysical principle in support of the heart's wisdom; (In photography language, fill light is secondary light from a lamp or reflector that helps illuminate areas that have shadows.);

Filter(s): our five physical senses; our brain; our previous choices and experiences;

Finch Features: being able to make ebullient forecasts; maintaining a positive outlook; expressing joyfulness; being celebratory and optimism;

Fingerprint(s): verification of the extent of our physical activities and whereabouts;

Finish Line: for our physical bodies it is the end of one of our incarnational experiences; for our spiritual selves, as far as we know, it is the culmination of each cusp of consciousness in whatever dimension of being we find ourselves;

Fire: illumination; truth; the fiery serpentine energy; purifying one's thoughts; intense spiritual energy; truth that consumes the dross of materialism and sense appetites; *destructive fire* represents hypercritical attributes and qualities of the unenlightened human mind; a *pillar of fire* symbolizes the kundalini force (fiery serpentine energies of the Holy Spirit, the *paraklete, speirema*) rising in our spinal cord to purify our spiritual energy centers (chakras); consciousness itself;

Fire Ball(s): incendiary thoughts and violent emotions;

Fire Drill: the practical application of, well, Fire; (See Fire);

Fire Eater: our spiritually-attuned self absorbing the fiery illumination of truth principles;

Fire Engine, Fire Extinguisher(s), Firefighter(s): denotes the immediate need for putting out destructive inner fires; (See Fire);

Firefly: intermittent intuitive moments; flashes of insight;

Fire Walking: the ability to achieve higher states of spiritual awareness without being consumed by the ego's corporeality;

Firewall: denials (statements that deny the power of outer appearances); (In the IT world firewalls limit the data that can pass through them and protect a networked server from damage by unauthorized users);

Fireworks: the spectacular brilliance of sudden aha's and phenomenal, life-changing insights; the fully aroused serpentine energies that quicken each of the chakras as we move toward the moment of achieving our enlightenment;

Firing Range: practicing poignant, to the point, laser-like sound bites to prepare for getting our message across;

Firmament: consciousness;

First Lady: the Eternal Sophiac Wisdom; Eve;

First World: our super-conscious;

Fir Tree Qualities: displaying resilience and strength; achieving longevity;

First-Born: newly initiated spiritual thought or idea; 'birth' into a higher level of awareness and/or into a newly attained incarnation; the Eternal Presence expressing Itself in physicality as the Cosmic Christ in the creation of universes;

First-Born From the Dead: the illumined mind is the first-born from the dead (our lower, phrenic mind) having been crucified on the cross of matter as an incarnated being;

First Coming: Spirit (Eternal Presence) descending into matter as the Christ in each of us at the instant of our birth in human form; God becoming incarnate in us, through us, as us; (See Second Coming and Third Coming);

Fish Bowl, Fish Tank, Fish Pond,: the human experience with its fish bowl perspective;

Fish Capacity: achieving intellectual illumination; generating divine ideas; establishing the union of will and love; seeking the Christ Conscious aspect of human consciousness; organic life immersed in inorganic matter (our being divine souls [products of organic evolution] immersed in a sea of inorganic evolution [suffering under muddy water]); (The origins of the fish symbol appear to have been Nordic and/or Hyperborean); [The form of a fish (*Matsya-avatara*) is one of the manifestations of Vishnu. When the fish is considered as a symbol for the Christ, its Greek name is Ichthus]

Fishers of Men: spiritual thoughts that positively influence ordinary thoughts;

Fish Hook(s), Fish Net(s), Fishing Rod: our ability to grasp divine ideas;

Fish Market: spent ideas that lay the foundation for current ideas;

Five Wounds of the Christ as Jesus: the five physical senses; (The most common number of wounds lists the nail wounds in Christ's hands and feet as four wounds, with the spear-puncture in his side as the fifth wound. However, this does not count Christ's circumcision as a boy, the crown of thorns with its scores of puncturing wounds, his sweating blood in the Garden of Gethsemane, or his being flogged at the hands of the Roman soldiers which no doubt produced numerous wounds.);

Fixed Costs: the karmic debts we pay for our errant thoughts, words, choices, and actions unless we re-cause our experience; (In marketing terms, fixed costs are things like salaries and rents that are paid monthly as the costs of doing business);

Flag(s): high ideals; *red flags* are base inclinations;

Flag Pole(s): male energy directed at achieving high ideals;

Flaming Sword: the white heat of truth that awakens the Third Eye; the flaming sword issuing from the mouth denotes the 'word of power' that slays the illusion of materiality's permanence; (See Third Eye);

Flammable Error: when error thoughts, words, and actions are exposed to the white heat of truth;

Flashback(s): life reviews; past life regressions; (See Life Review);

Flash Knockdown: quickly composing ourselves despite being 'knocked down' or derailed by a disappointment or setback; (In boxing terms, a flash knockdown occurs when a punch from an opponent knocks a boxer down, but the boxer gets back on his feet before the referee begins the count.);

Flashlight(s): focused awareness;

Flash Mob: a sudden outburst of unspiritual-like, hurtful, rude, negatively-charged thoughts, words, and actions coated with malicious intent; (In IT language, a group of people summoned by e-mail or text messaging to a predetermined location at a specified time to perform a specific action before dispersing);

Flat Hatting: our tendency to attempt to bring a highly esoteric spiritual principle down to earth very quickly, but are unable to do so because we don't quite understand it enough to be grounded in it; a religious or spiritual teacher's habit of taking a higher truth and sharing it at such an elevated level that people are unable to grasp it; (In FAA terms, flat hatting means flying an airplane at too high a speed dangerously close to the ground);

Flea Market: recycled (used, pre-owned) religious and/or spiritual teachings;

Flea-ness: our penchant for jumping from one thing to another; quickly leaping from one conclusion to another; flea bites denote being agitated and irritated at bits of knowledge or experience that cause pain or discomfort;

Flesh: physicality; the material (quantum) expression of Spirit; *eating flesh* represents comprehending eternal truths through the sciences and/or through one's spiritual practice, intellectual absorption of spiritual knowledge; an attempt to comprehend spiritual truths; symbolically *eating the flesh of Christ* means becoming illumined by understanding divine truths and comprehending the highest spiritual laws;

Fleur-de-lis Quality: telepathic ability; transcendence-oriented;

Flexitarian(s): people who have a primarily vegetarian diet but occasionally eat meat, cheese, and fish;

Flibbertigibbet Fluff: scatterbrained thoughts;(In social media, fibbertigibbets are frivolous, flighty, or excessively talkative people);

Flight Recorder: (See Black Box);

Flint-like: our impulse toward spontaneity and creative insights;

Flocks: spiritual concepts; a collection of spiritual sayings;

Floodlight(s): immense spiritual understanding in the midst of darkness;

Forget-Me-Nots: the power of remembrance; gratefulness;

Flying Fish: an extremely compelling spiritual idea;

Flying Saucer(s): esoteric ideas and concepts of unknown origin;

Fly Paper: our ability to keep from succumbing to small annoyances or letting petty nuisances get in the way of our spiritual growth;

Fly Quirkiness: developing pesky habits and behaviors; succumbing to small annoyances; letting petty nuisances get in the way of our spiritual growth;

Flyswatter Rebuttal: posting an immediate counterargument to someone's religious belief without any chance for engaging in protracted debate;

Fog-ish: denotes lack of clarity and/or understanding; also implies the need to slow down when we can't see the big picture;

Fohat, Chokmah: the Universal Life Force; fiery energy of creation; (In Tibetan cosmology, Fohat is the energetic aspect of the Supreme Spirit);

Food: subsistence; *healthy food* denotes spiritual truths, laws, and principles; *unhealthy food* represents error thoughts, words, and actions;

Food Court: a buffet of spiritual and religious ideas, insights, and concepts;

Food Fight: various faith traditions defending their own religious views;

Food of the Gods: divine wisdom; superior intuition; spiritual discernment; higher knowledge; etc.;

Food Poisoning: false spiritual and religious teachings;

Food Processor: the study and application of spiritual and religious principles; personal introspection;

Footnote(s): daily experiences; minor disappointments and irritations;

Footprints: discovering others have preceded us on the path; the emotional impact of previous spiritual and/or religious ideas;

Forbidden Fruit: the illicit pleasure associated with an incarnational experience; skin school experiences in general;

Forceful Projection: transferring the consciousness of a person who is dying out of his/her physical body to "somewhere else" so that the disembodied consciousness can "live on" in a 'host' nearby in the physical world (This transfer of the 'software of consciousness' requires compatible hardware (a brain with a similar operating system);

Forehead: the seat of superior perception;

Foreign Languages, Foreign Land(s): for a spiritually attuned consciousness error thoughts, inclinations, intentions, and ambitions are foreign languages; for our egocentric consciousness spiritual thoughts, inclinations, intentions, and aspirations are foreign languages;

Forelsket Reaction: the euphoria we feel when we first come across a compelling spiritual truth and see its implications for transforming our lives; (Forelsket is a Norwegian term that refers to the euphoria we experience when we first fall in love.);

Forest-like: being on the edge of disorientation and/or bewilderment; (See Wilderness Wooziness);

Forest Ranger(s): truth principles; our natural higher instincts;

Forgery, Fraud: pretending to be something we're not; an unenlightened ego; a false teaching;

Forgiveness: giving up the false for the true; going from *bitter to better*; no-fault discourse; giving up our fixation with fiction (the kind of fiction I'm referring to is our attachment to any falsehood which blocks our spiritual growth); pardoning error; (Forgiveness, it seems, is a universal human need. At its core it is the need to be pardoned, to be released from the emotional strain of having wronged someone or having been wronged by someone. Forgiveness requires an emotional correction. It is an empathic response to a wrong doing. It constitutes an act of extraordinary consideration which oftentimes seems much too lenient, if not down right foolish. But forgiveness is not doormat theology. Spiritually, forgiveness means giving up the false for the true. Another way of saying that is it means giving up our fixation with fiction. The kind of fiction I'm referring to is our attachment to any falsehood which blocks our spiritual growth);

Fork in the Road: recognizing the difference between the spiritual path and the material path; duality;

Formaldehyde Beliefs: dogmatic beliefs that remain preserved in our consciousness;

Fornication-ish Whims: the debasement of our consciousness with divisive and corrosive error thoughts;

Fort, Fortress: an egocentric consciousness (the safe house for our materialistic appetites);

Fortean Phenomenon: strange naturally occurring phenomena that science cannot yet define or explain (levitation, poltergeist, teleportation, spontaneous ignition of a human being, unexplained disappearances);

Fortuitous Fork: choosing the spiritual path over the material path;

Fortune Cookie(s): good intentions;

Fortune Telling: wishcraft; hopeology;

Fossil-like: our tendency for preserving old habits, life patterns, and ideas;

Fountains, Springs: the inexhaustible flow of ideas, insights, and inspirations from the reservoir of Spirit;

Fountain of Teaching: when a spiritual teaching flows (morphs) into heuristic interpretations;

Four Beasts: Represent the four fixed points on the zodiac (Leo, Aquarius, Scorpio and Taurus); [These are the strongest signs of the zodiac which also correspond to fire, water, earth, and air]; [They also symbolize our four human aspects that relate to the four directions or winds: North corresponds our emotions. East is our spiritual nature. South corresponds to our physical nature, and West represents our intellect]; (See Four Elements);

Four Cosmic Chauffeurs: the containers we choose as unfoldment vehicles; (The incarnational sheaths (bodies) we employ to 'move around in' on our extended trip 'back home.' They are: the etheric [memory body]; the mental body, the desire body, and the physical body. The *etheric sheath* houses all that we have ever thought, been, or done. It is the cosmic carbon print of our physical existence. The mental sheath is the 'vessel' of our cognitive genealogy. The desire sheath is the imprint of all of our spent desires and current urges. The physical sheath is the vehicle that allows us to travel around in material form);

Four Elements: denote the hidden power of the cross '+' and its psychic and psychological symbolism (air [mobility], fire [temperature], water [fluidity], and earth [solidarity] – Also, Air [*Gemini, Libra and Aquarius*],

Fire [*Aries, Leo and Sagittarius*], Water [*Cancer, Scorpio, and Pisces*], and Earth [*Taurus, Virgo and Capricorn*]);

Four Horsemen of the Apocalypse: The *white horse* represents dogma that limits our spiritual growth and blinds us to greater truths; the *red horse* stands for the chemicalization that occurs when our old beliefs and assumptions are rocked by cognitive dissonance (Our thoughts war against each other as we try to grasp compelling spiritual insights); the *black horse* symbolizes our going through the 'dark night of the soul' as old beliefs and life patterns are challenged and then released; the *pale horse* represents the demise of our worldly, Adamic consciousness which does its best to resist the inevitable spiritual transformation which is occurring; The four horsemen also represent the archetypal world, the psychic world, the material world, and the phantasmal world); The four horsemen of the Apocalypse may also signify the four main divisions of human life: *Birth* is represented by the rider on the white horse who comes forth conquering and to conquer; the impetuosity of *youth* by the rider on the red horse who took peace from the earth; *maturity* by the rider on the black horse who weighs all things in the scales of reason; and *death* by the rider on the pale horse who was given power over a fourth part of the earth. In the Hindu cosmology these horsemen signify the four *yugas* (ages, epics) where the universe is destroyed once every 4 to 8 billion years (one full day and night for Brahma).

Four Noble Truths: suffering (*dukkha*), its causes, its cessation, and the path leading to its cessation; (These truths are the central doctrine of the Buddhist spiritual tradition and provide the framework for all Buddhist thought);

Four Seasons: Spring (the beginning of our spiritual resurrection, realignment), Summer (awakening to our divine nature and spiritual powers), Autumn (the opening of our heart center and mastery of our lower, sense nature), Winter (our purification and preparation for rebirth);

Fourth Coming: when people the world over realize that the Christ Presence is incarnated in everyone else at h/her birth and we all are the human expressions of the Planetary Christ. (See First Coming; Second Coming; Third Coming);

Fourth Dimension: the next higher frequency range just beyond the earth's physical essence;

Foxish: cleverness; cunningness; resourcefulness;

Foxglove-ish: our susceptibility for having positive, sincere, and faithful thoughts and emotions as well as hypocritical, negative, and deceptive thoughts and emotions; denotes the subtleties associated with moving from the head to the heart;

Frankincense: affirmative prayer and meditation which lift us above worldly concerns;

Frashokereti: transforming our coma consciousness into our divinely-attuned consciousness; (In Zoroastrian eschatology, *frashokereti* symbolizes the final renovation of the world. In other words, the apocalypse);

Free-For-All: brainstorming; each new day's possibilities;

Free Radicals: materialistic thoughts that cause us all kinds of trouble; (In the nail care industry, free radicals refer to excited molecules that cause many kinds of chemical reactions, including polymerization of acrylic nails.);

Free Style: the power of individual choice; the course we chart for each day;

Free Will: multi-incarnational influenced self-conscious and self-expressive choice; contextual self-imposed destiny;

Freeze-Dried Fallibilism: believing that no belief, theory, supposition, thesis, view, or postulation can be proven with absolute certainty;

French Kiss: our infatuation with physicality and its sensual nature;

Frequency Fence: our neural real estate tuned to the repetitive imprinting of dogmatic thinking, making it difficult to 'hear' the higher frequencies of esoteric thought; three frequency fences are our subconscious, waking conscious, and super-conscious; the vibes between our multidimensional selves (human, astral, mental, ethereal, cosmic, etc.);

Frequent Fliers: those who have a habit of enjoying astral travel, flying in their dreams, and experiencing hypnogogic visions;

Friars Orders: walking our chosen spiritual path;

Friend(s): thoughts, inclinations, proclivities, words, choices, and actions that are in concert with our stated beliefs and values;

Friendscaping: eliminating old habits and beliefs (friends) that used to define our old materialistic selves in favor or new habits and beliefs that are more in line with our spiritual growth; (In social media terms, friendscaping refers to the act of 'trimming' our friends lists down to a reasonable number);

Fringe Time: communicating with someone who seems to have extremely far-out religious and/or spiritual views;

Frisbee(s): field tested ideas;

Frivolous Lollygagging: plodding along and inching our way through each incarnation without the slightest inkling that we are spiritual being having a human experience;

Frog-like Inclinations: being fertile in our thoughts, words, and actions; harnessing our yin energy; encountering good luck; enjoying a safe return; undergoing metamorphosis; experiencing resurrection;

Frontier: a major growth edge; brand new, never before attempted mental, emotional, and physical territory;

Frozen Food: striving for prepackaged personal growth and spiritual enrichment advice that are advertised to be the definitive answers (cold, hard facts) to our quest for truth;

Fruit: the choices and intentions that 'fall' from our consciousness and the actions that are the result of our choices;

Fruitfulness: illumination; increasing spiritual awareness and interest;

Frying Pan: our earth experience; our incarnational experiences in the physical plane as well as in other dimensions of being;

Fuchsia-like: spiritual groundedness; devotion to esoteric knowledge;

Fugitive(s): ingrained habits that we are trying to outgrow;

Fungus: the consequences of negative choices, behaviors and emotions;

Fundamental Falsification: error thinking, being, and doing;

Fundamentalist Skullduggery: hell fire and brimstone sermons;

Funeral: the deliberate attempt to bury an old habit or world view and/or celebrate putting to rest a talent, skill, or ability that no longer serves our higher good;

Furnace-like : the fiery action of truth which incinerates the dross of error from our consciousness; matriculating through an incarnation;

Furniture: fairly fixed ideas, beliefs, and attitudes that serve as the basis for our world view; *rearranging furniture* implies changing our ideas, beliefs, and attitudes; furniture in disrepair implies beliefs and values that need modification, revisiting, reaffirmation, and reconsideration;

Gaia Bias: knowing that when Mother Nature is mistreated she usually returns the favor; (The Native American term for Gaia is Agisegwa);

Galaxy, Universe: our super-consciousness with its plethora of highly esoteric thoughts, concepts, and ideas;

Game Changer: a compelling spiritual insight; comprehending a new esoteric teaching;

Gammadion, Gammadia, Cross of the World: the meeting place [decision point] in consciousness where we decide if we want to be a spiritual or material being; (Four try-squares, the right-angled summits that are turned toward the center which forms a cross or intersection. The intersection forms the meeting place of water to the north, fire to the south, wood to the east, and metal to the west, with earth as the center. Also represents the Christ as the center and the four Evangelists, and the four beasts in the vision of Ezekiel and of the apocalypse as the four directions.); [See Perpendicular Path];

Gang: a collection of negative, combative, and belligerent thoughts based on self-interest and fear;

Gangrene: longstanding error thoughts and tendencies; impure, carnal, divinity-denying thoughts and actions;

Ganymedes: the most promising worldly ideas that can potentially be elevated to their higher spiritual essences; (In Greek mythology, *Ganymede* is a divine hero whose homeland was Troy);

Garage-like: learning fundamental principles and then neglecting to apply them on a daily basis; committing ideas to memory for future use;

Garbage: unethical, sacrilegious, immoral, disrespectful, perverted, satanic, self-negating, divinity-denying, blasphemous, inhumane – thoughts, words, choices, and actions;

Garbage Can: a materialistic consciousness that supports all kinds of temporal refuse; (See Garbage);

Garbage Disposal(s): affirmative prayer, meditation, positive affirmations and mantras, spiritually-attuned visualizations, sacred rituals and ceremonies;

Garden of Eden: the etheric realm of super-consciousness; the 'cosmic heart' of God; an organized sphere of divine consciousness; the Universe and the Multiverse;

Gardenia-like: penchant for brevity;

Gargantuan Encroachment: when an enormous worldly thought with gigantic implications for interrupting our spiritual growth enters our consciousness;

Garment(s): our physical body (thought sheath, somatic spacesuit); belief system; mental concept; static perspective; *shedding (changing) garments* symbolizes clearing one's consciousness of encrustations of dogmatism, duality, and religious biases, adopting new spiritual perspectives; *tearing garments* implies a strong desire to change our perspective; *giving garments away* represents willingly sharing our perspective; a *seamless garment* denotes the complete alignment of our human personality with our Christ individuality and/or the indestructible unity of life; *garment of light* is our imperishable spiritual essence; the *garment of darkness* is our physical form;

Gas Chamber: a toxic consciousness; evil as a form of error expressing itself;

Gas Mask(s): truth principles that protect us from toxic intellectual and emotional environments;

Gasoline-like: feeling the vim and vigor of transformational ideas; experiencing the get-up-and-go of energizing concepts; also denotes the possibility of explosive emotions and/or dangerous actions;

Gate: attaining or leaving a degree (level, benchmark) of spiritual understanding and/or evolvement; (For example, two of the types of gates we pass through are earthly birth gates and earthly transition gates);

Gate, narrow: a spiritually-oriented mindset; the illumined mind;

Gate, wide: sense consciousness; a materialistic mindset;

Gate of Entrance: total union with the Absolute, the Eternal Presence;

Gate of Exit: reincarnation;

Gauntlet of Forgetting: the repetitive parade of human incarnations and reincarnations;

Gazebo: openness and receptivity toward the natural rhythms of an earth experience;

Geber: a compelling spiritual insight;

Geebatic Nonsense: backbiting; gossiping; malicious scuttlebutt; (Geebat is an Islamic word for backbiting, particularly in political arenas);

Geek Chic: the clothing and spiritual/religious paraphernalia associated with "the look" that it takes to appear mystical and godly; (In geek language, the dress and personal appearance, and cyber-gadgetry associated with computing and technology enthusiasts that is regarded as stylish, highly fashionable, and current);

Gehenna: in our quickened consciousness the white heat of truth that burns off the dross of error; (See Hell);

Geko: exoterically, monk responsible for discipline in monastic communities; spiritually, our conscience;

Geller Effect: one or more psi talents that enable the user to bend metal objects without physically touching them; (Named after Uri Geller);

Geloscopy: receiving psychic impressions about someone from h/her laugh;

Gene Doping: symbolizes the intentional mistranslation of scripture to create a watered down version of the truth; (In sports medicine, the transfer of genes or genetically modified cells into an athlete to illicitly enhance athletic performance);

Geode-like: our capacity to see the big picture and shape our own future;

Geometry of Mediocrity: thinking negatively, constantly talking about mundane things, refusing to let go of the past hurts and ills, fearing the future, neglecting to take care of our health, failing to exercise, worrying about things in general, forfeiting periods of rest and relaxation, and staying too busy for our own good;

Geranium-like: cultivating a renewed sense of positivity and optimism; self-sufficiency;

Germs, Bacteria: error thoughts, impulses, and urges;

Ghetto: self-defeating, subconscious life patterns; a collection of thoughts derived from the same perspective (world view);

Ghost Dance: a dance that would reunite the living with the spirits of the dead and bring peace, prosperity, and unity to Native American peoples throughout the region;

Ghosts (Ghouls) of Unfoldment: base material thoughts and karmic patterns that haunt us as we progress toward our enlightenment; (These ghouls denote unfinished business and/or unfulfilled wishes that must be mastered);

Ghost Busting: using positive affirmations and denials to offset the negativity caused by repressed material (ghosts) that has resurfaced;

Ghouls: anti-Christed thoughts and tendencies;

Ghoulish Abandonment: total denial of our innate divinity;

Giants: exaggerated thoughts and emotions; over-emphasized assumptions; hyperbole; much ado about nothing;

Gift Card Millionaire: esoterically, denotes the invisible wealth available to us in Universal Substance that is ours by right of consciousness' (In social media circles, this phrase refers to people who have significant amounts of money tied up in gift cards, store credit, and a wide variety of vouchers);

Gilgoolemic Dilemma: the mindless, repetitive cycle of rebirths;

Gilgul Nesahmot: the Kabbalistic term for reincarnation;

Gimilic Glimpse: heavenly thoughts;

Gimmickry: the promises, ridiculous testimonials, and pseudo-science retailed by unscrupulous prosperity gurus;

Gingerbread: familiar feelings;

Ginger-like Qualities: being able to digest difficult information; being passionate about achieving health and wealth;

Ginnungagap: the 'cup of illusion' that describes our attachment to materiality; the unmanifested potential of an emerging thought; (In Norse mythology, *Ginnungagap* [mighty gap] was the vast, primordial void that existed prior to the creation of the manifest universe);

Giraffe-ishness: gracefully striving; being entrepreneurial; acquiring an over-arching vision; having noticeable elegance;

Girl Scout(s): the evolving emotions associated with personal growth;

Giving Consciousness: having an open palm instead of a closed fist; (A giving consciousness means realizing that our personal and professional success and happiness are never more than a thought or act of generosity away. Neuro-biologically speaking, a giving consciousness is nestled within the same frontal regions of the brain which are activated by awe, wonder, transcendence, and joy. An internal coherence results, which fortifies our immune system, strengthens the neural pathways in the frontal lobe, and arrests the feelings of fear and uncertainty which are the products of the amygdala. A giving consciousness is one of our deepest connections to our Extraordinary Self. It acknowledges our oneness with and appreciation for the Authentic Us. It is the realization that there is more to us than the circumstances we face. It is the recognition that we have a capacity to give that outshines any thoughts of lack. It is one of the seven core abilities that characterize the Extraordinary Us, our Christ Self.); [Research at the University of California, San Diego and Harvard University provides laboratory evidence that cooperative behavior spreads between people. Those who benefit from kindness tend to find it contagious – and "pay it forward" by helping others. James Fowler, an associate professor of political science at UC San Diego, and Nicholas Christakis, a Harvard sociology professor, showed that when one person gave money in a "public-goods game" to help others, the recipients were more likely to give money away in the future. The domino effect continued as more people were swept up in the tide of kindness and cooperation.] (See Extraordinary You);

Gizmo(s): quick material fixes; assumptions;

Glacier(s): cold, harsh feelings that are just the 'tip of the iceberg' when it comes to the depths of their meaning;

Gladiolish: nobility in thinking;

Glasses: our capacity to expand our vision, gain more clarity, and see beyond the veil of the obvious; correcting near-sightedness when we can't see the big picture and adjusting our far-sightedness when our immediate perspective over-looks nearby opportunities;

Glass House: transparency; feeling we have nothing to hide;

Glass Jaw, Glass Chin: being unable to take criticism for our spiritual and/or religious beliefs; (In boxing lingo, a glass jaw means being unusually susceptible to a knockout punch.);

Glass Slipper(s): clear understanding;

Glider: thoughts that characterize our going with the flow;

Glitches: error tendencies;

Globe: our incarnational crib;

Global Warming: raising the level of respect and love and goodwill and trust and humility and compassion and common sense and spirituality to transform this planet into a kinder and gentler and more loving place in which to live. It's the kind of global village that can turn hatred into loving… hunger into harvest… disease into healing… violence into vapor… war into peace. It's the kind of global warming that's characterized by handshakes and hugs... helping hands... reciprocating helping hands ... lending someone a hand... walking hand in hand... and praying hands;

Globesity: over-filling our consciousness with materialistic thoughts and attitudes;

Gloom and Doom: the preaching tactics of religious fundamentalists; a consciousness centered on doubt, lack, fear, doubt, and guilt;

Gnat(s): small annoyances and irritations;

Gnome-like: perceptions that interpret and guard our accumulated knowledge;

Gnosis: hidden spiritual knowledge; the knowledge we acquire through our own experience, as opposed to knowledge based on theories that we are given and told to mindlessly believe;

Gnostic Church: experiential knowledge; (According to Gnostic tradition, the Gnostic Church is comprised of all the perfect beings in existence, who are called gods, angels, buddhas, masters, etc.);

Gnosticism: the belief that we can know and understand universal truths:

Goal Post, End Zone: accomplishment; achievement;

Goat Proclivities: resisting spiritual truths or religious tenets; intellectual stubbornness; rigid thinking; stubbornness;

Gobbledygook: the claims made by charlatans;

Goblin(s): life perspectives that work against us;

God: Supreme Sacred Unity, Universal Cosmic Oneness, the Infinite Isness, the One Indefinable Reality; the One Eternal Presence; the Absolute; the Perfect Perfection;

Goddess: universal feminine energy; the feminine, receptive force through which creation occurs, symbolized in many of the world's faith traditions by figures such as Eloah, Isis, Mary, Maya, Tara, Isobertha, Rhea, Cybele, Gaea, etc.; the formless-force-matter symbolizing Mother Nature;

God of the Gaps: believing that because science cannot explain some events or phenomenon then it is reasonable to believe that an anthropomorphic God is responsible for whatever is and/or happens;

God Particle: the Christ Principle; God's essence in physicality; (On July 4, 2012, physicists announced they found evidence of the 'God particle.' The head of the world's biggest atom smasher, Rolf Heuer, said physicists discovered a new particle that is consistent with the long-sought Higgs boson known as the 'God particle.' The 'God particle' is believed to give all matter in the universe size and shape. The phrase 'God particle' was coined by Nobel Prize-winning physicist Leon Lederman in the 1950's, as a non-technical way of explaining how mass in the subatomic universe works. The 'God particle' was found in the $10 billion Large Hadron 17 mile long proton-smashing Collider on the Swiss-French border. Until now the 'God particle,' or Higgs Boson, was a theoretical particle. "We have now found the missing cornerstone of particle physics," Rolf Heuer, director of the European Center for Nuclear Research (CERN) announced);

God's Will: God's 'isness' expressing Itself in endless forms and patterns in both manifest and unmanifest realms of being and non-being; (Humankind's conscious recognition that we are indivisibilized expressions of God at the point of us and the disciplined actualization of our Christhood is the will of God);

God Wink: usually performed when we want to suggest a coincidence to be of divine origin;

Gog: thoughts that deny our innate divinity;

Gogynfeirdd: our penchant for using poetic words to describe the effects of a spiritually active life; (In Welsh literature, gogynfeirdds are court poets);

Going Upstream: ascending toward our illumination which necessitates our struggle to swim against the currents of our errors and limited earthy perspectives; going downstream represents giving into our material attachments;

Gold: vitalized spiritual energy; our ability to transform material consciousness into spiritual consciousness; durability and malleability; perfection; spiritual refinement; enlightenment; liquefied spiritual fire; (See also the Philosopher's Stone);

Golden Baton: ancient wisdom being passed from spiritual teacher to student, who becomes a spiritual teacher who passes it on to his/her student, who passes it on, etc.;

Golden Bough: the safety and security of an enlightened consciousness; a Christed Consciousness; a Universal Truth Principle; (*The Golden Bough* is an epic tale written by Virgil that narrates the underworld adventures of the Trojan hero Aeneas who is directed by Deiphobe, the sibyl of Cumae, to obtain a golden bough in order to enter the underworld.);

Golden Dawn: denotes our being at the cusp of illumination;

Golden Egg, Golden Womb, Universal Gem: the source of the creation of the universe or of all manifestation in Indian cosmology. (In the Upanishads it is called Hiranyagarbha or the 'Soul of Brahman or of the Universe);

Golden Gate, Gate of Mercy, Beautiful Gate, Gate of Eternal Life: Christ Consciousness; total and complete illumination;

Goldenrod-like: harvesting our thoughts; congested attitudes;

Golden Wedding Garment: the etheric body; soul body;

Goldilocks Zone: the Kingdom of God is the Goldilocks Zone and the Goldilocks Zone is Christ Consciousness, and Christ Consciousness is within us; (It is in our super-consciousness and we have constant access to It through 'right living, being, and doing.' The Christ in us is the God in us in the Kingdom of God in us, which is our spiritual address the Goldilocks Zone);

Golgotha: the place in consciousness where we cross out error (crucify); the brain (which is in the skull) is transformed by the power of the mind at the moment of our enlightenment; the Crown Chakra;

Go-No-Go: going back and forth from silly to serious thoughts in an attempt to forestall being serious-minded;

Good and Evil, Error: good is all that is in alignment with truth; evil – a form of error – is all that is out of alignment with truth;

Good Samaritan: our innate divinity; spiritual wholeness; illumined self;

Good Samaritan Story: When we choose to leave the peace and serenity of our spirituality (Jerusalem) and follow the temptations of our material sense consciousness (Jericho), we rob ourselves of our strength and vitality. Our error thoughts (robbers) can take us over dangerous emotional and physical ground, oftentimes resulting in life-threatening illnesses. [Our spiritual wholeness (Good Samaritan) will be restored when we are receptive to Christ-centered thoughts (the Inn) and accept the wisdom and encouragement that comes from our Christ Nature which gives us comfort through the Holy Spirit];

Goofy Gullibility: believing the wild claims of televangelists;

Google, Yahoo: cyber juggernauts; electronic Akashic Records;

Google Surfing: aimlessly and randomly looking for religious and/or spiritual material online when we're bored or looking for something inspirational;

Goosebumps: yin and yang; excitement and/or fear;

Gospel Goose Bumps: discovering a life-changing spiritual, esoteric, theosophical, anthroposophical, allegorical, and/or metaphorical interpretation of a scriptural passage;

Gospel Magic: actually applying the spiritual and/or religious truths we know; (In magic circles, gospel magic is a branch of magic that uses magic effects to present and reinforce fundamentalist Christian concepts.);

Gourmet Gospel: spiritual, metaphysical, esoteric, theosophical, anthroposophical, allegorical, and metaphorical interpretations of the higher truths contained in the gospels;

Government: legislated obedience and leashed freedom; the belief in an organized set of laws and rules to ensure morality and control when human character is not at the height of its spiritual essence;

Grace: divine benevolence, favor, and generosity; consideration in returning to wholeness; (We experience grace every time we think a Christed thought, have a Christed intention, make a Christed choice, and take a Christed action);

Grace Period: the time between the thoughts we have, the choices we make, the words we use, and the actions we take: (In debt collection terms, the grace period is time period we have to pay a bill in full and avoid interest charges.);

Graffiti: opinionated, sometimes hostile, thoughts and feelings;

Grandchildren: newly formed thoughts and feelings;

Grandfather Clock: conventional, perhaps even outdated, thoughts, concepts, and/or views;

Grand Jury: all of the spiritual laws and truth principles that exist; the 85 billion cells in our brain and the 100 trillion cells in our body; (In legal circles, a grand jury is a body of 16-23 citizens who listen to the evidence presented by the prosecutors in criminal allegations, and determine if there is probable cause to believe someone committed a punishable offense.);

Grandparents: our preference for established customs, prevailing beliefs, and conventional thinking;

Grape(s): foundational concepts that lead to wealth and leisure;

Grasshopper-like: our fancy for delivering glad tidings and joyful news; also represents our preference for being lucky, creative, and resourceful; also implies our susceptibility for losing focus and having a short attention span;

Gratitude: the acoustics of thanksliving; the harmonics of thank you's; (The Father of Positive Psychology, Martin Seligman reminds us that people who write down at least three things to be grateful for each day are happier and more optimistic than people who choose not to record what they are grateful for.); (See Spoice);

Grave(s), Graveyard: spent ideas (graves) that have been put to rest in our subconscious (graveyard);

Graven Gulag: the history of errors we have sculpted because of our worldly thoughts that make our living laborious, unfulfilling, and inharmonious; (In Soviet political parlance, a gulag was the government agency that managed the forced labor camps during the Stalin era);

Graven Image: an anthropomorphic God; (Anytime we attribute more power to something other than holding our relationship to the Eternal Presence as supreme, we are literally and figuratively bowing down to graven images);

Gravity: the magnetic power of attraction between thoughts, ideas, and concepts;

Gray-ness: implies our compulsion for ambiguity, vagueness, equivocation, and even double-entendre when we feel pressured; conservatism; practicality; status quo;

Great Battle of Life: the 'war' between our carnal and the spiritual elements in our nature is fought in the sodium chloride (saltiness) in the blood within our physical bodies; (See the Red Sea);

Great Breath, Divine Breath, Life Breath: our divine pneumatic umbilical to the omni-activity of the Eternal Presence; it is the pneumatic exchange of divine energy between our human soul and the particular dimension of being in which we find ourselves; [Becoming conscious of our breath brings us closer to the Consciousness that animates our soul and the greater process that we share with it]; (See Holy Spirit);

Great Depression: going from spirit into matter;

Greater Jihad: self-cleansing; self-purification; (In Islam means the religious war waged within ourselves against our evil desires and bad qualities);

Great Ordeals: our skin school experiences;

Great Trilemma: an argument voicing three dilemmas regarding the divinity of Jesus; (It is sometimes referred to as '*Lunatic, Liar,* or *Lord*', or as '*Mad, Bad,* or *God.*' According to Rabbi John Duncan "[Jesus] either deceived mankind by conscious fraud, or He was Himself deluded and self-deceived, or He was Divine. There is no getting out of this trilemma." On the other hand C.S. Lewis asserted, "You must make your choice. Either this man was, and is, the Son of God, or else a madman or something worse. You can shut him up for a fool, you can spit at him and kill him as a demon or you can fall at his feet and call him Lord and God, but let us not come with any patronizing nonsense about his being a great human teacher. He has not left that open to us. He did not intend to. Now it seems to me obvious that He was neither a lunatic nor a fiend: and consequently, however strange or terrifying or unlikely it may seem, I have to accept the view that He was and is God); While it is perhaps the most important argument in Christian apologetics, the same argument can be applied to us since we are the human expressions of the Christ at the point of us;

Great Voice: the still small voice;

Great Wall of China: protectiveness; restrictiveness;

Great White Brotherhood: a highly evolved order of Western and Eastern adepts throughout the ages who have fully realigned themselves consciously with their divine natures. They have ascended into the higher planes of being and are known as ascended masters. Their calling is to assist and guide incarnated beings on their journey to Christhood (Buddhahood, Krishnahood, Vishnuhood, Allahhood, etc.) The descriptive word 'white' refers to the aura of white light that cocoons their forms and does not have anything to do with race or ethnicity);

Great White Throne Judgment: the final transformational moment when all remaining error thoughts are consumed by the white heat of Spirit as our egocentric consciousness gives way to an enlightened consciousness;

Greed Giddiness: the wobbliness we feel when we've overdosed on copious amounts of stinginess, self-interest, and self-indulgence;

Greedom: being bulimic with gluttony, greed, and excess;

Greenhouse: growth and transformation; love for nature; an ecologically and environmentally-focused awareness;

Green-ish Traits: being conscious of chronological time and aware of the flow of life itself; green also implies our desire for growth and wellness; green also implies protectiveness, envy, and even jealousy; generosity; good luck; renewal; (Green is the color of the heart chakra. It also stands for the natural us – that is, humankind);

Greeting Card: sense of community; friendliness; sociability;

Gremlin(s): old habits that we haven't outgrown yet;

Grenade: an explosive thought and/or volatile emotion;

Grievous Body Harm: our errant practice of abusing our physical body by thinking harmful thoughts, using harmful words, eating unhealthy foods, and engaging in dangerous and harmful actions; (In law enforcement terms, grievious body harm refers to dangerous and harmful actions by someone against someone else);

Grigoric Preferences: our penchant for astrology [cosmobiology], forms of divination, herb craft, and magic;

Grim Reaper: an anti-Christed conclusion;

Grinches: thoughts that steal our joy and happiness;

Grinding Stone: an incarnational experience;

Groceries: food for thought;

Grocery Store: a marketplace for food for thought;

Groovy Grooves: When we think similar thoughts and experience similar events over and over again, we form neurological pathways (grooves). The more repetitive the experiences the deeper and more imprinted the grooves become. In effect, we create neural highways, established neural routes (patterns), the more we repeat particular words and/or phrases;

Gross Billing: paying off two or more huge karmic debts in one lifetime; (In advertising terms, gross billing is the cost of advertising at the highest advertising rate.);

Group Hug: the highly loving practice of a number of people embracing one another simultaneously, for the express purpose of providing support and solidarity;

Growing Edge Donnybrook: (See Chemicalization);

Growing Edge Real Estate: the largest room we have - the room for our own improvement;

Growl(s): the anger, disappointments, and dissatisfactions associated with our base instincts;

Grumpy Eulogy: saying good-bye to a long-standing personal habit that we're going to miss even though it negatively affected our spiritual growth;

Crystal Sea: purity; without blemish;

Guardian Angels, Guardian Wall: powerful, protective, spiritual thoughts (gifts, abilities) that guide us out of danger when we are swayed by error thoughts;

Guardian of the Threshold: our conscience; the Extraordinary Us; the Authentic Us; the Sentinel of our subconscious and conscious selves; our Cosmic Portal to the Unseen universes of higher awareness;

Guerrilla Hug: a bad habit we thought we'd gotten over announcing its resurrection;

Guillotine: our built-in temperament for losing our head when we become frustrated or angry;

Guinea Pig(s): new spiritual concepts, ideas, and practices that we try on for size because someone said we should, but we doubt very seriously we'll adopt them as enduring practices;

Gunas: the three expressions of matter – Tamas (inertia), Ragas (activity), and Sattva (harmony); (In Sanskrit philosophy, these three gunas are associated with creation (sattva), preservation (rajas), and transformation (tamas);

Gunpowder: the explosive potential for setting off our anger and rage;

Guru: spiritual law and/or principle; an epiphany; a highly intuitive thought; a transformative life experience; (In her book, *The Wizard of Us*, Jean Houston sees the word *guru* as an acronym: G̲ee, yo̲u a̲re yo̲u);

Gussied Up Handcuffs: dogma coming from highly respected clergy;

Gymnast Traits: desiring to achieve and/or maintain our flexibility, strength, and life balance;

Gymnosophistic Propensities: highly mystical thinking, being, and doing;

Hacker(s): subconscious material that gains unauthorized access into our waking consciousness;

Hades: a hellish state of consciousness; (See Hell, Sheol Prerogative);

Hail: the condensation, psychically, of our auric substance;

Hair: vitality; charismatic holiness; spiritual strength; freedom; mastery over the human experience; personal power; *shaving one's head* represents renunciation of material appetites or surrendering one's human self to one's Divine Nature (pigtails also symbolize surrender to a higher power); *cutting* *one's hair* implies conformity or allegiance to a disciplined pattern of thinking that makes one's vitality aligned with a higher authority; (It also symbolizes a disconnection with past patterns and habits; a *lock of hair and pigtails* imply a set of strong beliefs; *disheveled hair* represents intellectual virility and idiosyncratic genius;

Hajj: a sacred pilgrimage to Mecca; (In Islam means a sacred obligation or duty);

Hallucinations: the belief in original sin; evil; an anthropomorphic God; incurable illnesses; duality; separation between Spirit and matter;

Halo: the aura of a spiritual thought; enlightenment; goodness;

Halo Collective: the pool of our spiritual thoughts, ideas, concepts, inclinations, aspirations, attitudes, beliefs, etc.;

Hamartias: error thoughts, words, choices, and actions that interfere with our spiritual progress; (Hamartias in Greek mean mistakes and/or errors in judgment);

Hammer: constructive thoughts and attitudes;

Hammock: leisurely thoughts; relaxed demeanor;

Hand(s): conduits (transmitters) of power; our ability to transmit spiritual, psychic, and physical power and energy; the *right hand* represents masculinity, yang energy, assertiveness, giving; the *left hand* symbolizes femininity, yin energy, receptivity; an *eye in the palm* denotes clairvoyance; *hands clasped or folded together* denote friendship, allegiance, support; different *mudras* (hand positions) designate various divine powers; *long fingernails* represent femininity and royalty; *short fingernails* denote being used to the daily grind and labor intensive work; laborious service;

Handcuff(s): negativity and a lack consciousness; harsh judgmentalness; fear; doubt; laziness; feeling unworthy; rudeness; lack of diplomacy; cussedness; chronic nay-saying; passivity; pretentiousness; repulsiveness; materiality; malevolence; maliciousness; not putting limits on limits;

Hand-Me-Down(s): our current incarnation; dogmatic perspectives; conventional religious and spiritual beliefs;

Handshake(s): denote trust and cordiality; also represent the willing alignment between our human self and our Christ Self;

Hang Gliding: astral travel; freedom;

Hangover: the dizziness, giddiness, and headaches we feel when we compromise our authentegrity;

Hanky-Panky: trying to fit square religious beliefs into round spiritual wholes;

Happiness: the hum of good choices;

Happiness Eclipse: belief in the necessity of suffering;

Harbor: emotional stability; refuge;

Hardpan: our subconscious patterns and repressed material; (In gardening terms, hardpan is the impervious layer of soil or clay that lies beneath topsoil.);

Harmaceutical(s): disparaging words like "unbelievers" and the "unchurched," used by mainstream religious groups to describe people who aren't members of their religious affiliation - and the people on the receiving end of those insulting descriptors find themselves even more turned off by mainstream religion; (Medically speaking, an FDA approved medication released for public consumption by a pharmaceutical company which is re-called and becomes the subject of a class-action lawsuit because of its previously unreported dangers.);

Harem: a collection of associated sensual impulses and propensities;

Harlot, Prostitute: to prostitute the mind, and thus, our spirituality to matter;

Harmonic Convergence: the entrainment of our human self with our Christ Self;

Harmony: love at its highest, most spiritual azimuth; [The harmonious relationship I invite you to get really, really, really serious about is the one between your human self and your Christ Self (Buddha Self, Krishna Self, Allah Self, etc.)];

Harmony of the Spheres: our cellular symphony; the compatibility between our super-conscious and our waking conscious;

Harp-ness: unifying our ordinary consciousness with our Christ Consciousness by harmonizing our psycho-emotional-spiritual vibrations;

Harpoon: male energy; confronting superficial emotions;

Hashmalling: our ability to know when to speak and when to be silent when it comes to being tactful in religious conversations; (Hashmal is the Kabbalistic term for balancing speech and silence);

Hashtag: a spiritual and/or religious concept that becomes a meme; (In social media, a hashtag is a word or an unspaced phrase that is prefixed by a pound sign #. Hashtags make it possible to group messages so people can search for a particular message and add h/her comments relating to the message); [See Meme; Internet Meme];

Hasnamussic Dilemma: the propensity to cultivate a divided consciousness, one characterized by our egocentric nature and our divine nature; (Coined by Gurdjieff, means a person with a divided consciousness: part of which is free and natural, and part of which is trapped in the ego.);

Haumaic Tendencies: self-centeredness;

Haunted House: our consciousness when self-defeating ideas, self-negating thoughts, and stale beliefs surface that we thought we had outgrown; our subconsciousness;

Hawk-ishness: focus; distraction-free; immense concentration; exceptionally visionary; a keen sense of partnership; our soul;

Haymaker: an unconscionably hurtful criticism, verbal attack, or life situation that can totally rock us off course by knocking the props out from under us; (In boxing terms, a haymaker is a wild swinging punch thrown with all of the opponent's weight behind it in an attempt to knockout the other boxer.);

Headaches: pessimistic attitudes; negative outlooks; self-negating habits; our thoughts are out of alignment with our professed values and beliefs; a result of the struggle to comprehend complexity;

Head Candy: spiritual teachings;

Healing: physical, mental, emotional, and spiritual *wholing*; the elimination of dis-ease; the body's natural pharmacy at work; the movement toward wholeness; *absent healing* represents the process of nonlocal *wholing* on the mental plane;

Health: oneness with our Christ Nature; wholeness established in body, mind, and soul;

Hearing Genealogy: the lineage of oral teachings from master teacher to disciple;

Heart: center of wisdom, truth, love, spiritual understanding, and intuition; the fountain of immortality; conscience; moral courage; (The 'cave of the heart' is a spiritual center alluding to initiation into the greater mysteries. The Sanskrit word *guha* refers to a cave, but also represents the inner cavity of the heart as the vital center for enlightenment); [In the *Upanishads III.14.3*, the heart/cave analogy is clarified: "The Principle which resides at the 'center of the being' is smaller than a grain of rice, smaller than a grain of barley, smaller than a grain of mustard, smaller than a grain of millet, but also at the same time larger than the earth, larger than the atmosphere, larger than the heavens. And larger than all the worlds together." Spiritually, the aspect of smallness applies to relativity and largeness designates absolute reality.);

Heart Bypass: using our left-brained, logical, intellectual thinking only;

Heating the Crucible: (See Chemicalization);

Heathens: error thoughts; divinity-denying base instincts;

Heather-like: courageous; brave;

Heaven, Kalani, Hemel, Ciel, Himmel, Cyu, Parayso, Celestyn, Celeste: living joyfully, confidently, faithfully, and lovingly at the speed of our Christ Consciousness; Christ Consciousness (the Kingdom of God); fully enlightened super-consciousness; the state of consciousness that is underwritten by purity, sacredness, reverence, universal love, harmony, and unity with the Eternal Presence; our default state of consciousness; when *heaven opens* it means a higher level of spiritual awareness is achieved; *in the midst of heaven* means an enlightened perspective; (The original Greek word used for Heaven is *ouranos* which literally means *expanding, widening, magnifying, maturing*. So Heaven is a process. It's an adverb not a noun. It's not a physical place. It's a state of consciousness); [The concept of a physical heaven probably originates from our deep inner knowing that physicality is not our 'home' and that we are destined to 'live' on a much higher plane of being]; (In *Quantum Theology*, Diarmuid O'Murchu tells us: "We have come to understand heaven, hell, and purgatory as states of being, not places, within the one world. According to the old theology, in death, we humans became a-cosmic, that is, cut off from the cosmos. In our new understanding, we become pan-cosmic – we enter into a new relationship with the whole cosmos." Pg. 181);

Heaven and Earth: Christ Consciousness is heaven and our egocentric human consciousness is earth;

Heel: the intersection between comprehension and understanding; the leverage point (first contact area) when our cosmic consciousness meets our coma consciousness (physical incarnation); an *injury to the heel* symbolizes the vulnerable position we've put ourselves in when we chose another incarnation and/or reincarnation, it also signals an injurious setback in our quest for immortality; a *winged heel* represents substantial progress toward our immortality; an *uncovered heel* symbolizes surrendering to our incarnational vulnerabilities for the purpose of understanding and then mastering physicality;

Heimlich Method, Heimlich Maneuver: forcing new life into a stale religious experience;

Heir-ing It Out: aligning our human self with our Christ Self (Buddha Self, Krishna Self, Allah Self, etc.);

Heirship: our incorruptible, inheritable, fully available and accessible Divine Nature;

Heisenberg's Uncertainty Principle: we have both position (are human in physical form) and velocity (are connected to Spirit) at the same time; (When we chose this human incarnation we dumbed down our awareness (thinking we could clarify our *position*) to justify our notions of duality and separation. Unfortunately, our spiritual *velocity* was also slowed down because of its encasement in the physical bodies we created to experience physicality);

Helicopter: elevated religious ideas, fancies, and urges;

Heliocentric: Christ-centric; our whole psychology revolves around our divine extraordinariness;

Hell, Hades, Gehenna, Jahannam, She'ol, Demonios, Maldito, Cehennem, Zum Teufel!: a consciousness fixated solely on material things, personal aggrandizements, and the denial of our innate divinity; a consciousness bivouacked in error; a consciousness of duality and separation topped off with faith deprivation; (Hell is not a geographical location 'down there' ruled by a red-garbed being with horns, tail and pitchfork, where people scream in agony and are tortured endlessly in eternal flames. The notion of this kind of hell, which comes from pediatric theology, has been popular for centuries. If you happen to have been brought up in a traditional Christian home, chances are this kind of 'hell' was passed on to you at a very early age. If it was, and if it is still your dominant belief about hell I invite you to suspend that hellish belief as soon as possible); The "hell" referred to in the *Gospels* represents the word *gehenna*, which was in a valley southwest of Jerusalem, where the refuse and filth of the city was burned. It was actually the city dump in Jesus' day; it was a smoky, smelly, gruesome place. Centuries earlier it was even a worse place! Certain idol-worshipping kings of Israel had practiced appalling religious rites in Tophet, sacrificing children in the fires to Baal. The region was called the Valley of Hinnom, which means "groans and anguish." A perfect name for such a grisly site, don't you think?;

Hellish Halitosis: cursing; taking the name (nature) of God in vain;

Hellish Hyperbole: the intensified progression of errors that seem to feed off each other making the consequences of those errors more exaggerated and harmful;

Helmet-like Capacities: being protected by our intellectual superiority, intuition, and reasoning abilities;

Hemispheric Guffaw: during a guided meditation when we respond to suggestions involving mental imagery that take us first to one brain hemisphere then to the other in order to stimulate both sides of our brain;

Hemlockish: self-injurious attitudes; self-deprecation; self-denial;

Hemorrhage: losing our spiritual and/or religious convictions;

Hepatitis: feeling intensely vulnerable and powerless; learned helplessness; (Learned helplessness is a giving-up reaction, a quitting response that follows from the belief that whatever we do doesn't matter. Explanatory style, coined by psychologist Martin Seligman, is the manner in which we habitually explain to ourselves why events happen. It is a great modulator of learned helplessness. An optimistic explanatory style stops helplessness, and a pessimistic explanatory style spreads helplessness. Our way of explaining events to ourselves determines how helpless we can become, or how energized, when we encounter everyday setbacks and defeats.);

Herbology: a form of healing where healers employ herbal formulas to help bring about results. In some cases, this can mean creating elixirs and tonics from an infusion of herbs in a liquid that are ingested. (It can also mean other methods, such as using them to treat wounds and illnesses);

Heredity: our own personal karma; life thread that runs through our successive incarnations; our own psychic genealogical tree;

Heresy: false teachings that go mainstream; (See Heretical Thoughts);

Heretical Thoughts: error thoughts that deny our innate divinity and the spiritual principles that characterize it;

Hermeneutics: interpreting sacred scripture using grammatical and historical, contexts, the meaning of words, the form of sentences, and the peculiarities of idioms of the original language;

Hermetic Principles: in psychic circles, these are seven principles of Western thought that are considered as the great foundation for all life and creation on the physical plane. (For mystics and psychics, these foundations are Mentalism, Polarity, Rhythm, Correspondence, Vibration, Gender, and Cause and Effect);

Heroes: courageous ideas; spiritual thoughts entering an egocentric consciousness for the first time; positive affirmations that turn our lives around;

Heterodox Actions: behaviors that deviate from (contradict) our professed beliefs and values;

Hibiscus-like: superior intuitiveness; precognitive ability;

Hiccup(s): error thoughts, poor choices, and childish actions;

Hidden Curriculum: the repressed material in our subconscious that influences and impacts our conscious learning;

Hidden of the Hidden, Concealed of the Concealed: highly mystical esoteric knowledge; incomprehensible secret knowledge;

Hierophants: the highest, most elevated spiritual thoughts;

High Blood Pressure: anger and resentment tied to doing something we feel pressured to do but feel we shouldn't have to do or aren't meant to do;

Higher Consciousness Flickrs: sharing riveting New Thought and spiritual insights with others; (In social media, a flickr is online sharing of grouped photos and short videos with others);

Higher Education: esoteric studies;

Higher Self: our Christ Self; our Extraordinary Self; (See Deeper Self); [In *Stages of Faith: The Psychology of Human Development*, James Fowler says that "the more we contemplate life's meaning, our notions of our (Deeper Self) will evolve from concrete ideas to mythical beliefs, and from there toward more universal values of social responsibility");

Highfalutin Escrow: the amount of prayer we put into any undertaking;

High Priest: a major religious concept and/or principle;

Highway(s): denote neural pathways that connect relatively distant regions of our nervous system with another; (They usually consist of bundles of elongated, myelin-insulated neurons, known collectively as white matter);

Hijacking: emotions trumping reason;

Himalayas: an exalted state of consciousness;

Hippie(s): freedom of expression; disrespect for, and rejection of, authority;

Hippopotomonstrosequippedaliophobia: literally, the irrational fear of long words; metaphorically, the irrational fear of pursuing spiritual knowledge;

Hippopotamus: quick-tempered; easily aroused; impenetrable;

Hitchhiking: the magnetic qualities of powerful positive thoughts and contagious negativity that take closely related thoughts and emotions along for the ride;

Hiwyai' Bisha': our carnal thoughts and emotions that deny our innate divinity; (In Chaldean, Hiwyai' Bisha' stands for the evil beast);

Hoarding: the fear of letting go; a 'catch and release' phobia;

Hobo-ing: keeping in touch with being out-of-touch;

Hochoian Consciousness: sense consciousness that produces subject-object, dualistic thinking; (Hocho is a Japanese term for dualism);

Hocus-Pocus: the shenanigans of televangelists;

Ho-hum Probabiliorism: believing that when in doubt we must always choose the most likely answer;

Holarchic Being: the allness of God is the simultaneous eachness of us and our eachness is the simultaneous wholeness of god;

Hole(s): empty areas in our body of knowledge;

Holiness: divinely-oriented thoughts; the *way of holiness* means absorbing divine knowledge;

Holistic Medicine: employing both tradition and non-traditional healing techniques and technologies;

Holistic Thinking: the belief that reality is contingent on the understanding of unified wholes that are greater then the sum of their constituent parts;

Holly-like Penchant: having a high degree of protectiveness; acquiring soul work through dreams;

Holotrophic Breathwork: a non-drug enhanced mental practice that uses breathing, group process, intensified breathing, evocative music, focused body work, and expressive drawing to access non-ordinary states of awareness to enhance self-exploration; [The practice was developed by Stanislav and Christina Grof as a "cartography" of the psyche.];

Holy City: a fully Christed personal and/or collective Christ Consciousness demonstrated and lived 'religiously';

Holy Grail: Christ Consciousness (Buddha Consciousness, Krishna Consciousness, Allah Consciousness; Vishnu Consciousness, Great Spirit Consciousness); (Also, the Grail is our heart which is the somatic cup [vase] that dispenses our blood throughout our body. Christ's heart is also the Grail because it dispenses the vital force to all beings. Our physical body can also be considered the Grail because it houses our spirit and the Spirit of the Eternal One); [The Grail legend probably originated in Celtic and Druid traditions]; (The Grail's various manifestations include, but are not limited to: the Lost Paradise, an illumined mind, a giving heart, the eternal Word of God, spiritual centers built by humankind, Arthur's Round Table, the Book of Life, the blood that flows from someone who sacrifices h/her life for others, a downward-pointing triangle, 'cupped' flowers, the calyx of a flower, the Cosmic Egg, the sacrificial cup containing the Vedic Soma, the lunar crescent, etc.);

Holy Ghost: the omni-activity aspect of the Eternal Presence; (See Holy Spirit; Holy Trinity; Holy Spirit); [In The Holy Science, Yukteswar explains, "The Holy Ghost, being the manifestation of the Omniscient Nature of the Eternal Father, God, is no other substance than God." pg. 6];

Holy Ground: a Christed (holy) consciousness (ground);

Holy of Holies (Adytum): a fully Christed consciousness; the Kingdom of God;

Holy Land, Pure Land, Land of the Saints, Land of the Blessed, Land of the Living, Land of Immortality, Supreme Country: an illumined consciousness; Christ Consciousness; Kingdom of God; (In Sanskrit it is *Paradesha*; in Chaldean, *Pardes*; in the West, *Paradise*);

Holy Rood (Haly Ruid): a piece of the true cross on which the Christ as Jesus transcended human form;

Holy Spirit: the omni-activity of the Eternal Presence expressing Itself in physicality; (There is an Intrinsic Life Force that permeates all that is. It is the Eternal Presence animating Itself in the manifest and unmanifest realms of being. The Hindus call it *'kundalini.'* The Japanese call it "*ki*", the Chinese "*chi*" and in Christianity, it is known as 'Holy Spirit,' the Comforter (*parakletos* or *speirema*. Its highly-charged energies ascend and descend in our spinal cord (the alchemical serpent), depending on our level of enlightenment. The white heat of Spirit travels up and down our spinal cord through powerful energy centers (chakras), purifying, cleansing, and activating these spiritual transformers. I believe John 3:14 and 15, as well as other New Testament passages, refer to this *kundalinic* rise of serpentine energies: "14. *And as Moses lifted up the serpent in the wilderness, even as the son of man be lifted up*, 15. *That whosoever believeth in him should not perish but have eternal life*."); the Feminine Principle; Ruach Elohim;

~ *Spiritually Speaking* ~

Holy Trinity: Spiritually, means the Eternal presence in three aspects: God, Christ, Holy Spirit: Also, denotes Mind, Idea, Expression; Religiously, implies Father, Son, Holy Ghost; (Tanga-Tango is the Peruvian Trinity);

Holy Vitamins: positive affirmations, affirmative prayers, truth principles, acts of kindness; spiritual visualizations; sacred rituals;

Holy Water: the Spiritual Life Force that permeates all physicality and non-physicality;

Homecoming Hankerings: meditation; affirmative prayers; positive affirmations; sacred rituals; spiritual visualizations; (See Practicing the Presence);

Home Improvements: filling our consciousness with spiritual thoughts;

Homicide: killing off the better parts (aspects, qualities, talents, higher essences) of ourselves to pursue materialistic appetites;

Homogenized Experience(s): when our behaviors mirror (represent, are the image of) our spiritually-attuned consciousness;

Homelessness: (Spiritually, homelessness is a misconception. We are never homeless. We carry our spiritual home with us all of the time. It's called the Kingdom of God within us);

Homework: matriculation through each skin school experience;

Homosexuality: similar sensual thoughts feeding off each other in the pursuit of connecting the dots in a particular human experience; (See Lesbian(s);

Honey-like Aptitude: obtaining divine wisdom through transmutation (spiritual alchemy); extracting the nectar from the flowering of human experience; *extracting honey from a carcass* represents sublimation of the creative force;

Honeymoon: the nine months, or so, we spend in the womb as we begin a new human experience; the time we spend learning basic New Thought teachings; the time between a clergyman/woman's acceptance of a new church appointment and the date h/she actually starts;

Honeysuckle-like: telepathic abilities; esoteric adeptness;

Honoring the Silence: moving away from the imprecision of words;

~ Spiritually Speaking ~

Honor Your Father and Mother: (The well-known scriptural phrase "honor your father and mother" needs some much needed spiritual clarification. Let's take a closer look at the word *honor* which comes from the Hebrew root word *hâbad* – which means "burdensome." Add to that the spiritual perspective for "father" (which means established conventional thoughts) and "mother" (which means normally expected feelings) and you begin to see the esoteric implications of this often repeated phrase. Looking at it from an expanded spiritual perspective this phrase really implies: "Have the courage to move beyond the burdensome (honor) perspective of any previously established thought (father) or normally expected feeling (mother) that interferes with your spiritual growth." As you can see, the emphasis is on the quality of your 'family' of thoughts and emotions and not about the genealogy of your family relationships);

Hoodwinked: believing in the embedded theology of our youth; (See Fib(s), Fiction); mindlessly giving power to outer appearances;

Hooligans: impure thoughts and corrupt inclinations;): error thoughts, words, and actions that bash our truth walk; [See Mob, Thug(s)];

Hoop of the Nation: a spiritual perspective (hoop) that unifies our consciousness (nation); [In Native American spirituality, that which binds the Lakota nation together];

Hope: spiritualized wishing that seems to be a necessary prerequisite for faith-lifts; patience that leaves the light on for you;

Horizontal Contentment: adopting hammocks, gazeboes and Jacuzzis as soul catchers;

Hornet-like: experiencing stinging remarks; angry, needling negativity;

Horn-ish Attributes: having powerful aspirations; displaying fierceness in conviction; having defensive thoughts; the *horn of salvation* symbolizes the power of exerting spiritual thoughts and aspirations over material thoughts and ambitions; procreative fertility; denote luminous rays;

Horoscope: displaying inbred tendencies; indigenous naturalness; *wishcraft*;

Horse-like Traits: experiencing the cosmic life force; having considerable mental power; *white horse* represents superior intuition and intellect operating quickly and gracefully at their highest essences; a *winged horse* represents complete mastery of our mental faculties (subconscious, conscious, and super-conscious);

Hosannas: the hum of spiritualized thoughts;

Hospice: allegorically, denotes the reverential thinking we engage in when we put certain attitudes, habits, beliefs, and behaviors to rest; (Clinically, the care for the terminally ill with an emphasis on pain relief, emotional and spiritual support, and dignity);

Hospital(s): a collection of healing thoughts and feelings; a medley of healing affirmations that alleviate our health concerns; our consciousness itself because of its transforming placeboic power to heal; the wound site on our physical bodies; (In medicine, hospitals are the places where we get private rooms and public gowns);

Hostage(s): repressed emotions and life patterns;

Hot Air Balloon(s): an elevated intellectual mindset; a higher spiritual perspective;

Hotel(s): refers to our brain with its many regions (frontal lobe, parietal lobe, occipital lobe, temporal lobe, brain stem, etc.); also refers to our consciousness with its three main floors (subconscious, conscious, and super-conscious);

Hotline(s): meditation and affirmative prayer; Aha's and intuitive flashes;

Hot Swappable: calling for (plugging in) prayer in the middle of a heated conversation at a church board meeting; (In IT language, *hot* means *powered on* or *active*. A swappable device can be added and/or removed while a computer is running);

Hot Zone: a highly controversial spiritual and/or religious subject that would ignite tempers and be seen as a 'theological contaminant' by some of the people involved; the intersection of an egocentric mindset and a spiritually-attuned mindset; (In firefighting terms, a hot zone is a specific contaminated area containing HAZMAT that must be isolated.);

Hour Glass: the Hayflick Limit; (the Hayflict limit is the number of times a normal human cell population will divide until cell division stops. The concept was developed by Leonard Hayflict in 1961 to show that our physical cells have limited potential for continued replication, disproving immortality and anti-aging theories.);

House, Home: consciousness; our somatic envelop (body);

House Arrest: keeping our thoughts to ourselves;

House Cleaning: removing error thoughts, inclinations, and intentions from our consciousness;

House Guest(s): every thought, idea, and inclination that comes into our conscious awareness;

House of Shadows: a consciousness filled with carnal, base, lower, material, error-prone thoughts;

House Warming: filling our consciousness with spiritual thoughts, ideas, and ideals;

Housework: self-improvement; (See Homework);

Huascarán: a very high state of consciousness; (The name of Peru's tallest mountain at 22,205 feet);

Hucker(s): diving headlong into religious dogma without considering how much such a plunge will dampen our understanding of our divine nature and detour our enlightenment; (In snowboarding terms huckers are people who uncontrollably throw themselves into the air without regard to their safety, the safety of others, and property damage.);

Hullabaloo(s): our skin school experiences; leaving a mainstream faith tradition and taking a New Thought route to spiritual growth;

Humankind: Spirit's 'skin school' address; cosmic consciousness trapped in matter; the collective biological address of the Christ Presence;

Humble Bragging: a self-deprecating, wry remark about ourselves that also reveals how famous, wealthy, spiritual, religious, or important we think we are;

Humdinger Levitation: base instincts being raised to their higher spiritual inclinations;

Humility: knowing that pinnacles of pride are always lower than the sod of unpretentiousness; (The word humility comes from the Latin word, *humus*, which means, the "soil." Perhaps humility is derived from the soil because being human entails a stooping and returning to earthy origins. It calls for a naturalness and reverence for everyday life. We find in it the vitality and spiritual richness unnoticed by people who merely hydroplane across the surface of life, missing its essence, and losing their connectedness with their essential being);

Humming Bird-like Qualities: total immersion coupled with varied interests; ability to focus and quickly refocus; compartmentalized concentration; controlled energetic quickness; playful agility; congruence with continuity and eternality;

Humpty Dumpty: bifurcation;

Huna Perspective: creating our own reality through a well-developed internal locus of control; (People who have internal locus of control believe that the outcomes of their actions are results of their own abilities. Internals believe that their hard work would lead them to obtain positive outcomes. They also believe that every action has consequences, which makes them accept the fact that things happen and it depends on them if they want to have control over it or not. *Externals* attribute outcomes of events to external circumstances. People that have external locus of control believe that many things that happen in their lives are out of their control);

Hunkered-Down Faith: mature faith;

Hurricane(s): the fiery energies of the Holy Spirit leveling, flooding, and tearing asunder (transforming) our sense-soaked consciousness (houses and buildings); (See also Chemicalization);

Hush Money: tithing to a church or donating to a worthy cause simply to ease our guilty conscience;

Hwergelmiric Furnace: where the white heat of Truth crosses out error;

Hyacinth-like: parasitical tendencies;

Hybrid Christianity: an integration of mainstream Christianity, New Thought faith traditions, and science. (Hybrid Christianity takes mainstream Christianity back to its spiritual and mystical roots. It is a highly integrative treatment of the various New Thought faith traditions that have sprung up over the religious landscape over the past 200 years. It incorporates the latest findings of scientific disciplines such as epigenetics, quantum physics, neuro-psychology, neuro-biology, evolutionary virology, neuro-theology, molecular biology, and positive psychology to amplify spiritual truths);

Hybrid Hoaxes: perpetuating the belief that there is an anthropomorphic, goodie god in the sky who favors some people and punishes others and/or an anthropomorphic devil that is evil, horned, red, and sports a tail;

Hydromancy: a type of scrying divination that uses the patterns of moving water as the medium for interpretation;

Hyena(s): the consequences of error;

Hylozoism: believing all things, animate and inanimate, have some sort of life sense and/or essence; (Hylozoism is a Milesian school term that means all matter, animate and inanimate, has latent powers);

Hyper-aesthesia: having exceptionally acute sensory awareness;

Hyperbole(s): the belief, and rhetoric that accompanies it, that we are condemned to everlasting hellfire, that we are the products of original sin, and that we are to fear a vengeful god;

Hyper-hypochondriacs: the flurry of self-deprecating and demeaning thoughts that run through our heads telling us how sinful and good-for-nothing we are;

Hypnagogic Filters: experiencing a transitional state of consciousness just before and immediately after sleep. (However, the 'sleep' I'm referring to is the unawareness of, and outright refusal to believe in, our innate divinity);

Hypnotists: extremely alluring sense appetites;

Hypocrisy: denotes an air of piety;

Hypocrite: egocentric thoughts dressed in spiritual clothing;

Hypostatic Union: the uniting of our human consciousness with our Higher Consciousness (Christed, Buddhic, Allahic, Krishnic Consciousness);

I Am: the Christ individuality within us; (Each time we affirm our "I-Am-ness" with the Universal Presence we strengthen our neuro-connections. Also, pleasant thoughts, positive and optimistic inclinations, sitting meditations, and affirmative prayers are all dopamine triggers); [In his Divine Comedy, Dante Alighieri expressed that the purpose of creation is to awaken the divine 'I am' in all creatures];

Ibis-like: birth; fertility; (According to local legend in the Birecik [Macedonopolis] area, the Northern Bald Ibis was one of the first birds that Noah (rest) released from the Ark (our super-consciousness) as a symbol of fertility);

I-Catching: aligning ourselves with the Indwelling Christ Presence (Buddha Presence, Allah Presence, etc.); (In the brain, every manifestation of self is impermanent. The small 's' self is continually constructed, deconstructed, and reconstructed again and again. It's not so much that we have a self, it's that we do self-ing. The brain strings together heterogenous moments of self-ing and subjectivity into an illusion of continuity. The small 's' self is a fictional character);

Iceberg: a cold, unfeeling attitude that is generally caused by a deeply hidden hurt;

Ice-cream: enjoying simple pleasures and contentments in life; cheerfully opting for a little *joie de vivre*;

Ice Skating: denotes our ability to remain above cold, narcissistic harshness and icy emotional states;

Icicle(s): ice cold intentions that hang around until they are used or forgotten;

Icky Double-Talk: pretending to be spiritual or religious when we're not;

Ida and Pingala: the believable (ida) and the true (pingala);

Idiot(s): unforgiving thoughts; harsh, hurtful thoughts delivered to destroy someone's self-esteem, sense of security, or happiness; beliefs that foster the denial of our innate divinity;

Idolatry: addiction to material forms; an external locus of control; giving the world of outer appearances precedence over our spirituality;

Idols: the false 'gods' of greed, covetousness, jealousy, avarice, deceit, etc.; material things when we choose them over spiritual things;

Idyllic Introspection: letting the parts of us ripen that sow the seeds for tomorrow's version of the spiritual 'us' today;

Igloo: an outwardly cold, tactless, and heartless attitude that is really an attempt to be 'hard now to be kind later';

Illegal Drugs: destructive, base instincts and negative karmic influences that we carry from one incarnation to another until we refuse to give power to them;

Illegitimate: cancerous, toxic, diabetic, hyperglycemic, prostatic, cardiac failure-ish kinds of thoughts – all of which are not true of our Real Nature;

Illness: the body's version of tough love; reminder of the need for self-care;

Illuminati: enlightened thoughts;

Illumination: enlightenment; nirvana; a Christ-centric (Buddha-centric, Krishna-centric, Allah-centric, Great Spirit-centric, Vishnu-centric) consciousness;

Illusion: seeing a particular incarnation and our experiences in that incarnation as the only reality;

Ilungaic Intrusions: allowing an error thought or inclination to intrude into our consciousness the first time, tolerating it a second time, but eliminating its influence thereafter; (In Bantu terms, ilunga refers to a person who is willing to forgive abuse the first time; tolerate it the second time, but never a third time.);

Image of the Beast: the anthropomorphic god of exoteric religions;

Imbas Forasnaic Vision: precognitive foresight; (*Imbas forosnai*, is a special gift of clairvoyance believed to be possessed by the Druids);

Imma: the beginning of everything; the Divine Mother (corresponding in the Qabbalah to 'Abba' (father); the Multiverse (her children are the universes that the Multiverse spawns);

Immaculate Conception, Immaculate Reception: the divinely inspired result of our intuitive intelligence, love, and receptivity to our innate divinity being raised to their highest and purest spiritual essences so that we immaculately conceive a pure, inviolate Christed Idea;

Immigrant(s): every thought that morphs into its higher spiritual essence;

Immobilities: addictions that keep us stuck in our stuckness;

Immortality: timeless and eternal beingness (unfoldment) that is our movement toward total alignment with our divine nature; (We are already immortal beings – that have been evolving even before the Big Bang that created our universe. Our beingness is characterized by timeless and eternal progress because we are God's Presence expressing Itself as us. As we subordinate the personal ego, the particular 'garment' we wear in each incarnation, we will see our eternalness more clearly);

Immortals: spiritual truths; illumined thoughts;

Impaired Hearing: not hearing our own excuses when it comes to explaining why we haven't taken our truth walks seriously;

Impaired Vision: seeing the world through our physical senses only; adhering to a literal interpretation only when reading sacred scripture;

Impeachable Oath: realizing that our promises may be empty if they haven't been field-tested;

Impious Contradictions: thoughts, words, choices, and actions contrary to our stated religious beliefs;

Implants: medicines ingested into our physical bodies; spiritual ideas that enter our egocentric awareness; metaphysical teachings placed along side religious teachings to deepen them; positive, optimistic thoughts placed into negative attitudes to lighten them;

Imposter(s): deceptive thoughts and attitudes meant to hide our impure motives;

Imprecatory Prayer(s): positively framed and/or negatively laced affirmations;

Imprisoned Splendor: our repressed Christ Nature;

Imprisonment: a consciousness completely filled with the fetish of materialism;

Inaugural Moment: the moment we realize we are the human expression of the Christ Presence;

Incarceration: every skin school experience;

Incarnation: Spirit descending into matter as us; the ancestor becoming heir and the heir becoming ancestor; our spiritual essence becoming a quantum being; our willful embodiments and re-embodiments in skin school;

Incense: prayers, affirmations, and mantras lifted up when we are in an elevated state of consciousness;

Incest: commingling, fusing, cross-pollinating, and jumbling highly carnal and expressly lascivious error thoughts that deny our innate divinity;

Inconvenient Truths: realizing that the same Christ Presence that expressed Itself as Jesus of Nazareth over 2,000 thousand years ago is the same Christ Presence that expresses Itself as us today; the Only Begotten Son is the Christ Presence; we don't have to die a physical death to go to heaven – or hell;

Incubator: our consciousness for our spiritual enlightenment; the world for our involution;

Inculpatory Evidence: our body's reaction to the errant choices we make and the divinity-denying actions we take; (In legal lingo, inculpatory evidence is evidence that indicates a defendant actually committed the crime.);

Indecent Exposure: an error thought that surfaces in our conscious awareness;

Indentured Servant(s): our misguided inclination to 'sell' our human personality to a warped, totally materialistic ego;

Independence: complete alignment with our Divine Nature, the Extraordinary Us;

Indigestion: the guilty feeling we get when we give into our error thoughts; the consequences of our error thoughts, words, and actions;

~ Spiritually Speaking ~

Indigo-ness: denotes highly spiritual qualities, superior intuitiveness, wisdom, prestigious tones of royalty, and sincere loyalty; acting dignified and above board; having a high degree of authentegrity; enlightenment; honor; mysticism; (In stained glass, indigo unites the "wisdom" of blue and the "love" of red); [meditation is heightened when practiced in an indigo light]; (Indigo is the color of the Third Eye Chakra);

Ineffable Name: Since 'name' means the 'nature of' the ineffable name is giving no name to the illusion that we are separate entities from the One Presence. There is no need to even voice such an illusion;

Inertia: spiritual inactivity; letting our thinking, being, and doing sink into the status quo; spending time in too many successive incarnations;

Infants: newly formed ideas;

Infection(s): error thoughts and inclinations that let to body, mind, and soul difficulties;

Infidel: any belief or conviction arising out of our egocentrism that denies our innate divinity or the divinity of others;

Inflammatory Infidelity: compromising truth principles by choosing base sense appetites that we know we should have outgrown;

Infant Damnation: the banishment of a newly formed spiritual (infant) thought in an egocentric consciousness;

Infant Mortality Rate: the number of newly formed spiritual ideas (infants) that 'die' in an egocentric consciousness everyday;

Infestation: when error thoughts become error choices and error choices become error actions and error actions become an error-ridden lifestyle;

Infidelity: anytime we neglect, abandon, dishonor, misrepresent, misalign, are prodigal with, renege on, transgress, malign, and maroon ourselves from our Divine Nature;

Inflatable Bed: having too much materialistic praise (hot air, infatuation, longing) for our earth experience (bed);

Infringement: any iota of a thought concerning the errancies in the Bible is considered by mainstream, religious fundamentalists as unforgivable infringement;

In-Group Bias: believing own religious affiliation is better than others;

Inheritance: our innate Christness;

Initial Evidence: the fact that we have incarnated in human form suggests that we are continuing our quest to align our individual consciousness with the Eternal Presence;

Initial Mutation: the first time we had the thought of incarnating into a human form as spiritual beings;

Injurious Gravity: the painful fallout from error thoughts, words, and actions;

Inkisaric Discipline: being humble by 'breaking the ego' or showing repentance; (In Hindustani terms, *inkisari* means obedience and humility);

Inn: our incarnational experience;

Innate Wisdom: opening from the inside out, learning to look for answers inside, going deep into our hearts and souls where we can connect with our Christ Self and receive guidance from within to transform our lives. Innate wisdom is using our intelligence to seek the common good by balancing our own interests with those of other people. It means knowing what is most important in life and how to get it, knowing what constitutes the meaningful life, and intuiting how to plan for and manage such a life. It is one of the seven core abilities that characterize the Extraordinary Us, our Christ Self. (See the Extraordinary You);

Inner City: the repressed areas of our subconscious;

Inner Heat Yoga: a yogic practice that uses psychic energy to create inner warmth and resistance to extreme external cold temperatures;

Inner Parts of the Earth: our subconscious, waking conscious, and super-conscious);

Inner Strength: using our internal resources, our mental skills, and our physical capabilities to confront difficulties of all kinds. It means meeting any challenge, difficulty, and disappointment with a high degree of confidence and poise. This core ability is the epitome of tenacity, determination, and fortitude which we already possess at a deep level. Commitment, resolve, and stick-to-itiveness are present. We will not give up on a commitment no matter what mood, emotion. or roadblocks we might be facing. It is one of the seven core abilities that characterize the Extraordinary Us, our Christ Self. (See the Extraordinary You);

Inoculations: meditation; affirmative prayer; spiritual visualizations; positive affirmations and resolute denials; the support of friends and family; a positive attitude; an optimistic spirit;

In One Accord In One Place: our cohesive thoughts; it could also refer to our human self being in complete 'accord' with our Christ Self;

Inquisition: the worldly ego's attempt to silence our quest for enlightenment;

Insanity: attempting to negate our innate divinity; worshipping dogma, believing in an anthropomorphic God or a satan 'out there'; praying to a 'goodie god out there' instead of praying from our own God essence; expecting answered prayer when we pray with an unforgiving heart; believing we can achieve spiritual ends through material means; trying the walk the spiritual path on material feet; believing heaven and hell are physical places we go to; thinking we have to die to go to heaven – or hell; believing all good things come to an end; trying to erase error with error; blaspheming the Holy Spirit; fasting from something we enjoy as penitence during Lent; hesitating to walk the spiritual path on practical feet;

Insect-ish: small spiritual inclinations; brief spiritual insights; on the other hand, they can also represent bothersome inclinations and impulses;

Inside Voice: It is a voice we must listen to when we are facing difficulties, when we suffer major setbacks, when we run into ten miles of bad road. It is a voice we must listen to if we are to grow spiritually. It is a voice we must pay attention to if we are to master the art of living. It is the voice of Spirit within. It is the *Still Small Voice*;

Insurance Policies: our spiritual practices;

Intelligent Design: The imprints of an Intelligent Designer are certainly compelling. The threads of traditional science and the dogma of pediatric theology are obviously wearing thin and are in need of triage. Their days are numbered. The narrow-minded nihilism of traditional science and the arrogant divisiveness of dogmatic religion have kept underlying universal truths hidden, ignored intelligent design, and have pushed us toward division and separation. (Fortunately, there are a growing number of scientists from the fields of quantum physics, neuropsychology, biology, neurotheology, astrophysics, and parapsychology who are collaborating with metaphysicians, mystics, and spiritual leaders throughout the world to pull us out of the dark ages);

Intention Deficit Disorder: unactualized spiritual growth intentions; our failure to follow through on our spiritual enrichment;

Intercom(s): meditation; affirmative prayer;

Interfaith Dialogue: the integration of the teachings from the world's faith traditions into our conscious awareness which makes us eclectic in our thinking, being, and doing;

Interfaith Traditions: I believe in freedom for people in matters of faith. The essence of spirituality, as well as religion, is a higher consciousness of the Eternal Presence called God. There are seeds of truth in all the world's religions. Different faith traditions are like spokes on a wheel with the hub being the Universal Presence we call God. They may be set apart by a variance of beliefs and approaches, different shades of theological interpretation, and a variety of rites and practices, but they are all seeking the One God (the One Presence, the One Reality, the Infinite Isness) at the center of all life. All spiritual/religious paths are valid expressions of honoring the Sacred. (I honor all faith traditions to the degree that they do not injure others, infringe upon interfaith spiritual and religious rites and practices, or attempt to force their theology on others);

Interior Decorating: our desire to add higher, more spiritual thoughts and feelings to our psyche; (See Internal Medicine);

Interiorization of Ignorance: an unquickened consciousness that is unaware of our divine nature;

Internal Hard Drive: our brain that registers and records the mind's input; (In IT language the internal hard drive stores the user's software and personal files);

Internal Locus of Control: operating from the knowledge that we're in charge of our life. If we succeed, we believe our skills, talents, and abilities had a great deal to do with it and if we fail, we take personal responsibility. If our orientation is an external locus of control, however, we believe other people, the environment, outer circumstances, or a higher power controls what happens – essentially we feel dependent on something outside of us or even helpless at times. People with a high sense of self-reliance (internal locus of control) believe that events in their lives are the result of their own actions. Internal locus of control is one of the seven core abilities that characterize the Extraordinary Us, our Christ Self. (See Extraordinary You);

Internal Medicine: meditation; affirmative prayer; positive affirmations; healthy, wholesome food and drink; positive attitude;

Internet: the modern day version of the Library of Alexandria; the evolving electronic equivalent of the Akashic Records (astral cloud); an electronic noosphere; our consciousness;

Internet Memes: concepts and/or behaviors that spread from one person to another across entire continents (Facebook, MySpace, email, #hashtags, tweets, etc.); [As we Tweet, post, like, share, and pin, are our brains registering our digital frenzy and shape-shifting accordingly? Preliminary research suggests yes. We also know that our digital life can alter our processing of thoughts. Psychologists have come up with the phrase "popcorn brain" to describe this phenomenon. It's that rapid-fire succession of thoughts we have when we're in our digital mode, which for some can make life offline seem unbearably mundane by comparison. In more extreme cases, like Internet addiction, studies have found actual changes on brain scans, though what these changes mean clinically is not yet known." Nerurkar, A., Can Tweeting Affect Our Biology?, *Huffington Post*, May 16, 2013];

In the Hold of a Ship: We have been Jesusing and Jonahing around ever since we got here (in a skin school experience). Like Jonah in the great fish's belly and Jesus falling asleep in the hold of a ship that was being tossed around by a storm we have been sleeping in the 'hold' of our human experiences. (The implications are obvious. We must awaken to our divine nature and become the best Christ we can be);

Intoxication: obsession with materiality in all of its forms;

Intrapersonal Violence: succumbing to our paranoid ego's habit of killing spiritual ideas, denying our innate divinity, and negating any and all inclinations to move in a more spiritual direction;

Intuition: logic in a hurry; absolute knowledge expressed relatively; a tweet from our Deeper Self; spiritual wisdom downloaded in an instant;

Invalid(s): self-deprecating thoughts and attitudes;

Invasion: negative thoughts, error tendencies, and toxic habits that enter – and disrupt - our waking consciousness and daily lives; (According to positive psychologists by willfully treating invasive urges and compulsions as errant neurochemistry we can alter those areas in the brain that produced them and put ourselves on the road to positivity);

Involution: mindful movement (descent) from our pre-human state of elevated consciousness toward our incarnational state of awareness; the infolding (downward arc) of our continuing spiritual self-expression;

Iolite-like: our capacity for visioning and forecasting;

Iota Management: fussing over non-essentials; (Trivial pursuits minimize the value of the moment. They squeeze out the important stuff and fill priceless moments with pettiness and unnecessary distractions. Trivialities are just that – trivialities. Attending to minute details has its place, but chronic immersion in details can become an exercise in futility. Tedium for tedium's sake wears us out. Quantitative data has its place. You won't get any argument from me there. It is the excessive need for irrelevant, "nit-picking," excessive, extraneous information that doesn't give us time for the growing edge that will bring us enlightenment);

iPad-ness: our capacity for instant connectivity; (See Computer Traits);

iPause: the length of time it takes to deliver a Sunday message in which congregants are asked to turn their iPads, iPhones, and iPods, etc., off;

iPhone-ness: our aptitude for near instantaneous communication and connectivity with other people and information networks locally and over long distances;

iPod-like: our ability to listen to our own lyrical impulses, appreciate our melodious qualities, and pay attention to the wisdom and advice of others;

Iris-like: our aptitude for peacemaking, collaboration, and diplomacy; nurturing tendencies; feminine qualities;

Irksome Heebie-Jeebies: the unsettling feeling we get when we cop out on our spiritual growth;

Iron-like Susceptibilities: our lower, base emotional nature;

Iron Deficiency: not feeling whole within ourselves without the support and approval of others;

~ *Spiritually Speaking* ~

Irreconcilable Differences: attempting to believe in truth and error at the same time; expecting answered prayer with an unforgiving heart; an anthropomorphic god in the sky mentality and spiritual wisdom; attaining Christ Consciousness and lusting after material addictions; maintaining a white-knuckled grip on separation, duality, and dogma and an open-palmed approach to universal oneness; pronounced and arrogantly perpetuated warfare between the world's faith traditions and world peace and civility; mindless defense of literal interpretations of sacred scripture and the acceptance of the heuristic value of metaphysical interpretations of the same scripture;

Irritable Bowel Syndrome: suffering so much from the "pain in the ask" that we hesitate to ask for help and hold back to our detriment;

Irritable Vowel Syndrome: the irritating practice of mainstream ministers and televangelists who accent certain syllables in words during the delivery of their sermons to the faithful; (In social settings, where we find ourselves with so many vowels on our rack in a Scrabble game that we can't make a new word, or the only word we can make is to add a vowel to an existing word for a low score);

Irritainment: annoying and irritating, but funny, consequences of errant thoughts and actions that remind us we're not as spiritual as we think;

Isagogics: interpreting sacred scripture using its cultural and/or historical context;

Island: an isolated thought;

Itsy-Bitsy Infections: the little lies we tell;

iTunes: our penchant for appreciating mobile audio music nearby and far away;

Ivory-like: expressing aloofness; displaying purity of character and of thought; exhibiting rarified thinking that rises above concrete thought; pleasantness;

Ivory Tower: mercantile aloofness and hierarchical distinction; superior business acumen;

Ivy-ish: having plenty of durability; attaining enviable interdisciplinary acumen;

Jackal(s): manipulative attitudes and behaviors;

Jacob's Ladder: the orderly sequencing of involution and evolution; *each rung* represents a higher – or lower – level of initiation, and/or adeptship; (In the mythology of many faith traditions, a seven-runged ladder, whose foot rests on the earth and whose top reaches to heaven. Angels continually ascend and descend upon it rungs. It is symbol of moral, spiritual, and intellectual perfection accomplished by a succession of steps, gates, or degrees of initiation. In Hermetic Masonry, the seven steps represent Justice, Equality, Kindness, Good Faith, Labor, Patience and intelligence. A ladder's two vertical uprights represent the duality of the Tree of Knowledge or in the Hebrew Kabbalah, to the two columns on the right and left of the Sephirothic Tree.); [Ladders are unified by the rungs that join the two uprights, and resemble DNA links (rungs). The rungs represent the different levels or degrees of initiation and/or dimensions (heavens) in consciousness]; (In the Mithraic mysteries the esoteric ladder had seven rungs and climbing these rungs symbolized the achievement of each successive level of initiation); [A double ladder and/or spiral staircase imply that an ascent is to be followed by a re-descent and can be analogized to our DNA's double helix];

Jack-in-the-Box: subconscious patterns surfacing unexpectedly;

Jackpot: illumination;

Jacuzzian Urges: riding ourselves of negativity and releasing error-prone toxins;

Jade Emperor: the Universal creator; the Supreme deity of Taoism;

Jade-like Properties: adopting positivity as our chief behavioral perspective; being insightful as a normal reaction;

Jadoo: hurting and scaring people by misusing spiritual gifts for personal gain;

Jail, Incarceration: living with a materialistic ego; fear; lack consciousness;

Jalopied Spirituality: literal only Biblical interpretations which turn out to be lower, more superficial, incarnations of religious exclusivism; (They are a *jalopied spirituality* at best – limited to short trips into dogma and judgmentalness, but entirely unsuitable for longer, more open-minded excursions into the higher truths hidden within them. No matter how intellectually gifted we are we must learn to listen to the wisdom of the heart if we want to be illumined spiritually. The wilderness referred to in most sacred scriptures represents the state of confusion caused by our dogmatic ego which keeps us from opening our heart to esoteric truths);

Jamais Vu: the experience of having seen something and experienced something before but feeling as if it is being experienced for the very first time (similar to amnesia); this feeling characterizes our inability to remember our previous incarnational experiences; (In psychology, *jamais vu* experiences refer to events we know we should recognize, but seem to be unfamiliar. The phenomenon is similar to déjà vu experiences);

Jamboree Junction: the collaborative intersection between the Sunday Truth Talk and the special music during the service;

Japaian Mantra(s): repeating affirmations, the Name of God, key spiritual words, and/or mantras aloud or silently as a spiritual practice;

Jasmine-like: goodwill tendencies; collaborative; diplomatic;

Javelin: male energy;

Jazzy Jargon: cute, inventive, and witty wording used in a particular line of work that describes the work, but is unfamiliar to those outside of that line of work – much like some of the terms used in this metaphysical dictionary;

Jeremiad Sewage: denotes the tendency to complain, lament, and prophesy doom and gloom;

Jericho to Jerusalem: the road from material attachments (Jericho) to spiritual enlightenment (Jerusalem);

Jerusalem Effect: going within into the field of peace and tranquility and becoming consciously one with our Christ Self; finding that inner peace that passes 'all misunderstanding' in the midst of whatever is going on around us;

Jesus: the person, born of Mary over 2,000 years ago, who perfectly understood His divine nature, who fully demonstrated His innate divine potential, and who fulfilled His divine purpose on Earth by completely aligning His human self with His Christ Self; (He assured us that the same Christ Presence that expressed Itself as him is the same Christ Presence that expresses Itself as us today); He saved us from the delusion of duality and separation; (He saved us from the absurd belief in an angry and vengeful white-bearded, white robbed God in the sky); He saved us from the fantasy that we have to die to go to heaven – or hell; (He saved us from the self-deprecating belief that we are unworthy, no good sinners); He became consciously one with the Only Begotten Son of God; (As far as I know Jesus, the man, never wrote anything down. He never had a bestseller. Never wrote an autobiography. Never scribbled anything on an envelope. Had no use for a Mont Blanc pen. Never e-mailed, tweeted, or 'text-messaged' anyone! He did write something in the sand that no one knows to this day what He wrote except the church leaders for whom it was written. However, what he 'wrote' was a biography of the evolving spiritual consciousness of the human race – through His example. What He 'wrote' was our future through His Christed actions. What He 'wrote' was a roadmap of how we can align ourselves fully with our Christ Nature); the reincarnation of Adam, Enoch, and Melchizedek;

Jet(s): compelling spiritual ideas, insights, revelations;

Jewelry: precious attitudes; priceless thoughts; expensive tastes; highly evolved spiritual discernment; our priceless divinity;

Jewelry Box: our waking consciousness;

Jewels, Precious: spiritual virtues and psychic abilities; hidden truths revealed; spiritual teachings;

Jigsaw-ing: mastering one spiritual concept and then placing it along side another for contextual clarity so we can see the big picture;

Jinn, Djinn, Genies: psychic and/or cosmic abilities; (In Muslim theology jinn are spiritual creatures made of smokeless and 'scorching fire' that have qualities similar to humans, but have the power to travel large distances at extreme speeds);

Jinx Junk: error thoughts, words, and actions that sabotage our health, wealth, and happiness;

Jivan Mukti: believing we can achieve spiritual liberation during our lifetime and not necessarily only on our (transition) physical death; (In the Advaita philosophy of Hinduism, jivanmukti means one who has assimilated knowledge of the Self and becomes liberated while living in a human body);

Jodo Shin: the Kingdom of God; Christ Consciousness; (In Japanese Buddhism Jodo Shin means 'True Pure Land');

Joke(s): calls to let our inner child out; invitations to lighten up;

Joker(s): thoughts with a jovial fix;

Jokester: the unenlightened, vertically-challenged ego;

Jomo: exoterically, a woman of high spiritual attainment; metaphysically, superior intuitive ability;

Jouissance: absolute, unadulterated, ecstatic joy; (What we've learned about joyful experiences, says psychologist Barbara Fredrickson is that the playful urges they carry build resources, and in times of trouble, these gains in resources can spell the difference between life and death);

Journeying: seeking spiritual growth by trying out different faith traditions to find a good fit;

Joystick: our highly synchronous hand and eye coordination that brings us the happiness and joy of accomplishment; (In IT language, a joystick is an input device commonly used to control what goes on in video games);

Joy Touch: the brush of angel wings; the warmth in the region just behind the heart center during intense meditation;

Judgment Day(s): periodic self-assessments of spiritual progress; every time we choose truth over error; each time we make a choice or take an action (set causes into motion); (We are "punished" by the deed itself. Our thoughts and deeds are continually producing results either 'for' or 'against' us. No one escapes the 'Day of Judgment,' because it is taking place every day, every moment of our lives);

Juggernaut of Dogma: getting caught up in the harmful, oftentimes calamitous, and destructive effects of die-hard religious dogma;

Juggle Knots: our susceptibility for dealing with too many thorny life issues (knots) at the same time;

Jukebox: nostalgia generators; our collection of past beliefs that can replay whenever we request them;

Jukebox Religion: holding onto old time religious teachings; replaying old familiar teachings without realizing the impact they still hold;

Jungle-like: our uncivilized instincts and notions; our untamed dispositions that we have allowed to contaminate our neural real estate, emotions, and behaviors;

Junk: useless, encrusted habits; obsolete life patterns;

Junketeer(s): our penchant for pursuing pseudoscience, unscrupulous gurus, false teachings, bling for bling's sake, etc.

Junk Food: violent TV shows, DVD's and movies; gossip; profanity; racial and sexist comments;

Junk Mail: incoming error thoughts that characterize our desire to resurrect old habits and world views;

Junkyard: our subconscious;

Jurassic Theology: dogma, which one day will asphyxiate on its own lack of depth. (Thankfully, it's becoming so extinct in New Thought circles that it's on the endangered species list);

Jury-like: denotes feeling pressured, judged, or possibly misunderstood by peers; *being on a jury* represents our feeling the need to conform, compromise, and/or deciding to opt for independent thinking; (See Courtroom);

Ka: spirit guide; guardian angel;

Kaaba: the Kingdom of God; God Consciousness; (In Islam, Kaaba is a giant black stone cube that stands at the center of Islam's most sacred mosque, Al-Masjid al-Haram, in Mecca, Saudi Arabia.0

Ka'bah: universal feminine energies;

Kabbalah, Cabala, Quabbala: Kabbalah is the Hebrew body of mystical tradition that contains techniques such as gematria, notariqon and temura, drawing on numeric equivalences of letters, numerology, permutations of letters, forming new texts by picking first letters of words and other kinds of text manipulation to derive higher spiritual meanings;

Kachinaian Genealogy: remembering past ideas and spiritual thoughts (ancestors) that were important for our growth and influenced us; (In Hopi spirituality, Kachinas are spirits or personifications of things in the real world);

Kafiric Beliefs: irreligious perspectives; atheistic thinking; (In the Swahili religious tradition, kafiri means pagan);

Kakodaimon: misplaced genius; ill used prodigiousness; (This Gnostic term denoted the nether pole of the dual serpent – tempter and/or ally);

Kaleidoscopic Thinking: creative, out-of-the-box, lateral, metaphorical, spiritual, allegorical, metaphysical, anthroposophical, theosophical thinking;

Kama-Loka: a consciousness of attachment to material things and especially physical existence;

Kami: vital life force; (In Japanese cosmology Kami is the nature god of Shintoism);

Kangaroo-like: our willingness to protect newly formed spiritual insights from undo criticism; having strength and considerable balance;

Kapukiric : stinkin' thinking; (In the Amazon, *kapukiri* comes from the archaic Quechua *kiri,* which means 'that which stinks.');

Karaoke: spontaneous embellishment;

Karma: past life oppression; the movement of cause and effect (chain of causation); *kudzu* to the uninitiated, and a matter of choice to the wise who know they can re-cause their experience and avoid the effects of a karmic hangover; incarnational noise; [According to quantum physicists, upward causation (cause moves from micro to macro) is only capable of producing material waves of possibility for nonmaterial consciousness to choose from, and consciousness has the ultimate power (downward causation) to create reality by freely choosing among the possibilities offered];

Karma-Marga: attaining salvation through our works and deeds instead of faith (bhakti-marga) or knowledge (jnana-marga);

Karmic Report Card: our incarnational thoughts, words, choices, and actions are adjudicated by our right of consciousness before and after each incarnation. Our karmic baggage (allotment), our next incarnational assignment, and our entry point (portal) into each incarnation are all determined by our accumulated karmic history);

Kayaking: demonstrating how emotionally stable, composed, and well-balanced we are in whatever circumstances we find ourselves;

kDebt Ceiling: the amount of karmic baggage we carry in a particular incarnation;

Keepsake Knuckleheads: recognizing that no one is completely useless – he/she can always serve as a bad example;

Kenosis: voluntarily restricting the selfish use of our spiritual and psychic powers;

Kerosene-like: hurtful, uncomplimentary, inflammatory remarks, barbs, innuendoes, and pot shots;

Keurig Moment: enjoying a cup of Joe; a caffeine moment that heralds peacefulness, rest, and inner satisfaction;

Key(s): denote access to certain kinds of knowledge, success, and opportunities; *finding a key* suggests being in a position for a future opportunity; *losing a key* symbolizes losing opportunities and/or access to opportunities; a *golden key* implies gaining the way to enlightenment; a *silver key* suggests using our will and resoluteness to become enlightened; a *rusty key* implies knowing, but neglecting to take advantage of the path to higher knowledge and greater opportunities;

Keyboard: our six basic senses along with the other 'higher, more psychic' senses; (In IT parlance, a keyboard is basically a board of keys used as an input device on a computer);

Keyboard Shortcut(s): using multiple senses to "speed up" our awareness of what we perceive to be real; (In IT language, keyboard shortcuts are key combinations that perform certain commands, such as closing a window or saving a file);

Keyhole: limited knowledge; narrow, blindered perspective;

Keystone Species: meditation, prayer, positive affirmations, and denials are "keystone species" that are necessary conditions for spiritual growth and development; (Without these technologies, our spiritual practice will collapse. They are essential spiritual technologies); (From an ecological perspective, keystone species play critical roles in maintaining the structure of an ecological community relative to the keystone species biomass. Examples of keystone species are: sea stars, jaguars, elephants, grizzly bears, sea otters, prairie dogs, and beavers);

Kha: our physical body which is cast off when we make our earthly transition; a mental perspective that we set aside when it becomes obvious it is obsolete; (In Egyptian cosmology, *kha* refers to the unimportance of the physical body in our afterlife development);

Khulqic Virtue: noble temperament; moral religious character; (Khulqui is an Arabic term for nobility);

Ki, Chi: universal life energy;

Kidnapping, Hijacking: allowing a worldly thought to sway us, to influence us, to detract us from pursuing a more spiritual path; putting the spiritual us in material form in order to do physical things;

Kidney Failure: our melancholy with the heaviness and fruitlessness of life causes us to give up and release any attachment we feel for our current skin school experience;

~ *Spiritually Speaking* ~

Kidney Stones: suffering from such intense frustrations with relationships and irritating life circumstances that we allow our displeasure to fester inside of us;

Killer(s): divinity-denying thoughts, choices, and actions behaving baaaaadly;

Kindergarten: a thoroughly literal-only religious perspective;

Kindle, Nook: our sensory connectivity with our brain; knowing we have immediate access to hidden knowledge and resources;

King-like: displaying divinely sanctioned power; having temporal, but authoritative thoughts; showing a high degree of masculine power;

Kingdom: ruling (guiding) principle (in Aramaic – *malkutah*); attaining the vision of the One Being;

Kingdom of God (Sanctum Regnum): Christ Consciousness; supreme illumination; eternality;

Kingdom of Heaven: our innate divinity; the deeper, more spiritual level *of* us; the Christ dimension of us; the somatic home of our Eternal Cosmic Self; the vernacular of spiritually-charged ideas; spiritual headquarters;

Kingdom Within: the living presence of the Eternal Presence expressing in our consciousness; (See the Kingdom of God and the Kingdom of Heaven);

Kiosk: Universal Substance; the Akaskic Records; the Internet;

Kirlian Clarity: seeing beyond the obvious;

Kiss: the blending of giving and receiving, positive and negative, matter and spirit, love and desire; instinctual unity and harmony; the *kiss of Judas* symbolizes the human desire to entrap its own cosmic divinity and identity in matter and thus betray (entomb, restrict, imprison) its own divine origins;

Kitchen-ness: our desire for nutritional experiences that require our intentional preparedness;

Kite-like: our aptitude for seeking higher spiritual insights while keeping our feet on solid footing;

Klutzy Karaoke: the evangelical proselytizing of fundamental religious fanatics; (See Proselytizing Smog);

Kneeology: letting prayer lower your body and elevate our spirit;

Knife-like: having steeled will and/or resolute thoughts; being good at having cutting insights;

Knight(s): chivalrous, protective thoughts and inclinations; loyalty; strength of character;

Knot(s): perceived restraints and restrictions; addictions; dogma;

Knots of Nots: the result of tying ourselves up into knots: knots of not being good enough, not having enough, not feeling prosperous enough, not letting go enough, not holding on long enough, not listening enough, not releasing anger enough, etc.:

Knotty Knee-Knocking: asking if it's opportunity we hear knocking or our knees – especially when it comes to moving beyond the embedded theology we grew up with and embracing metaphysical thought;

Knowledge Sniffing: our attempts, covert and/or overt, to see how much someone knows about h/her expertise area;

Know Thyself: "Know thyself" is an Ancient Greek aphorism). It is inscribed in the *pronaos* (forecourt) of the Temple of Apollo at Delphi. Its Latin equivalent: *temet nosce* means "Thine own self thou must know." Fifteen hundred years later William Shakespeare paraphrased the ancient dictum by reminding us: *"This above all – to thine own self be true."* Know what self? Be true to what self? Our true Self, of course! Our Divine Self, our Christ Self! Our capital 'S' Self! The I Am Presence within us that works in, as, and through us. *"To thy Christ Self be true,"* Willy might have said. And then after Willy says: *"And it must follow, as the night follows the day, thou canst not then be false to that self."* In other words we must walk our talk. We must be authentic. Real. Genuine. The product of the teachings we study;

Koi No Yokan: hearing a spiritual truth for the first time and realizing that it is going to have a transformative effect on our lives; (Koi No Yokan is a Japanese term that intimates an inevitable love relationship in the future.);

Kol Dmamah: our capacity to embrace the power, majesty, and reverence of silence; (In Kabbalistic terms *kol dmamah* means the sounds of silence);

Kookaburraian Hilarity: good-natured merriment; (In Aboriginal Austrailian terms kookaburra is a rather large bird that has sounds that echo hysterical human laughter); (Neuro-theology must admit the crucial importance of laughter in understanding the human mind and its ability to deal with an ever changing and confusing world. In fact, says neuro-theologist Andrew Newberg, "it may be humankind's greatest legacy to be able to look upon an incredibly short lifespan, often filled with anxiety, fears, loss, suffering, and death and still find some way of laughing at ourselves and at the very world which causes us so much angst.");

Koran: our soul journey of unfolding enlightenment; literally, the sacred religious book of Islam;

Kuan Yin: compassion and loving kindness; (In Chinese cosmology Kuan Yin is the Bodhisativa of Compassion);

Kufaarian Thoughts: error thoughts; (In Arabic, *kufaar* means non-believer);

Kundabuffer Energies: our negatively polarized, descending, sensual energies housed [along side the kundalini energies] in our spinal cord that characterize our desire for sensory experience;

Kundalini, Speirema, Bhujangini: the coiled up, serpentine, super-physical Supreme Life Principle encased in our spinal cord and nervous system; the spiritual voltage (serpent fire) of our chakras; the fiery energies of the Holy Spirit; the amperage of our spiritual practice; (Kundalini is a compound word: *Kunda* which reminds us of the earthy kundabuffer energies, and *lini* which is an Atlantean term meaning 'termination.' kundalini means the termination of our sense-addicted kundabuffer nature); [Theosophist, Alice Bailey in *A Treatise on White Magic*, uses the phrase 'Golden Rod of Power' to describe the spinal column after kundalini has risen in it];

Laboratory: our earth experience;

Labor of Love: moving through each incarnation by helping ourselves and others on our way to enlightenment;

Labyrinth: our consciousness and its physical vehicle, our body; walking the unicursal (one way in and one way out) labyrinthian path represents a yogic journey that unites our body, mind, and soul; the *winding pathways* represent our trek from ordinary awareness to illumination; the path of rebirth;

Laceration(s): selfish and hurtful actions; injurious gossip; malicious 'fun'; spiteful rhetoric; poisonous jealousy; cutting remarks; leaching comments;

Lack Consciousness: never missing an opportunity to miss an opportunity; whenever we repeat (*imitate*) self-defeating thoughts and behavior, we *limit* what we can be; an anesthetized awareness of the omnipresence of abundance; (The word *limitation* has the words *limit* and *imitation* in it. It doesn't take a giant leap in insight to see that whenever we repeat (*imitate*) self-defeating thoughts and behavior, we *limit* what we can be. We limit our good because we limit our access to Spirit);

Lackadaisical Excuseitis: the unfortunate habit of proving that an excuse is the line of least persistence;

Lackology: belief in chronic and perpetual inadequacy, scarcity, paucity, and deprivation;

Ladder-like: our measured progress toward attaining higher knowledge; (See Jacob's Ladder);

La-Di-Da-ing: Making melodramatically false claims about a prosperity message that is based on materialistic promises and predictions;

Ladybug(s): prosperity; abundance;

Lagoon, Tidal Pond, Bayou: repressed emotions in our subconscious warehouse;

Laity: religious, not spiritual, thoughts and perspectives; worldly thoughts and inclinations;

Lake of Sulphurous Fire: the white heat of Truth consuming the negativity of falsehood and error; the rejected elements of our animal nature return to the elemental kingdom which was their origin;

Lamb, the: Christ Consciousness; the Christ Principle; the Kingdom of God; (The use of a lamb is indicative of the Persian origin of Christianity, for the Persians were the only people to symbolize the first sign of the zodiac by a lamb. The lamb is used for its innocence and purity. The lambskin apron worn by the Freemasons symbolizes that purity);

Lamborghinian Propensities: denotes our desire to live life in the fast lane coupled with its wealth, opulence, and power;

Lameness: error-prone attitudes that severely restrict our movements;

Lamp(s), Lantern(s), Lamppost(s): being devoted to the truth; having divine insights; being able to orchestrate dedicated vigilance; our chakras;

Lampooning: engaging in activities that misrepresent our divine nature;

Lance-like Aptitude: employing powerful generative male energy to make a point; symbolic of the Solar Ray; one of the stabilizing aspects of the World Axis;

Land: the human body; the subconscious mind; *dry land* means settled convictions and fixed ideals, the status quo;

Landfill, Dump: the repressed regions of the subconscious;

Landing Zone: the human portal through which we enter another incarnational and/or reincarnational experience;

Land Mine(s): false teachings that seem down to earth;

Land of Ahs: being wonder full; a consciousness filled with an openness to awesomeness;

Landscape-like: the bustling panorama of our thoughts, emotions, actions, talents, skills, and knowledge; our physical bodies;

Landslide-like Impulses: allowing the accumulated sediments of past false beliefs and assumptions to come unglued unexpectedly and momentarily block our progress at a time in which we can pause to reflect on the continued efficacy of the direction we're going;

Language of the Birds: esoteric truths, metaphorical truths, mystical truths, cabalistic truths, theosophical truths, anthroposophical truths, and metaphysical truths

Lapis Lazuli, Lapis Exili, Stone of Destiny: our ability to open the Third Eye; enhanced psychic abilities; the 'stone fallen from heaven' in Parzival that is called the Holy Grail; (See Holy Grail); the 'fallen stone' that must reascend to heaven;

Laptop(s): electronic recall and projection; electronic stream of consciousness; our brain in recall mode; knowing we have immediate access to the Akashic Records; (In IT language, laptops are portable computers. They include a screen, keyboard, and a track pad or trackball, that serves as the proverbial mouse);

Laryngitis, Hoarseness: denotes our difficulty in conveying the message we want; indicates the lack of personal power and influence; suggests the fear of speaking up;

Laser Printer: our optical nerve (photoreceptor) that transforms sensory input into 'readable' language via our brains;

Last Rights: the most recent 'right things' we've thought, said, or done;

Laughable Leakage: mindlessly and spontaneously saying or doing something that is outlandishly out-of-sync with our spiritual growth;

Laughing Stock: the accumulated benefits of good-natured giggling and laughing;

Launch Sites: each newly-formed thought, word, or action;

Laundromat: cleaning up our perspectives; paying attention to the image we project; a place of spiritual enrichment that offers education and support;

Laundry Chute: keeping well-worn perspectives in their place;

Lavender-like: femininity and grace; elegance; wisdom;

Law Abiding: applying spiritual principles;

Law Breaker: any thought, word, choice, promise, or action that is not in accordance with our professed spiritual or religious beliefs;

Lawn: a domesticated perspective;

Lawn Furniture: intellectual mobility;

Lawn Mower: recognizing the need to keep up appearances; clarifying and fine-tuning our perspectives;

Law of Mind Action: Thoughts held in mind produce more of the same kind of thoughts. (Similar thoughts produce similar intentions, and similar intentions produce similar choices, and similar choices create behaviors consistent with the original thoughts which started the process. And those enlightened behaviors produce actions consistent with a spiritually attuned consciousness);

Lawsuit(s): seeking vindication for feeling judged, criticized, and/or defensive for our actions;

Lawwamaian Discipline: being able to resist carnal desires; (In Islamic religious conviction, *lawwama* refers to our repentant self);

Laya Yoga: altering consciousness using sounds and rhythm;

Laying on of Hands: a healing practice in which healers' hands are in direct contact with the people receiving healing;

Lead With Our Chin: sharing highly esoteric knowledge with fundamentalist Christians: (In boxing, leading with our chin means leaving our chin, a vulnerable point, unprotected.);

Leaflet(s): suggests our openness to new ideas and/or opportunities;

Leak-Proof Faith: absolute trust in our indivisible status as human expressions of the Eternal Presence;

Leaky Roof: obvious 'holes' in our spiritual and/or religious conviction;

Leash: common sense; conscience; discipline;

Lecture(s), Keynote(s): our openness to new ideas, concepts, and learning;

Leeching Killjoys: our divinity-denying thoughts, inclinations, and tendencies;

Left Hand Path: the way of materialism; the egocentric perspective that is fixated on worldly attachments and desires;

Leftovers: unprocessed thoughts, concepts, and teachings;

Legos: thoughts, creative concepts, and teachings that become building blocks on our path toward mastering our human experience;

Lein Air: exploring esoteric faith traditions while holding onto our current religious ideologies; (In snowboarding terms, lein air means grabbing the heel edge of the snowboard with our front hand and leaning out over the nose of the snowboard);

Lemon-like Susceptibility: expressing bitterness and/or disappointment;

Lemuria: the continent that preceded Atlantis, the last remnants of which are Australia, Borneo, Madagascar and Easter Island. It was on this continent (race) that the 'spark of mental capacity' was implanted in humanity;

Lens: our mind; clarity of perspective;

Leper(s), Leprosy: impure, unclean, socially unacceptable thoughts and emotions;

Lesbian(s): similar sensual emotions feeding off each other in the pursuit of connecting the dots in a particular human experience; (See Homosexuality);

Lethe: loss of memory; forgetfulness that leads to repeating past self-defeating practices;

Letters, Envelopes: thoughts that enter our waking consciousness;

Leviathans: recurring (cyclic) antagonistic mental and emotional life patterns that tend to block or dampen our spiritual progress;

Levitation: opposing the gravitational pull of sense consciousness; lifting a worldly thought to its higher spiritual essence;

Lexicon, Dictionary, Glossary: the extent of our vocabulary;

Ley: Alignments and patterns of powerful, invisible earth energy that connect a variety of sacred sites, such as churches, temples, stone circles, megaliths, holy wells, burial sites, and other physical sites of spiritual magnitude;

Liar(s): false teachings;

Liberation, Deliverance: emancipation from the pull of materialism; freedom from the illusion of duality and separation;

Libido: psychic energy that drives us toward sensual pleasures;

Libramancy: a form of divination that uses incense;

Library: our brain with its short-term and long-term memory storage, recall, and encoding capabilities; (See also the Internet and Akashic Records);

License: the power of choice;

License Plate: a rite of passage;

Lickety-Split Leprechauns: instantaneous emotions (gnomes) that surprise us with their unannounced arrival and remind us that we haven't gotten over a past hurt or slight;

Lie Detector(s): Universal Spiritual Truths;

Life: the continuous vital substance of the One Presence manifesting in limitless macrocosmic and microcosmic ways and forms throughout infinitesimalness;

Lifeline: the Silver Cord: (See Silver Cord, Antahkarana; Sutratma; Umbilical Cord);

Life Review, Lifecasting: having flashback memories of our whole life's experiences; (In social media language, lifecasting is a continual broadcast of events in a person's life through digital media.);

Life Saver(s), Lifeboat(s), Lifeguard(s): Universal Spiritual Truths;

Life Sentence: a life of endless possibility, vitality, joyful beingness, vibrant on-goingness, expanded awareness, higher consciousness, exuberant unboundedness; a life without restriction, worry, or limitation;

Light: higher wisdom and superior knowing; illumination; divine awareness; illumined intellect; The Light of the World is the Christ

Presence within our human consciousness. We are the Light of the World dressed up as us! We are divine beings having a 'skin school' experience. Within our being – within our body, mind, and soul – there is a Divine Presence which lights up our inner landscape. It guarantees the awakening of our human consciousness (the world);

Light-bearers, Light-bringers: spiritual thoughts;

Lightbulb(s): highly illuminating spiritual insights; aha's; creative and innovative ideas;

Lighthouse(s): spiritual guidance; spiritual, metaphysical, esoteric truths, ideas, beliefs, and teachings; acts of generosity and kindness; a forgiving heart;

Light of the World: Christ Consciousness;

Lightning, Thunder: compelling spiritual insights; powerful spiritual convictions; the movement of fiery, transformative spiritual energies (kundalini); generative male energy;

Lightweight Interpretation: a literal only interpretation of scripture;

Like-Gating: being able to comprehend basic esoteric teachings before we venture into an understanding of advanced spiritual principles; (In social media, like-gating is the practice of blocking users from certain content on a Facebook page unless they first "like" the Facebook page);

Lilithian Obstinacy: our rather harsh refusal to submit to the left brain's logical and methodical nature coupled with our desire to experience the totality of the physical senses even though it means trying to compromise the integrity of virtuous thinking, being, and doing; (Lilith is depicted as the first wife of Adam before Eve and refuses to take a secondary role to Adam. She flees from him in pursuit of sensory experiences. She appears in Chaldean mythology, Talmudic texts, the Jewish Midrashic tradition, and the medieval Zohar.);

Lily-like: attaining purity; expressing piety; enjoying rightness; honoring fertility; respecting femininity; faithfulness; spiritual unfoldment;

Lilliputian Thoughts: dwarfish, small-minded, judgmental sentiments;

Limbic Lingering: the emotional state of staying in a highly nervous, overwrought, and oftentimes irrational emotive state of mind;

Limbic Lingo: the language of fear, guilt, shame, and negativity used by fundamental faith traditions;

Limbic Theology: fostering frontal lobe deprivation by keeping people in a fear-based, guilt-ridden, dogmatized state of mind;

Limbo, Nowhere: the nanosecond before we decide to take a Christed action or an ego-saturated action; the innocent unawareness of our divine status;

Limitless Chalice: our consciousness; (Our consciousness is a borderless container of enlightenment. It can hold immense potential. So, the potential to be realized that flows from the 'Field' into the chalice depends on how much the 'cup' can hold at any point in awareness);

Lingam: male generative energy;

LinkedIn: establishing a strong spiritual connection with the 'business end' of our spirituality – our Higher Self; (In social media, Linkedin allows professional business people to engage in business-oriented networking. It is akin to an online resume. Companies can have their own profile pages listed.);

Lint-Free Living: The L I N T I'm talking about is an acronym which stands for *listless impoverished negative thinking*. It's the kind of thinking that spoils our consciousness and soils our spiritual walk. It's the kind of thinking that negates our goodness and conceals our Godness. *Listless, impoverished negative thinking* comes from a consciousness of lack and fear and anger and hopelessness. People who have PhD's in this kind of LINT say things like: "I can't do that!" "I'm not good enough." "I'm too old." "I've been a failure all of my life." "I don't have much to offer." "I don't ... I can't ... I'm not ..." When we wear our LINT like a badge *listless, impoverished negative thinking*, in its lowest form manifests as racism, sexism, violence, gossip, envy, and jealousy. (These forms of LINT are corrosive. They embed themselves in the fabric of our consciousness and are difficult to extract. Living LINT-free is the answer, of course);

Lion-like Virtues: harnessing the inner cosmic fire; displaying considerable courage, having fierce strength when it comes to doing the right thing;

Lip Synching: parroting the teachings of others as if they were our own; trying to live up to the expectations of others; counterfeit expertise;

Liquid(s): emotions;

Liquor: liquid courage; the false sense of security false teachings give us; (See Alcoholism);

Listless Loitering: sampling the teachings of various faith traditions without putting any of them into practice;

Literalbot: a person who is fanatically robotic at interpreting sacred scripture from a literal standpoint only;

Literal Interpretations of Sacred Scripture: Literal interpretations of sacred scripture have their place, but when we find stories about burning bushes that talk to you, the Sun standing still, the Main Character of the New Testament walking on water, and water being turned into Manischewitz wine at a marriage in Cana we question the literal validity of these events. Our intuition – and common sense – tell us that bizarre literal interpretations are like pop up ads on Internet Home Pages telling us to look for deeper spiritual teachings associated with those accounts;

Litigation: the reaction of our body to our mistreating it; (In legal terms, litigation simply refers to a case, controversy, or lawsuit.);

Litter, Garbage, Junk, Trash, Rubbish: false teachings;

Litter Box: a false doctrine;

Litter-Free Environment: a Christed Consciousness; a spiritually-attuned perspective;

Liver Problems: the chronic intensity of toxic emotions like bitterness, resentment, rage, anger, and jealousy have a disastrous effect on our being able to mediate their effects, causing us to deceive ourselves and judge ourselves too harshly;

Living Dead: soulless thoughts; sense-soaked memories that lie dormant in our consciousness waiting to be surfaced for a material purpose;

Lizard(s): our primal, reptilian instincts that spring from the amygdala;

Llama-ness: strength; endurance;

Loan(s): our physical bodies;

Lobhaian Impulses: covetousness;

Locksmith: our super-consciousness;

Locust-like Propensities: having destructive, toxic, corrosive thoughts;

Logic Error(s): thinking we can walk the spiritual path on material feet; (Thinking the Bible story of Shadrach, Meshach, and Abednego surviving Nebuchadnezzar's fiery furnace actually happened; thinking the Biblical story about the sun standing still actually happened; thinking there is an anthropomorphic god in the sky or a satanic presence that micro-manage human affairs; etc.); (In IT terms logic errors are mistakes in a program's source code that result in runtime errors that produce the wrong output or cause the program to crash);

Logos, Nous: Cosmic Christ; Only Begotten Son; Word; Vibration; cosmic intelligence within us; the realm of divine ideas and/or sacred archetypes (eternal patterns within the manifested universe); [The Logos-figure described in the Book of Revelation is a composite of the seven sacred planets: He has the snowy-white hair of Kronos (Father Time), the blazing eyes of wide-seeing Zeus, the sword of Arcs, the shining face of Helios, and the *chiton* and girdle of Aphrodite; his feet are of mercury, the metal sacred to Hermes, and his voice is like the murmur of the ocean's waves (many waters), alluding to Selene, the Moon-Goddess of the four seasons and of the waters];

Logosophy: psychic thoughts leading to enlightenment; the neuroplasticity of spiritual revelation;

Lokian Proclivities: fiery thoughts; enlightened thoughts; (In Norse mythology, Loki is a shape shifter god and a god of fire);

Lollipop(s), Candy: opting for lighthearted indulgences; enjoying a delicious 'kernel' of truth;

Longversation: the persistent self talk we have in our heads about the self-improvement things we should do, but never get around to doing;

Loon-like: our ability to search within for the answers we feel we need;

Looney Tunes: any mainstream religious assertion that diminishes, minimizes, subordinates, and debases the value, status, and importance of women, people of color, and same sex couples; the songs we 'sing' to ourselves in our heads that are composed of self-defeating, self-negating, and self-diminishing lyrics;

Loose Religious Rap: unabashed proselytizing;

Lord's Day: the moment of illumination and/or enlightenment; (It does not refer to a day of the week. It is an announcement of heightened awareness);

Lord's Supper: the conscious union between our human self and our Christ Self; (A sort of spiritual alchemy takes place as symbolized by the bread and wine. And it takes place in the Upper Room which signifies a high state of spiritual consciousness. When we are in an 'Upper Room' state of consciousness we have the wisdom to know the difference between sacred truths and falsehoods. We know the difference between the centrifugal force of materiality and the pull of Spirit);

Lost Generation(s): a group of purely worldly thoughts that characterize our refusal to honor our innate divinity and the divinity in others;

Lost Soul: a human personality that is fixated purely on egocentrism;

Lost Word: unveiled or unexpressed secret knowledge; our unrealized innate divinity; our latent Christ Self;

Lottery: our belief in the availability of abundance; Universal Substance; our super-consciousness; the full spectrum of our talents, skills, and abilities;

Lottery Ticket: the wise application of spiritual teachings;

Lotus: the rise of the manifest from the unmanifest; divine matrix revealed; manifestation manifesting itself; positivity springing from negativity; the universe springing into universalness; our higher nature developing from our lower nature; birth and rebirth; our unfolding illumination; the rise from darkness into the light; immortality; the realization of our own innate divinity;

Loudness: the compelling nature (volume) of a newly formed spiritual insight;

Love: universal union and harmony; God's Isness in expression; the rock, the foundation, the eternal harmonics of our spiritual and human happiness; the ultimate expression of our belief in our oneness with Spirit; the spiritual glue that unites us with the 7 billion expressions of it around the world; the open sesame to the mastery of our human experience; the Eternal Presence expressing Itself as the Christ in physicality and in super-physicality;

Loveseat: an invitation for intimate conversation;

Love Triangle: Father, Son, Holy Spirit; (Divine Order: Mind, Idea, and Expression);

Low Blood Pressure: feeling drained and over-worked by being forced to do things we'd rather not do;

Lower Frequency: our subconscious mental processes;

Lower Quaternary: our four dense material qualities (vehicles) – mental, emotional, etheric, and physical;

Low-Voltage Congregants: church goers who have Ph. D's in passive involvement;

Luciferic Thinking: light-bringing ahrimanic revelations of what human incarnation means; realizations of what it means to reject spiritual thoughts and cling to materialistic thoughts;

Lukewarm Camouflage: keeping religious and political conversations basic and light so we won't have to divulge how we really feel about what is being said;

Lullaby: protecting our innocence;

Lull of Attraction: believing our prosperity comes to us instead of through us;

Lunatic Fringe: fanatical, irrational, absurdly extreme, bigoted, headstrong, insanely preposterous thoughts;

LSD, Angel Dust, Yellow Sunshine: a counterfeit awakening; an altered 'state' of consciousness; (Experts in every field of psychology and religion agree that drug-induced spiritual experiences do little to create a spiritual foundation from which to live one's life (D. C. D'Souza, G. Braley, R. Blaise, M. Vendetti, S. Oliver, B. Pittman, M. Ranganathan, S. Bhatkta, Z. Zimolo, T. Cooper, and E. Parry in "Effects of haloperidol on the behavioral, subjective, cognitive, motor, and neuroendocrine effects of Delta-9 tetrahydrocannabinol in humans," *Psychopharmacology*; 2008, Jan. 29);

Lucky Charm(s): giving power to something outside of ourselves for our abundance and prosperity;

Lullabies: the stories we tell ourselves to ease the fears and concerns of our skin school experience;

Lurker(s): worldly thoughts that are leaning toward their higher religious essences and religious thoughts that are unfolding into their higher spiritual essences; (In social media, lurkers are people on social networks who listen and watch, but choose not to participate in online conversations.);

Lycanthropy: innocent thoughts becoming transformed into carnal, self-aggrandizing, psychotic thoughts;

Lynx-like: having a sharp, penetrating vision;

Lyre Proneness: thoughts and emotions that remind us of the musicality and rhythm of our connection to all things; the ability to divine our peace and tranquility;

Macabre Regime(s): the compulsion to mindlessly organize our day around one error thought and action after another; (In *The Voice of the Silence*, Theosophist, Helena Blavatsky says that " wrong thought must be slain, ere desire can be extinguished." Pg. 84);

Mace: an intentional insult; undue criticism; standoffishness; repugnant speech;

Machine Gun, Assault Rifle: extremely hostile thoughts and 'rapid fire' anger;

Macintosh, Microsoft, HP, Dell, Gateway: our thinking capacity; our brain; (In IT parlance, desktop and laptop computers are operating systems to capture, retrieve, and record all types of data);

Macro Lens: applies to clairvoyance as well as remote viewing; (See Clairvoyance; Remote Viewing);

Maddening Undertow: the riptide of error thoughts, words, and actions that pull us into a downward spiral of self-deprecating emotionality;

Mafia: our extreme resolve to eliminate inner turmoil, dissention, and conflict;

Magi, Wise Men, Sage, Wizard: the wisest, most spiritually discerning of thoughts;

Magic Carpet: astral travel; out-of-body experience;

Magical Roughhousing: engaging in a heavy New Thought conversation by tossing delightful spiritual and metaphorical truths around to stimulate higher thinking and joyful dialogue;

Magician-ish: endorsing manipulative and distracting thoughts; being illusive;

Magog: concepts and theories that attempt to disprove our innate divinity;

Maggot(s): impure thoughts that eat away at our character;

Magnetic Center: the energy we send out, based on our level of consciousness, that attracts those who have similar energy (affinities, interests, knowledge, world views) – religious fundamentalist has the magnetic center of religious fundamentalism, the metaphysician has the magnetic center of metaphysics, the neuroscientist has the magnetic center of neuroscience;

Magnified Mediocrity: the words, choices, and actions that accompany our warped thinking;

Magnifying Glass: spiritual discernment; close examination and introspection; spontaneous life review; autobiographic journaling;

Magnolia-like: illumination; desire for spiritual knowledge;

Magpie-ness: our tendency for acquiring bling and chasing after material things; our penchant for flamboyance and glamorous artifacts; our paradoxical tendency to be both reclusive and sociable;

Mahat: feminine energy; the Holy Spirit; (In Sanskrit mahat is the source of birth in the material world);

Mainframe: our mind with the brain as its recording device;

Mainstream Conglomerate: the predominate host of conventional faith traditions;

Mainstream Religious Hagging: mainstream religious sermons delivered to frighten congregants 'out of their sleep' when it comes to their religious growth;

Majestic Make-believe: the conventional belief in an external, anthropomorphic god in the sky;

Majuscule Aspirations: having grand, huge, gigantic thoughts and aspirations instead of minuscule ones; (Linguistically, majuscules are very large letters used in printing);

Majzubic Devotion: being disciplined enough to curb worldly concerns and desires;

Makeshift Salvation: thinking we can jerry-rig our way to nirvana by adopting slipshod and rickety religious practices along the way to justify our lack of real commitment toward spiritual growth;

Making Amends: back-paddling to get ahead of the rough edges in relationships;

Making-One's-Mark: choosing truth over error or choosing error over truth;

Maladjustment(s): judgmentalness; chronic error thinking; unapologetic selfishness; pathological lying; settling for one reincarnational 'fix' after another; perpetuated bad habits;

Malefactor(s): error thoughts that dampen our spiritual growth;

Malignant Mimicry: the mindless parroting of fanatical, dogmatic views without any thought given to their narrow-minded implications;

Mall(s), Shopping Center(s): a smorgasbord of spiritual and/or religious teachings; material appetites;

Malnutrition: adopting a literal-only perspective of sacred scripture; depending only on religious dogma for answers;

Malware: false teachings; anti-Christed perspectives; error-prone tendencies; (In IT language, malware is short for 'malicious software.' It is software employed to disrupt computer operation, gather sensitive information, or gain access to private computer systems);

Mamma Grizzly: a highly volatile emotion that is a ferocious attempt to defend a new idea and/or insight from what we consider to be undue criticism;

Mammon Misery: obsessive materiality;

Mana Nature: our wise nature; our highly spiritual nature; (Mana is a Melanesian word that means 'holy' and/or 'divine');

Manacled Miniaturization: the price we pay for mindless, religious conformity;

Mandala-like: expanding the circumference of our individual thought universe in order to attain a particular level of spiritual unfoldment; enlarging the scope of our current enlightened perspective;

Manger, Cradle: our inclination toward baser human instincts and emotions; also denotes new beginnings and the foundation for increasing our potential;

Manhole: a portal to our subconscious;

Maniacal Retailing: melodramatic and overbearing proselytizing; (See also Klutzy Karaoke; Proselytizing Smog);

Manmukhic Thought: a self-aggrandizing thought or inclination; following whichever way our mind leads us; (In Sikh scripture *manmukhs* are people who only care about worldly things);

Manna: high spiritual teachings explained (brought down to earth) in such a way that the unenlightened can understand; esoteric knowledge which descends as *divine wisdom* from heaven (our super-consciousness); [Manna is called 'the bread from heaven' and was the chief food of the Israelites when they fled from Egypt];

Mannequin(s): hollow religious thoughts that appear substantive but lack depth;

Mansion(s): consciousness;

Manure, Buffalo Chips, Cow Chips: the consequences of error thoughts;

Manuscript: our accumulated earth experience; our Quantum Self;

Many Mansions: states of elevated consciousness;

Many Worlds Interpretation: an infinite number of versions of us are inhabiting simultaneous worlds, each triggered by choices we make each-consecutive-moment-of-now? For example, when we choose to go to a certain movie, there is an aspect of us, a quantum version of us, who chooses to go to a different movie or no movie at all. Once a choice is made there is a natural progression of events – and choices – associated with each choice in each "world" (parallel universe). Suppose when the Christ as Jesus said, *"In my Father's house there are many mansions"* he meant, "It is the nature of the Sacred Unity's (Father) Consciousness (house) that there are many levels of heightened awareness (mansions)." What if our universe, like the billions of other universes, is simply a thought in the mind of the Eternal Presence we call God? Like thoughts, each universe can expand and grow and produce something phenomenal when those thoughts become actions. What if our dreams, nightmares, and déjà vu experiences are merely time warps where we pick up fragments of experiences from the other versions of us that are living simultaneous existences in their own universes? (From a quantum physics perspective, the Many-Worlds Interpretation, introduced by Bryce Everett in 1957, views reality as a many-branched tree where every possible quantum outcome occurs. Each "world" branches endlessly in direct proportion to the incidence of choices made. Everything that can happen *does* happen somewhere); [In the many Worlds Interpretation of quantum mechanics, according to astrophysicist Bernard Haisch, every human being creates a billion times a billion times a billion alternative universes every second];

Map(s): an initiation process; intuitive revelation; spiritual teachings;

Marathon: the cosmic involution and evolution process; aligning our human self with our Divine Nature;

Marauding Rascal: a devilish thought;

Marginal Bliss: when laughter, giggles, and smiles are foreign languages;

Margin of Error: the soul leakage between a spiritual thought and a worldly thought: (In statistics, the measurement of the accuracy of the results of a survey or research study);

Marigold-like: domesticity; service; passion; creativity;

Marijuana, Cannabis, Hashish, Maryjane: one of our manufactured, drug-induced shortcuts to oblivion;

Marionette(s): religious and spiritual practitioners who blindly follow a guru's teachings;

Marketable: truth principles that are believable, timely, reliable, and relevant;

Mark of Cain: our karmic debt (our Cain-ness represents our highly acquisitive and self-aggrandizing nature which has its karmic price but also its saving grace, a grace (mark) that reminds us in each incarnation that we have a divine nature and are fundamentally good);

Marksmanship: walking the spiritual path on practical feet; living at the speed of our Christ Consciousness; honoring our authentegrity;

Marriage: union of our ordinary waking consciousness with our Christ Consciousness; total alignment of our human personality with our divine individuality; the complete harmony of our human self with our Christ Self; the indissoluble union (at-one-ment) between Spirit and matter, between Universal Consciousness and human egocentric consciousness; a *dissolved marriage* (separation or divorce) represents our decision to forego enlightenment, to deny or reject our divine nature; a *premature marriage* symbolizes our immature and/or juvenile attempts (our unreadiness) to grasp esoteric knowledge;

Martyr-like Symptoms: immediately censoring a spiritual thought when it enters our egocentric awareness; mindlessly choosing salty water [reincarnational experiences] over ethereality [spiritual illumination];

Mary Magdalene: superior intuition and wisdom; (In Gnostic teachings she was the priestess-spouse of Jesus of Nazareth. She, as well as Salambo, Matres, Ishtar, Astarte, Aphrodite, and Venus all represent the priestess-wife energies which we must unite with in order to awaken the serpentine fire of the Holy Spirit); (The energies referred to are the natural harnessing of our latent psychic and psychological energies, making them active and harmonious with our Divine Nature. These energies are the combination of our cognitive and affective powers.);

Mashup: combining a number of spiritual concepts to arrive at a completely new concept; (In social media language, a content mashup contains multiple types of media drawn from pre-existing sources to create a new work.);

Maskunfusion: We hide behind masks of fear, guilt, unworthiness, anger, jealousy, worry, envy, revenge, greed, hatred, anxiety, pride, and suffering. These are the masks we wear to give our power away. They are the masks we wear when we allow ourselves to be fooled by outer appearances. They are the masks we wear when we accept lack and limitation. They are the masks we wear because we think we deserve to suffer;

Masochism: following a dogmatically, literal-only interpretation of sacred scripture;

Masquerade: pretending to align ourselves with our Divine Nature; our physical form burdened by an unenlightened ego bent on staying unenlightened;

Masquerade Attack: someone who pretends to subscribe to our particular theology, but covertly does everything h/she can to subvert our belief; (In IT security language, a masquerade attack is a type of attack in which one system entity illegitimately poses as [assumes the identity of] another entity.);

Massacre: killing off any and all spiritual thoughts that enter our waking awareness;

Masterful Mettle: knowing that fact-facing is just as important as fact-finding when it comes to expanding our theology; understanding that wishbones and backbones are two different things; realizing we want to hold onto the right end of half-truths;

Master's Voice: our conscience; our superior intuition; the 'still small voice';

Matador: the courage to be vulnerable;

Matchmaking: aligning our human self with our Christ Self;

Materialism, Worship of Bling: vertically challenged horizontal consciousness; a sense-soaked consciousness; the worship of form; an attachment to externals; the neglect, repression, and denial of our spiritual nature;

Materialistic Burr(s): error thoughts that stick to us (interfere with our good) through many life experiences;

Materiality: a form of energy burdened by matter; (The suffix 'ity' in the word 'materiality' implies a 'state or quality of being.' Thus, materiality is composed of degrees and densities that go beyond the quantitative limitations of matter. There are different gradations [densities] of materiality that are determined by the rate at which the atoms vibrate that comprise it. Each density (level) has its own characteristics and the matter on one plane may not be considered 'material' from the perspective of a lower plane. Thus materiality is relative, as is matter and energy. What is material at one level may be considered non-material at a lower level, and what may be considered non-material at a lower level may be considered as material on a higher level. The nature of materiality, from lower orders of being to higher orders of being, becomes less clear since matter and energy are really just aspects of visible world with which we are all familiar. As we ascend to higher orders of being, matter and energy blend into each other and become less dualistic because we become less dualistic);

Material Spontaneity: being swayed by a ticker tape parade of immediate gratification. The confetti is diabetes, heart failure, ulcers, high blood pressure, failed relationships, obesity, shoplifting, credit card debt, bankruptcy, etc.;

Maternal Deprivation: a patriarchal religion;

Matriculation: our involutional and evolutionary journey toward becoming fully enlightened;

Matryoshka Doll: our Quantum Self: (See Quantum Self); (Matryoshka dolls are Russian dolls of decreasing size that fit inside each other);

Matter: frozen Spirit; crystallized thought; a dense form of materiality;

Mausoleum, Crypt, Catacomb: our subconsciousness;

Mauvaise Foi: the practice of deceiving ourselves by refusing to take responsibility for our choices and actions;

Maverick(s): our wild, untamed base instincts;

Maya-like Susceptibility: mindlessly expressing our sensory perversion of reality that is based on a host of illusions, fabrications, fantasies, hallucinations, and delusions; (Maya comes from the Sanskrit root *ma* which means "to measure, to effect, to form, to limit." Its esoteric significance is prompted by the limited, sense-soaked lens we use to understand reality that 'sees' things unclearly from an unenlightened eye);

May Day: the instant one of our cells goes from a healthy state to an unhealthy state and sends a signal to the brain announcing its distress; the instant our conscience kicks in, announcing its discomfort with one of our errant thoughts and/or actions; (In police, fire, military, and rescue operations of any kind a may day is a radio call for immediate help and assistance.);

Maze-like: our desire to move through the nuances associated with progress and change; (See the Labyrinth);

Mechanical Commitment: unfeeling, routine-mired, allegiance to a religious practice;

Medical Hexing: the practice of a medical authority pronouncing that a patient has a 'chronic,' 'incurable,' or 'terminal' illness and/or saying our healing affirmations, spiritual practices and prayers won't or can't work; (Diagnoses, especially hexed diagnoses, are rigid medical boundaries. They are the ego's medieval walled city, erected out of limitation and maintenanced by fear); (See Spiritual Growth Hexing);

Medical Posse: employing both traditional and nontraditional medicine to assist in our healing;

Medicinal Smiles: medicine for an ailing spirit; (Neuroscience research tells us that smiles and laughter stimulate the frontal cortex in our brains and build neurons that strengthen our axons and dendrites);

Medicine: the wisdom of healing;

Medicine Bag: a bag containing medicinal stones, minerals, plant and animal parts used for healing; a 'bag' of healing techniques (methodologies) used for healing;

Medicine Cabinet: our body's immune system;

Medicine Men, Medicine Women: our body's army of cells that fight off infections;

Medicine Wheel: in Native American Indian spirituality, this 'wheel' was a circle made of stone that represented the spiraling galaxy, even prior to knowledge of the galaxy being spiral in nature; (In this particular circle, it is a place of prayer, understanding, ceremony and study of the stars);

Meditation: psycho-somatic medication; mental nutrition for the body, mind, and soul; (According to astrophysicist Amit Goswami, meditation allows us to become witnesses to the mental phenomena that arise in awareness, to the conditioned-response parade of thoughts and feelings. It creates a gap between the arousal of mental responses and the urge physically to act on them and thus enhances our capacity of free will to say no to conditions acts); [In *Freedom From the Known*, Krishnamurti describes the meditative experience: "Meditation is to be aware of every thought and of every feeling, never to say it right or wrong but just to watch it. It that watching you begin to understand the whole movement of thoughts and feelings." Pg. 115-116];

Meditational Smudging: using smudges of burning sage, sweet grass, and/or juniper to cleanse the atmosphere;

Mediumship: having highly spiritualized thoughts that bring passive worldly thoughts into automatic alignment with their divine qualities;

Megaphone: our conscience; the power and clarity of our authentic voice;

Melodrama: each skin school experience;

Melodramatic Repellant: a highly materialistic thought, word, or action that bluntly and brazenly denies our innate divinity and the divinity in others;

Melting Pot: our human personality;

Meme(s): concepts and/or behaviors that 'spread' virally from one level of our consciousness to another (beliefs, preferences, attitudes, memories, etc.);

Memorabilia: our past thoughts, feelings, choices, and actions; previous reincarnations, incarnations, accomplishments, and achievements; our karmic baggage;

Memorandum(s): thoughts that remind us of our natural mastery over the world of outer appearances;

Men, Beau(s), Guy(s): thoughts; masculine propensities; paternal instincts;

Menacing Miscue(s): finding ourselves on the wrong end of a misguided choice;

Mental Cinema: visualization;

Mental Disorder: the abject denial of our innate divinity;

Mental Health Geode: psychotherapy; psychoanalysis; spiritual counseling;

Mental Indigestion: error thoughts, inclinations, and intentions which surface from a consciousness addicted to things that aren't good for us;

Mental Kudzu: Kudzu is an insidious vine that can absolutely take over an area. In fact, it has been nicknamed the "foot-a-night vine," the "mile-a-minute vine," and "the vine that ate the South!" Error thoughts can do the same thing to us! They start out small, but they can quickly dominate our thinking. Grudges, resentments, hurts - if we let them have space - will soon clutter our mental landscape! (I call these mental intrusions *mental kudzu*);

Mentally Challenged: those who subscribe to a dogmatic, literal only view of sacred scripture and not know that it is a limited perspective (It is one of the most debilitating forms of mainstream religious practice);

Mental Mall: our subconscious, conscious, and super-conscious;

Mental Mercenaries: unprincipled, money-grubbing thoughts that represent our covetousness for material things;

Mental Shampoo: spiritual beliefs that wash the materialistic film off our thinking;

Menu Bar: learned behavior patterns; our penchant for organization and order; (In IT parlance, menus bars are horizontal strips that contain lists of available menus for certain programs. These bars are always fixed at the top of the screen and/or the top of each open window);

Melchizedek: the fully awakened Christ Nature within us; Christ Consciousness;

Mercedes Benz: denotes status, wealth, luxury, and safety;

Mercenary Quibbling: being caught between puzzlement and anger when it comes to testy religious discussions;

Mercury-like: quickly expressing spiritual wisdom; having intellectual fluidity; exercising the ability to serve as a capable liaison;

Mercy Seat: the medial longitudinal fissure which is the deep groove that separates our cerebral hemispheres;

Merkabahic Travel: astral travel; (In Jewish mysticism *merkabah* means a 'thing to ride in, cart, chariot' and is closely associated with Ezekiel's vision in Chapter 1 of the four-wheeled vehicle driven by "the Likeness of a Man.");

Mermaid Tendencies: being enchanting and alluring; practicing elusiveness; honoring femininity; displaying a rebellious spirit; opting for independence, nonconformity, and privacy; expressing our sensuality; accepting our peerless beauty;

Merry-Go-Round: the wheel of rebirth; reincarnational cycles;

Messiah, Anointed One, Savior: the Christ Presence (the Only Begotten Son) within; our Christ Mind; our enlightened super-consciousness that has been elevated to its Christ Consciousness awareness; an extremely highly evolved (anointed) spiritual thought which transforms our entire consciousness;

Messing Up: choosing to ignore our Divine Roots;

Metafissle: metaphysical malpractice; (See Metaphysical Malpractice);

Metamorphosis: reincarnation; episodes of birthing and rebirthing;

Metanoia: exoterically implies repentance, spiritually denotes our transformation from mortal (sense) consciousness to immortal (enlightened) consciousness;

Metaphysical Bible Interpretation: Metaphysical Bible interpretation is an esoteric treatment of scripture that finds the deeper spiritual meanings of Bible passages. (It takes the text beyond the literal translation and sees people, events, and places as aspects of human consciousness);

Metaphysical Conceit: our tendency to use unlikely combinations of metaphors, puns, similes, hyperbole, imagery, analogies, and oxymora (paradoxes) to describe metaphysical truths so 'regular' people can comprehend those truths;

Metaphysical Exegesis: applying the principles of metaphysical scriptural interpretation to extract esoteric truths from sacred and secular writings;

Metaphysical Hors d' Oeuvres: basic metaphysical principles; the same thing applies to basic theosophical, anthroposophical, allegorical, and metaphorical principles;

Metaphysical Malpractice: purposefully misinterpreting truth principles for egocentric and monetary gain and using that warped perspective to create guilt, blame, and fear (example: asking someone who is sick, "What did you do to cause your illness?" Metaphysical malpractice can become kudzu to an evolving spiritual practice, putting a coating of false assumptions on Truth that can be difficult to climb out from under);

Metaphysical Rolphing: sharing no-holds-barred metaphysical truths in such a way that produces high degrees of cognitive dissonance;

Metaphysical Sophrology: combining key metaphysical principles, meditation, yoga, and physical exercise to unite the mind, body and soul;

Metaphysical Tai Chi: combining metaphysical concepts with mirrored body movements to align our human self with our Christ Self; (Tai Chi is an ancient Chinese martial arts discipline that combines mental focus and controlled graceful movements to unite the mind and body.);

Metaphysician's Sense: the intuitive ability of metaphysicians to deduce esoteric meanings of people, places, things, and events;

Metaphysics, Ontology: study of being as such, questioning the meaning of existence and the nature of mind, bodies, god, space, time, causality, unity, identity, dualism, universals, etc.; [In *Jung*, Jacobi and Hull quote Swiss psychologist Carl Jung: "Because of the incarnation of the Cosmic Christ we are involved in a new responsibility. (We) can no longer wriggle out of it on the plea of (our) littleness and nothingness, for the dark God has slipped the atom bomb and chemical weapons into (our) hands and given (us) the power to empty out the apocalyptic vials of wrath on (our) fellow creatures. Since (we) have been granted almost godlike power, (we) can no longer remain blind and unconscious. (We) must know something of god's nature and of metaphysical processes if (we) are to understand (ourselves) and achieve gnosis of the divine." Pg. 363];

Metensomatosis: assuming 'body after body' as we incarnate in one dimension after another (However, these 'bodies' may not be physical bodies like the ones we possess in our earth experience. The bodies (somatic garments) we inhabit in other dimensions may be more ethereal and luminous than the bodies of flesh we burden ourselves with in skin school);

Meteorites: shooting spiritual inclinations that enter our corporeal consciousness as bursts of enlightened thought;

Metronomic Sacrifice: discerning when to sacrifice our needs for someone else's wants, or our wants for someone else's needs;

Mettlesome Rubbish: the syrupy, insincere attentiveness we show when we're not the least bit interested in what someone is saying about a particular religious topic;

Microblogging: quoting religious scripture [sound bytes] as our contribution to the conversation in which we are involved in at the moment; (In social media terms, microblogging is the act of broadcasting very short messages, such as on Twitter, where posts are limited to very few words.);

Microcosm: a thought; an intention; a cell; a molecule; our mind; our physical body;

Microphone, Mic, Mike: denotes clear, powerful speech; assertiveness;

Microscope: suggests introspection;

Microwave: represents quick thinking with actionable results;

Mictlanic Darkness: the unknown regions in our subconscious; (According to Aztec legends, *mictlan* is the underworld);

Midget(s): passing inclinations; brief impulses; newly-formed spiritual concepts;

Midnight: gross misuse of spiritual knowledge for material gain; dense materiality;

Midrashic Thinking: using allegory to fill in the gaps that appear in terse biblical text; (The Midrash is an anthology of rabbinic scriptural commentary);

Mildewed Principles: watered down religious and/or spiritual teachings;

Milk-ness: wanting to be spiritually nourished; honoring fertility and motherhood;

Millstone-like Disposition: championing any error-laced thought, intention, inclination, choice, word, or action;

Mind: an attribute of Divine Mind; Consciousness in action as mentation; (In *God and the New Physics*, Paul Davies states that "the essential ingredient of mind is information. It is the pattern *inside* the brain, not the brain itself, that makes us what we are." pg. 98);

Mind Action: purposeful, positive thinking centered on creating Christed outcomes; (Neuropsychologists are telling us that neurons which fire together wire together. These 'wired' neurons not only create new neural structures, their 'firing together' can actually leave lasting impressions on our brains – even from fleeting thoughts and feelings. So, what we think and feel are critically important for our health and wellbeing, and for our spiritual growth. We are not only the alchemists of our thoughts we are the alchemists of our neural real estate); [In research by psychologist Melanie Greenberg, we become what we repeatedly think. Over long periods, our patterns of thinking become etched into the billions of neurons in our brains, connecting them together in unique, entrenched patterns. When certain brain pathways – connections between different components or ideas – are frequently repeated, the neurons begin to 'fire' or transmit information together in a rapid, interconnected sequence. Once the first thought starts, the whole sequence gets activated. Over time, because of the nature of our consciousness, we can begin to change the wiring of our brains so our prefrontal cortex (the executive center, responsible for setting goals, planning and executing them), is more able to influence and shut off our rapidly firing, fear-based amygdala (emotion control center)];

Mind Auction: doing mindless things like: allowing our busy schedule to push prayer and meditation off our schedule; slipping into old habits of doubt, fear, and weariness; reliving hurts caused by someone close to us without wanting to let them go; and allowing excuses to take the place of healthy life styles;

Mindfulness: attentive awareness; moment to moment awareness of present events; being fully present; concentrated attention; (Research by Schwartz and Begley tells us that the most noteworthy result of mindfulness, which requires directed willful effort, is the ability it affords practitioners to observe their sensations and thoughts with the calm clarity of an external witness. Through mindful awareness, we can stand outside our own mind as if we are watching what is happening to another rather than experiencing it ourselves);

Mindless Madness: our knee-jerk response to maya;

Mind Over Molecules: our placeboic power as spiritual beings in human form to effect self-healing – with and without conventional medicine;

Mind Raider(s): subconscious propensities and repressed material that surface in our waking consciousness and hijack our good intentions;

Mine, Quarry: our subconscious;

Mine Field: a collection of divinity-denying thoughts, impulses, and intentions;

Ministerial Quackery: any sermon and/or ecclesiastical edict that denies or negates the divine nature, intrinsic value and worth, and equality of women, same sex couples, and people of color;

Minority: spiritual thoughts in an egocentric consciousness or material thoughts in a spiritually-attuned consciousness;

Minusing Ourselves: denying our innate divinity; denying we are the human expressions of the Indwelling Christ; consistently allowing enjoyment vacancies to appear on our calendar;

Miracle(s): cosmic snapshots of higher spiritual truth principles at work; proof of our inseparability from Spirit; probabilities and possibilities morphed into realities; *out*picturings of higher spiritual principles expressing as natural laws at work in our everyday lives;

Miracle-Making: turning tragedies into trajectories, scars into stars, *heeling* into healing, knots into bows;

Mirage: the phenomenal world;

Mirror-like: moon; reflectiveness; having foresight and farsightedness; our human self that reflects our Christ Self; the Christ Self and Holy Spirit which reflect the Eternal Presence; our consciousness which is a reflection of our Christ Consciousness; the universe mirrors the Logos; psychic scrying;

Misdemeanor(s): error thoughts that remain thoughts; (In legal circles, misdemeanors are offenses punishable by one year of imprisonment or less.);

Miser: thoughts that characterize our stinginess and hoarding penchant;

Miskinian Mannerisms: lowly, humble, submissive, meek mannerisms; (In Islam means a poor person who doesn't own property);

Misological Quirk: the fear, distrust, or even absolute distain for reason; anti-intellectualism; letting emotions trump reason;

Missing Link: The missing link is the missing link itself, because there is no missing link. Our physical bodies are the outpicturing of spiritual refinements which raise our bodies to higher degrees of perfection using each skin school experience as a laboratory;

Missile of Awareness: an illumined lightning bolt; a spiritual epiphany; a higher consciousness bombshell;

Mist-like: cultivating worldly attachments that make it difficult for us to grasp spiritual truths; spiritual cataracts;

Mistletoe-ness: experiencing rebirth; attaining immortality; undergoing regenerative experiences;

Mixtecian Altruism: believing that renewal and fertility of the world are only possible through acts of self-sacrifice; (A Mixtec belief. Mixtecian peoples were a branch of the Otomanguean family of Mexican people); (Higher than normal levels of oxytocin could explain one of the most important traits of human, as opposed to animal society: we are altruistic towards people we do not know, are proud of being Good Samaritans, and are generous and charitable when we do not have to be. The study was published by Prof Paul Zak of Claremont Graduate University);

Mob Bonding: our penchant for hanging around other people who share our love for riotous thoughts and murderous intentions;

Mob-like Disposition: riotous thoughts; subscribing to error thoughts; blinded by cruel intentions, murderous inclinations, impure intentions; following unillumined promptings;

Moj*ology*: taking distinct advantage of a distinct advantage;

Mokshaian Freedom: being liberated from the cycle of continuous incarnations; the dissolution of the sense of a separate self; (In Sanskrit, *moksha* is the liberation from *samsara* [the cycle of death and rebirth]);

Molehill Management: keeping molehills *molehills*;

Monastery: religious practice without worldly involvement;

Monastic Thinking: the kind of thinking where we remove ourselves from daily routines in favor of spiritual contemplation alone and/or with like-minded people; (See Eremitic Tradition);

Monetary Mockery: recognizing that dollars and sense don't always travel together;

Money: materialistic thoughts that are the currency of an egocentric consciousness; an exchange in perceived value; the fiscal union of wants and needs; a convenient end of bartering; materialistic energy; *tribute money* represents the materialistic value we place on life's necessities;

Monism: everything that exists stems from the same Source which is distinct from what exists;

Monkey Mind, Ego Chatter: the pesky voice inside our mind that gives us an incessant, judgmental chatter characterized by criticism, self-doubt, feelings of unworthiness, and doom and gloom; (Our minds are abuzz with thousands of thoughts each day, all of which compete for our attention. The Buddhists call this untrained mind of buzzing thoughts the Monkey Mind. The Monkey Mind, the ego mind, constantly flickers between conscious thoughts of love and unconscious thoughts of fear. This non-focused flickering is an intentional tool of the ego used to perpetuate confusion, attachments to duality and a resulting state of suffering. The ego's life depends on a consciousness of confusion, for with stillness and peace comes enlightenment and death to the ego's supremacy. The untrained mind is tempted by the allure of trivialities and other intruding thoughts. The ego, sustained by the consumption of such thoughts, enslaves our consciousness. The result of our egocentrism is attachment, an unconscious sleepwalking from which our materialistic tendencies bring suffering and separation); (See Chatter Bomb);

Monkey-ness: experiencing instinctual sharpness; enjoying playfulness; having mobility; being known for our swiftness; (In *Why Adults Need to Play*, Lenore Terr says that "play is essential to maturity. It gives us pleasure, a sense of accomplishment, of belonging. It reduces our stresses. If we are already accustomed to playing, we must upgrade our play. Why? Because it unlocks the door to ourselves." Pg. 126);

Monster(s): anti-Christed thoughts and impulses;

Moodle: our innate programming for lifelong learning; our desire for virtual learning; (In IT environments Moodle [Modular Object-Oriented Dynamic Learning Environment] is an open source, virtual classroom management system);

Moon: femininity; mortal consciousness; a *crescent moon* denotes expansiveness, unity, the feminine principle;

Moral Ontology: determining how morality exists and what sort of morality it constitutes;

Moral Whisper(s): the distinctive, hushed buzz we hear from our conscience; (When it comes to making moral choices many voices call on us: the voice of our own conscience, the cries of our families, the whispers of our ancestors, the yearnings of our children, the taunts of our adversaries, the temptations of our appetites, reminders of the truth principles and spiritual laws we have studied);

Morgue, Mortuary: the repressed patterns and feelings region in our subconscious;

Morning Glory: dawning spiritual awareness; new beginnings;

Morning Star: the Christ; (Morning Star is a name for the planet Venus);

Mortgage: our current mental, emotional, and physical makeup;

Mosque, Masjid: religious devotion;

Mosquito-ish: our susceptibility for letting small irritations, bothersome inconveniences, and swarms of negativity interfere with our happiness (suck the blood out of us);

Mother: a previous emotion that spawns and/or exacerbates a current emotion;

Mother-in-Law: an emotional state that creates feelings that contribute to our reacting positively or negatively to our current experience;

~ *Spiritually Speaking* ~

Mountain-ish: attaining a high state of spiritual awareness;

Mouthwashing: keeping our language clean;

Mount Sinai: Spiritually, Mt. Sinai represents a *highly-attuned and exalted state of spiritual consciousness*. It symbolizes a heightened awareness of the Christ Presence within us. Mt. Sinai is in here (I'm pointing to my head). It is a spiritual state of consciousness not a material waste of consciousness. (The same thing can be said for three of the world's highest mountains: Mount Everest, Qogir (K2), and Kangchenjunga. Mountains are primordial symbols for high states of consciousness);

Mouse-ness: being prolific in word and action; able to mediate spiritual aspirations and material ambitions; modeling modesty and shyness; having a great amount of adaptability;

Mouth: verbal self-expression;

Mrityuloka Crib: the physical world; physicality; the universe; (In Sanskrit, means the world of death which is the physical world);

MSTR: an acronym that defines people who consider themselves More Spiritual Than Religious; (See SBNR: Spiritual But Not Religious. According to recent Pew Forum and Barna Group polls there are a growing number of people of all ages worldwide (25-33%) who identify themselves as "more spiritual than religious." And among the Millennials (Generation Y – people born between the 1980's and early 2,000's) a survey by *Time* magazine found that 72% of this cohort consider themselves to be "spiritual and not religious.");

Muktic Thoughts: liberating thoughts; liberation from repeating incarnations; (In Hindu eschatological thought, *mukti* or *moksha* is liberation from *samsara* (the cycle of birth and death);

Mule-ishness: being willfully stubborn; showing how headstrong and hardheaded we can be; championing our cantankerous cussedness;

Multi-Asking: the juvenile practice of repeatedly petitioning an external, anthropomorphic goodie god in the sky for the things we want;

Multi-Homed: being a spiritual being with a physical address; (In IT security language, multi-homed describes a situation where our network is directly connected to two or more ISP's.);

Multi-Hop Journey, Multi-Leg Trip: our route toward enlightenment is filled with a myriad of incarnational and reincarnational experiences; (In airline lingo, in a mulit-hop journey passengers do not simply fly between two airports to reach their final destination, but stop en-route any number of times, and usually spend time in each of the destinations before they take off again);

Multinational Incorporation: adopting the spiritual and/or religious teachings and practices of selected faith traditions worldwide;

Multi-Storied Self: The part of us that wants to write, or dance, or paint, or sculpt, or yodel. It is that special dimension that's hard to reach, that wants to fix broken things, to end world hunger, to teach, to discover the cure for heart disease, cancer, or diabetes. It's that part of us that's not satisfied with where we are. It wants us to take risks, seek new insights, try novel experiences, test our limits, make better choices. It's the spiritual us, the divine us, the cosmic us;

Multitasking: enjoying a game on an iPad while sitting in a pew with our family during a sermon delivered by a religious fundamentalist (I'm messing with you ☺); the multi-functioning of the cardiovascular system; digestive system; endocrine system; nervous system, etc.; trying to play the materialistic "card" and the spiritual "card" at the same time; meditating and listening to music at the same time; (See the Twelve-Gated City);

Multiverse: the Garden of Eden; (For most of its history, the idea of a Multiverse was the domain of science fiction and some rare speculation from physicists. In recent years, though, the idea that our Universe may be just one among many has gained traction in two different areas. String theorists think it may help explain why, if there are a huge number of possible universes, we ended up in one with the properties we see around us. Meanwhile, cosmologists are realizing that cosmic inflation, which is the only way we know of to get from the Big Bang to our current Universe, necessarily implies the creation of other universes spawned by a Multiverse);

Mummified Tenets: dogmatic monuments and doctrinal shrines to religious close-mindedness (See also Religious Relics);

Mummy-like Urges: preserving dysfunctional life patterns, habits, assumptions and behaviors by embalming them as outposts in our minds;

Muraqabaic Practice: watching over or taking care of our spiritual heart (or soul), and acquiring knowledge about it, its surroundings, and its universal creative Source; (Muraqaba is a Sufi term that means to watch over, as in meditation);

Murder of Innocents: blocking or 'killing' newly formed spiritual ideas;

Museum: the full spectrum of our subconscious patterns and tendencies;

Musical Chairs: trying out one religious and/or spiritual practice after another;

Music of the Spheres: our physical and mental bodies are constantly in motion and emit a symphony of sound that defines our spiritual isness and beingness; our collective vibrations;

Music to Noise Ratio: the preponderance of useful spiritual and/or religious teachings verses marketing hype communicated by workshop presenters; spiritual thoughts (music) verses gross materialistic thoughts (noise);

Mustang: a wild, out-of-the-box, non-conformist thought;

Mustard Seed: a newly-formed idea (a profession of faith, a compelling spiritual intention) that grows in consciousness until it becomes the foundation for incredible transformation and soul growth; symbolic of the Divine Principle in unactualized potential; the unmanifest and manifested activity of heaven on earth; (See Divine Principle);

Mutant(s): underdeveloped ideas;

Mutasawwific Understanding: basic understanding of spiritual truths; a novice; (A Sufi term for perfect saints and spiritual adepts);

Muted Eloquence: realizing that speaking from the heart makes up for the imprecision of words, especially when we're being criticized for our religious and/or spiritual beliefs; (Some things will always remain beyond the grasp of mere words. Love is one of those things - and so are respect and trust and compassion and sacrifice);

Myrrh-like Qualities: letting go of anything which is no longer needed for our higher good; releasing impediments that interfere with our spiritual growth; emancipating ourselves from the illusion of duality and separation;

MySpace: our preference for social networking and staying in touch with a worldwide community;

Mystai: candidates (veiled ones) for initiation; a readied consciousness;

Mystery Cults: collections of mystical concepts that float around in our consciousness and synergistically contribute to our spiritual knowledge and growth;

Mystery Schools: centers of spiritual thought within our own consciousness that are collections of associated thoughts which become concepts of higher learning;

Mysticism: our conscious awareness stepped up to its super-conscious azimuth so we can become consciously aware of our oneness with the Eternal Presence; (Evidence suggests, say neuroscientists, that the deepest origins of religion are based in mystical experiences. Religions persist because the wiring of our brains continues to provide believers with a range of unitary experiences that are often interpreted as assurances that a Universal Presence called God exists);

Mystic Rose: heart chakra; our Higher Self; the seat of immense wisdom; *an open rose* is the quickened heart chakra;

Mystic Tie: the Indwelling Christ Presence within all of us;

Mzee(s): traditional, conventional thoughts; (A Swahili term for a respected old person and/or older parents);

Nails: *five nails* represent the five human senses that bind Spirit to the cross of matter (human physicality);

Nakedness: innocent thoughts; openness to higher truths; intellectual reticence; emotional vulnerability;

Namaste: beholding the Christ in every person we see. We don't need to do anything outwardly special, just make the conscious decision to behold the Christ, the good, within them - no matter whether it is our best friend, a loved one, the person who cuts us off on the beltline, the customer who becomes totally irrational, or the homeless person who is holding up a sign on the street corner. (That conscious moment of beholding the Christ in that person will magnetize the oneness we share with the Indwelling Christ);

Name: the nature of something; the mind's penchant for closure and categorizing experience; *changing a name* signifies attaining a new level of consciousness;

Name Badge: identifying ourselves with where we are;

Namshe: consciousness that continues from one incarnation to another;

Nam Simran: remembering God through disciplined meditation; (A Hindu word for disciplined devotional practice); [A comprehensive study by Lutz, Creischar, Rawlings, Ricard, and Davidson revealed that when experienced Tibetan practitioners go deep into meditation, they produce uncommonly powerful and pervasive gamma brainwaves of electrical activity, in which unusually large regions of neural real estate pulse in synchrony 30-80 times a second];

Nanometer: measuring our spiritual progress each-consecutive-moment-of-now; the distance between our thoughts; (In IT language, a nanometer is a unit of measurement [one billionth of a meter] for measuring integrated circuitry);

Nap(s), Siesta(s), Forty Wink(s): each incarnational experience;

Narcolepsy: compulsively daydreaming our way around enlightenment; falling into a temporary state of denial that refuses to accept our divinity; [Narcolepsy is a sleep disorder that affects 1 in every 2000 Americans by making them excessively sleepy];.

Narrative Theology: dependence on the study of the nature of God and religious truths as outlined in religious stories and parables;

Narrow-Mindedness: seeing our spiritual growth as a condiment instead of the main course;

Narrow Way, the: the spinal column;

Narthex: our initial willingness (interest, curiosity, route followed) to become enlightened;

Nastikaian Refusal: denying the truth or the validity of divine revelations; (A Hindu term for atheist);

National Security: protecting our tri-level consciousness (nation) from foreign invaders (error thoughts);

Nation(s), Empire(s), Republic(s): collections of thoughts, ideas, concepts; the three aspects of our mind (subconscious, conscious, and super-conscious); our body, mind, and soul;

Nativity: descent of Spirit (Cosmic Christ) into matter; a new level of spiritual awareness is born; the Christ (Brahma, Buddha, Allah, Krishna, Vishnu) expresses Itself in human form as us;

Nausea: the feeling we get from an error overdose;

Navel: center of the universe; central philosophy;

Navigation Bar: spiritual principles and teachings; (In IT terminology, navigation bars are user interfaces within a webpage that contain links to other sections in the website);

Navigation Equipment: truth principles and spiritual practices; positive affirmations;

Nearsightedness: not seeing beyond a literal-only interpretation of holy scripture;

Nefelibatan (fantasizer) Attributes: our tendency to "walk in the clouds" and stay considerably outside the proverbial box in our thinking, being, and doing;

Nefesh Elokit: our Extraordinary Self (Christ Self, Buddha Self, etc.); (In Kabbalistic terms, our Godly Soul);

Nefesh HaBehamit: our base instincts; (In Kabbalistic terms, our animalistic soul nature);

Negative Holder: the amygdala which focuses on the negative; (In photography terms, a negative holder is a clamp-like device that fixes a negative in position in an enlarger);

Negative Thinking, Pessimism: whineology; Some people have Ph.D's in negativity. There are people who wear negativity like a badge of honor. Others wear it like a straight jacket and struggle to get themselves out of a negative disposition. Negativity comes from a consciousness grounded in lack, and fear, and anger, and hopelessness. Here's the thing. All of us have been exposed to negative environments. We've been told we're not good enough, that we're failures, that we can't do certain things or have certain things. And there's a part of us, that wounded child part of us, that says – what if they're right! I put a positive spin on that kind of malpractice by saying – negation is simply a choice we don't have to make. And we certainly don't have to allow it to form outposts in our mind. [In *Learned Optimism*, Martin Seligman emphatically asserts that "twenty-five years of study has convinced me that if we habitually believe, as does the pessimist, that misfortune is our fault, is enduring, and will undermine everything we do, more of it will befall us than if we believe otherwise. I am also convinced that if we are in the grip of this view, we will get depressed easily, we will accomplish less than our potential, and we will even get physically sick more often. Pessimistic prophecies are self-fulfilling." Pg. 5]; (See Negativity Bias);

Negativity Bias: our penchant for living in the amygdala instead of the neocortex; over-protectiveness; living in fear and doubt; (The reason negativity is so detrimental to our spiritual growth – and human happiness – is that it causes the hippocampus to embed the perceived negative experience into our long-term emotional memory. The stress hormones and neurotransmitters that are released send our defense mechanisms cascading through the brain, making indelible limbic imprints in our consciousness);

Neighbor(s): our body, mind, and soul; our subconscious, conscious, and super-conscious; our human self and our Christ Self;

Negligible Numbing: slipping back into an old habit, but noticing it in time to prevent wholesale slippage;

Nemesis Nonsense: lackadaisically choosing error thoughts over spiritual thoughts so that those very sense-laden thoughts become our chief adversaries against an enlightened path;

Neophyte, Postulant: a newly formed spiritual idea; newly-formed philosophical, mystical, and metaphysical ideas;

Net: our subconscious, conscious, and/or super-conscious;

Netiquette: our desire for respecting other people's privacy in public places; common sensical separation between spiritual practices and public displays of how spiritual we are; (In IT language, netiquette refers to etiquette online. Good netiquette means not doing anything online that annoys, frustrates, demeans, and/or spams people);

Neuro-Musculoskeletal Massage: (See Yoga);

Neuroplasticity: denotes the brain recording what our mind already knows; [The brain's adding new neural real estate mirrors the elasticity of the mind. Because of the brain's neuroplasticity, our thinking, emotions, and memory formation *matter* well beyond their momentary, subjective impact. Our brain restructures itself based on the indelible impact of these events. So, the neurochemistry of thinking Christed thoughts, filling our days with loving and nurturing feelings, and remembering positive experiences has therapeutic effects on our bodies; (According to neuroscience, neuroplasticity is brain's incredible capacity to perennially learn and, thus, constantly change structurally and functionally); [In *Train Your Mind, Change Your Brain*, Sharon Begley says that "the hardware of the brain is not fixed at birth." Pg. 48];

Neurotheology: the marriage between psychology and theology; (Neurotheology's very name and essence demands a mutual co-interaction between science and religion. Thus, anyone engaging in neurotheology must be open to both perspectives. As a matter of fact, a crucial element of neurotheology, which really should be true for all academic fields, is a passion for spiritual inquiry with an emphasis on its relationship to our brain's functioning. Neuroscience has proven beyond a doubt that even fleeting thoughts and feelings can leave lasting impressions on our brain. When you add the amperage of the spoken word as a vocal expression of those thoughts and feelings you literally change the neural structure of the brain. Positive thoughts and affirmations are not only essential for spiritual growth but they are necessary ingredients for emotional and physical wellbeing and for rewiring the brain);

Neutralizing Negation: not giving power to negative thoughts, words, or actions;

Never-Never Land, Neverland: the religious 'real estate' called heaven and hell which are not places we go to after our physical transition, but states of consciousness we grow each-consecutive-moment-of-now; (See Heaven, Hell, When Hell Freezes Over, Everlasting Hell, Gehenna, Hades);

New Jerusalem, Holy City: the transformation of our human consciousness into its higher spiritual equivalent, a fully enlightened super-consciousness (Christ Consciousness); an abiding consciousness of inner peace, deep reverence for the regenerated and perfected life, and sacredness characterized by an enlightened consciousness; *entry into Jerusalem* means the realization – during waking consciousness – of our human self as the Christ expressing Itself as us; [The foundation of the Holy City consisted of 144 stones in twelve rows which denotes the mystic symbol of humankind (144 reduced to the number 9) and also the number of initiation]; the twelve gates of this symbolic dodecahedron are the twelve major orifices in the human body; (The trued *ashlar* in Masonry);

New Money: newly-formed ideas and concepts that we deposit into our consciousness;

Newseum: our short term memory; our tendency to not only make ourselves aware of current events, but to want to remember those events;

News Feed: our stream of conscious thought that helps us connect our spirituality with the world in which we live, move, and have our being; (In Facebook terms, a news feed is the continually appended feed of status updates that appears on our Profile home page. It shows the most recent activities from our Friends and Pages that we follow.);

Newspaper(s): our penchant for keeping ourselves informed and aware of the world around us;

New Thought, Higher Thought: believing that the Eternal Presence called God is a supreme, universal and everlasting presence that underwrites the manifest and unmanifest; believing that consciousness is the ground of all being; believing that human beings are spiritual beings having a human experience; believing that divinity indwells in every person, animal and plant; believing that sickness and dis-ease originate in the mind; believe in mind over molecules; (New Thought is really Old Thought in the sense that its teachings have been around for centuries. Some of the earliest proponents of the New Thought Movement were Phineas Quimby, Warren Felt Evans, Emma Curtis Hopkins, Charles and Myrtle Fillmore, Nona L. Brooks, William Walker Atkinson, Malinda Cramer, Ernest Holmes, Annie Rix Militz, Helena Blavatsky, Anne Besant, Alice Bailey, Rufus Douglass, Eric Butterworth, and Joel S. Goldsmith to name only a few);

Night: spiritual unreceptivity; unawareness of and/or ignorance of spiritual principles; spiritual blindness; the *oncoming of night* means willfully resisting and/or blocking spiritual growth; spiritual cataracts;

Nightlight: the Christ Light, the Extraordinary Us; (See Extraordinary You);

Nightmare, Tribulation: choosing materialism over spirituality;

Nimbus-like: attaining a high state of enlightenment;

Nirvana: an error-free consciousness; Absolute Consciousness; Christ Consciousness; (In Hindu philosophy, nirvana means the permanent cessation of suffering and its causes. When our mind-stream has liberated from the causes of suffering, it will naturally vibrate at the level of Nirvana [heaven]. Nirvana, say Hindu mystics, can be attained through millions of births and deaths, but it can also be attained by means of a shorter path called the initiation route);

Nishmat Haim: In Kabbalist terms, the breath of life;

Noah-ing: According to neuroscientists, our brain first quantifies physical objects into pairs and then separates the pairs into opposites (night and day, good or bad, short or tall) in order to set the dualistic parameters of the polarity. That could very well be what was going on when the Biblical character Noah rounded up the animals two-by-two and named them. As part of the story of our evolving spiritual consciousness this Biblical episode could be referring to an early phase in our neurological development. Because we are born with two brain hemispheres that see the world in two different ways this account clearly suggests that we have the wherewithal to integrate both hemispheres to conceive a unified whole. [Vishnu appears in the form of a fish to Satyavrata who, under the name of Vaivasvata. Vishnu announces that the world is to be destroyed by a flood and orders Satyavrata to construct an ark and enclose seeds which will become the post-flood world. Sound familiar to Noah's commission?]; (We can also compare this story to Jonah, where the whale [fish] takes the place of an ark and transports Jonah in its belly. Jonah's emergence from the belly of the whale [ark] denotes resurrection and immortality.); [As far as we know the only way to grasp the totality of life is to move from an intellectual perspective that tends to be reductionist in nature to a more heart-centered (mountaintop) perspective that is able to sense unified wholeness];

Noble Sanctuary: the Kingdom of God (Headquarters) within us;

Nocebo Effect: negatively-charged mind over molecules;

Nocializing: a religious organization's practice of not including guests (visitors) in the 'meet and greet' time during the Sunday service by ignoring them while we socialize with fellow congregants;

No If's, And's, or But's: being very clear about who we are – the human expressions of the Christ Presence expressing as us in physicality;

No-Fault Discourse: amicable conversations between open-minded truth seekers;

Noise: egocentric chatter; religious proselytizing;

Noise Reduction: eliminating the 'chatter' of the daily grind by meditating and/or saying affirmative prayers; (In photography terms, noise reduction generally switches on automatically at slow shutter speeds to prevent grainy pictures);

Non-Dischargeable Debt(s): karma that accumulates from one reincarnation to another; (In legal circles, non-dischargeable debts cannot be eliminated in bankruptcy.);

Nonjudgmentalness: being a spiritual lighthouse instead of a religious flashlight;

Non-Locality, Spooky Action at a Distance: the One appearing as the many; (The many are simply different degrees (expressions, aspects) of the One. Each of us is a Christ-bearer. We are eternal beings who have chosen to wear temporal clothing. Our relationship *with* God [the Eternal Presence] is nonlocal. It has always been that way because we have always been indivisible expressions of God from the beginning. The allness of God expresses Itself as the eachness of us whether we choose an incarnational or reincarnational experience. That being said, our connection with God has been unbroken, and remains unbroken and nonlocal); [In quantum physics language, non-local influences do not diminish with distance. They are as potent at a million miles as at a millimeter. Their influences are instantaneous and the speed of their transmissions is not limited by the velocity of light. A non-local interaction links one location with another without crossing space, without decay, and without delay. A non-local interaction is, in short, unmediated, unmitigated, and immediate];

Non-Transferrable Ticket: our own special 'ticket to ride' (individual consciousness) on our flight to illumination; (In airline industry terminology, a non-transferrable ticket is a ticket specifically for just one passenger and cannot be used by anyone else.);

Nonversation: the awkward, meaningless dialogue between New Thought practitioners and religious fundamentalists when their views are shared with each other;

Noon-like State: experiencing a revelation; achieving the absence of doubt, conflicting thoughts, or confusion about spiritual aspirations;

Noose, Strangulation: a life of unadulterated denial of our innate divinity;

Normal Science: working within the parameters of existing paradigms;

Norns: the three *fate*ful sisters (the Past, the Present, and the Future);

North Star: a central spiritual teaching;

No-Show: having a chance to do the right thing, but not doing it; (In airline industry terms, a no-show describes passengers or either arrive late or fail to arrive at all to travel on their booked flight.);

Nostalgic Newness: being used to personnel changes, especially when it comes to finding volunteer replacements for church volunteers who have resigned and/or rotated out of their volunteer positions; the reverence, joy, and peace of the next sunrise;

Nous: our higher faculty of superior intuition; (Nous, according to the mystery schools, is a super-conscious capability that makes clairvoyance possible);

Nouvelle Cuisine: esoteric truth principles and spiritual teachings topped off (coupled) with quantum physics tenets, neuroscience findings, genetic and biology research, and neurotheology revelations;

Nowhere Sermon: a sermon that doesn't ever go anywhere or have a point;

Nowologist, Present Tense Champion: living each-consecutive-moment-of-now from our elevated Christ Consciousness;

Now*ology*: finding the heart of the moment, so we can find the soul of our day;

Ntsahakee-like Awareness: spiritual clarity and divine awareness of the natural order as reality;

Nuclear Bomb, Nuclear Armageddon: collective hostility and fear resulting in a global death wish;

Numbers: the science of numerology comes from the study of numbers and their relationship to the divine, mystical, and spiritual meanings of things. Numbers have many different interpretations and contexts. Here are a few of the generally accepted meanings:

0: infinity; boundlessness; universality; the movement around a sacred object; allness and nothingness; feminine principle; cycles; expansiveness and limitation; the center; the Source of all and sourcelessness; an elliptical path; descent and ascent; involution and evolution; the *fons et origo* of all that is; when added to another number it emphasizes magnitude, vastness, enormity, fullness; the Universal Field; the unmanifest and manifest;

1: fundamental unity; divinity; the positive activity of Spirit; the unmanifest made manifest; selfhood; from nonbeing to becoming; masculine principle; positivity; physical and mental energy; new beginnings; self-reliance; internal locus of control; the One Eternal Presence (also: the Indwelling Divinity within us, the incarnated Logos, the human ego at its lowest essence); individuality; the polarity between height and depth; singularity; yang; the prime mover; the coming into something from nothing;

2: male and female; spiritual and material; Spirit and matter; the manifest and unmanifest as dual aspects of the divine; antithesis; balance; the need for choice indicated; discernment; polarity; duality; human self and Divine Self; yin; creative principle; opposites; thoughts and emotions; seeing Christ as immanent and transcendent; theory and practice; what is and what isn't; the observer and the observed; the beginning, middle, and end; the two hemispheres of our brain; our higher mind and lower mind;

3: Divine Order (mind, idea, expression); trinity; creativity; the three levels of human consciousness (subconscious, conscious, super-conscious); body, mind, and soul; the physical dimensions of length, breadth, and height; fecundity; past, present, and future; the thinker, formative thought, and creative thought; teleological harmony; the breaking of inertia; the Buddha, Dharma, and Sangha; (Vedic trinities include Brahma, Vishnu and Shiva with their consorts Saraswati, Lakshmi and Kali); creation, destruction, preservation; unfolding, maintaining and concluding; the Three Norns: Mani, Nyi and Nithi;

4: foundational creation; the time of preparation; reality; solidarity; groundedness; the four aspects of being (spiritual, mental, emotional, and physical); the material universe; the cross (human incarnation); realization of our true identity; spiritual unfoldment; the Divine Quaternity; the four cardinal directions; the Damba Tree of Life has four limbs and from its roots four sacred streams of Paradise; (In Chinese Buddism there are four celestial guardians of cardinal points: Mo-li Ch'ing [the East, with the jade ring and spear], Virupaksha [the West, the Far-gazer, with the four-stringed guitar]. Virudhaka [the South, with the umbrella of chaos, darkness, and earthquakes], and Vaisravenna [the North, with the whips, leopard-skin bag, snake, and pearl]); the Four Gospels; (Taoist: There are four celestial guardians: Li, with the pagoda; Ma, with the sword; Cho with two swords; Wen with a spiked club);

5: the five senses (touch, taste, sight, smell, and hearing) and their higher spiritual sensory vibrations (clairvoyance, clairaudience, clairalience, clairsentience and clairgustance); sense consciousness (coma consciousness); the middle; mediation; compromise; unpredictability; material connectedness; humankind; impersonal law of cause and effect; the cosmic quintessence giving birth to all matter; (the marriage of the *hieros gamos* as feminine and the masculine: feminine being even, as 2, in frequency and masculine being odd as 3 in frequency = 5); (In alchemy, the five petaled flower and five pointed star symbolize quintessence); five wounds of Christ as Jesus on the cross;

6: equilibrium; symmetry; harmony; diplomacy; the psyche; masculine and feminine reciprocity; an enlightened perspective; imagination; telepathy; cooperation between the brain's hemispheres; going from an amygdala (Sobek) theology to a neocortex (Horus) theology; the union of polarities; the six-pointed star; (In Chinese, six represents Universe, with its four cardinal points, plus Above and Below, making a total of six directions); six days of creation; [Sobek and Horus are Egyptian gods. Sobek is associated with the reptilian brain and Horus with the neocortex];

7: impending completion; moving toward perfection; enlightenment; comfortable with mystery and ambiguity; interest in esoterical and spiritual truths; the seven major chakras (represented by the seven churches mentioned in the Book of Revelation: Ephesus, Smyrna, Pergamum, Thyatira, Sardis, Philadelphia, and Laodicea); the seven step creative process; the realization that consciousness is the ground of all being; the fusion of divine order (mind, idea, expression) with the four quaternaries of physicality (earth, air, fire, and water); reintegration; synthesis; rest; seven houses in the underworld, as depicted in Egyptian myths; there are seven branches to the Tree of Life each having seven leaves; (According to the chronology of Johannes Trithemius of Sponheim, there are seven distinct repetitive periods where archangels [Universal truth Principles] rein throughout our evolutionary history: Oriphiel, Anael, Zachariel, Raphael, Samuel, Gabriel, and Michael); there are seven beatitudes in the Book of Revelation;

8: infinity; karmic conformity, balance and adjustment; momentum; probabilities; distributions, tendencies, and sequences; constellations of experience; processes; magical alignments; interrelationships between cycles; the ebb and flow of patterns and states of being; eccentricity; extraordinariness; the clearing away of obstacles and barriers; paradise regained; regeneration and rebirth; solidarity and stability; prosperity; abundance; the eight-pedaled lotus; eight major chakras [7 physical chakras plus an etheric chakra known as the Chakra of the Soul]; the eight great gods of the Vedas: Surya, Candra, Agni, Yama, Varuna, Indra, Vâyu and Kubera; there are eight trigrams in the Chinese pakua; madalas are constructed on an 8x8 symbolism; in Islam, the throne that encompasses the world is supported by eight pillars; there are eight Taoist immortals; (In St. Hildegard's *Scivias*, the divine throne is represented by a circle supported by eight angels);

9: influential difference; trinity of trinities; every level of being in heaven (super-consciousness, Christ Consciousness) and earth (egocentric human consciousness); superior attainment; the cusp of one level of consciousness and its succeeding level of consciousness; regeneration; revelation; precognition; premonition; pure intelligence; there are nine underworlds;

10: perfection; total mastery; the allness of allness; the synthesis of fundamental unity and universality; the union (entrainment, alignment) of egoic consciousness and super-consciousness; the completion of an important cycle in our spiritual unfoldment; the attainment of enlightenment; the Philosopher's Stone; the cosmos; whole of manifestation; completion of journeys and returns to origins; the sum of the number nine of the circumference plus the one in the center denoting perfection; there are ten commandments in the Decalogue; (In Qabalism ten is the numerical value of Yod, the Eternal Word); infinite expansion;

11: wholeness of body, mind, and soul; male and female equality and unity; unfailing balance; highly reflective thought and advanced awareness; congruency; refinement;

12: completed soul work on each plane of being; spiritual adeptship; divinely ordered advancement at each stage of one's soul development; zodiacal influences; a complete cycle; cosmic order; (twelve disciples followed Jesus, there are twelve astrological signs in the zodiac, there are twelve months in the year, and a clock is divided into two groups of twelve hours, twelve fruits of the Cosmic Tree, twelve days of Yuletide and Christmas, twelve gates and foundation stones of the Holy City); there are twelve gods and goddesses of Olympus; there are twelve descendants of Ali in Islam; Mithra had twelve disciples;

13: the end of something and the beginning of another; denotes transitioning from one state of being to another; (There are 13 circles in Metatron's Cube); (Superstitions about Friday the 13th may have originated in a Norse myth about twelve gods having a feast in Vahalla. The mischievous Loki crashed the party as an uninvited 13th guest and arranged for Hod, the blind god of darkness, to shoot Baldur, the god of joy and gladness, with a mistletoe-tipped arrow. Baldur was killed and the Earth was plunged into darkness and mourning as a result); (our 13 major articulations (ankles, knees, hips, wrists, elbows, shoulders and neck);

14: our capacity for adapting to change, even unexpected change; seeking equilibrium, balance, and harmony;

15: our inclination for breaking free of constraints, restraints, restrictions, and confinements;

16: recognizing that the moment of enlightenment will take our unsuspecting ego by surprise as the diverse levels of awareness (heavens) become unified in an undivided whole;

17: represents the intellectual awareness and illumination that comes from divine ideas;

18: implies reflectiveness, intuitiveness, and empathy;

19: our preference for independence, self-reliance, and self-sufficiency;

20: our impulse for refined thoughts and emotions; also denotes a discerning disposition and sound judgment;

21: our tendency for closure and an orderly and systematic finishing up;

22: being grounded in what we know and have experienced; having an internal locus of control that primes us for personal, professional, and spiritual achievements; (There are 22 pairs of human autosomal chromosomes. In the divinatory tarot, 22 is considered a master number);

23: the desire for improving ourselves; depending on our five physical senses for keeping us aware of our surroundings and of our relationship to those surroundings;

24: honoring both our thoughts and emotions as legitimate expressions of our personhood;

25: seeing vagueness, uncertainty and ambiguity as 'friends' as we seek to make ourselves comfortable with exploring higher truths and the transformations in our thinking they bring with them;

26: our resolve to cross out error ; (There are 26 ganglions of the sympathetic system in the human body);

27: our ability to see light in darkness; seeing daylight at the end of the tunnel;

28: denotes an appreciation for the cyclic nature of things;

29: discernment and sound judgment;

30: recognizing the limitations associated with concrete operational thought;

31: the holographic nature of things;

32: our ability to manage karmic implications;

33: having achieved a Christ-centric consciousness; illumination; (the age of the Christ as Jesus when he made his earthly transition);

34: our capacity to move past the exoteric into the esoteric;

35: having a sense of unfinished business;

36: our internal locus of control rooted in the knowledge that we can divinely order our experiences;

37: recognizing the interplay between synergy and compatibility;

38: the ability to turn our scars into stars; (When a highly spiritualized thought [angel of God] enters our consciousness [baptismal pool] it creates an energetic reaction in our thought currents [stirs up the waters]. Spiritualized thoughts influence future thoughts by elevating them to their higher spiritual essences [heal them of dis-ease]. What usually happens is there is at least one well-established, although limited, thought pattern [an invalid], which is the product of sense consciousness [coma consciousness]. This anemic thought pattern affects the harmonics of both our human and spiritual aspects [represented by the number thirty-eight which is 3 + 8 or 11]. The question we must ask ourselves is how long do we want to allow discordant thoughts to pollute our consciousness with *sense sludge*?);

39: recognizing that base instincts and other materialistic thoughts and tendencies will rise to their higher spiritual essences as they are purified of their material dross, and our human consciousness (the earth) and all of its mental real estate shall be transformed into its dynamic illumined form;

40: completion; a radical transformative cycle;

41: denotes an above average ability to master skin school experiences;

42: realizing that one day we will have achieved such spiritual adeptness that our human personality, with its materialistic ego will be transformed into an expanded consciousness (new heaven);

43: discerning what intentions and inclinations will contribute to our being on the right path when it comes to our spiritual growth;

44: introspection over the expectations associated with completing a cycle of spiritual development;

45: the mental bridge between our divine capacities and our human capabilities;

46: our strong inclinations toward preserving spiritually enriching experiences;

47: being humbled by the depth and practicality of esoteric teachings;

48: seeing trust and mature faith as hope all grown up;

49: recognizing that our five senses do not tell the complete story and are simply sensory filters that register what we think we see;

50: the five physical senses operating at a high level of spiritual functioning without letting the ego unduly filter our experiences so that our enlightenment becomes more difficult; direct knowing and intuiting; a more spiritually awakened humankind;

51: intentional movement toward more spiritual pursuits than egocentric habits;

52: being able to consistently live in the moment;

53: recognizing that unforgiveness blocks our good;

54: attaining above average precognitive abilities;

55: universality of perspective;

56: our capacity for habitual divine revelation experiences;

57: able to sense the full spectrum of spiritual growth opportunities in any given incarnation experience;

58: understanding that when we pretend to practice truth principles and, at the same time, deny our oneness with Spirit, we compromise our spiritual growth;

59: recognizing that every circumstance invites us to be who we are;

60: sense consciousness (coma consciousness);

61: having the courage to move beyond the embedded theology of our youth;

62: able to have unconditional positive regard for anyone seeking to heighten h/her spiritual acumen;

63: our penchant for being able to resurrect unused, under used, and/or repressed talents and skills;

64: having the talent for recognizing our uniqueness;

65: coming into the understanding that if we practice the truth principles we know (walk in the light) our thoughts, words, and actions will be in congruence with the truth of who we are;

66: being more positive and less moody when it comes to handling life's challenges;

67: seeking out enriching spiritual opportunities that guarantee us a growing edge;

68: seeing, hearing, and feeling our oneness with nature;

69: apprehending that the same life force that was actualized in the fully illumined Jesus through his conscious oneness with the Christ can be actualized as us too;

70: the end of an era or cycle;

71: knowing that when we get *us* right our world will be right;

72: recognizing that when we stop denying our oneness with the Eternal Presence (God) we begin to consciously align ourselves with our Christ Nature;

73: knowing that we are works-in-progress;

74: recognizing that self-discovery is really Self-recovery (the small 's' is our human self and the capital 'S' is our Divine Self);

75: our willingness to make normal life more fulfilling;

76: having the self-assurance to know that each challenge we face requires us to think, choose, and act from the truth of who we are;

77: knowing that we have dormant greatness within us;

78: believing that it is us that determines our successes or failures and not external circumstances;

79: denotes our willingness to move beyond worn-out perspectives;

80: authoritativeness, efficiency; achievement;

81: seeing the value in moving beyond our human imperfections and limitations;

82: recognizing that when we study truth principles and then neglect to raise worldly thoughts to their higher spiritual values, we essentially deny (are in darkness) our inherited divinity;

83: knowing it is our innate wisdom that allows us to understand wisdom;

84: our ability to see both science and spirituality as twin paths to an illumined perspective;

85: believing in our wholeness as spiritual beings embodied in human form;

86: taking our skin school experiences in stride;

87: our ability to respond to difficulties with awareness, poise, and resilience;

88: being able to mediate the effects of karmic baggage by making Christ-centric choices and taking Christ-centric actions in our current earth experiences;

89: paying attention to our thoughts, words, choices, and actions so we can monitor our spiritual growth;

90: the meeting point (decision point) between spirit and matter;

91: recognizing that we learn more from unanswered questions than unquestioned answers;

92: knowing that an open palm instead of a closed fist is one of the roads to world peace;

93: recognizing that we have the innate ability to understand incomprehensible paradoxes, human dilemmas, and inexplicable concepts;

94: recognizing that we are connected to everything because everything is connected through us by right of consciousness;

95: living in the neocortex instead of the amygdala;

96: realizing that when we grow spiritually our egocentrism diminishes along with its excessive sensory appetites and our consciousness becomes Christ-centered and we enjoy an expanded spiritually-attuned beingness;

97: seeing completion as an ongoing process;

98: attaining a level of awareness whereby we don't confuse our self-worth with our net worth;

99: knowing that a giving consciousness puts us into direct alignment with our Extraordinary Nature, our Authentic Self;

100: complete harmonization of Spirit and matter;

101: realizing that as we come close to enlightenment divine ideas (children) will flow, our patient anticipation heightens and there will be a surge of perverse thoughts (many antichrists) that pour out of an overall denial (the antichrist) of our innate divinity;

102: our selfless concern for the welfare of others;

103: our disposition for speaking our mind, knowing we can influence others, but at the same time respecting the personal space and spiritual beliefs of others;

104: having a high degree of conscientiousness when it comes to honoring our divine impulses;

105: our proclivity for acting courageously in trying circumstances;

106: recognizing that lower vibratory egocentric thoughts are part of our overall human makeup, but they are the products of a self-aggrandizing, petulant ego;

107: our ability to recognize the fundamental unity in all things;

108: the normal number of cycles (reincarnations) in a skin school-prone spiritual being's enlightenment portfolio; also, denotes ultimate reality which is composed of only one thing, no things, and/or everything;

109: using our physical and mental energy for unity and harmony instead of division;

110: denotes our fancy for enjoying serendipitous experiences;

111: our ability to discard preconceived assumptions and opt for new learning;

112: being able to delay our gratification when it comes to material things;

113: using our five senses for exploration and the power of observation;

114: our ability to work with others by practicing social adroitness because we believe in fundamental unity and harmony;

115: having a natural curiosity for spiritual teachings;

116: denotes our ability to manage polarities;

117: our preference for rejecting any religious perspective that teaches dogma and duality;

118: our tendency to lead from the heart instead of the head;

119: realizing, without a doubt, that the antichrist is not a person or personage, but is any thought or inclination which denies that we are the Christ (the Only Begotten Son) expressing Itself in human form as us;

120: our preference toward striving toward agreeableness and likableness;

121: recognizing that our mere presence can have an effect on others since what quantum physicists call non-locality is a very real phenomenon that connects us all;

122: always acting on the dictates of our consciousness and conscience;

123: our ability to distinguish between courage and foolhardiness;

124: seeing dogmatism as a walled city that locks spiritual growth out;

125: believing that all faith traditions should be honored and respected;

126: having a high degree of impulse control when it comes to our nonattachment to material things;

127: being able to discern charlatanism, false prophets, and quackery;

128: recognizing the importance of aligning our human self with our Divine Nature;

129: being able to draw our good from Universal Substance by right of consciousness;

130: the ability to control our narcissistic tendencies;

131: realizing that the Good News (our innate Christhood) is the Christ Presence (Son of God, [God in physicality]) underwrites all beingness in every dimension of deific manifestation so that, eventually, we will outgrow our spiritual cataracts, becoming consciously aware of our own divine nature;

132: having a high degree of empathy;

133: showing considerable hardiness and resourcefulness;

134: denotes the uncanny ability to turn scars into stars by applying truth principles and practices;

135: having a high degree of extraversion, but recognizing that not everyone is not as outgoing as we are;

136: seeing the 'wait' time for bringing the unmanifest into manifestation as up to us;

137: honoring both our masculinity and our femininity;

138: recognizing that when we align our human self completely with our Christ Nature in body, mind, and soul we will have established such inner harmony and unity that each thought we have will eventually be transformed into its higher spiritual octave;

139: being able to control our impulsivity and whimsicalness;

140: our capacity for altruistic inclinations and sense of wholeness when it comes to honoring individual differences;

141: allowing our internal locus of control to guide us toward self-definition;

142: quick thinking and responsiveness;

143: denotes our independence and nonconformity;

144: having the initiative to look beyond literal interpretations of sacred scripture to find hidden metaphysical meanings; (This particular personality trait helps us "save" ourselves from the falsehoods and misinterpretations perpetuated by a literal-only focus on scriptural content); (The foundation of the Holy City consisted of 144 stones in twelve rows);

145: having an inner sense of wholeness and completeness;

146: having a healthy respect for esoteric truths and metaphorical perspectives;

147: acting with authentegrity and honesty in all of our dealings;

148: seeing the scientific method as a legitimate search for the truth, but also respecting our personal experiences and revelations as equally valid indicators of what is real;

149: seeing our skin school experiences as only one part of our overall spiritual growth;

150: recognizing the difference between absolute and relative realities;

151: being faithful to a given tradition of spiritual and/or religious values;

152: seeing masculinity as only one of our internal compasses, with femininity as the other;

153: striving to be in complete harmony with the Trinity of Trinities; (Our super-conscious awareness is limitless in its capacity to comprehend the Infinite, the One Reality, the Eternal Isness, Divine Mind because we have moved beyond any notion of duality and separation);

154: curbing our narcissistic tendencies because we realize we are still works in progress;

155: seeing a negativity bias for what it is, distrust in our own innate talents and skills and lack of faith in our indivisibleness with the Eternal Presence;

156: believing that charitable giving is a necessary condition for enlightenment;

157: recognizing that while our body is our biological address our consciousness is our permanent home;

158: realizing that an unhealthy ego is the poster child for close-mindedness;

159: discovering that religion is embedded in the amygdala while spirituality is enveloped in the neocortex;

160: being absolutely convinced that meditation is a form of medication;

161: seeing fashions and fads as materialistic distractions;

162: our penchant for expecting the best possible outcome for any given situation;

163: believing that the allness of the Infinite Isness is in the eachness of us;

164: recognizing that chronic passivity is akin to trying to run to second base with our foot on first base;

165: seeing insincere self-abasement as sham modesty;

166: growing into the awareness that omnipresence, omnipotence, omniscience, and omni-activity are only aspects of the Eternal Presence according to our limited understanding of the Whole as parts of the Whole;

167: being willing to release anything that no longer contributes to our health and wholeness;

168: seeing the value in having more willpower than won't power;

169: acknowledging spiritual teachings as a form of higher education;

170: believing that our optimistic spirit is based on an inner knowing that the universe is wired in our behalf;

171: knowing that perfectionism is protectionism in its pathological expression;

172: seeing a lack of confidence as a form of idolatry because it puts the world of outer appearances ahead of our connection with our innate divinity;

173: viewing entrenched dogma as rebelliousness and stubbornness that block our growing edge;

174: coming to know that seeing an anthropomorphic god in the sky is idolatry;

175: seeing metaphysics and quantum physics as kissing cousins;

176: realizing that the 'ruts' we find ourselves in from time-to-time are 'rigid unyielding thinking' that slow our progress;

177: not confusing our self-worth with our net worth;

178: seeing each incarnational and/or reincarnational experience as a growth experience;

179: not being shy about sharing metaphysical truths;

180: knowing that a giving consciousness is in our spiritual DNA;

181: believing that what we call heaven and hell are simply states of consciousness that we possess in whatever dimension of being we find ourselves;

182: seeing vengeance, vendettas, and violence as the underbellies of the human condition;

183: recognizing the value – and necessity – of applying the truth principles we know;

184: seeing error thoughts as insurgents and intruders;

185: showing a strong inclination to 'practice the Presence' everyday through meditation and affirmative prayer;

186: taking grumpiness, sourness, and cheerlessness out of our vocabulary;

187: our ability to act rightly in the face of popular opposition to our being more spiritual than religious;

188: not being combative when it comes to engaging in conversations with religious fundamentalists;

189: seeing apathy and indifference as deterrents to our spiritual growth;

190: apprehending that the Christ Principle as the Eternal Presence in physicality, has two complementary aspects; (One aspect takes the form of physical entities (humans, animals, plants, rocks, insects, etc.) that have a conscious mind that changes and varies at the slightest stimulus that presents itself. The other aspect is the soul-ized divine energy (blood) which is the outflow of the vital force of the Godhead;

191: realizing that we are the universe becoming more conscious of itself;

192: recognizing we can divinely order our experiences by applying the truth principles we know;

193: seeing diversity as unity in disguise;

194: denotes our tendency to stay focused when we immerse ourselves in highly complex spiritual material;

195: denotes our ability to be discreet when we are around people who have not studied and/or are not interested in higher esoteric teachings;

196: having trust in our ability to prosper in spite of outer appearances to the contrary;

197: denotes our commitment to spiritual growth and exploration;

198: having perfect vision on the astral plane;

199: our earthly passions having been subdued, we have little to no difficulty mastering our human experience;

200: an ingrained tendency toward duality, opposites, and polarities;

201: realizing we are both the observer and the observed;

202: becoming adept at balancing and integrating our maleness and femaleness;

203: recognizing that successfully crossing out error is a prerequisite for our continuing unfoldment;

204: seeing our idiosyncrasies as part of our connecting the dots toward Selfhood;

205: seeing every cell, each molecule, each atom as a sacred tabernacle of Spirit; (These sacred tabernacles are connected. There is no denominational sparing. Their biology is their theology. When we realize the significance of this invisible connection we will honor the human soul's relationship to Spirit. When we acknowledge this connection, from soul to cell, our body becomes the highly-charged sacred ground of our being. When we achieve this perfect synchrony we experience the inner peace, joy, health, and wholeness which are the truth of us);

206: recognizing that duality and separation are human inventions;

207: knowing that everything that has form has its origin in Spirit;

208: intuiting that matter is frozen Spirit;

209: our capacity for successfully combining theory and practice;

210: realizing that the Multiverse is one of many 'mansions' in Cosmic Consciousness;

211: knowing that once a myth becomes dogma, it loses its capacity to enlighten and inspire;

212: recognizing we have spent many incarnations and/or reincarnations on the earth plane;

213: sensing that dogma is the principle vice of mainstream religions;

214: the awareness that religions which sell fear, shame, and guilt are based in the amygdala, keeping people in darkness instead of in the light;

215: the willingness to shed inadequate perceptions of what God is and what God is not;

216: realizing that the argument for a material god creating a material universe can only take us in circles the size of a pin head;

217: obtaining a full awareness that few material things are really necessary for joy, prosperity, and happiness;

218: realizing that our Innermost Self is the Cosmic Christ as the Planetary Christ as us in human form;

219: realizing our subconscious must become conscious, and our conscious must become super-conscious if we are collectively going to master the human experience;

220: recognizing that when mainstream religions marry traditional theology with metaphysics and quantum physics we will have returned to our mystical roots;

221: knowing that our prosperity flows from the inside out, and that if we believe it comes from outside of us we've gotten the direction wrong;

222: denotes our ability to know that at the unmanifest, quantum level, nothing is ever lost, only transformed;

223: coming to the realization that duality is really do-ality reduced to its material form;

224: recognizing that beginnings and endings are human constructs because we insist on believing in duality;

225: realizing that the God of the limbic system is a frightening God, but the God of the anterior cingulate is Love Itself;

226: having the awareness that fasting, from a higher perspective, is fasting from error;

227: reaching the realization that we are the mirror as well as the face in it;

228: the ability to release our skepticism about the value of spiritual perspectives;

229: believing in the power of our visualizations;

230: knowing that all of us have at least a pinch of eccentricity;

231: seeing the importance in letting our inner child out;

232: consistently seeing the Christ (Buddha, Allah, Krishna, etc.) in others;

233: knowing that a little frivolity is good for the soul;

234: understanding that our theology is mirrored in our biology;

235: recognizing that, in a very real sense, unconventional theology is mainstream theology;

236: realizing that our best, brightest, most prodigious thinking is only an approximation of the way things are;

237: our strong disposition toward knowing that time we affirm our "I-Am-ness" with the Universal Presence we strengthen neural connections in our neocortex;

238: realizing that once our spiritual awareness is expanded we can't unexpand it;

239: recognizing that our five physical senses confirm our world view;

240: recognizing that one of our ultimate achievements will not be establishing a tranquility base on the moon or on Mars, but within us;

241: intuiting that to continue to believe in a limited view of sacred scripture and not know that it is a limited perspective is unrecognized suffering. (It happens to be one of the most debilitating forms of mainstream religious practice);

242: feeling a compunction to develop our psychic abilities;

243: seeing nothing fundamental in religious fundamentalism;

244: sensing that the 'volume control' of our beliefs is usually determined by our reactions to life experiences mediated by the amount of influence significant people have on our lives. (If we're not careful religious beliefs fall under that form of mass indoctrination and the 'fever pitch' is usually deafening);

245: discovering that when people let their Christ Lights shine they emit a luminescence that can be seen by those on the receiving end of their inner radiance;

246: understanding that pleasant thoughts, positive inclinations, sitting meditations, and affirmative prayers are all dopamine triggers. (Dopamine, the pleasure chemical, is produced when we see the world as a safe, life-enriching experience);

247: knowing that when we *rust* in our connection with our innate divinity instead of *trust* in our divine connection we limit our spiritual growth and put a damper on working things together for good

248: recognizing that what we call the "self" is the ego's rendition of our human self which is the product, quantumly speaking, of a tangled hierarchy;

249: realizing all dogmatic beliefs are "walled beliefs" which are filled with smidgeons of false assumptions, pinches of inaccuracies, and light touches of misconceptions concerning the nature of things;

250: seeing ourselves as more spiritual than religious;

251: knowing that consciousness is not an epiphenomenal effect of biology;

252: realizing that what the majority of people call 'death' refers to the discontinuation (emancipation) of our flesh and blood physical bodies from physicality;

253: coming to terms with the realization that the abject refusal and adamant disbelief in concepts such as God, angels, original blessing, absolute good, and metaphysical truths cause significant cognitive dissonance in the frontal lobe. (Such strongly held resistance makes it extremely difficult for those who bury themselves in disbelief to have a spiritual or mystical experience. Such disbelief creates an unfortunate neurological barrier that will most likely require many lifetimes to dissolve the dissonance);

254: believing we are God stuff becoming conscious of our God stuffness;

255: knowing fully well that finding spiritual truths in a haystack of religious dogma takes discernment, determination, and discrimination;

256: becoming aware that the unenlightened ego and an anthropomorphic God concept reinforce each other's otherness;

257: using our power of discernment to discover that the very idea of a spiritual path, or truth walk is misleading. (Both focus on the idea of futurity, on something that has physical distance. Enlightenment, the Kingdom of God, is readily accessible NOW! All we have to do is awaken from our illusion of separation and duality);

258: our recognition that the God of our understanding is an eternal, timeless, limitless, universal Presence that underwrites all that is;

259: seeing the punitive, revengeful, anthropomorphic god of the *Hebrew Testament* as a limbic God, the God of our primitive reptilian brain;

260: discovering that our egoic self-awareness is the localized version of our nonlocal, unitive cosmic consciousness which is available to us through intense meditation and spiritual practice;

261: denotes our ability to comprehend that using God's name in vain and cursing the Eternal Presence when things don't go as we want are the kind of *tongfu* that will delay our enlightenment;

262: represents our recognition that there are parts of us that are over 15 billion years old and areas that are nanoseconds old. (We are comprised of stardust and God essence);

263: denotes our ability to 'get' that graven images are Self-negating attitudes and beliefs that we carve into our consciousness;

264: believing that acts of kindness, prayers, positive affirmations, and hugs have halos over them. (If you pay close enough attention you can see them);

265: undergoing a change in consciousness that recognizes that those who are oblivious to their divine 'hologramness' are running around as 'hollow movements' without any real appreciation of their oneness with Spirit;

266: recognizing that there are many levels of Biblical interpretation, many perspectives, many shades of meaning in everything we think, do, and say;

267: realizing that health concerns and illnesses are only footnotes, not chapter titles in our lives;

268: discovering that what the majority of people call 'death' is the passage of a limited human form into one or another of its higher vibratory essences;

269: recognizing that our value is priceless and that our potential is unlimited;

270: denotes the recognition that we can be God expressing or God repressing;

271: fully realizing that there is no gray area when it comes to accepting our divine nature. (According to the best minds in neuroscience there are no neuro-receptors that distinguish gradations of gray);

272: realizing that we are localized 'islands' of 'nonlocal' consciousness;

273: discovering that the longest trip we will ever take, the most lengthy journey upon which we will embark, is the spiritual journey toward Selfhood. (This 'journey' is not a point A to point B journey in physical space, but a higher consciousness journey in inner space);

274: coming to the realization that we are frozen Light. (That is, we are Light expressing itself as dense matter in the form of us);

275: having the absolute conviction that total dependence on dogma is awfulizing scripture;

276: coming into an awareness that we begin each incarnation with the 'karmic baggage' of many previous lifetimes; (Our brains come equipped with the neural real estate to draw from that 'karmic bank' of experience whatever we think we need to understand the current world in which we find ourselves, particularly since each present skin school experience is an attempt to discover who we really are);

277: the astute realization that every obstacle and challenge in life is a 'take home' quiz. (The *home*, of course, is the spiritual sanctuary within us called the Kingdom of God);

278: achieving the awareness that to believe in incurable dis-eases is to elevate the amygdala to god status;

279: the recognition that our human self is but a quantum phase of our Spiritual Self. (Much like a wave – large or small, lengthy or abbreviated – is merely an aspect of an ocean, both the self and the wave are conditional states of being. Each enjoys a span of temporal beingness before it returns to its greater, more transcendent beingness);

280: knowing that the ego's awareness is the small "s" self-awareness;

281: realizing that our consciousness determines our beingness: our denseness or airiness, ephemeralness or enduringness. (When we leave this vibration we call the physical us (the human us), we will move on as another impermanent version of us in another dimension of being. How long we remain as the next version of us depends on our level of awareness and our purposefulness in that particular dimension of being);

282: coming to understand that mainstream religions have turned the wise men into wise guys and tried to kill the true meaning of Christmas;

283: discerning that intense meditation may be one of the "doors" into the many mansions (states of higher awareness) the Christ as Jesus assured us are readily available to us;

284: the recognition that there is no parochialism in metaphysics;

285: realizing that we are the One Presence showing up as us in human form;

286: denotes our full knowledge of our consciousness as borderless container of enlightenment;

287: coming into the awareness that the reason traditional neuroscientists cannot explain how a nonmaterial mind can rise from mere biological functions is because 'mere biological functions' arise from the mind; (Our biology, you see, is the effect of mind action);

288: grasping that perhaps one of the sources for so much violence, unrest, and greed in the world is that we have misspelled "one" by spelling it "won";

289: denotes our newfound awareness that the curvature of dogma is so deafeningly circular and filled with such critical myopic mass that it constantly implodes upon itself;

290: recognizing that our next dimension of being will be consistent with our level of spiritual ripening in the previous dimension;

291: apprehending that practicing the Presence requires a distraction-free consciousness.

292: comprehending that the practice of praying to an external, anthropomorphic God "out there" perpetuates the illusion of our separation from Source;

293: discovering that we have the opportunity with every thought, word, and action to realign (vibrate in phase) our human self with our Christ Self;

294: coming to terms with the human failing that whenever we worry about finances, fret over the news, complain about politics, blame others for our troubles, or are fearful about our own health and well-being we are bowing down to the graven images we have created;

295: the belief that the Eternal Presence, the Infinite Isness, God, Ein Sof, the One, Divine Mind – cannot be packaged in anthropomorphic terms;

296: our conviction that as long as the embers of an anthropomorphic god or devil in the sky are fanned by dogma the relevance of mainstream Christianity will continue to erode;

297: realizing that what the majority of humankind calls 'death' is the exiting release from our incarnational human-ness into a more expanded cosmic existence – an existence that has become accustomed to many iterations as we unfold into the next version of us);

298: discovering that we are the total spiritual package who doesn't know we are the total spiritual package

299: recognizing that our skin school experiences are somatic apprenticeships. (For some, leaving skin school is a graduation – it signals the end of a limited state of awareness into a higher, more profound, level of consciousness, making the earth experience no longer necessary for soul progression. For others, transitioning out of a 'skin school' experience means there will be more – many more – 'skin school' experiences based on the quality of awareness the particular soul possesses. In each dimension of our being we are held there by the gravity of our spiritual awareness);

300: mastering the ability to cross out error by divinely ordering the experiences we want by right of consciousness;

301: intuiting that a sense of oneness requires seeing beyond labels and boundaries;

302: having the awareness that compromising our mental, physical, emotional, and spiritual health dampens our ability to consciously become one with the One;

303: grasping that most people confuse 'reel-ality' with reality; (That is, most people replay their old self-defeating tapes like 'B' movies, keeping them stuck in the reincarnational merry-go-round);

304: the deep realization that our quantum selves (our incarnated selves) are strung like beads on a thread of quantum nonlocality;

305: becoming clearly aware that dogmatic thoughts, belief in the inerrancy of scripture, and the mindless worship of literal interpretations of sacred scripture are cathedrals of illusion;

306: recognizing that mainstream religions champion duality and separation – we are 'here' and God is 'there' wherever 'there' is;

307: grasping the truth that a life lived on the basis of an unenlightened ego's whims is a life riding on a carousel of dysfunction;

308: discovering that a dogmatic mindset, lack of physical exercise, anger, and religious myopia are all egocentric distractions that keep us off center and out of balance;

309: apprehending that satan is a fig Newton of our imagination;

310: recognizing that each 'death' experience is a lifting of the veil of illusion. (Whether we reincarnate into a human form again or incarnate into a new dimension of higher beingness, our life task will be to become consciously aware of who we really are – the One Presence expressing Itself as us);

311: understanding that our cells, atoms, and molecules are conscious beings;

312: recognizing that our physical bodies serve as our somatic 'space suits' for each incarnational experience;

313: seeing that we must plumb the depths of ourselves and repot ourselves as often as necessary, so that we can allow the Infinite Us to help the finite us matriculate through the human experience with as much grace and poise and purposefulness as possible;

314: realizing that spiritual and religious sophistry will get us nowhere, that we must always be open to honest and genuine New Thought inquiry;

315: electing to expand our thinking past the literal interpretations of our particular faith tradition so we can soar into the esoterical and metaphysical "cloud of knowing" that will someday revolutionize human thought and raise our collective human consciousness to its highest spiritual octave;

316: coming into the awareness that God (the Eternal Isness, Absolute Good, the One Reality) manifests [so loved] Itself as the Cosmic Christ [Only Begotten Son] in human (Adamic) consciousness [the world], and whosoever comes into that Christed awareness [believeth] will move beyond the illusion of separation and duality [will not die] and shall attain Christhood [eternal life];

317: recognizing that there is no dividing line between the universe and us, because we are the universe expressing itself as us through the Christ Vibration;

318: grasping clearly that 'intention deficit disorder (IDD) can block our spiritual growth;

319: the deep realization that each incarnation is an evolutionary installment (the next phase or version) of the quantum self (that which is the composite of all of our past and concurrent selves);

320: recognizing that the light of dogmatic lampposts keeps many people in the dark;

321: understanding that worry, guilt, shame, and doubt have no nutritional value;

322: comprehending that our consciousness is the true lottery, and that we can manifest what we want to manifest by right of consciousness;

323: realizing that things and events in and of themselves do not bless us, but that we are blessed by the choices we make as responses to those things and events;

324: discerning that once we get away from the superficial 'digs' of pediatric religious studies, our excavations into our evolving spiritual consciousness become more mature and expansive, propelling us toward a new era of spiritual, not religious, growth;

325: comprehending that our human incarnations can be numbing experiences. (We go 'numb' because it's the soul's way of dealing with another skin school experience);

326: coming upon the deep understanding that mainstream religion has aimed too low, that it continues to sell fear, guilt and shame as its "trinity of control" to bully believers into conformity, submission and mindless fiscal obedience;

327: recognizing the great truth that as spiritual beings we created the universe as a safety net to catch our fall from grace; (The Buddhists call this safety net the Net of Indra. The Hopi Indians call it the Spider Grandmother's Web);

328: coming into the awareness that there is no need for us to look 'out there' for a Super Hero because there is a Super Hero within us waiting to be unleashed;

329: having enough life experiences to know that we will not achieve what we want to achieve, be what we want to be, and do what we believe we are put here to do until we get in sync with our Core Essence;

330: a deep knowing that we keep forgetting ourselves into another incarnation;

331: recognizing that our spiritual understanding must always be a step ahead of our technology;

332: comprehending that divine ideas [children] do not come from the human personality but from the Kingdom of God [Christ Consciousness] within us;

333: reaching the cosmic understanding that the same Christ Presence that incarnated as Jesus, Buddha, Krishna, Joan of Arc, Geoffrey Hodson, Albert Einstein, Alice Bailey, Charles and Myrtle Fillmore, Thich Nhat Hanh, Emma Curtis Hopkins, the Dali Lama, Corinne Heline, Billy Graham, and John and Jane Doe, etc. is the same Christ Presence that incarnates as each and everyone of us, in any time and in any dimension of being;

334: the understanding that the ubiquitous Christ Presence underwrites all beingness, including human beingness which is generally unaware of its innate divinity;

335: realizing that our intellectual perception of Truth [our John the Baptizer quality] is a necessary prerequisite for the expanding awareness of our divine origin. (In our illumined awareness, the Jesus of us, we understand that we are embodied Christs. It is this Perennial Quality which underwrites our very existence);

336: coming to know clearly that our human personality is a facade, a mask, a cosmetic cover-up. It is not who we really are. (We eventually realize that our intellect is only a soul song in our Christogenesis);

337: recognizing that corrosive, negative thoughts, intentions, and inclinations are ballast and the self-defeating habits that are housed in our sub-consciousness continue to weigh us down, producing a thought universe mired in surplus thoughts we can do without;

338: discerning that we must trust the urges and promptings of our divinely-charged interior energies which receive their vibrancy from Spirit;

339: knowing that our inborn superior intuitive receptivity prepares our body, mind, and soul for their sacrosanct unfoldment;

340: having the astute awareness that we must opt for spiritual growth over religious parochialism. (Our theology must seek to outgrow dogmatism, demolish all dualisms, transcend all human conceptual limitations, and pursue an expanded cosmic awareness that honors our mystical and metaphysical roots);

341: the awareness that our consciousness is filled with as many discordant materialistic thoughts as there are spiritually-oriented thoughts;

342: coming into the realization that the fusion of enlightened thoughts and stale belief systems causes an internal emotional combustion which sends specks and flecks of our ego's insecurities to the surface, uprooting our materialistic tendencies and our dependence solely on man-made solutions dissolved;

343: coming into the awareness that there is a tendency within us, our fundamental religious perspective to cling to encrusted theological biases and dogmas that can define our over-all religious outlook if we're not careful;

344: having made the decision that meditation, affirmative prayer, visualization, positive affirmations, personal introspection, right eating, scientific and metaphysical studies – all form the *prima materia* of our truth walks;

345: recognizing that aligning ourselves with our Christ Self through visualization, meditation, affirmative prayer, positive affirmations, spiritual study, a consciousness of giving, and eternal optimism are all important stops on our truth triptych;

346: having developed the full recognition that error perpetuates error;

347: the ability to consistently revitalize our thought universe by filling our sub-consciousness, consciousness, and super-consciousness with Christed thoughts, insights, and ideas;

348: having grown into a level of spiritual maturity where toxic thoughts and bleaching beliefs which can contaminate our higher consciousness are forced out before they compromise our spiritual growth;

349: coming to understand that our illumined intellect [our John the Baptizer quality] is only capable of cleansing [baptizing] error thoughts out of our current consciousness;

350: the deep realization that our dreams, *deja vous*, and past life regressions are conscious nonlocal recollections of our 'other' selves (beads) on the thread of the interconnectedness of life expressing Itself as us;

351: recognizing that when we resolutely strive toward our Christhood [believe in the Son] we shall attain Christ Consciousness [eternal life], but, if we choose to remain attached to sense pleasures and material addictions [reject the Son] we will delay our Christhood [will not see life] until we suffer through what has been described as the dark night of the soul (the process of overcoming our sense attachments). [This purging process (karmic matriculation) is called the wrath of God];

352: grasping that the truth of the matter is, when we depend only on the intellect's *gnosis* [drink from man-made wells] we will not comprehend hidden Truths [remain thirsty];

353: understanding that when we apply the truth principles we know our entire consciousness will be revitalized with the transformative amperage of Spirit which will lead to our eventual Christship [eternal life];

354: grasping on a deep emotional level that a sense-veneered intellect is incapable of providing spiritual wisdom;

355: grasping the timeless truth that we are the Eternal Tree leafing Itself as us in human form;

356: recognizing that our spiritual unfoldment depends on our willingness to allow the healing flow of divine ideas from our super-conscious reservoir of ideas to penetrate our conscious and subconscious filters;

357: apprehending that by centering ourselves in the peace which passes all *mis*understanding we create a psychic channel for Christed thoughts to bathe our senses with healing (wholing) energies;

358: the ability to have moved beyond the embedded theology of religious fiefdoms which seem content with selling a punitive, vengeful, goodie God 'out there';

359: attaining the full recognition that if our consciousness is not grounded in Spirit our sense-veneered thoughts [infirmities] will not be able to correct the disequilibrium caused by such infirmed thinking; (Consequently, we quarantine ourselves from the quantum field [pool] of divine ideas);

360: apprehending the deep knowing that each time we affirm our wholeness and oneness with our Extraordinary Nature we establish the inner harmonics it takes to unite body, mind, and spirit. (This *at-one-ment* which recognizes the unity between our *self* with our *Self* is simply one thought, one intention, one choice away);

361: the realization that as we continue to grow spiritually, stale religious beliefs will surface which deny our divine heirship. (These thoughts spring from an unenlightened and paranoid us who not only fears a spiritually alive mindset but is traumatized at the prospect of our coming to the realization that we are the Cosmic Christ expressing at the point of us;

362: coming to the realization that we must elevate our consciousness from its Adamic, sense-soaked state to its higher super-conscious orbit;

363: seeing that when we truly understand who we really are we will elevate our awareness to a spiritually alive state of consciousness instead of settling for a materially wasted state of consciousness;

364: having reached a more mature spiritual perspective we realize that as we continue to raise our spiritual awareness all twelve of our spiritual faculties will become so enriched that our physical senses will become enriched as well;

365: recognizing that affirmations are conformations not causative agents;

366: understanding that if we depend only on our human abilities, no matter how resourceful or creative they may be, we will fail to appreciate the power of our actualized Christ potential to elevate us above negativity;

367: realizing that our unfolding Christ Consciousness (eternal life) depends on our ability and interest in discerning Truth from error;

368: apprehending that our innate *spiritual wiring* is our birthright and comes from the Christ of us;

369: recognizing that until we fully embrace the Truth of our Indwelling Christ Self we will tend to look for evidence 'out there' instead of experiencing the transformative energies within;

370: reaching a stage in our spiritual unfoldment where we have gotten past looking for spiritual sustenance (manna) through old egocentric filters which have kept our spirituality arid and sterile;

371: coming to the awareness that we do not draw Universal Substance *to* us because it comes *through* us;

372: grasping the truth that we must remind ourselves that we are the Christ expressing at the point of us;

373: recognizing that satisfying our spiritual curiosity from an intellectual standpoint instead of experiencing the spiritually-charged transformative effects that come from *practicing the Presence* is a dumb program;

374: 'getting' that it is the Cosmic Christ which underwrites our physical existence so that we can comprehend eternal truths (the bread of life);

375: grasping the eternal truth that whenever we center ourselves in prayer and become consciously one with the Christ Presence within us we will move toward attaining Christ Consciousness [eternal life] and receive clemency for our pre-Christed error-prone thoughts and actions;

376: becoming completely honest with ourselves that we must not seek to satisfy overly-consumptive material appetites but strive instead to understand universal truths;

377: discovering that when we actualize our Christhood (as Jesus did) we will discover that we are flesh and blood expressions (quantum editions) of Eternal Truths (the bread of life);

378: the recognition that we must move beyond the inertia of mortal consciousness;

379: knowing that eternal truths are spiritual *food* and conscious realization of our divinity is an enlightened drink;

380: realizing that there is no shortcut to enlightenment;

381: having complete trust and an abiding faith that our *indivisibleness* with the Cosmic Christ is an eternal truth;

382: knowing that when we religiously follow eternal truths we will spiritually arrive at our destination;

383: apprehending that we hamper our spiritual growth by remaining unaware that the Cosmic Christ is God [the Father, the Infinite Invisibleness, the Absolute)] expressing Itself in physicality as the Cosmic Christ;

384: realizing that, much too often, we simply intellectualize our *heirship* instead of feeling it from a body, mind, and soul perspective;

385: knowing that because of the nature of our physicality (having chosen human form and, thus, subject to the temptations of human experience) we will need to discipline ourselves to master the human experience;

386: apprehending that our adeptship is purely an inside-out process;

387: comprehending, from a deep level, that if we look for spiritual sustenance (manna) through old, stale belief systems we will miss underlying eternal truths;

388: realizing that our journey to become a fully accomplished Christ is a journey of disciplined volition;

389: recognizing that when we truly comprehend Universal Truths, we will want to learn, and then apply, truth principles that help us expand our spiritual awareness;

390: fully grasping that sometimes we allow a sense-addicted ego (our Adamic Consciousness) and its protégé, an unenlightened intellect, to prevent us from comprehending our *indivisibleness* with our Christ Nature;

391: discovering that as we become more spiritually inclined some of our thoughts may be the result of a clairvoyant capacity; (We sense there is more to us than mere flesh and blood);

392: coming into the astute awareness that as we attempt to sort out our divine heritage, especially our Messiahship, we realize that, at our core essence, we have been anointed at birth with the Allness of the Eternal Isness (God, the One Reality) *indivisibilized* as us;

393: recognizing that as we continue to expand our spiritual awareness we will have many opportunities to transform stale thoughts and beliefs into their highly attuned spiritual counterparts;

394: having moved past our ambivalence about our divine nature so that we don't doubt our divine genogram;

395: realizing that it is our own dogmatic tendencies which limit our openness and teach-ability;

396: having gotten really good at catching the nuances of Spirit;

397: knowing that if we continue to orphan ourselves from our innate divinity we will fail to actualize our Christ Individuality;

398: recognizing that our next Christed thought, Christed choice, or Christed action can elevate us to a greater awareness of our eventual illumination;

399: having moved beyond a 'letter of the law' religiosity;

400: the fully-integrated four aspects of our being (spiritual, mental, emotional, and physical);

401: our impeccable ability to discern truth from error;

402: recognizing that our Christ potential [the Jesus of us] permeates every fiber of our being, bathing our consciousness with Its presiding tactility and grace;

403: discovering that our descent into human form is fused with divine energies which come from the unlimited and perpetually expansive spiritual substance of God essence;

404: not doubting for a moment that our Christ potential fills our consciousness with its high voltage presence;

405: recognizing that eternal truths (bread) are essentially spiritual laws expressed in their quantum forms which can be expressed through disciplined practice to elevate our consciousness;

406: believing we can transcend any and all human limitations;

407: knowing that our worldly appetites will keep us from hearing the 'still small voice' and its wise guidance;

408: realizing that those perspectives which are still the products of sense-sludge will have to be transformed into their higher spiritual essences through disciplined study and faithful actions;

409: reaching an intentional practice of filling our consciousness with spiritual thoughts and inclinations;

410: understanding that it will take the formative power of faith to help us move beyond sense entrapments;

411: knowing that it is our self-aggrandizing nature that springs from a purely acquisitive, selfish, overly-ambitious side of us that is prone to compromise our spiritual growth;

412: apprehending fully that the Good Shepherd (Eternal Isness, God, the Infinite Invisibleness, the One Reality) embodies Itself in human form [lays down its life] to raise our thoughts [sheep] to their highest spiritual essences;

413: perceiving that if we remain influenced by an error-oriented ego we may consider any thought of our divine heirship as disrespectful [blasphemous] of the ego's sovereignty;

414: understanding that the knowledge of our *indivisibleness* with the Eternal Isness (God, the One Reality, the Absolute) takes a leap in faith;

415: knowing full well that a material consciousness is not the kind of *soil* which brings enlightenment;

416: realizing that our adeptship gets its vibrancy from an interior connection to Spirit and not from external sense attachments;

417: understanding that thoughts produced by a sense-soaked ego deny the expression of any spiritual thoughts, preferring mortal appetites to spiritual attunement;

418: apprehending that, although we re-embody with our higher spiritual faculties in tact at a super-conscious level of awareness, we tend to forget we are spiritual beings having another human experience;

419: recognizing that if our current belief system is framed around encrusted religious beliefs and biases it will be difficult for us to receive Christed ideas;

420: realizing that our reincarnational experiences are not necessary conditions for enlightenment;

421: having reached a level of understanding that knows our material attachments (horizontal missteps) keep us vertically (spiritually) challenged;

422: knowing that our spirit-filled thoughts invariably operate at a higher obit than earth-bound thoughts coming from the ego;

423: realizing that the hard, rigid, materialistic beliefs and biases produced by a recalcitrant ego will never bring us the clarity we need;

424: being mature enough not to allow a cattle drive of materialistic thoughts [thieves and robbers] to form outposts in our mind;

425: recognizing that until we mature in our spirituality there may be times when rudimentary inclinations demonstrate our impatience in forcing greater expressions of the divine powers we believe we have;

426: understanding that consciousness, not matter, is the ground of all being;

427: becoming mindfully aware that a worldly ego is very good at keeping Christed thoughts out of a spiritually quarantined consciousness;

428: recognizing that despite its neglect, our Christ potential remains the foundation of our physical, mental, and spiritual health;

429: sensing there is that within us, a superior inner knowledge, which 'documents' who we are but we fail to see the casual relationship between our current error thinking [sins] and our previous incarnational baggage [negative karma];

430: knowing without a doubt that, by its very nature, our Christ potential equips our consciousness with the powers of discernment and discrimination [judgment] to see rightly;

431: realizing that from our old, sense-veneered perspectives we are clueless as to how spirited ideas originate;

432: knowing, without a doubt, that nothing is lost in Spirit;

433: discovering that when our openness is genuine our Christ potential can be released;

434: understanding that sometimes we get so caught up in our devotion to service that we neglect to recharge our spiritual batteries;

435: recognizing that when we raise our awareness to the Christ Standard we shall attain Christhood (eternal life) and move beyond any and all limitations associated with the particular incarnation in which we find ourselves;

436: realizing that each time we actualize our Christ potential we literally bring to life the dormant vital forces that are instrumental in raising our energies to their Christed vibrations;

437: discovering that until we have fully embraced our divine nature we tend to let newly formed, spiritually-charged ideas fend for themselves in a spiritually anorexic materialistic consciousness;

438: understanding that we are usually limited by a thin veil of intellectual awakening as we grapple with our divine potential;

439: knowing that when we seek truth, even though we initially fail to see our divine connection, we will gain the clarity we need to fully demonstrate our divinity;

440: realizing that we have opportunities in each re-embodiment to discover our innate divinity and unfold into our Christhood;

441: recognizing that we must transform our rudimentary sense perceptions into refined spiritual insights;

442: having the courage to express our Christ Nature each-consecutive-moment-of-now;

443: discovering that the longer we remain calcified in cosmetic theology and unduly influenced by the world of appearances we will find it difficult, if not impossible, to see the *indivisible* connection between Spirit and matter;

444: completely grasping that a fully Christed life is our divine birthright;

445: our ability to be fully aware that from the viewpoint of our fossilized ego it is better to deny any possibility of our Christ potential than allow the thoughts of our divine heirship to supplant a materially-fixated consciousness;

446: recognizing that if our truth walk is not underwritten by faith our Christ potential will not unfold;

447: discerning clearly that there is a difference between the faith that knows and the desire to know, which is *wishcraft*;

448: having the distinct awareness that in the totality of the Eternal Isness' quantum and cosmic beingness (Father's house) there are many levels of awareness or states of being (rooms/mansions);

449: knowing that when we peripheralize (deny) our divinity and remain attached to materiality, we remain oblivious [blind] to the spiritual principles that can set us free from the gravitational pull of error;

450: fully recognizing that the ego, with its knothole perspective, is unable to comprehend even a brief intermezzi of enlightenment;

451: being consciously aware that we must not be surprised to find that encrusted dogmatic views and deep-seated religious biases may surface from time-to-time;

452: despite our focus on outer forms of spiritual growth we have a growing sense in the inviolate omnipresence of Spirit (God, the One Reality, the Absolute);

453: recognizing the transparency and malleability of the physical universe to gain the clarity we need to remember our spiritual origins;

454: understanding that once we surrender to our Christ Nature and demonstrate our trust and faith in the transformative powers of our Christ potential, a deeper understanding [feet] and ability to craft [hands] a Christed outlook will go a long way toward the necessary reformation of our ego personality;

455: knowing that the foundation of our evolving Christhood is firmly set within us from birth;

456: recognizing that when we fully attain our Christhood, as did Jesus, we will obtain conscious *indivisibility* with the Cosmic Christ [the Way], God [the Truth] and the Holy Spirit [the Life];

457: discerning that the quality and maturity of our faith determine our readiness to move from one *cusp of consciousness* to another;

458: understanding that there is an egocentric part of us that worships the sensory accouterments of religious practice and the material world and refuses to leave its hedonic perch (our Adamistic penchant), favoring materiality over spirituality;

459: seeing that it is through our conscious connection with the embodied Cosmic Christ (the Only Begotten Son) that we are able to attain conscious oneness with the One Reality;

460: attaining the incredible truth that the self of us which remembers our past lives and concurrent lives in other dimensions of being is our Quantum Self, the composite of all of our human and intra-dimensional incarnations;

461: the ability to imagine what we could accomplish as a global society of practicing Christs;

462: coming into the understanding that when we recognize our unity with all life it is the out-formation of our clarity of vision and the ability to rise above old patterns of thought;

463: discerning that when we are faith-conditioned and add to that the spiritual capital of a disciplined and reverential Truth walk, we will achieve an extraordinarily high level of awareness which will make it possible for us to exceed anything we could ever have accomplished at the level of the ego personality;

464: the recognition that when we achieve a Christed awareness we will be able to harness the incredible power of the vital energies which emanate from the inner fire [Holy Spirit, Counselor, Advocate] within us;

465: having the knowledge that our disciplined adherence to divine principles makes it possible for us to harmonize (love) our human self and Christ Self;

466: recognizing that divine laws are readily available to us, but their absorption and receptivity depend on how attached we are to material appetites;

367: coming to terms with the realization that sense consciousness [the world] is so rooted in matter that it is oblivious to any connection we have with our Spiritual Essence;

368: being fully aware that we can call forth the serpentine energies (the Advocate, Counselor, Fire Spirit, *kundalini*, Holy Spirit) which lie latent within us waiting for expression at any moment;

469: apprehending that when our ego consciousness is fully Christed, our thoughts are in alignment with our Christ Nature and raise any and all unquickened spiritual thoughts to their higher vibrations;

470: having learned that by our very thoughts, words, and actions we either affirm our innate divinity or mock it;

471: understanding that if we are inconsistent in aligning our ego personality with our Christ Individuality we may compromise our Christ potential by giving into sense attachments, particularly those which are covetous and overly consumptive;

472: we have gotten to the point in our spiritual growth where the belief in duality and separation is no longer part of our consciousness;

473: recognizing that those perspectives and beliefs which we truly want to elevate depend on our desire to raise them to their higher spiritual essences;

474: unfolding into our Christ-likeness on three levels of consciousness: the super-conscious, subconscious, and our waking conscious;

475: perceiving that when we are in absolute and total sync with our Christ Nature there is no consciousness of separation between our Christed Self and our emotional, mental, physical, and spiritual selves;

476: realizing that unless we have highly developed qualities of discernment and spiritual intuition, there is that within us which denies our divinity and clings to such a belief in lack that it covets materiality over spiritual growth;

477: coming into the awareness that no matter how illumined we may think we are, the struggle to erase the staining effects of error (betrayal by our aggrandizing Judasness) will occupy more of our time than we might think;

478: knowing without a doubt that as we deepen our spirituality there are three inner qualities which can help solidify our ability to cross out error: superior intuition, the ability to divinely order our experience, and our uncompromised devotion to loving service;

479: having reached the level of spiritual growth that the bitterness of our self-imposed incarnational sojourn gives way to the sweetness of our conscious oneness with Spirit;

480: recognizing the interplay between Spirit and matter that propels us toward the understanding that the material universe is an illusion we have created to sustain us while we grapple with the deeper, more cosmic (spiritual) dimensions of our being;

481: apprehending that once we have become fully Christed, even the most penetrating of materialistic thoughts is transfused by the power of high potency universal love;

482: comprehending at a deep level that if we discipline ourselves to remain at a high state of awareness our universality of love and mature faith will become even more potent and powerful;

483: understanding that in a heightened state of illumination, our psychically-sharpened intellect and highly spiritualized intuition will characterize our initial unfoldment experience;

484: recognizing that if our consciousness is defined by its egocentric narcissism, we tend to pride ourselves in grandiose materialism and generally refuse to 'cross out' material addictions we view as harmless consumptions;

485: coming into the awareness that if all we are is flesh and blood (belong to the world) we would only resonate with the material appetites of a self-absorbed ego and sense-addicted consciousness (the world);

486: realizing that if we are not careful we may allow our devotion to serving others to become a substitute for the inner work we need to keep our consciousness at a Christed orbit;

487: understanding that spontaneous at-one-ment and chimeric purification lay the foundation for a newly Christed consciousness;

488: feeling we have mastered our incarnational calling;

489: attaining the realization that we must learn at each pre-Christed level of awareness to release current knowledge so we can expand our capacity for greater knowledge;

490: discerning that when we reach a certain level of unfoldment our vital energies rise to their spiritually-charged counterparts as we continue our wholing (healing) process;

491: recognizing that we must add to our spiritual resume with every thought, word, and action;

492: coming into the awareness that in order to fully understand the dynamic process of going from Spirit into matter and from matter back to Spirit we must harmonize all of our spiritual qualities;

493: realizing that when we maintain a level of heightened awareness we transcend ego limitations and remain at a Christed level of thinking, feeling, being, and doing;

494: comprehending that we must turn intellectual knowledge into spiritual understanding;

495: recognizing that it is in the nature of our initial unfoldment, regardless of our degree of illumination, to want proofs of the efficacy of higher truths;

496: knowing that our spiritual growth requires both disciplined introspection and Christed actions;

497: realizing that if our consciousness is Truth-centered our ability to remain in the world but not of the world, will provide many opportunities to master the art of living on any plane of being;

498: realizing that our demureness and reticence are only temporary speed bumps on our way toward proclaiming the truth of who we really are;

499: apprehending that transforming potential into actuality, or thoughts into things, is a seven step process (initiation): initial awareness, insight, imagination, resolve, wisdom, love, and stillness.

500: having elevated our five physical senses (sight, hearing, smell, touch, and taste) to their higher sensory vibrations: clairvoyance, clairaudience, clairalience, clairsentience and clairgustance;

501: recognizing that from a Christed orientation we can draw divinely-inspired ideas [fish] from Universal Supply at will;

502: intuiting that walking on water means much more than simply staying above negativity because it means remaining above worldly thoughts, temptations and addictions;

503: coming to know that when we are at an illuminated level of enlightenment we must make it a practice to Christize [feed] all of our thoughts, words, emotions, choices, and actions;

504: understanding that it is our unenlightened resistance to our innate divinity which causes us to deny any spiritual thought, inclination, or insight which threatens our egocentricity;

505: being fully human yet recognizing that our human-ness doesn't have to interfere with our spiritual growth;

506: knowing that the thoroughness of our spiritual will come from diligence and discipline as we apply higher knowledge;

507: recognizing that on whatever plane of consciousness we are operating (physical, astral, ethereal, etc.) we can divinely order our good by using our highly-charged spiritual capacities to master our temporal experiences;

508: realizing, without a doubt, that the strength of our faith depends on the depth of inner knowing and confidence we bring to any life experience, regardless of which plane of consciousness we find ourselves;

509: having learned not to question the value of any potentially viable spiritual perspective, no matter how benign it may seem, because it generally dims our spiritual perspective;

510: understanding that when we sense that our egocentric thoughts are being consistently raised to their higher spiritual essences we may wonder how long it will take us to totally align our human self with our Christ Self;

511: grasping that we unfold according to the parameters set by our own capacity for expressing our Christhood;

512: knowing we must be careful not to anthropomorphize the source of our divine nature;

513: recognizing that our fixation with material appetites (our Judas penchant) produces mercenary thoughts and dogmatic biases which are characterized by intellectual thirst for worldly knowledge, caustic pragmatism, and fear-laced self-preservation;

514: seeing that since we are spiritual beings in *ego suits* we will need to remain very disciplined when it comes to using the powerful spiritual energies that enliven us;

515: knowing when we reach the 'high pitch of enlightenment' every one of our thoughts is a Christed thought;

516: having experienced that when we allow God (the Christ and the Holy Spirit in expression) full expression as us we can comprehend many levels of divinely-inspired truths;

517: having felt, from personal experience, that the wonderful thing about the electrifying serpentine energies within us is that all thoughts and feelings coalesce into a cohesive whole;

518: recognizing that if we remain true to our Christ potential and deepen our faith we will use our knowledge of truth principles wisely and prudently;

519: knowing fully well that the journey we have taken to actualize our Christhood is the same process we undergo each time we move from spirituality to materiality to spirituality again;

520: understanding that once we become serious students of spiritual teachings we will be able to comprehend the deeper mysteries of Christology that will be revealed to us;

521: having been a serious truth student we know that because our spiritual nature is the truth of who we really are, it doesn't matter how ingrained our deceptively woven sense thoughts and intentions are, or how faulty our desire to discern the difference between sufficient and necessary conditions for spiritual growth is, or how much we repress our divine nature, because we have the power to overcome all of that negativity and achieve Christhood;

522: realizing that when we fully quicken all of our spiritual centers we will enjoy an incredibly keen sense of interior perception that minimizes the subconscious patterns and influences which we have allowed to stifle our spiritual growth;

523: recognizing that when we fully quicken all of our spiritual centers we will feel the rush of the fiery serpentine energies (power of the Holy Spirit) and shall feel the transformative power that comes from a consciousness operating at an optimum state of spiritually potent harmonics and divine sensitization;

524: knowing that as we reach a high level of spiritual maturity our fully-attuned faith quality will still underwrite all of our quickened spiritual abilities;

525: realizing that spiritual nonchalance usually leaves us settling for mindless material fixes;

526: recognizing that our overall awareness is raised as we attune our thoughts, words, and actions with our inherited Godness;

527: having learned very carefully that if we allow ourselves to be overly influenced by the world of outer appearances we may tend to question the strength of our faith;

528: coming into the awareness that as we mature in our understanding of Truth principles we readily see the necessity of quickly supplanting error thoughts with spiritually sound ones;

529: understanding that unless we have bridled the ego it will be difficult for us to gain ground in a contentious consciousness;

530: learning that it is from the very nature (name) of our innately ordained, spiritually-attuned consciousness (heaven) that we are able to transfuse our thinking, being, and doing (be saved);

531: recognizing that we must choose our heart-centered energies to guide us instead of allowing our purely human penchant for employing material means to accomplish spiritual ends dampen our progress as we unfold our Christ potential;

532: having learned from personal experience that as we journey through our *skin school* experience there have been far too many times when we believed we could attain spiritual ends by material means;

533: knowing that if we remain the product of sense consciousness [love this life] we will not receive the spiritual insights we need to master the art of living;

534: learning that as we become devoted to transforming our thinking all of our newly formed thoughts will supplant any and all remnants of error thinking, being, and doing;

535: comprehending that if we remain attuned to each inner spiritual prompting in spite of the ego's denial of our innate divinity, we can regain the clemency we need to raise mere mortal thoughts (people) to their higher spiritual essences;

536: reminding ourselves that our purely material thoughts and penchant for worldly fixes from an egocentric viewpoint can be transformed through our Christ connection;

537: giving ourselves permission that until we feel comfortable with our indivisible relationship with Spirit we will tend to question any and all spiritual inclinations in light of the ingrained religious beliefs which spring from our embedded theological roots;

538: having grown beyond the self-imposed blinders we placed on ourselves when it came to processing spiritually enriched scripture or religious instruction, we have learned not to dismiss spiritual perspectives that used to threaten enthroned dogmatic beliefs;

539: recognizing that most outcomes of material appetites prove to be hollow monuments to empty aggrandizement;

540: discovering that when faith and love are active in our waking consciousness we can divinely order an amazing amount of goodness and prosperity;

541: the ability to remind ourselves that spiritual growth demands a purging of all sense attachments before any appreciable progress can occur;

542: the ability smooth out the rough edges in our pediatric theology;

543: resolving not to put ourselves in a position to experience an incredibly disconcerting inner alarm which signals our failure to walk our talk;

544: remembering that it is better to follow Christed thoughts which enliven us than egocentric inclinations that ossify into empty formulas;

545: reminding ourselves that not only are we are born as Christed beings [as was Jesus of Nazareth], but that it is an eschatological truth;

546: recognizing that spiritually unreceptive thoughts, beliefs, and biases are the fruits of a vehemently materialistic and unenlightened ego [devil] which prides itself in sense appetites that feed personal ambitions, not spiritual aspirations;

547: seeing that the process of conscious spiritual unfoldment leads to self-knowledge and Self-knowledge;

548: when we achieve a certain level of spiritual wholeness or "cosmic office" we will we demonstrate our readiness to actualize our spiritual heritage;

549: exemplifying the joy of manifesting the visible from the invisible;

550: having attained the knowledge that as we feel the interior harmonics for the first time we will experience the awesome universality of Spirit in the form of a mesmerizing cosmic hum or vibration (the still small voice) that fills our entire being, sealing the connection between body, mind, soul, and Spirit;

551: coming to the realization that our purely human penchant for giving expression to sense-sludge will lower our vibration and pollute our inner beingness with the residue of unprocessed life energies;

552: realizing that our ability to divinely order our human experience is an evolutionary ability;

553: becoming fully aware that the first time we experience a heightened state of super-conscious awareness we may not grasp the full extent of our *serpentine moment*;

554: having reached the understanding that if we are prone to question the viability of any spiritual perspective, we may be unduly influenced by another equally error-ridden line of reasoning as we struggle to eliminate worldly attachments;

555: recognizing that when our love for the Truth is pure and unrestrained in its simple elegance we can gain such clarity and depth of spiritual understanding that our entire consciousness [house] will be filled with the harmonics of absolute bliss;

556: having arrives at the universal truth that we must toss aside any limiting thoughts that cloud our understanding and realize we are Christed beings standing on holy ground in human form;

557: coming to know – and experience – that our very countenance will show that something very special is happening within us on a spiritual level once we are connected;

558: realizing that when we align our conscious and subconscious mind with the Christ of us through our super-conscious energies we will feel the rush of the fiery serpentine energies of the omni-activity of the Holy Spirit;

559: arriving at the insight that as we continue our 'climb' we become more sure of the proper steps to take;

560: achieving the awareness that the journey from sense attachments to spiritual enlightenment is not for the faint of heart;

561: having no doubt that the way to return to spiritual integrity is through right thinking and elevating our materially-focused human acquisitiveness to spiritual capital;

562: the recognition that our sense-soaked thoughts and inclinations remain strong influences as long as we seek skin school experiences;

563: understanding that as we continue to subordinate our ego personality to our Christ Nature we will find that our previous interest in the laminated dogma that filtered our previous reality gives way to the clarity of spiritual insights;

564: knowing that the more we allow ourselves to fully trust the promptings of Spirit the more we will unfold into our divine nature and enjoy the spiritual perspectives that come with it;

565: realizing that because we are going through a human experience we may allow past experiences, beliefs, and habits to form outposts in our consciousness;

566: coming to understand that when we patiently allow hardened dogma to soften into a broader, more spiritual perspective, we will re-establish the inner peace and harmony we need to bathe our consciousness with light;

567: knowing that the more immersed we become in our spiritual growth the greater our reverence for beautifully articulated spiritual concepts;

568: being clearly aware that elevating our thinking from a purely worldly perspective to an enlightened one oftentimes unfolds initially as over-exuberance because we are super-charged with the fiery energies of the Holy Spirit and can readily access the realm of divine ideas;

569: recognizing that a consciousness that is darkened by egocentric tastes fails to experience the unfolding of its Christ-permeated beingness in spite of occasional nudges from spiritual insights;

570: having learned from personal experience, we know that we can raise our spiritual awareness despite our reticence to believe we can attain enlightenment, or our reluctance to sensitize ourselves to receiving divine inspirations, or doubting we can demonstrate divine Substance, or the failure to appreciate our pre-wired connection with the Eternal Isness, or the hesitation to move beyond stale beliefs and stagnant religious biases;

571: having the common sense to know that we must give legs to our Truth walk;

572: discovering that unchecked service to others without the necessary self-care and spiritual nourishment can lead to sickness, exhaustion, and even life-threatening illness;

573: knowing that the ability to outgrow old paradigms can be difficult and immobilizing at times as we seek to integrate spiritual truths into our material consciousness;

574: understanding that the more protracted our journey the greater the need for an extended *faithlift* that aligns the human us with the spiritual us;

575: recognizing that when we subordinate our ego and put the I Am Presence within us first by aligning our human consciousness with our Christ Nature we will see the world with opened eyes;

576: coming to know that as we put faith into action and stand firm in our spiritual practice we will be able to transform unquickened worldly thoughts (beasts) into their spiritual equivalents (saints);

577: realizing that keeping our consciousness at a higher azimuth will help us keep our human acquisitiveness in its proper place;

578: knowing that as we journey from one cusp of consciousness to another our previous belief system will be expanded and augmented so we can grasp the new spiritual material contained in our super-consciousness;

579: attaining the awareness that when we reach the level of elevated spiritual perception we will enjoy the clarity that comes from the absence of ego 'shadows'; (It is not unusual in this highly-accelerated cognitive atmosphere to drift above our normal mental acoustics and find ourselves in an extraordinarily enriched gamma state);

580: recognizing that before we become enlightened we tend to be fixated on over-amplified dogma and ready to censor any and all Christed thoughts; (In such a state of diminished capacity our default response is to hide behind religious convention and orthodoxy);

581: recognizing that from a lackluster state of diminished awareness we will miss opportunities to take advantage of the spiritual gifts that are innately ours;

582: having reached the level of spiritual awareness that if we listen carefully to our inner guidance (the still small voice) we will know that there is only unity and wholeness;

583: knowing that a materialistic view of the world has no conception of the omnipresence of divine substance in *potentia*;

584: having the common sense to know that by exercising faith and trust in our divine connection there may still be a residue of unquickened worldly thoughts which are the result of our not seeing the connection between public demonstrations of selfless service and our need for continued soul growth;

585: knowing that whenever we find ourselves in dire circumstances we must deny the power of outer appearances and affirm our oneness with Spirit;

586: apprehending clearly that if we lower ourselves to unabated egocentric rulership, the negatively-charged shift in consciousness will dominate our thinking, being, and doing and prevent us from going from coma consciousness (egocentricity) to a higher state of being (our super-conscious);

587: having arrived at the truth that every divine idea comes from the Universal Consciousness that is the ground of all being;

588: understanding that as we become more aware of our divine connection our thoughts and inclinations will be more Christ-like and less egocentric and, certainly, less religiously biased;

589: recognizing that our baser, more temporal, instincts hold the illusion that only the physical universe and the sense delights that go with it is real;

590: fully realizing that our egocentricities, products of sense consciousness, produce warped beliefs that keep us sense-centered instead of Christ-centered, thus compromising our spiritual growth and slowing our progress toward the union with our I-Am-ness;

591: our ability to readily jettison error thoughts out of our consciousness;

592: grasping the truth that as we seek new spiritual horizons we must be willing to move through current error patterns of thought like water through a colander to find higher spiritual ground;

593: realizing that the inner resolve to organize and ritualize our spiritual practice is in our spiritual DNA;

594: knowing that there will come a time when our spiritual sterility, defined by our worship of sense attachments and egocentric sovereignty will contaminate our consciousness and then our personal space;

595: recognizing that the process of error erasure is the interplay between struggle and discernment;

596: understanding that when we enthusiastically devote ourselves to uncovering spiritual truths our sagaciousness and ability to use our intellect and love for Truth as complementary qualities will help deepen our spiritual roots and broaden our higher conscious perspective;

597: realizing that once we shed light on our false assumptions we can embrace and begin to use the higher spiritual powers of a tenacious spirit and sagacious soul;

598: coming to know from personal experience, we realize that being true to our spiritual nature will help us move past any reluctance to claim our divinity, or settle for conflicting thoughts and emotions as to our spiritual origins, or remain in spiritual darkness, or tolerate spiritual staleness by boarding ourselves up behind walled beliefs and immovable religious biases, or allowing our recalcitrant human willfulness to continue to choose the material over the spiritual, or permit undisciplined and unproductive thoughts, attitudes, and emotions to rule our consciousness;

599: attaining a high level of equilibrium and harmony;

600: realizing the great truth that unlike our sense-dependent intellectual knowing which must re-acclimate itself as we go from one *cusp of consciousness* to another, our harmonizing capacity (our heart-centered, intuitional understanding) has a built-in integrative *switch* which allows us to sense our unity with all that is at each plane of being until we can grasp the nature of our Christness at that level of quantum being;

601: recognizing that if we want to be more spiritual than religious we will need to purposely access key realizations of Truth in order to elevate our awareness from immersion in a particular faith's group mind to a broader, even more eclectic, esoteric perspective;

602: knowing that intellectualizing our devout intention to seek spiritual truths and our sincere desire to purge ourselves from error thinking, being and doing, must be followed up with our surrender to our Christ Nature;

603: seeing that when our dedication meets our resolve our spiritual energies spring into action, and we can begin to understand metaphysical, esoteric, and theosophical truths;

604: recognizing that if we are serious about our spiritual growth our error proclivities and error patterns will cease to be a part of our expanding consciousness;

605: denotes our willingness to broaden our spiritual perspectives to protect us from closed, rigid, dogmatic belief systems that promise Nirvana but deliver Alcatraz;

606: understanding that there are times in our lives when we experience bouts of spiritual lethargy;

607: recognizing that spiritual teachings will challenge deeply ingrained dogma and conventional religious beliefs;

608: knowing that when we resolutely connect with the I Am Presence (God, the Eternal Presence) within us we can comprehend the subtleties and call into action highly dynamic and robust spiritual forces;

609: recognizing that our ego is not wired to fully comprehend our inner transformation;

610: realizing that in a state of illumined awareness we are highly receptive to the descent of divine ideas into our waking consciousness despite the ego's predisposition toward dampening our awakening;

611: comprehending that higher spiritual insights are evidence of our growing alignment with Spirit;

612: coming to know that we do not have to allow the poisonous ignorance of a feverish belief in separation and duality to immobilize our Christed choices and actions;

613: recognizing that as we unfold into our Christhood we will realize that error thoughts that might have dominated our thinking and caused spiritually potent ideas and insights to be short-lived will be purged from our consciousness;

614: having the deep understanding that God's only begotten Son [the Cosmic Christ] expresses Itself as the Planetary Christ in human form as us;

615: understanding that by our very nature we are divine;

616: having gotten to the place where we realize that because we are innately divine, our habitual desire for accumulating sense experiences will be interrupted by inevitable bursts of inner clarity;

617: recognizing that we need only to seek our higher spiritual nature through prayer and meditation in order to awaken our vital energies and gain the understanding we need to continue our spiritual unfoldment;

618: having the awareness that each-consecutive-moment-of-now we have an opportunity to elevate our thoughts, words, and actions to a consistently Christ-centric octave;

619: knowing that when we become fully conscious of our divine nature (as did Jesus) we will be able to align our human self with our Christ Self (as Jesus did) so that we can express our I-Am-ness (as Jesus did);

620: denotes our ability to know that the Eternal Presence(Infinite Isness the One Reality, God, Divine Mind) underwrites all that is;

621: recognizing that the natural outgrowth of our core divine nature purging the dross of error from our consciousness;

622: knowing that if we allow ourselves to completely repress our divine nature we will experience such spiritual hollowness that our body, mind, and soul will lose their vitality;

623: seeing that we can lift our purely human thoughts to their highest spiritual octaves instead of allowing them to become the products of base sense appetites;

624: realizing that new spiritual insights create cognitive dissonance that upsets old patterns of thinking, being, and doing;

625: having come into the understanding that fixating on over-amplified dogma is our way of 'protecting' ourselves from any spiritually awakened thought (men) or divinely inspired feeling (women) that epitomizes the Christed perspective (the Way);

626: becoming aware that we attempt to justify our fall from grace by depending on our purely human aspirations, base impulses, and primordial survival instincts;

627: recognizing that no matter how sheathed in materiality we appear to be, we can call upon our inner resolve and restore our immense capacity to become one with our Christ Nature;

628: becoming aware that we experience spiritual refinement and deepening when each of our thoughts is Christ-centric whether it applies to orthodox religious perspectives or to purely temporal concerns;

629: understanding that cutting off materialistic bents and tendencies will benefit us if we are consistent in living truth principles on a daily basis;

630: realizing that once we choose darkness over Light and put our dependence solely on outer appearances instead of the Indwelling Christ we have essentially mortgaged our divinity;

631: becoming convinced that ceasing to put sense appetites first is an inside-out process that involves a consciousness grounded in Truth principles;

632: recognizing that once we become religiously spiritual we realize that our elevated awareness does not come from worldly thoughts but from our I-Am-ness;

633: coming the deep metaphysical understanding that the Sacred Unity (God, the Eternal Presence) which underwrites the physical universe expresses Itself in physicality through the Christ Principle (Son), thus confining Itself in the world of matter, space, and time before we existed on the physical plane;

634: understanding that when we honor our divine roots by thinking, being, and doing Christed things each thought represents a tithe to our Christ Nature;

635: realizing that from a purely sense-soaked perspective we tend to justify our materialistic bents through elaborate 'exculpatory' rationalizations to assert the ego's rulership over any and all spiritual pursuits;

636: perceiving that a Christ-centric thought tends to raise the vibration of the thoughts that follow;

637: knowing that we experience rickets (tribulation and anguish) of the soul when we choose error over Truth;

638: understanding that we can repress the Christ of us by blocking our Inner Light to such an extent that our vital energies can be thrown totally out of phase; (This derogation can throw our body, mind, and soul connection into spiritual fibrillation);

639: becoming aware that as we become more aligned with our Christ Self the less sense-coated our thoughts, words, and actions will be;

640: gaining the recognition that at some point on our spiritual journey we will come to a full realization that it is the wisdom of the heart that serves as the petri dish for newly formed spiritual insights;

641: denotes our understanding that our entire consciousness (subconscious, waking conscious, and super-conscious) expresses the amount of God essence we allow;

642: knowing that when we fully express our innate divinity we will be conscious Christ permeated beings;

643: realizing that although we are, for the most part, subject to the limitations of human form we can transcend any and all human limitations by aligning our thoughts with our Divine Nature;

644: recognizing that if we have not fully attained conscious oneness with our Christ Nature there may be lingering doubts and thoughts that are counterproductive to our evolving Christhood;

645: knowing that the Christ is enfleshed in, as, and through us;

646: having transcended the sterility of literal interpretations of holy scripture;

647: understanding that our inner awakening transforms our thoughts and inclinations from their temporal sense vibrations to their higher, more spiritual essences through the activity of the Indwelling Christ;

648: knowing that once we assume human form there are limits to our human personality because of the parameters we have built into the human matrix itself;

649: intuiting that we have the capacity to rise above all of our human frailties and worldly bents to become one with our Christ Nature;

650: recognizing that each time we raise a temporal thought to its higher spiritual octave we elevate our Christology;

651: having experienced that when our actions match our thoughts there is harmony in our body, mind, and soul;

652: coming to know without a doubt that there will come a time when we realize we have mastered all human frailties, addictions, and sense appetites;

653: realizing that if we are wise enough to resolutely affirm our divine connection with the Indwelling Spirit and believe that we truly have the wherewithal to raise our Christ potential from the depths of our egocentric nature we shall cleanse our consciousness from error;

654: becoming aware that it does not matter if our ego personality is a product of staunch religious orthodoxy or encrusted worldliness, because at the core of our being we are one with our Christ Nature;

655: knowing that if we give into the self-aggrandizing thoughts of our worldly ego nature the sense addictions that are the outgrowth of our human personality will keep us from fulfilling our divine potential;

656: the ability to recognize that if an emotion moves from a base desire we have an opportunity to restore it to its core spiritual aspiration;

657: being firmly convinced that the white heat of Spirit will strengthen our will for the soul-deepening work ahead;

658: understanding that we must not censor (kill) divine ideas or spiritual impulses;

659: recognizing that although our inner harmonization transforms the human self its effect is to ground the human soul in its Authentic Expression;

660: knowing that all error thoughts that deny our innate divinity will succumb to the inner Light of understanding that has been with us since our birth;

661: always affirming our ability to transform an error thought into its higher spiritual value by purposefully and consistently choosing truth over error;

662: apprehending that we can turn our Christ potential into our actualized Christhood;

663: coming to know the great truth that even before we could comprehend deeper, more universal truths, sharpen our receptivity for ancient wisdom, or open the portal of universal harmonization our consciousness has already been pre-wired for our eventual Christogenesis;

664: having transcended the numbing effects of past habits and belief systems that perpetuate the illusions of separation and duality;

665: knowing that before we become enlightened our thoughts and emotions are ruled by the filters of worldly views and beliefs perpetuated by an ego that dines on unquickened religious and dogmatic orientations and sense appetites;

666: coming to know this number as representing the number of the 'Beast' (humankind's shadow side, Sorat, the Sun Demon) in our collective consciousness; [It is also the number of *Hakathriel*, or the Angel of the Crown, and of Sorath, the solar demon]; (An interesting Biblical relationship to Phi is the number of the Beast 666. First, let's calculate phi. Phi is equal to the square root of 5 (diagonal of a one by two rectangle), which is equal to 2.2360679775. Next we add 1 which increases the number to 3.2360679775. The next step is to divide by 2, which equals 1.61803398875. If we divide Phi by two again (the musical octave) we get 0.8090169943749. Now here is where it gets interesting. If you take the sine of 666, you get negative -0.8090169943749 and multiplying this by 2 (musical octave) equals – 1.61803398875! For anyone that needs a little refresher course, the sine function gives the ratio of the opposite side of a given angle in a right triangle to the hypotenuse. Also remember that Phi is calculated from the hypotenuse of a 1 by 2 rectangle. From this mathematical exercise, it appears that the Beast is the exact opposite process of Phi, where Phi represents growth, light and life and negative Phi represents decay, darkness and death); [Also, the number of a name is the sum of the numerical values of the letters comprising it. The numerical value of the lower mind, phren (the Beast), is 666]; the inability to understand occult (esoteric) mysteries;

667: recognizing that even as we begin to awaken we will find it difficult to grow into a mature appreciation for higher spiritual knowledge as long as we settle for the 'world of bling';

668: being under no illusion that the Indwelling Christ has always underwritten our being;

669: coming to know that when the reasoning is faulty the emotions generally corroborate the misguided logic, attempting to make a mockery out of the latent potency of our spiritual powers;

670: knowing that our consciousness is a malleable instrument that can be transformed into an authentic higher consciousness instrument;

671: intuiting that it is best not to cultivate a practice of giving energy to spiritually prodigal thoughts;

672: realizing that just because we can think worldly thoughts, choose worldly things, and *want* worldly things does not mean we have to *do* those things;

673: understanding that we must refrain from telling partial truths (bearing false witness) to satisfy purely materialistic urges;

674: knowing that the Truth is still the Truth, despite our misguided attempts to deny it;

675: realizing that if we pretend to follow truth principles and harbor impure thoughts, or crave one error impulse over another, or habitually choose sense pleasures over spiritual laws, or gamble on material means to spiritual ends, or are consistently intoxicated by materiality, or are swayed by competing sense appetites we will not understand or honor our sacred connection with our spiritual nature;

676: recognizing that the true essence of our human consciousness is to express our divine nature;

677: coming to know that as our faith matures we will cease blocking the fiery energies of the Eternal Isness (God, Divine Mind) in physical action (the Holy Ghost) and adamantly refrain from compromising or altering truth principles to suit our egocentric whims;

678: being very much aware that we are not our human envelopes;

679: realizing that Christ-centric consciousness requires uncompromised discipline, discernment, and devotion to truth principles;

680: comprehending the great truth that we will accelerate our enlightenment once we realize that God creates, the Christ formulates, and the Holy Spirit animates;

681: seeing clearly that corporal thoughts are an indication of our railing against the Core (Christ) of our being;

682: knowing that error dissipates (perishes) in the presence of wisdom;

683: recognizing that we must not crave (covet) sense sensations over spiritual experiences;

684: grasping fully that if a highly potent spiritual insight causes a great deal of cognitive dissonance that upsets a current belief system and leads to chemicalization it is best to allow the new learning to simmer for a while because we have just 'poured new wine into old wineskins'; (Chemicalization is the sobering spiritual growth process which takes us from 'ouijaing around' in mindless materialism to a state of enlightened spiritual perspectives. New spiritual insights create cognitive dissonance that upsets old patterns of thinking, being, and doing sending us in inner turmoil, questioning, and finally into spiritual realization);

685: intuiting that the Universal Field is Divine Substance;

686: being aware that the Source of the Only Begotten Son (the Christ) is Its Universal Creative Dimension (God), the One Presence, the Eternal Isness, Divine Mind);

687: discovering that when we have risen completely above the sense attachments of an unenlightened ego we will experience a wonderful transfusion in consciousness;

688: possessing the wherewithal to believe in our ability to produce thoughts that lead to our wholeness (healing);

689: recognizing that even if we give up all of our temporal attachments and cultivate a consciousness filled with Christed thoughts but fail to apply what we have learned, we will not have deepened our spiritual growth;

690: understanding that our dependence on certainty (knowledge) will be transformed into a new definition of certainty when we realize that we *are* the universe becoming more aware of itself;

691: realizing that once our thoughts are spiritually quickened we see things from a spiritual perspective (put away childish things);

692: the ability to recognize that our thoughts (husbands) are the precipitating causes of our emotions (wives);

693: seeing that once we are fully actualized we understand that as we attain one level of unfoldment, then another, and then still another we essentially return to the truth of who we really are;

694: intuiting that our *me-ness* is our Godness;

695: recognizing that when we believe in the omnipresence of Universal Supply and affirm its availability we literally stir the invisible ethers that create the manifested substance, turning potential into actualized substance;

696: realizing that there are three foundations to our spiritual practice: trusting that we can divinely order our good; desiring that our good will manifest with speed, ease, comfort, and joy; and working to bring about universal harmony and sacred unity (love);

697: apprehending that we must strive to become consciously one with the harmonious rhythms that permeate the universe and endeavor to express divinely inspired thoughts and abilities in our daily lives;

698: knowing that our increased spiritual worth brings with it the privilege and responsibility to help others 'get' back home, too;

699: becoming fully aware that in the Realm of the Absolute (the Eternal Presence) there is no imperfection, only equilibrium and universal harmony;

700: the rising of the vital energies through the seven major chakras;

701: realizing that if a feeling (wife) is out of sync with the thought (husband) that produced it, we can allow the feeling to run its course or acknowledge the disparity and move toward congruence;

702: learning that we may think we can justify our sense attachments by falling into old error habits, but denying our divinity is not the answer;

703: recognizing that when we chose this incarnation, Spirit descended as us and subjected Itself to the limitations associated with human form;

704: discovering that whatever we manifest is an *out*picturing of our attempt to concretize the Divine Idea that galvanized the ethers to produce it;

705: realizing that our spiritual unfoldment is a work in progress;

706: recognizing that an attempt to turn truth principles into dogmatic instruments is metaphysical malpractice;

707: having the awareness that when we fully unfold into our Christ Mind we will have achieved conscious oneness with the Eternal Isness;

708: grasping the truth that we have become physical incarnated beings who have the wherewithal to return to our pre-quantum, etherealized angelic forms;

709: recognizing that our Adamic consciousness with its mortal body will unfold into its Christ-centric consciousness (immortality) because that is our spiritual birthright;

710: seeing the truth of who we really are is hidden from most people because they have not gotten in touch with their divine beingness;

711: having discovered that when our consciousness becomes Christed our egocentric filters are transmuted into their divine counterparts and our more elevated beings and doings are now our natural (true) state;

712: understanding that while it is important for all of us to understand multi-storied truths we must be able to share them in such a way that others understand and can apply them;

713: coming into the awareness that the illusions of separation and duality were created to perpetuate a false relationship between our human self and our Christ Self;

714: realizing that dogmatic beliefs are embalmed beliefs;

715: recognizing that our skin school experiences are divine envelopes;

716: arriving at the conclusion that right thinking (righteousness) and wayward inclinations (lawlessness) are irreconcilable;

717: knowing that the application of the Truth Principles we know from a consciousness of transcendental oneness will help us move well beyond the limitations of worldly biases and sense-coated addictions;

718: understanding that as we progress toward becoming a fully enlightened being we must be aware that an occasional error thought or inclination will surface from time-to-time lowering our vibration in proportion to the karmic weight of the error thought;

719: discerning that the failure to apply spiritual truths is as unpardonable as unrealized potential;

720: realizing that every idea we have has the potential to prosper us;

721: knowing that when we have completely burned off the dross of error we will have become living and breathing Christed beings;

722: in order for the One to become the 'many' the Eternal Isness (God, the Universal Presence) lowered Its vibration becoming Its formative aspect, the Cosmic Christ (Son), and became enfleshed (born of a woman) according to the Principle of Divinely Ordering physicality from potentiality;

723: remembering that we are not human beings being spiritual, but spiritual beings being human;

724: recognizing that we have the innate capacity to generate an endless number of divine ideas;

725: knowing that purely worldly teachings bring us a great deal of struggle because the ideas worldliness brings keep us bogged down in material density;

726: recollecting that as long as we choose worldly ambitions we will remain in a sort of unenlightened wilderness that keeps us unsettled so that we keep confusing activity with accomplishment when it comes to our spiritual growth;

727: being familiar with the truth that we have within us a highly-attuned Beingness that is centered in a perpetual state of equilibrium and peacefulness;

728: realizing that our higher, more spiritually-attuned thoughts and feelings are the products of a fertile, spiritually-attuned consciousness;

729: knowing that if we seek to become one with our Indwelling Christ Nature and strive to fully demonstrate our innate divinity we will elevate our consciousness even though we have much more work to do in cutting off habitual error tendencies;

730: discerning clearly that our unwaivering trust in Spirit that will lead us to the universal spiritual harmonics necessary to transform our worldly thoughts into their higher spiritual essences;

731: acknowledging that being able to divinely order our good comes down to this: We must establish sacred unity between our human self and our Christ Self, our Authentic Self, our Deeper Self;

732: consciously experience the out-picturing of our Christ-likeness;

733: comprehending that as we fill our consciousness with Christed thoughts we begin to expiate the errors and sense-sludge (passions and desires) from our karmic baggage;

734: recognizing that even though we have chosen another human experience we can cross out much of the error we have accumulated;

735: having an accelerated sense of rightness, joy, tranquility, and peace;

736: noticing that we can complicate our daily lives by unnecessarily causing momentary jaundice of the soul through discordant actions;

737: honoring the spiritual essence of all things;

738: acknowledging the foundational Sacred Unity (God, Eternal Isness, the One Reality, One Presence) underwrites our existence;

739: recognizing that the core of our being is Christed which is that eternal *exousiai* part of us (before the world's foundation) that is without karmic baggage or material attachments of any kind because its essence is universal harmony and love; (*Exousiai* refers to the Earthly spiritual dimension of life forces, spirits of form, and sun beings);

740: apprehending that because we are spiritual beings in human form we are already Christed beings;

741: realizing that our eschatological inheritance is imprinted in our evolving Christology;

742: having confidence in the divinely ordered processing of experience;

743: noticing that once we open ourselves up to our true Christ Nature we have immediate and eternal access to the realm of divine ideas;

744: understanding that as we come into conscious awareness of our Christ-centric nature we have many opportunities to vivify the exquisitely pure divine energies within us so that our entire consciousness, including our sense-contaminated thoughts can be cleansed of error and raised to their spiritually-enriched mintage;

745: coming to the awareness that there is only one Consciousness and one Eternal Presence (Spirit, God, the One Reality, Divine Mind) and we are Its quantum (human) expressions;

746: deciding to do no harm;

747: recognizing that our inevitable Christed unfoldment is the disciplined result of cleansing our consciousness of the toxic thoughts and bleaching beliefs of encrusted error;

748: comprehending that sense-soaked thoughts and inclinations generally characterize a consciousness steeped in over-amplified sensory addictions;

749: trusting in the immediate access to Universal Supply;

750: realizing that once we become physical (quantum) beings, the process of divinely ordering our return – the 'many' becoming the One again – is assigned to each of us according to the degree of our enlightened awareness in applying the metaphysics of Mind Action;

751: apprehending that immoral, impure, self-aggrandizing, and covetous thoughts are ballast;

752: understanding that the Cosmic Christ 'stepped down' Its super-charged energies to become compatible with the lower, more dense energies of physical form;

753: recognizing that everything physical comes through God's Formative Aspect, the Cosmic Christ;

754: knowing that when our thoughts and emotions are in sync (the two become one) our spiritual growth will become delightfully exponential;

755: having reverence for all things;

756: having the awareness that we must constantly remind ourselves that good orderly direction ensures many opportunities to quicken our human consciousness and raise its vibration to a more Christed level;

757: ensuring that our spiritual antennae alerts us to anything we think, say, or do that ignores or denies our innate divinity;

758: recognizing that our spiritual growth is dampened by worldly thoughts;

759: understanding that when we confidently stand in our truth any and all error patterns ossify into empty paradigms;

760: realizing that we must constantly Feng Shui our thinking, being, and doing so that the Truth Principles we know support our truth walk;

761: respecting the limits of our current spiritual awareness;

762: underwriting our spiritual growth with Christed actions;

763: having the awareness that deep within us a Central Sun (the Christ Light) that creates equilibrium and harmony;

764: having the full knowledge that every cell, each molecule, every atom in, as, and of our bodies is a Christ-permeated being;

765: reminding ourselves not to allow encrusted conventional beliefs and thought patterns to short-circuit new spiritually-attuned ideas and insights;

766: denying the preponderance of errant thoughts that spring up from our evolutionary belief in separation and duality;

767: declaring the abundance of Universal Supply;

768: constantly walking our talk and talking our walk;

769: recognizing that thoughts of lack are generally the products of subconscious patterns and faulty life scripts that surface, retailing our insecurities and fears;

770: acknowledging that our true nature is our Christ Nature, and to subordinate our human personality to our divine nature is to ready ourselves for the marvelous joys enlightenment brings;

771: moving beyond the compunction to see the value in limiting ourselves to sense pleasures;

772: surrendering all of our thoughts to their higher, more spiritually-enriched essences;

773: recognizing that our resolute desire to become fully Christed is our incarnational calling;

774: knowing full well that we have complete and unadulterated heirship to the domain of the divine (heaven);

775: apprehending that as we open ourselves up to the spiritually pure energies of the Indwelling Christ Presence our human consciousness and its perceptual filters will be transformed into their Christed octaves;

776: realizing that while we may not have fully actualized our innate divinity, we can be assured that our previous, more worldly, level of awareness that defined our 'old self' is evaporating;

777: understanding that perfection underwrites all levels of being (mental, emotional, physical, astral, quantum, planetary, cosmic, intergalactic, universal, Multiversal, etc.) and that the cycles of involution and evolution lie within the parameters of that primordial perfection; (In the first verse of the Bible, it is written: "*In the beginning God created the heavens and the earth.*" (Genesis 1:1) This verse has three key names: God, heavens and earth. The sum of the numerical value of these three words is 777: God = 86, paradise = 395 and earth = 296, which makes 86+395+296 = 777); [The number 777 appears only once in the Bible: Genesis 5:31, "*Lamech lived a total of 777 years, and then he died.*" Spiritually, Lamech means Vital Life Principle]; knowing that we have reached the extraordinary "portal of consciousness" where we have attained complete and absolute conscious *union with the Divine*;

778: coming into the awareness that getting in sync with our higher nature is a necessary condition for our enlightenment;

779: having full knowledge that the Cosmic Christ is the Only Begotten Son (firstborn) of the Eternal Presence;

780: realizing that in order to become more illumined we must fill our consciousness with thoughts that are raised to their higher spiritual values, emotions that complement spiritually-attuned thoughts, inclinations that are unimpeachable, motives that align with Truth Principles, intuitions that resonate fully with higher order thinking, and actions that correspond to professed adherence to spiritual teachings;

781: recognizing that sense-sludge tendencies keep us bottled-up in a world of duality and denial (darkness), causing warped assumptions to filter our choices through defective egocentric lenses;

782: realizing that we must be careful that we do not allow a worldly thought or inclination to lead us astray;

783: seeing that we have plenty of opportunities to cut off self-aggrandizing tendencies as we seek to cleanse our consciousness of worldly thoughts;

784: recognizing that we must not see practices that lead to spiritual understanding, mastery over esoteric teachings, higher spiritual insights, ability to refrain from worldly thoughts and concerns as ends in themselves instead of the means toward spiritual enlightenment;

785: noticing that once our consciousness has been elevated from coma consciousness (worldly, egocentric consciousness) we can see clearly that we are anointed by the Holy Spirit;

786: perceiving that as we turn from our egocentric bents and consecrate ourselves to full-filling our destiny as Christed beings we shall unfold into our spiritual perfection;

787: having the awareness that our eternal quest for illumination has many forms and shades which are essentially gradations of enlightenment. (For example, having superior intellect and/or adopting conventional thinking, cutting off materialistic tendencies and our attachment to materiality, slipping into uncouth behaviors and unrefined inclinations, having sense attachments, or seeking spiritual aspirations – are homogenized steps and/or missteps toward our ultimate enlightenment;

788: affirming that we must not let encrusted beliefs and religious biases dampen our enthusiasm for new spiritual insights;

789: being aware that as Spirit descends into matter It lowers Its cosmic vibration from Its Absolute aspect (heaven) to Its quantum (relative) aspect;

790: seeing the Christ as the Underlying Vital Life Principle;

791: recognizing that as our error thoughts decrease and our spiritually-attuned thoughts and inclinations increase we will experience the universality of peace and tranquility (heaven) while we are alive;

792: coming to know that the greater or lesser degree of our spiritual enlightenment depends on how well we are able to cleanse our consciousness of each error thought, and every discordant thought that denies our divinity;

793: knowing that the outpouring of rarified divine energy made possible by the physical incarnation of the Christ in human form makes it possible for us to achieve the sacred unity which is our birthright as spiritual beings;

794: realizing that the moment of enlightenment will occur suddenly and will come unannounced for everyone;

795: acknowledging that just when we think we've gotten it figured out, a higher level of awareness will come and transform our previous level of awareness;

796: recalling that error thoughts come from a consciousness that sees duality and separation;

797: understanding that as we elevate our truth walks the dross of discordant thoughts, words and actions will burned from our consciousness by the Fire of Spirit;

798: knowing fully well that we have dominion and control over an unenlightened, sense-addicted ego (the evil one);

799: apprehending that the Cosmic Christ underwrites the manifest and unmanifest realms of being;

800: karmic liberation and extraordinary spiritual attainment;

801: recognizing that learning new truths without sharing them in a way that others benefit or understand is centripetal and implosive;

802: apprehending that enlightenment is more verb than noun, process than event;

803: recognizing that feelings, emotions, and intuitions of one who is enlightened are generally based on truth-centered motives, down-to-earth interpretations of truth principles, and disciplined intentions;

804: coming to the realization that as receptacles of divine knowledge and universal truths we can best access higher spiritual principles and align ourselves with Spirit by going into the Silence;

805: realizing that we are not separate from the Christ, merely physical (quantum) extensions of It;

806: grasping the great truth that the sequencing of thoughts before feelings is in our cosmological DNA. (When we incarnate into human experiences our Adamic consciousness [Adam] grows attached to physicality and becomes very egocentric. Our emotional struggle to regain [restore] our perfect state of cosmic consciousness [symbolized by Eve] naturally follows our egocentricity;

807: recognizing that a great deal of our incarnational struggle involves our being in relative Absoluteness;

808: our ability to see the sacredness in all things;

809: realizing that fixating all of our being (body, mind, and soul) on the self-aggrandizing manifestation of material substance (money) is the underbelly (root) of all error (evil);

810: our soul's task is to establish seamless alignment with our Christ Self;

811: knowing that allowing errant thoughts permanent residence in our unfolding consciousness tends to compromise our disciplined progress toward enlightenment;

812: becoming soberly aware that our intoxication with materiality is usually what sends us back into a skin school experience;

813: recognizing that our non-separability (indivisibleness) with our God essence is guaranteed because we are the Christ expressing at the point of us;

814: having the awareness that if an errant thought surfaces that retails duality and separation we should thank it for sharing and give it no more energy;

815: comprehending that the Christ Presence in us, and *as* us, is not subordinate to the limitations religious thoughts and denominational biases place on Its rich spiritual significance; (It is not something one faith tradition can "own, offer, or withhold" from others);

816: understanding that the Eternal Presence (God, Brahman, Allah, Great Spirit, etc., in physicality) is the highest order of consciousness (the Melchizedek Order) that exists;

817: realizing that all of our thoughts, words, and actions create vibrations in the ethers (all we do is 'recorded') because everything in the universe is connected to everything else in the universe;

818: recognizing that we are super beings who need no fictional super hero to 'save' us;

819: seeing clearly that there can be no error triage without elevating our consciousness to a higher spiritual octave:

820: recognizing that a Sabbath (rest) experience unites our waking consciousness with our God Essence;

821: discerning that by Its very nature the Indwelling Christ frees us from the penalties of error (sin) each time we have a Christed thought, make a Christed choice, and take a Christed action;

823: knowing that thoughts implode in the presence of truth;

824: moving from a perfunctory understanding (tent) of spiritual principles to a clearer, more reverential perspective;

825: having total confidence in our divine heirship;

826: recalling that the assurance (faith) a spiritually-charged super-consciousness gives us is that there is no leakage between our human self and our Christ Self;

827: recognizing that when we build a spiritually quickened consciousness our ego-filtered consciousness (world) loses its dominant influence in our lives;

828: enjoying a variety of metaphysical landscapes;

829: experiencing that our spiritual exuberance can raise the quality of our spiritual understanding and mediate the effects of a sense-coated consciousness;

830: grasping the universal truth that the Red Sea is our blood; (It is the physical manifestation of a universal form of spiritual energy that gives us life on the material plane. It underwrites our physicality and makes it possible for us to function in the material universe); (See Red Sea);

831: resolving not to give energy to temporal thoughts and actions;

832: expressing our unfailing love for the truth;

833: the ability to employ faithlifts anywhere and anytime;

834: adroitly deflecting the sharpness of cutting remarks and edgy biases that are leveled at us to kill our spirit;

835: transcending any and all regimented beliefs that deny our innate divinity;

836: monitoring our emotions for their spiritual resonance and making the internal shifts necessary to elevate base emotions to their higher spiritual essences;

837: not being stifled by rigid worldly beliefs;

838: recognizing that because we are the Christ expressing in us, as us, and through us neither denial of our divinity nor physical incarnation, nor the expanded awareness caused by higher spiritual thoughts, nor the misalignments caused by error thoughts, nor our current proclivities, nor future tendencies, nor anything in the world of outer appearances, nor exceptional knowledge, nor deeper understanding, nor anything else on the material plane can separate us from the sacred unity with our I-Am-ness;

839: having outgrown the anthropomorphization of God and an evil, horned, red devil with a tail;

840: knowing that a necessary condition for our state of mind that has a deep inner knowing that we know-that-we-know-that-we-know our oneness with Spirit can only take place by our having 'practiced the Presence' in a thoughtful, disciplined, devoted way everyday;

841: recognizing that a professed conviction (believing) is fiction unless our thoughts, words, and actions are in sync with it;

842: intuiting that Divine ideas are the chosen race;

843: realizing that "fallen angels" are error thoughts that deny our innate divinity;

844: coming into the awareness that one moment of illumination (one day) can be the result of a thousand thoughts and insights (years), and a thousand thoughts and insights (years) can be considered the genealogy of a moment of enlightenment (one day);

845: moving past the shackles associated with duality;

846: championing both our masculine and feminine qualities;

847: realizing that as we come close to enlightenment, there will be a final desperate push by a frightened ego which is the classic signal that tells us we are moving from an egocentric consciousness to a Christ-centered consciousness;

848: recognizing that what the Christ as Jesus saved us from was the illusion of separation from the Eternal Presence;

849: understanding that unless there is devoted practice *in* something, there is only knowing *about* that something;

850: able to cultivate a sense of personal 'all-rightness' and worthiness;

851: recognizing our prosperity comes through us and not to us;

852: knowing that no act of kindness is lost in the scheme of things;

853: realizing that lower vibratory egocentric thoughts generally remain perverse up to the moment of our enlightenment and become the last holdouts of a warped and fearful ego;

854: comprehending that perverse thoughts that deny our divine heirship are anti-Christed thoughts since they miss the significance of the Christ as God in physicality who becomes incarnate as each and everyone of us who is born into the flesh;

855: perceiving that a "right-thinking" thought universe epitomizes the sacred unity (love of God) that is the truth of us;

856: our ongoing capacity to be flexible, resilient, and adaptable;

857: recognizing our selfhood is achieved with our Selfhood;

858: becoming aware that have the choice to align ourselves with our Christ Nature or deny our Christed inheritance and remain a prisoner of physicality;

859: coming to know that we are 'here' (in skin school) by right of consciousness and that we can be 'there' (the Garden of Eden) by right of consciousness;

860: having the awareness that abject and total denial (the devil) of our innate divinity is most likely the result of a string of incarnations which feed upon previous incarnations' ignorance of our divine roots;

861: denotes innocence, chastity, and virtue;

862: grasping clearly that once our conscious alignment is established we can *feeeeeel* our oneness with the Eternal Presence;

863: ascertaining that it is difficult for our worldly ego to admit that the Christ as Jesus was the Torch Bearer and Way Shower who fully actualized his divine nature and assured us we can do the same;

864: recognizing that when we choose the Christ Standard we can affirm our good due to the nature of our indivisible Christ connection because we are in sync vibrationally with our divinity;

865: having more spiritual aspirations than worldly ambitions;

866: denotes our being unpretentious, humble, and modest;

867: the ability to realize that an unenlightened intellect, even if it is a superior intellect, will breed worldly thoughts and beliefs that make it difficult to truly understand higher spiritual teachings;

868: reminding ourselves that as we gain more and more esoteric knowledge we must be careful not to produce narcissistic and self-aggrandizing thoughts that supplant spiritual discernment;

869: recognizing that if we add the wisdom of the heart to worldly-oriented, but spiritually motivated, thoughts and beliefs we can raise their octaves to a higher, more spiritual azimuth;

870: believing that we should be honest, not out of duty, but because of our convictions;

871: acknowledging that in the depths of our soul the Truth resonates within all of us;

872: coming to know that at some point in our unfoldment we will cease placing so much value on worldly thoughts and addictions;

873: recognizing that our mature wisdom quality looks beyond outer appearances knowing that Truth always trumps error;

874: comprehending that there are three inclinations we must outgrow on our way to enlightenment: unbridled materialistic appetites, worldly thoughts that undermine and adulterate spiritual aspirations, and an insatiable penchant toward mindless sensory pleasures;

875: knowing that there is a deeper part of us, our divine sense of rightness that helps us move beyond any fears or doubts we may have;

876: comprehending that there is that all-pervasive I-Am Presence within us which is constantly ready to guide us if we are open to Its wise counsel;

877: seeing clearly that if we choose to ignore Spirit's counsel we will not understand the nature of our innate *heir power*;

878: intuiting that as we gain a perfect awareness of the Perfect Idea in human form raised to its divine essence, we will become consciously one with our Christ Nature and achieve the fullness, comfort, and grace that are our inheritance;

879: becoming aware that when mature love is raised to its higher intuitive expression our human soul feels a spiritual kick;

880: recognizing that when our memory-dependent intellect rights itself through direct communion with Spirit, it will surrender to the enduring love that underwrites our being and, thus, will become receptive to the healing nature of spiritual possibilities;

881: noticing that oftentimes we are tempted to fall back on our old intellectual reasoning to understand what is happening to us, but once we become more enlightened, we have a sense that we are operating at a much higher intellectual frequency;

882: sensing the distinction between our old intellectual perception and our heightened intellectual awareness;

883: showing our gratitude for our newly-found connection with the Omnipresent Source of our good;

884: not allowing our egocentric influence to become the ruling authority over every thought and activity within our consciousness and behavior;

885: reminding ourselves that our confinement in a sense-induced perspective (skin school) is a temporary condition and not a permanent reality on our way toward illumination;

886: seeing luck as an acronym: living under correct knowledge;

887: our penchant for advocating an unmaterialistic lifestyle;

888: apprehending that we already intuitively know the way;

889: recognizing that it is through quickening and combining our superior intuition and maturing wisdom that we become conscious of the Christ Seed in the midst of our baser human instincts;

890: our ability to put material things aside;

891: intuitively knowing that our Christ potential will generate many Christed ideas which will begin to dominate our worldly thoughts;

892: knowing that our 'salvation' comes from our next choice;

893: coming into the awareness that a Christ-centric Consciousness will disrupt the status quo of our sense-attached consciousness so much that we must be prepared to the eliminate destructive thoughts and inclinations which surface from our subconscious warehouse of repressed, sense-laden material;

894: 'getting' that our conventional beliefs cannot comprehend our spiritual reformation;

895: standing on principle no matter what;

896: not giving our executive will governorship over us at the expense of our spiritual growth;

897: knowing that truth penetrates the subconscious to righten discordant thoughts and reveals the facade and deceitfulness that are the trademarks of the illusionary nature of outer appearances;

898: understanding that our Christ Self constantly transforms us with love, purifying us and cleansing us with the *sushumnic* energies of Truth;

899: experiencing that when our material thoughts are purged from our consciousness, and our Christ potential is affirmed, we have direct access to the realm of divine ideas (heaven opens);

900: conscious oneness with the trinity of trinities;

901: recognizing that once we have sensed our spiritual wholeness and completeness we become dissatisfied with religious staleness and the emptiness it creates;

902: reminding ourselves that we can put unquenchable material appetites (devilish things) before our Godness, or we can put our innate Godness first;

903: reaffirming our *indivisibleness* with Spirit;

904: realizing that when we truly get serious about our truth walks and step out on faith, our spiritually attuned mind will be open and receptive to divine ideas which will make our journey on earth more in line with the truth of who we really are;

905: learning not to doubt our ability to manifest our good;

906: finding that even with a modicum of faith we can do amazing things;

907: knowing that if we buy into this world of duality (worship the carnal mind) we will place ourselves squarely in the tentacled web of our sense consciousness;

908: recognizing that he unenlightened ego's sense-driven instincts are generally oblivious to higher spiritual truths, even though these truths underwrite all of our human experience;

909: noticing that when we find ourselves experiencing *spiritual subluxation* (thought traffic that is characterized by paralytic, debilitating, emotional upheavals, religious dogma, repressed anger, subconscious hang-ups, etc.) we can reaffirm our Christ potential and the *heir* power it gives us;

910: coming to terms with the truth that we can ask ourselves if it is easier to deny thoughts that negate our divinity, or simply affirm our innate perfection and wholeness and live the lives we are meant to live;

911: understanding that while our Christed thoughts, words, and actions are in tune with Spirit, our egocentric thoughts, words, and actions must constantly undergo *truth triages*;

912: recognizing that one of our chief human tasks is to break karmic ties with our sense consciousness (coma consciousness) so we can stop missing the mark (sinning) when it comes to establishing a proper relationship with our Christ Self;

913: seeing beyond the unenlightened ego's penchant for deception;

914: recognizing that our externally-focused intellect, with its dogmatic exclusivity and well-manicured religious biases will play games with us;

915: fully realizing that purely human distractions usually spring from perfunctory and dogmatic perspectives that mindlessly question our spiritual progress and rationalize our shortcomings;

916: acknowledging that it is impossible for us to cast off our true nature no matter how much we deny our divinity;

917: realizing that there is only one kind of fasting relevant to our spiritual growth – abstaining from error thoughts which promote the illusion that we are separated from Spirit;

918: being aware that our unenlightened ego will raise its truth-deficient head (tempt us) from time to time;

919: acknowledging that although we may feel immobilized by what we consider to be dire circumstances, we must give ourselves an immediate *faithlift* by denying the illusionary power of outer appearances and the false impressions they create;

920: having an inner sense that we are more, much more, than mere specks and flecks of flesh;

921: coming into the awareness that we should not attempt to *pour* Truth principles into bottled-up religious beliefs or into fully-entrenched and embedded denominational theologies and expect to grow spiritually;

922: recognizing that it is important to remember that those who hide behind the fermented assumptions of blind convention tend to prefer the status quo instead of opening themselves up to the risks associated with unconventional spiritual territory;

923: avoiding religious intolerance of other faith traditions;

924: acknowledging that we will deepen our Truth walks if we extend unconditional love to every aspect of ourselves;

925: not giving power to personal attacks like: slights, ridicule, or false accusations against us;

926: making sure that we don't discount the unfailing accuracy of the Law of Life, because it applies to all of us;

927: realizing that whenever we give joyfully and freely we will never impoverish ourselves because true giving is receiving;

928: becoming more comfortable with the interior spiritual threshold which connects the spiritual us with the human us, by being sensitive to every high-potential spiritual idea which comes into our conscious awareness;

929: affirming the unlimited potential and goodness that can come from a divine idea no matter how dismal or hopeless outer appearances may seem;

930: becoming aware that truth falls through the cracks of myopic religious parochialism;

931: having gotten past questioning whether our elevated sensitivities come from our Christ Center (the illumined us) or are merely the rationalizations of a spiritually attuned, but naïve, intellect;

932: sensing that a highly attuned intellect, nourished by its receptivity to understand hidden truths is one of the first steps in actualizing our spiritual unfoldment. (However, the most advanced intellectual knowing pales in comparison to the wisdom of the heart);

933: knowing that, by their very nature, universal truths first appear in creative thought, then formative thought, and finally can be expressed for all to see in words, choices, and actions;

934: comprehending the great truth that despite numerous higher consciousness detours we may have taken, once we center our attention on the Christ of us and move beyond the debilitating illusion of separation from Spirit we can unfold into our wholeness;

935: turning from our naturally defensive human nature to the wise counsel of our Christ Self;

936: recognizing that pure, unadulterated love for the Christ of us creates molecular and cellular harmonization throughout our entire body;

937: not allowing lingering sense perceptions to cloud our spiritual understanding or compromise our spiritual growth;

938: harmonizing our spiritual powers and using them to transform our waking consciousness are two of our chief incarnational tasks;

939: reminding ourselves that when we appropriate higher knowledge, every aspect of our consciousness will be so enriched that the ideas we generate will produce more ideas which serve as seed ideas for even greater demonstrations of prosperity and abundance;

940: assuring ourselves that when we conscientiously and reverently connect (pray, meditate) with that level of our being called our Christ potential (our Extraordinary Nature) our spiritual powers will underwrite all of our thoughts, inclinations, choices, and actions;

941: fully recognizing ourselves as the physical dwelling places of the Christ Presence;

942: knowing that when we move from our head to our heart center, our soul consciousness becomes deepened by its feeling aspect which has moved beyond mere sense-orientations;

943: having the awareness that it takes more than the intellect's mechanics to fully comprehend spiritual truths;

944: grasping that a consciousness of consumption (gaining the whole world) is not a route to enlightenment;

945: recognizing that to actualize our Christ potential we must have the wisdom to purify our *subconscious*, the faith that our higher thoughts will have a place in bringing our *deified super-consciousness* down to earth, and the rarified love for the *conscious* pursuit of Truth no matter where it takes us;

946: realizing that unrestricted access to the never-ending goodness and Godness of our Christ Nature is our birthright;

947: reminding ourselves that, at the level of Spirit (the Kingdom of God), all is well;

948: allowing the Allness of God, *indivisiblized* at the point of us, to work in, as, and through us;

949: knowing that when we are able to transform literal thoughts into spiritual thoughts we will live, move, and have our being from a more Christed perspective;

950: coming to the realization that there is no geography in Spirit;

951: comprehending that we (humankind, the world and everything in it, the universe and Multiverse) are part of the densest aspects Eternal Presence;

952: intuiting that if it comes to a steady diet of well-meaning, but fanatical, service over developing a closer connection with the Christ of us, the wiser choice would be to put the clear understanding of our divinity first because when we get that right we will be able to work everything else together for good;

953: giving up our error consciousness (sins) and seeing others moving past their error consciousness (sins) as well;

954: knowing that because we are subject to Universal Laws our thoughts, words, and actions are always based on cause and effect relationships;

955: recognizing that when we eliminate a false belief (unclean spirit) from our consciousness, that is to say, deny its illusionary power over us, we censor its potential for growth and karmic damage;

956: understanding that after we become aware of our innate divinity we are no longer hand-cuffed by lactic thought patterns in our subconscious;

957: being careful not to postpone or erase opportunities to elevate our consciousness;

958: knowing that expressing our innate divinity is more important than knowledge *about* that divinity;

959: realizing that our complete trust and worry-free connection with Spirit will lead to our daily *flowering*;

960: recognizing, metaphorically, that our evolving spiritual awareness is like a highly spiritualized Lilliputian thought (mustard seed) which develops (expands) into an awesome spiritual epicenter (tree) composed of lofty insights (birds) and consciousness-expanding concepts (nests) that fill mental estuaries with unlimited possibilities of expression;

961: sensing the slippage of even the minutest aspect of our spiritual growth;

962: becoming familiar with the vibrational disturbances of sense-laden thoughts that arise from our human evolutionary mind (wilderness) so we can 'defriend' them from our consciousness;

963: not allowing regimented religious beliefs about the proper way to meditate or pray prevent us from taking immediate remedial actions to heal an emotional impediment (wound) that presents itself during our centering experiences;

964: honoring all of our spiritual qualities, especially the newly-developed ones;

965: not allowing longstanding emotional hang-ups to block our greater good;

966: recognizing that "material eyes" do not have spiritual lenses;

967: recognizing that the medicinal benefits of illuminated thoughts are mediated by our willingness or unwillingness to expunge error from our consciousness;

968: realizing that it is easier to push a large rope, through the eye of a needle than for our materially-minded human personality to still itself long enough to achieve Christ Consciousness [the Kingdom of God];

(The Hebrew word for rope is *gamla* [some texts misapply the word and use camel in this verse]);

969: coming into the awareness that from a state of grace we can move beyond our worldly ambitions and the human evolutionary mind which produces them and demonstrate a newfound willingness to surrender to the promptings of Spirit;

970: recognizing that when we grasp the essential nature of Divine Ideas we will understand that when we express a Divine Idea, no matter how insignificant it may appear, its medicinal value is greater than the most profound qualities and attributes of sense-veneered thoughts;

971: becoming consciously aware of the dissonance between the *spiritual us* and the *material us*;

972: comprehending that our consciousness (house) is the epicenter of communion with our Christ Nature;

973: recognizing that sacred scripture is the story of our on-again-off-again relationship with Spirit;

974: realizing the simple truth that that material thoughts produce material outcomes and spiritual thoughts create spiritual outcomes;

975: acknowledging the universal truth that sense attachments are the 'cup which must pass from us' as we seek to align our will with Divine Will;

976: denotes our willingness to move beyond embedded religious beliefs and dogmas, as well as the centrifugal pull of outer appearances in order to have any chance at enlightenment;

977: recognizing that once we master negation by affirming our oneness with the Christ of us, we can rise confidently and expectantly above old error patterns;

978: having recognized that when we deepen our connection with Spirit, we will be astounded at the awesome power of our innate divinity;

979: realizing that the absoluteness of our Christ nature always rattles the earth-bound ego that senses a very real threat to its temporal dominion;

980: reminding ourselves that we should not attempt to pour truth principles into bottled-up religious dogma, because the truth will fall through the cracks of exclusivity, parochialism, and religious intolerance;

981: realizing that when we are faced with demonic and entrenched negativity, we must understand that many of these tendencies come to us through our subconscious connection with the *wounds* and *bruises* of the collective consciousness;

982: discerning that it is not what is said or even done *to* us that contaminates our consciousness, but what comes *out of* our consciousness that shows the level of our spiritual maturity or immaturity, growth or stagnation, enlightenment or unenlightenment;

983: seeking to unify all of our universal, temporal, transcendental, and cosmic aspects in order to appreciate the importance of our multi-storied wholeness;

984: recognizing that when our get up and go has gotten up and gone, it is time for a Sabbath experience;

985: discovering that much like our stomach on the physical level digests healthy as well as unhealthy food our consciousness has the ability to absorb truth and dispose of error;

986: knowing that we have *passport free* access into the Kingdom of God;

987: remembering that the process of unfoldment involves going from a sort of *spiritual hibernation* to a perfect state of divine unfoldment;

988: reminding ourselves that we have not been created to be subservient to error;

989: being resolutely willing to cross out all forms of error (bear a cross) and being unequivocal in our commitment to follow inner teachings;

990: knowing that the Vital Force of the Universal Isness (the Eternal Presence, the One reality, God) sustains our newly enlightened consciousness as it did in our dense unenlightened mortal consciousness;

991: acknowledging that as we transform our thinking we will honor that great Presence within us, our I-Am-ness, which is mightier than our sense-burdened human personality;

992: not allowing the centrifugal force of appealing outer appearances catch us off guard;

993: recognizing that in order to attain immortality we must renounce all of our personal ties with error;

994: reminding ourselves that the mystic thoroughfare for enlightenment is surrendering to (aligning ourselves with) our Christ Nature;

995: realizing that at their highest level of development in our previous level of consciousness, our selfless love, superior intuition, and spiritual discernment pale in comparison to what they will become in their illumined state;

996: remembering that error thoughts are only a few remaining vestiges of our old consciousness; (Until our human personality fully integrates with our Christ Individuality a few sense-attached thoughts will arise to plead their case for the concepts of duality and separation);

997: allowing Spirit Its eternal ascendancy in every waking moment;

998: coming into the realization that if we dutifully and joyfully walk the principled path of spiritual unfoldment, encrusted religious beliefs and erroneous materialistic attachments which have burdened us for so long will be crossed out;

999: being fully aware, without a doubt, that through the Cosmic Christ all things – from Christ Consciousness (heaven) to human consciousness (earth), from quantum particles (visible) to quantum waves (invisible), whether planets (thrones), galaxies (dominions), universes (principalities) or multiverses (powers) - are given form and function; the Cosmic Trinity of Trinities;

1,000: seeing and expressing our transcendentalness and universality as spiritual beings having a skin school experience; fully recognizing that matter is frozen Spirit; the relative time between physical incarnations; our non-incarnational beingness; our non-incarnational and incarnational completeness;

1,290: denotes the realization that our daily sacrifice of having to cross out error will come to an end when our egocentric consciousness gives way to a Christ-centric Consciousness;

1,335: signifies our knowing that the veil of illusion has been lifted;

2,000: recognizing that polarities are dual aspects of singularities;

3,333: symbolizes the myriad of spiritual attributes of the Planetary Christ Presence; the boundlessness of Divine Order;

6,666: symbolizes the 'legions' of error thoughts and tendencies of the Beast, the Antichrist; (See 666);

7,777: symbolizes the innumerable aspects of perfection at all levels in the manifest and unmanifest realms;

33,333: symbolizes the limitless attributes of the Cosmic Christ Presence;

72,000: the number of nadis (channels for the flow of consciousness) through which, in traditional Indian medicine and spiritual science, the energies of our subtle body are said to flow, connecting with our chakras and also converging at our navel;

100,000: having actualized the all-conquering power of truth over error;

144,000: suggests universal completeness (12x12x1000); the 144,000 pedals (vibrations) of the crown chakra signaling the perfect marriage between mortal consciousness and Christ Consciousness; the fruition of spiritual ideas; (The number 144,000 can be reduced to 9 [the mystic symbol of humankind and also the number of initiation], for those who pass through the nine degrees of the Mysteries receive the sign of the cross as emblematic of their regeneration and liberation from the bondage of their own inferior, sense-soaked nature);

300,000: divinely ordering our good without the 'wait time' usually associated with the asking (declaring) and the receiving;

333,333: the Christ Presence incarnating a highly advanced soul (avatar);

777,777: perfection exponentially begetting perfection;

7 Million: symbolizes Relative (Planetary) enlightenment;

7 Billion: symbolizes Absolute (Cosmic) enlightenment;

Numbers, Unique:

Googol: denotes limitless knowledge and access to limitless knowledge; (Googol is the digit 1 followed by 100 zeroes. This unique number was the inspiration for the search engine Google. It also resulted in the word Googolplex, which is the namesake of Google's offices);

Rubik's Extravaganza: denotes the endless configurations, metaphors, ideas, acts of kindness, associations, and ways to serve others we can imagine; (Rubik's Extravaganza is the number: 43252003274489856000. It represents the total number of configurations we can create with this incredible 3D combination puzzle, invented by Erno Rubik in 1974);

Christ-Centric Number: our consciousness raised to its highest cosmic octave; (The Christ-Centric Number denotes Christ Consciousness and is the number: 3333333333333333333333, which is the number 33 repeated 11 times – the number of years the Christ as Jesus spent on earth before making His transition);

Human Wavicle: Spirit's out-picturing in human form; (Human Wavicle represents the number 50 trillion which is the number of cells in the human body);

Adamic Brain Power: our capacity for processing sensory experience on the earth plane; (Adamic Brain Power represents the 85-100 billion neurons in our brain which serve as the building blocks of our nervous system by transmitting information to and from our brain to the rest of our body);

Milky Way Galaxias: our cosmic capacity for creating our 'terrestrial crib' in the material universe along with our desire to explore the cosmos for the sensory delights it holds for us; (Milky Way Galaxias represents the 300-400 billion stars – with at least as many planets – in the Milky Way Galaxy);

Numbness: experiencing another human incarnation and/or reincarnation;

Numinosum: our capacity to experience illumination; (Numinosum was a term first used by Rudolf Otto to describe experiencing the divine as awesome and yet terrifying);

Numskull(s): irreligious thoughts that cause us to cut off our nose to spite our face;

Nurse-like: expressing our caretaking, nurturing, altruistic, and empathic qualities;

Nursery: mainstream, fundamentalist religion;

Nutritional Pivot: going from meat consumption to vegetarianism and/or veganism;

Nybble: a quick byte; a succinct sound byte that captures a spiritual and/or religious message [For example, another way of saying – *walk the spiritual path on practical feet* (byte) is *walk your talk* (nibble)]; (In IT talk, a nybble is a set of four bits, or half of a byte);

Nymph-like: recognizing that we have subconscious emotions awaiting expression when the time is right;

Oak Tree-ness: depending on our strength; seeing expansiveness instead of diminishment and limitation as our birthright; choosing esoteric doorways to higher thought; feeling regal; experiencing longevity; believing in eternalness; feeling powerful and well-grounded;

Oasis: refuge, support; a temporary sabbatical; a short term respite; rejuvenation;

Oath: commitment; dedication; devotion; enrollment;

Obelisk: male energy;

Obituary: an end to outdated beliefs, habits and allegiances; the cessation of old attitudes and preferences;

Objectionable Vagueness: not being able to understand what someone is talking about or trying to explain because the explanation is fuzzy, murky, or completely indiscernible;

Obscene Neutrality: living life from the perspective that is characterized by the unfortunate statement "It is what it is.";

Obscuram Per Obscuris: implies attempting to explain some difficult religious, spiritual and/or esoteric principle by using even more obscure reasoning;

Obscure Night: the 'dark night of the soul' that occurs just before our quickening; the phase of our unfoldment in which we question and experience our weaknesses and vulnerabilities so we can rise above human limitations and make the adjustments we need to prepare ourselves for the Golden Dawn; (See Golden Dawn);

Obstacle Course: the subconscious; another skin school experience;

Occult Perspective: an awareness of hidden esoteric and deep philosophical truths that explain our relationship with the manifest and unmanifest universe;

Ocean-like, Sea-like: symbolize the immensity of our emotionality and the ebb and flow of our emotions; *surfing* suggests being able to handle intense, and sometimes overwhelming emotions; *struggling against the current or undertow* implies allowing our emotions to overwhelm us and even pull us down;

Octopus-like: enjoying meditative depths; experiencing fluidity, agility, and focused movement in everything we do; being able to practically apply psychic and spiritual gifts; having the ability to cut loose excess baggage (self-defeating beliefs, perspectives, and habits); camouflaging our intentions; spinning illusions and distractions; subscribing to adaptability; harnessing our explosive potential;

Oddball(s): weird and/or kooky apparitions, visions, ethereal phantoms, anomalies, paradoxes, and hypnogogic episodes;

Odometer: refers to our initiatory progress;

Odour of Sanctity: an unexplained, beautiful, unearthly scent that is reported to have exuded from holy people, including two nuns: the blessed

Maria degli Angeli, an 18th century Italian nun and Sister Giovanna Maria della Croce. (At Rovereto in Italy in 1625 she took her symbolic wedding vows to Christ From the moment she put on the wedding ring, a beautiful scent emanated from her finger. Allegedly, everything she touched was left with a lingering smell for days. Eventually, her whole body, and even her clothing, exuded this mysteriously beautiful, unearthly fragrance);

Office(s): obligatory work-related thoughts and intentions; dutiful attitudes;

Offspring: our choices based on our thoughts, our actions as a result of our choices;

Oil: the bliss, love, joy, wisdom, superior intuition, and deep understanding that flow from an advanced state of spiritual consciousness; the Universal Life Essence that animates our consciousness and leads to illumination; if *oil is shared* (as in anointings) it symbolizes the expansion of the Universal Life Force (see also Anointing);

Ogre(s): harsh, self-critical thoughts;

Oh-No-Second: the fraction of a second in which we realize we've made a foolish mistake; (See Irritainment);

Old Age: Seasoned thoughts; ingrained thoughts and concepts;

Old Soul: an engrained belief; a fossilized thought; a person who has reincarnated many times;

Olive-ness: cultivating healing thoughts; producing regenerative ideas;

Olive Tree-like: sensing the restorative powers of our higher mental faculties;

Olympus Effect: using our super-conscious attributes to empower our thinking, being, and doing;

Om, Aum: the vibrational door to enlightenment; the highly sacred syllable of invocation, benediction, and affirmation of our oneness with the Eternal Presence; the sound of spirituality; (It is said that by prolonging the uttering of this holy word, both of the *o* and the *m*, with the mouth closed, the sound echoes in and arouses exquisite vibrations in the skull, and transforms, *if the practitioner is pious enough*, the different spiritual centers in the body into their highest spiritual energies);

Om Mani Padme Hum: affirming we can strengthen our human connection with our Divine Self [Buddha Nature, Christ Nature, etc.]; (A Buddhist phrase which means through a disciplined and devoted spiritual practice we can align our human self that is burdened with impurities with the body, speech and mind of a Buddha);

Omega: our perfected beingness after it has passed through the cycle of numerous incarnations and has become, once again, a superb, Christed spiritual consciousness; (See Alpha);

Omegatizing: being able to attain an appropriate ending, closure, discontinuance, cessation, resolution, adjournment;

Omen: an augury of what will happen in the future; prognostication;

Omniactive Revelation: realizing that the Eternal Presence is everywhere active;

Omnipotence Realization: recognizing that the Eternal Presence all-powerfulness personified;

Omnipresence Awareness: realizing that the Eternal Presence is everywhere present;

Omniscience Recognition: having the super-charged insight that the Eternal Presence is all knowingness;

Omnishambles: finding ourselves in a situation that has been completely mismanaged; a string of blunders and miscalculations;

Omnism: believing in the legitimacy of all religions;

Oneirology: studying dreams;

One Channel Religion: mainstream Christianity which follows a literal-only interpretation of scripture;

Oneness: unity; sacred harmony; the absence of separation and duality; (Not our past. Not our childhood experiences. Not our bad experiences. Not our most ingrained habits. Not our lost opportunities. Not the old tapes running through our heads. Nothing – No Thing - can separate us from our Authentic Christ Nature except our disbelief in our Authentic Christ Nature. In order for there to be oneness there are some irreconcilable differences that must be taken care of between people, and families, and countries.

~ *Spiritually Speaking* ~

Between science and religion. Between religions. Between us and Spirit. Between our human self and our Christ Self.); [As quantum physicists Rosenblum and Kuttner assert, as a result of Bell's theorem and the experiments it stimulated, a once purely philosophical question has now been answered in the laboratory. There is a universal connectedness. Einstein's "spooky interactions" do, in fact, exist. Any objects that have ever interacted continue to instantaneously influence each other. Events at the edge of the galaxy influence what happens at the edge of our gardens]; (In her *Collected Writings, vol. 10,* Helena Blavatsky reminds us of our oneness: "It is this sense of separateness which is the root of all evil" pg. 327. In *Divine Governance of the Human Kingdom Including What the Seeker Needs and The One Alone*, Sufi mystic Ibn Arabi says: "When the mystery of the oneness of the soul and the Divine is revealed to you, you will understand that you are not other than God … For when you know yourself, your sense of a limited identity vanishes, and you know that you and God are one and the same");

One-Way Street: linear thinking; being fixated on one solution, one way of doing things;

Only Begotten Son: the Cosmic and Planetary Christ; God's Core Essence in physicality; the Christ Principle; (The treasure that lies within us has been over-looked by the majority of people on the planet. Why? Because many of us have been taught that the Only Begotten Son was a Jewish carpenter named Jesus who was born 2,000 years ago. We have been led to believe that His 'only begotten-ness' was a one time occurrence and that we are to worship this gifted being called Jesus of Nazareth. Many of you, if not all of you, are aware of that naively fundamental Christian perspective. However, if you'll put on your dogma repellant, I'd like to offer a different perspective, a more enlightened perspective, of the true nature of the Only Begotten Son. It is a perspective that will put you on a higher plane of consciousness than 99% of the people on the planet. It is a perspective that will set you free. And it gives me no greater pleasure as a Unity minister than to share the following mind-stretching truth with you. From a higher consciousness perspective the Only Begotten Son is the Christ Presence (the Only Forgotten Son) within each of us. It is the same Christ Presence that was in Jesus. It is the same Christ Presence that was in His disciples, in His mother Mary. It was even the same Christ Presence that was in Pontius Pilate and Herod. It is the same Christ that was in Abraham Lincoln, Charles and Myrtle Fillmore, Mother Theresa, Princess Diana, Carl Jung,

Tammy Faye Messner, and Luciano Pavarotti. It is the same Christ Presence that is in you and me and in our children and grandchildren. It is the same Christ Presence that will be in the next child that is born); [In *Meister Eckhart and Carl Marx: The Mystic as Political Theologian*, Matthew Fox quotes Eckhart: "People think God has only become a human being in his historical incarnation – but that is not so; for God is here – in this place – just as much incarnate as in a human being long ago. And this is why God has become a human being: that God might give birth to you as the only begotten Son." pg. 541);

On the Ropes: feeling overwhelmed by a situation or event that seems to pin us in with no escape or solution; (In boxing terms, on the ropes refers to a boxer on the verge of defeat who has been knocked against the ropes and kept there by the opponent's incessant blows.);

Onychomancy: divining that interprets the reflection of sunlight on oiled fingernails;

Oomancy: knowing that the insights of tomorrow lie concealed in today's consciousness;

Oops Review: examining the nature and consequences of our error tendencies and then taking remedial actions to prevent future slippages;

Oort Cloudishness: the icy atmosphere we feel around some people who seem stand-offish and aloof; the iciness we feel when we read and/or hear divinity-denying rhetoric; (In quantum physics, an oort cloud is an hypothesized cloud of icy planetesimals that lies roughly 50,000 Au's [a light year] from the sun);

Opera-like: seeking approved emotional outlets that keep us connected with our sophisticated tastes and cultured habits;

Opium: our sensory experiences;

Optical Delusions: giving power to outer experiences; worldliness; (Many people are in a prison of sorts. They are incarcerated by optical delusions. Many people throttle back their consciousness by holding onto past beliefs and old scripts that keep them mired down in the shadows of rigid convention, religious dogma, and unhealthy assumptions. They live in a world of shadows, a world that gives power to outer appearances instead of inner transformation);

Optimistic Spirit: understanding that 'our lives - past, present and future - operate by laws of optimization and that the universe is wired in our behalf. It sees situations and events as being optimum, although the situation itself may not be fully understood. (Optimism is characterized by an attitude of hope for future conditions unfolding as optimal as well. Here's the neuroscience of optimism: As thoughts of happy future events flood our minds, two brain structures are strongly activated. The rostral anterior cingulated cortex [RACC] and the right amygdala areas are lit up. The RACC, it seems, works hand-in-hand with our emotional center, the amygdala, to actually downplay negative emotions, helping us stay more positive in the face of negative situations. An optimistic spirit is one of the seven core abilities that characterize the Extraordinary Us, our Christ Self.); (See Extraordinary You);

Oracle-ness: using precognitive divination; achieving prophetic revelations; precognitive thoughts;

Orange-ish Tendencies: our longing for sociability and community; usually denotes gregariousness, cordiality, an out-going nature, and hospitality and warmth; inclusiveness; extraversion; healing; community-centered; our need for social contact, status, and position; sacrum;

Orchard-ness: our need for growing, cultivating, and nurturing things; our aptitude for cultivating our thoughts and fertilizing our ideas;

Orchestra-like: our ability to coordinate, blend, harmonize, and synthesize our thoughts and emotions in order to achieve what we feel we need to accomplish;

Orchid-like: being loving, affectionate, and passionate; favoring exotic beauty; fleeting thoughts;

Orgies: our unwholesome penchant for brainstorming one carnal thought after another;

Original Sin: our initial descent into matter in human form; a newly-formed error thought; missing the mark (unawareness) of our innate divinity; We miss the mark (sin) every time we deny our innate divinity; (The term 'original sin' does not appear in the Bible. The concept of original sin is a human invention that originated from Tertullian's insecurities. Tertullian coined the phrase in the second century, and Saint Augustine followed his lead. It is a deliberate manipulative ploy to denigrate our innate divinity and create a 'curse' that falsely labels us as unworthy sinners. 'Sin' is an archery term. It means 'missing the mark (the bulls eye).' In Greek tragedies *hamartia* (missing the mark) signified tragic flaws, blindness, and misperceptions; Mainstream Christians think of original sin as the consequence of Adam eating the fruit in the Garden of Eden. For Augustine and Tertullian, however, the source of original sin is *not* that Adam and Eve ate the fruit, but that they engaged in sex for dessert. It was this subsequent sinful act, they contend, that caused the taint of original sin to 'infect' subsequent generations, and thus, rendering humankind incapable of achieving salvation without an external deity's grace);

Ornithomancy: divining that uses the flight patterns, habits, and songs of birds as the sources of interpretation;

Orphan: a spiritual thought that is rejected by a worldly consciousness and finds itself isolated from the surrounding pool of materialistic thoughts; our rejected divine nature;

Orphanage: a collection of rejected spiritual thoughts;

Orpheus Dynamic: the magnetism of higher thoughts to raise worldly thoughts to their spiritual equivalents;

Oryctomancy: divining that interprets the meaning of excavated artifacts;

Ostrich-like Tendencies: our proneness to bury our head in our defense mechanisms; burying our potential in our subconscious hang-ups;

Othering: our tendency to separate our spiritual life from our daily living; our unfortunate inclination to feel stronger tribal connections and allegiances to like-minded religious and spiritual groups than dissimilar faith traditions;

Other World, the: the deep recesses of our subconscious; each one of our three states of consciousness (subconscious, waking conscious, and super-conscious); our mind, body, and soul differentiations; the altered states of consciousness; (Many of the world's mythologies refer to the Other World as being supernaturally 'adjacent' to ours in mysterious ways. Even quantum physics refers to multiple universes, parallel universes, and the Multiverse);

Otter-ness: playfulness; gleefulness; (According to the National Institute of Play, play is the gateway to vitality. By its nature it is uniquely and intrinsically rewarding. It generates optimism, seeks out novelty, makes perseverance fun, leads to mastery, gives the immune system a bounce, fosters empathy and promotes a sense of belonging and community. Each of these play by-products are indices of personal health, and their shortage predicts impending health problems and personal fragility);

Ouiji-ing Around: backsliding; vacillating in our religious and/or spiritual interests;

Outcast(s): metaphysical thoughts and concepts rejected by mainstream religious practitioners;

Outhouse Material: impure worldly thoughts and inclinations; spiritual compost; [One thing is for certain we can't build castles out of outhouse material ☺] (See Outlaws);

Outlaw(s): error thoughts, choices, and behaviors that rob us of our joy, inner peace, and spiritual growth; dogmatic religious biases that bully us out of considering higher, more esoteric spiritual perspectives;

Outmoded Oomph: religious proselytizing; hell-fire-and-brimstone preaching;

Out-Of-Body Experiences (OBE's): instances in which a person becomes aware of h/her astral or spiritual body. Often, this can be involuntary, due to a state of trance or an accident of some kind, but can also occur when dreaming; our ability to astrally project and/or bilocate by temporarily leaving the confines of our physical bodies; (The term *out-of-body experience* was coined by G.N.M. Tyrrell. It is an experience that one-in-ten people experience sometime in their lives. There have been enough replicated OBE experiences, worldwide, to validate their subjective reality. The first extensive scientific study of OBEs was made by Celia Green. The first clinical study of near-death experiences (NDE's) in cardiac arrest patients was by Pim van Lommel, a cardiologist from the Netherlands. Many people report that they experience going out of their bodies during critical operations and/or serious accidents [near-death experiences]. They claim that during such forays, they can watch surgery being performed on themselves and/or see themselves hovering over their injured bodies at the scene of an accident. In the case of motor vehicle accidents, they are able to recall the accident as if observing it from a few feet above.);

Out-Of-Kilter: settling for purely materialistic wants instead of soul needs;

Out-Of-Phase Faith: saying we trust in the ready availability of Divine Substance and then spend our time worrying and fretting about its manifestation;

Out-Of-The-Box Thinking: also refers to thinking out-of-the-box, thinking beyond the box, lateral thinking, or the Eureka effect); a metaphor that means to think differently, unconventionally, or from a new, expanded perspective. The out-of-the-box thinking we're talking about is the process of creating something that is both original and worthwhile; Divergent rather than convergent thinking is involved so that creative ideas are not limited or stifled by reductionist thinking; the generation of multiple answers to a particular problem; one of the seven core abilities that characterize the Extraordinary Us, our Christ Self. (See Extraordinary You);

Outrospection: the chronic practice of mindlessly giving power to outer appearances;

Over-Active Judgmentalness: being quick on the flaw;

Overclocking: a metaphysician's natural penchant for quickly seeing hidden truths in literal interpretations of scripture; (In IT talk, overclocking means making a processor faster by increasing the clock speed of the computer's CPU past the rate at which it is designed to handle);

Overdose: too much of a religious and/or spiritual brain dump; too many simultaneous reincarnations without an incarnational intermission;

Oversoul, Ousia: the collective transpersonal human personality that defines the essence of where we are *en masse* in consciousness; (According to Martin Heidegger ousia means 'Being.');

Over-Toiling: repeated incarnations;

Owl-ishness: attaining superior wisdom and empowering discernment; having mystical inclinations; taking seriously our guardianship bent; achieving psychic propensities;

Oxygen: spiritual teachings; inter-dimensional travel;

Oxygen Mask: our Quantum Self;

Pacarimoc Runa: our very first thoughts about our spiritual journey; (In shamanic terms, pacarimoc runa refers to the first men who emerged on earth.);

Pacifier(s): dogmatic assertions; compromised values;

Pagan-ness, Paganism: having purely unadulterated materialistic thoughts;

Paha Sapa: a high state of consciousness realized; (In Lakota Sioux circles it is known as the Black Hills and is sacred ground. It is the center of the world where warriors and holy men sought visions);

Pain: the consequences of our no-holds-barred attachment to and worship of outer appearances; pleasure calibrated to its lowest possible setting; (It is the soul languaging its disappointment at our longing for things which do not contribute to our spiritual growth. In that sense pain is our ally. It tells us we have missed the mark in our evolution toward fulfilling our Christ Nature. From a spiritual standpoint, when one person is in pain, we all have an interior hurt that must be healed. Pain is part of the human condition because we are asphyxiated on our supposed separation from Spirit);

Pajamas: our earthly bodies;

Pakizgic Purity: cleansing our mind, body, and soul of error thoughts, words, and actions;

Palace: our super-consciousness;

Pallbearers: dogmatic religious tenets;

Palm-like Tendencies: honoring birth and fertility; feeling the transformative power of our flowering serpentine energies; respecting androgyny; believing in our restorative powers; rising above life's challenges;

Palmistry: interpreting the palms of someone's hands; chiromancy;

Palm Sunday: our conscious surrender to our Christ Nature; a 'depth charge' of enlightenment that stirs our entire consciousness (city in turmoil) and we sense there is something wonderful at work, but do not yet quite understand the full implications of increased spiritual awareness; (This 'explosion of inner quickening' intensifies and leads to the process of inner transformation and cleansing. That's what Jesus' driving the moneychangers out of the temple means from an esoteric perspective. Our job is to wave palm branches signifying the strength of our spiritual conviction, standing firm in our truth. That way, we can move through any situation with grace, dignity, and peace — regardless of outer appearances or internal ego-talk);

Palm Tree-like: tranquil thoughts; high spiritual aspirations; strength and flexibility;

Palooka: a lame brained excuse we keep using to justify our actions: (In the boxing world, a palooka is a lousy boxer with little-to-no ability who usually loses his fights in four to six rounds to boxers who are just beginning their careers. A comic strip created by Ham Fisher in 1928 featured a good-hearted, but slow-witted boxer named Joe Palooka.);

Pampering: receiving a prosperity shower; (See Prosperity Shower); being on the receiving end of non-traditional healing modalities;

Pandora's Box: the repressed material in our subconscious;

Panentheistic Thinking: believing that God is both immanent within all creation and transcends all creation;

Panglossian Stance: believing that all is for the best and that we live in the best of all possible worlds; (People who view every situation with unwarranted and unrealistic optimism. The word pangloss comes from Dr. Pangloss, a character in Voltaire's *Candide*);

Panpsychic: seeing consciousness as the ground of all being and non-being;

Panpsychism: the belief that every event is simultaneously mental and physical; asserting that the known universe is the sum total of psychic unities rather than physical matter;

Pansy Qualities: having fond romantic memories; gentleness; experiencing joyful recollections;

Pantheism: the universe and everything in it is God Essence;

Panthomorphos: the total constellation of thoughts, worldly and spiritual, that run through our heads;

Paper Bag: ordinary, unpretentious receptivity;

Paparazzi: persistent regrets; reoccurring bad habits; (According to psychologists Meyers, Stunkard, Coll, breaking bad habits, or habits in general, requires making them difficult to continue. They found, during the study, that they could cut cafeteria ice cream consumption in half by simply closing the lid of an ice cream cooler. When test subjects were required to wait longer than they thought they should, they moved on to something more convenient. Our best weapon against unwanted habits, the researchers report, is to make it harder for ourselves to succumb to bad habits we are trying to break);

Parabasic Moment: the moment we remove our worldly 'masks' and show others our Authentic Self;

Parachuting: denotes our ability to bring religious teachings 'down to earth' in such a way that they are understandable and practical;

Paraclete: Holy Spirit; (See Holy Spirit);

Parade of Ignorance: having one error thought after another; taking one foolish action after another;

Paradise: spiritual blissfulness; our spiritually-quickened super-consciousness in any dimension of being; a fully illumined consciousness in any of our states of being; our pre-incarnational beingness; Christ Consciousness;

Paradise Lost: our 'expulsion' into reincarnational and/or incarnational experiences;

Paralysis: dogmatic thinking; material attachments; being healed from paralysis means being liberated (cured) from religious orthodoxy;

Paralytic(s): highly judgmental attitudes that keep us from moving toward cementing relationships with those who have different religious beliefs than us; our own conventional beliefs that keep us from exploring higher esoteric perspectives;

Paraskevidekatriaphobia: unrealistic fears that can paralyze us; literally, the fear of Friday the 13th; (See Triskaidekaphobia);

Parent-like: foundational thoughts and beliefs that form the basis of future thoughts and beliefs;

Park-like Inclinations: the need for rest and relaxation; our preference for peace and quiet over the hustle and bustle of making a living;

Parking Lot(s): positioning ourselves for our next move; also denotes repressed memories; our subconscious as a whole;

Parole: our next choice;

Parties: our penchant for celebration, levity, and downright fun;

Passport(s): the reliability of our previous thoughts and ideas that makes it possible for us to enter a new line of thought confidently and purposefully; our current pool of knowledge that readies us for greater knowledge and insights; our Divine Nature;

Password: I am that I am;

Past-Life Regression: a healing technique used to create an altered state of consciousness to guide us to recall or re-experience past life experience in order to free us from blockages and/or limitations preventing our growth and wholeness;

Pastor(s): religious and spiritual ideas;

Path, the: the unfoldment process; (In a very real sense there is no external path – because path implies distance, and there is no distance between us and our Higher Spiritual Nature. The proverbial path is an inner transformation, a transcendental process of becoming consciously aware of our divine nature);

Pathological Procrastination: not being able to decide to become sober yet, or crime-free, or partisan-free, or racist-free, or entitlement-free, or litigation-free, or pornography-free, or alcohol-free, or child-abuse-free, or excess-free, or illness-free, or selfish-free, or excuse-free, or germ-free, or violence-free, or lethargic-free, or predatory-free, or status-free, or tax-free, or pollution-free, or slander-free, or negligent-free, or compulsion-free, or anarchy-free, or bad habit free, or depression-free, or ism-free, or façade-free, or prostitute-free, or cholesterol-free, or Pollyanna-free, or counterfeit-free, or irresponsible-free, or quarrel-free, or handicapped-free, or surgery-free, or prison-free, or flood-free, or uneducated-free, or obscene-free, or traitor-free, or political soft money-free, or safety hazard-free, or narcissistic-free … or truly free;

Pathology: matriculation through our self-imposed human experience; the projection (fabricated path) of our need to return to our cosmic sacredness without realizing we've never been separated from that sacred connection; failing to realize that we have invented the concept of a 'path' which doesn't exist because a 'path' implies distance and there is no distance between us and Spirit – only the delusion of distance;

Patriarchs: Highly spiritual principles, thoughts, and concepts;

Pauperish Pittance: giving money and material things to others instead of genuinely investing ourselves in the relationship;

Pauperization: the cultivation of a poverty consciousness; believing poverty is a virtue;

Pawikuy Orientation: believing we have to reincarnate to become enlightened; (In shamanic terms, pawikuy means to be confused);

Pawnshop: a hellish state of consciousness;

Payload: the esoteric (metaphysical, spiritual, metaphorical) content we receive when we attend a New Thought class; the insights we receive from a meditative experience; the mind, body, soul benefits we obtain from disciplined spiritual practice; (In IT terminology, data is referred to as the payload);

Pay Wall: private access to a guru, senior minister, and/or senior pastor is offered to top tithers only; comprehending higher truths and spiritual teachings is possible when basic teachings are understood; (In IT language, a way of blocking access to a protected part of the website that is only made available to members - paid subscribers);

Peace: the field of peace and tranquility within us that is the holy sanctuary referred to as the Kingdom of God within; (Entry into Jerusalem represents our conscious decision to commit to the eternal, indestructible, universal energies of our Christ Nature); *world peace* is the inner harmony and tranquility we experience that can be the precursor to peace on the planet earth;

Peacock-ishness: attaining immortality; achieving incorruptibility; able to show our true colors; having high self-esteem; becoming aware of our awesome divine nature resplendent with its hidden spiritual gifts (colors); knowing that when we misuse our spiritual gifts we can give up spiritual maturity for the flashiness of material appetites; being educated beyond our intelligence; experiencing pridefulness without strength of character;

Pearl-ness: our Christ Self (Buddha Self, Krishna Self, Allah Self, Extraordinary Nature, etc.);

Pear-like Qualities: being loving; enjoying longevity;

Pediatric Theology: mainstream, fundamentalist religion;

Pedicure: fine tuning our understanding;

Peephole(s): represents a very narrow perspective;

Peer Group: similar thoughts, feelings, words, and actions;

Peerless Perch: enlightenment; recognition of our uniqueness;

Pelagainistic Parachute: denying the existence of original sin; (Pelagianism, named after Pelagius, views the role of the Christ as Jesus as 'setting a good example' for the rest of humanity (thus counteracting Adam's bad example) as well as providing an atonement for our sins);

Pelican-like Capabilities: seeing self-sacrifice and selflessness as desired qualities; having the capacity to absorb higher knowledge; thriving on the ability to dive into the flow of life and come up with the ideas needed to master the art of living;

Pendulum: denotes our proneness to vacillate back and forth before we make a decision;

Penguin-ish: not being able to see the proverbial 'forest for the trees' when it comes to understanding higher thought; having a graceful demeanor and fluidity in emotional situations; a propensity for relying on patience and politeness;

Penitentiary: an egocentric, materially-addicted consciousness;

Pen Name, Pseudonym: the particular human body (name) we created to matriculate through our skin school experience to house (conceal) who we really are;

Pentecost: the fiery activity of the Holy Spirit (serpentine energies) within us; opening up to Spirit so that the fiery white heat of our inner Light shines. (Our five senses are raised to their highest spiritual essences so that our Earth experience is filtered through the eyes, ears, smell, taste, and touch of an enlightened being who has deepened his/her understanding of Eternal Truths. Pentecost is more process than event. More internal combustion than external commotion);

Penthouse Suite: our super-consciousness;

Peony-like: novice-like; an initiate;

Peopleware: the human element in any spiritual and/or religious practice; (In IT lingo, peopleware includes: individuals, groups, project teams, developers, programmers, end users, etc.)

Percipient: being aware of, intercepting, intelligibly perceiving and receiving telepathic or psychic impressions;

Percolator: our brain;

Peripatetic Enlightenment: becoming enlightened by wandering around;

Peripeteaian Moment: a sudden realization of a reversal in fortune as we enter a skin school experience;

Periscope: our Third Eye;

Perpendicular Path: the 'path' all of are on in each skin school experience; the ninety-degree intersection between Spirit and matter; the path of crossing out error;

Persecution Bias: believing in original sin and the devil;

Personal Penitence: taking a candid look at our counterfeit behaviors and replacing them with a much more spiritual dossier of habits;

Personal Trainer: our Divine Self (Authentic Self, Extraordinary Self, Fantabulous Self, Brilliant Self);

Personality Disorder: the refusal and/or outright denial of our innate divinity;

Pervert: an impure thought or action;

Pescatarian(s): vegetarians whose diets include fish;

Pessimistic Positivity: letting our positive attitude and optimistic spirit wane at the first sign of troublesome outer appearances; (According to positive psychologists Clifton and Rath ninety nine out of one hundred people would prefer to be around positive people. People believe that they work more productively when they are around positive people. Positive emotions are contagious so having a teacher or student who is positive can help the other students to be positive and work to the best of their abilities. If there is one negative person, it can ruin the entire positive vibe in an environment. Clifton and Rath believe that 'positive emotions are an essential daily requirement for survival');

Pessomancy: divining that uses colored pebbles;

Pests: the nagging consequences of error thoughts, words, and action that keep us distracted and annoyed;

Pest Management: our ability to be vigilant and take preventative steps to control, eliminate, and/or lessen the occurrence of error thoughts and actions that negatively affect our spiritual growth; (In landscaping terms, pest management means both insect and weed control);

Petrified Doctrine: fossilized dogma;

Petunia-like: peaceful; belief in goodwill for all;

Phablet: represents our ability to communicate above average spiritual principles but not advanced level teachings; (In IT circles, a smartphone that has a screen that is the size between a typical smartphone and a tablet computer);

Philalethistic Orientation: having a love for the truth, no matter where it leads;

Philosopher's Stone: the Christ Presence within each of us; the Eternal Presence that expresses Itself in, as, and through us; Christ Consciousness;

Phoenix-like: attaining both resurrection and immortality; experiencing re-emergence and transformation; achieving perpetual sustainability; gaining renewed clarity; attaining birth and rebirth; establishing a strong recommitment;

Phreaking: pretending interest in a particular spiritual and/or religious practice in order to "hack" into the discipline to attempt to debunk it, ridicule it, or cause hard feelings associated with it; (In IT language, phreaking describes "hacking" into analog phone systems to make free long distance calls);

Phrenology: divining the skull and head to tell someone's individuality and personality;

Physical Body: ego suit, skin school suit; collection of thoughts; a syllable of the incarnated WORD (frozen Logos);

Physical World: our collective whirled consciousness spun on the axis of our imaginations;

Piano-ness: like all musical instruments, reminds us of the beauty of the pitch, rhythm, and tempo of our continuing entrainment with our indwelling divinity;

Picture(s): denote validation of the mental and emotional impressions we have of the phenomenal world; *black and white pictures* suggest past impressions and/or our need to see things in 'black and white' (more clear-cut, the absence of gray areas); *color pictures* represent our desire to see things as close to perceived 'reality' as we can get; *abstract pictures* symbolize our preference for more creative, abstract, metaphorical thinking;

Picture Frame(s): represent our desire for closure, stability, adherence to guidelines, conformity, and normality;

Pidginic Consciousness: a consciousness filled with competing spiritual and materialistic thoughts (languages);

Pier(s): denote our patient plunge into expansiveness and transition;

Pietistic Leakage: being a bad commercial for the churchy, god-fearing, pious us;

Piggyback: making two or more statements about a spiritual or religious subject to invite listeners to see our point of view; (In advertising terms, piggybacking is slang for two of an advertiser's announcements that are presented back-to-back during a single commercial time segment);

Pillar: spinal cord; (see also Fire);

Pillar of Salt: the abrupt halt (turning back, petrification, becoming inactive) of serpentine energies (kundalini) in our spinal cord because of our return to another incarnation (salty body) with its over-indulgent sense appetites;

Pillow(s): truth principles that bring us comfort and rest; putting out intellect to rest;

Pilot: our enlightened mind;

Pineal Gland: the seat of our highest, most elevated, state of consciousness;

Pineapple(s): represent hospitality and warmth;

Pinecone(s): fertility; new pursuits; achievement;

Ping Pong: represent immediate feedback; what goes around comes around;

Pink-ish Qualities: expressing unconditional love, compassion, and happiness; pink also denotes joyfulness, sweetness, romance, tenderness, nurturing, and kindness;

Pinocchio: false representation; deceitfulness; façade;

Pioneer-like: relishing new adventures and discoveries; enjoying stepping-out on our own; the inclination to work and live outside of convention;

Pious Inflation: the unfortunate egocentric impulse of telling others how religious we are;

Pious Roughage: hypocritical forthrightness; pharisaical sincerity;

Pirate(s): the peculiarity of wanting to take something that isn't ours; irresponsible freedom; being comfortable with risk, adventure, and conflict;

Pirouette(s): balance and control; poise and grace;

Pistis Sophia: an evolving collection of enlightened thoughts that are seen as representing spiritual wisdom, superior intuition, and faith; (A Gnostic text discovered in 1773 that proclaims that Jesus remained on earth after the resurrection for eleven years. It is an allegory paralleling the death and resurrection of Jesus, and describing the descent and ascent of the human soul. It then describes important figures within the Gnostic cosmology, and lists 32 carnal desires to overcome before salvation is possible. It also identifies Sophia as being identical with the Holy Spirit, the Universal Mother, the Psyche of the world, and the female aspect of the Logos);

Pits, Holes: gross materialism; incarnation; glimpses into the subconscious;

Pixilation: the consequences of our errant choices and actions; (In photography terms, pixilation means that pixels in an image are visible.);

Placebo Effect: mind over molecules;

Place Mat(s): hospitality; social graces;

Plagiaristic Idolatry: our unabashed declaration that we are the sole authors of our accomplishments instead of attributing our alignment with our Christ Nature as the causative factor; (In *Practicing the Presence*, Joel Goldsmith defines idolatry: "To give power to anything external to consciousness is idolatry. It is to recognize a power apart from God. We must come to the inner conviction that power does not exist in form – any form, no matter how good, the form may be." pg. 51);

Plague(s): impure thoughts and self-deprecating actions that have wide-spread negative impact;

Plains (Level Land): waking consciousness; ordinary conscious awareness;

Plaintiff(s): the affirmative denials we make to serve notice to the illusionary power of outer appearances; (In the legal system, plaintiffs are the people who initially bring legal action against another (defendant) seeking a court decision.); (See Denialdom);

Planchette-like Decisions: choosing diddlysquat order instead of Divine Order;

Plane(s): highly introspective thoughts;

Plane Crash: a collection of highly introspective thoughts or set of beliefs that come 'crashing down to earth' when we realize they were based on false assumptions and will not take us where we want to go;

Planet(s): major intellectual concepts and theories; major religious tenets; premiere spiritual principles;

Plastic Surgery: a self-esteem lift; identity theft and/or identity retrieval;

Plateau(s): the status quo; normality;

Platypus: shyness, reservation, timidity;

Plausible Lie (s): original sin; the devil;

Playbook(s): Bible; Torah; Koran; Kabbalah; Vedas; Upanishads; Bhagavad Gita; Mahābhārata; Tipitaka; Zend-Avesta; Qur'an; Guru Granth Sahib; Kitab-i-lqan; etc.;

Playground: our inborn impulse to let our inner child out; our earth experience;

Pliers: expanding and strengthening our grip on a situation;

Plug(s): access providers and/or covers;

Plumb Line: the descent of Spirit into matter;

Plutoed: devaluing certain error thoughts, words, and actions, as happened to the former planet Pluto;

Pneumatological Insight: recognizing the omni-activity of the Eternal Presence in all things in physicality; (Pneumatology is the study of the Holy Spirit. In Greek, *pneuma* means 'breath, motile air, or incorporeal spirit. In Latin, it is *spiritus*, which means breath);

Pocket(s): receptivity;

Pocketknife: cutting edge discernment;

Podcast(s): show-and-telling our spiritual and/or religious experiences through storytelling, visualizations, and guided meditations; (In IT language, podcasts are audio and video broadcasts that use iPods and iTunes to play programs);

Podium, Lectern: a platform for influence;

Poinsettia(s): joyfulness; celebration;

Poison: thoughts, words, and actions that deny our innate divinity; false teachings;

Poison Ivy: non-productive behaviors, habits, and customs we need to avoid;

~ *Spiritually Speaking* ~

Polandry: an emotion that is coupled with two or more thoughts; (For example: joyfulness that 'marries' philanthropic and spreading the wealth thoughts);

Poles: male generative energy; the maypole represents a propensity of thoughts;

Polygamy: a thought that is coupled with two or more emotions; (For example: fantasizing about winning the lottery gets us feeling excited and glad that we bought a ticket);

Police, Law Enforcement: our sense of morality; conscience; our own unfailing authentegrity;

Political Rallies: religious denominations warring against each other over doctrinal superiority; our internal pitch for a certain ideology or belief;

Poll Booth(s): the power of choice;

Pollination: sharing ideas; allergic proselytizing;

Poltergeist(s): a German word meaning "noisy or troublesome spirit." (Poltergeist activity may include unexplained noises, movements of objects, outbreaks of fire, floods, pricks or scratches to a person's body);

Polysynthesism: sensing the profound homogeneity of the manifest universe;

Polytheism: believing in a pantheon of deities; internally, our integration of Truths from a variety of sources;

Pomegranate-like: expressing our sensuality; recognizing the oneness and unity in diversity; cultivating a strong and lasting marriage;

Pompous Stench: the puffed-up, portentous, pontifical pronouncements of a religious narcissist;

Pompous Witnessing: the egotistical grip of self-inflation;

Ponzi Scheme: stealing from Peter to pay Paul; justifying our actions by using statements of Truth;

Poor: worldly thoughts and inclinations;

Pope: religious orthodoxy;

Poppy-like: our fondness for remembering those who have died in wars; our quirkiness for having morphine-like thoughts that stifle our spiritual development and contribute to our sleeping through our earth experience;

Porcupine-ness: being a bit prickly or easily offended in matters where we feel vulnerable or unsuited;

Pornography: impure, carnal thoughts and tendencies;

Portrait(s): projected mirrors; our vision of ourselves;

Post-Apocalypse: the actualization of our Christhood (Buddhahood, Krishnahood, Vishnuhood, Allahhood, Great Spirithood);

Postcognition: Memories or flashes from past lives;

Post-it-Note(s): mental notes; cognitive reminders;

Potatoes: choosing the essentials in life; digging for the indispensable hidden truths in scripture;

Potholes: worn out attitudes and habits that interfere with our spiritual progress;

Potluck: brainstorming ideas;

Potpourri: a collection of spiritual and/or religious maxims;

Pottery: thoughts and emotions shaped by our consciousness;

Pottery Wheel: the human experience;

Potting Soil: spiritual and/or religious teachings; a faith community; (In gardening terms, potting soil is a nutrient-rich soil mixture designed for use in container gardens.);

Pout Rage: our proneness to pretend we're angry (false outrage) in order to obtain a personal, financial, and/or political advantage;

Power-Phrasing: using powerful quotes from famous people as affirmations;

Power Supply: the Eternal Presence; (In IT parlance, a power supply is a hardware component that supplies electrical power to electrical devices);

Powwow: Native American ceremony or tribal meeting; a time of personal introspection and/or decision-making;

Practicing the Presence: living from a state of grace and loving oneness in our hearts; connecting with our Christ Center; consciously connecting with the Eternal Isness; (In "The physiology of meditation: A review," *Neuroscience and Biobehavioral Reviews*, 1992, 16, R. Jevning, R.K. Wallace, and M. Beidebach report that "a quiet prayer, a stately hymn, or an hour spent in meditation, can activate the body's quiescent function that has been shown to enhance immune system function, lower heart rates and blood pressure, restrict the release of harmful stress hormones into the blood, and generate feelings of calmness and well-being." Pg. 415-424);

Prana: the breath of life; vital life force within our physical bodies;

Prayer: the world's number one antiperspirant; a spiritual Self-hug; the spiritual mortar that holds all of the other parts of our day together; connecting with our own God-potential; communion with that part of us which is the presence of God *indivisibilized* as us; a tool we use to build our awareness of God within and to bring ourselves consciously closer to our innate divinity; (Prayer is not an activity we do *to* a 'God out there,' or a ritual we perform to please an external deity. It is a deeply interpersonal experience in which we connect with our own God-potential. So, we do not really pray *to* God, rather we pray *from* a consciousness of our oneness with God within us. It is communion with that part of us which is God *showing up as us*).

Prayer-Conditioned: habitually employing daily doses of prayer as a spiritual practice; being prayed-up;

Prayer Err: praying with an unforgiving heart and expecting prayer to work;

Prayerful Parenthesis: bookmarking (sandwiching) each day with prayer;

Preachy Argumentativeness: a penchant for protracted debate;

Prebuttal(s): rebuttals to accusations before they are made (For example: someone might say, "You'all are going to think I'm prejudiced against same sex couples attending our church, but the Bible says homosexuality is a sin."); [Actually, the Bible does NOT say that! The above example is a warped perspective based on a literal-only interpretation of scripture];

Precious Ones: spiritual thoughts; divine ideas;

Predecessor(s): conventional thoughts, beliefs, attitudes, and emotions;

Predestination: our Heirship actualized; (See Free Will, Heirship);

Pre-exhausted: our penchant for programming negative outcomes because of the effort we believe will be required to accomplish whatever we feel we need to do; (In social media terms, pre-exhausted means feeling exhausted just by thinking about something laborious);

Pre-existence: our spiritual beingness before we chose our current incarnation;

Pregret(s): regretting things we're about to do anyway;

Premonition: conscious awareness of an unsettling impending event;

Pre-School: the space-time 'parking lot between skin school experiences: (See Quantum Veil);

Presence of God in Our Midst: our Divine Nature (our Christ Nature, Buddha Nature, etc.);

Prevailing Wins: using our existing spiritual knowledge and higher consciousness practices to live a more fulfilled, happier, prosperous, and healthier life;

Preventative Maintenance: pre-praying every day; pre-praying events, tasks, and important decisions;

Previsioning: seeing an event that is currently happening somewhere else or about to happen clearly in our mind's eye; prodigious foresight;

Prime Lens: either a Christ-centric perspective or an egocentric perspective; (In photography lingo, a prime lens is a fixed focal lens as opposed to a zoom lens.);

Principalities: foundational spiritual principles and/or laws;

Principle of Plenitude: believing that everything that can be, already is; believing in the universality of Universal Substance;

Priors: previous incarnational and/or reincarnational experiences; (In law enforcement terms, a prior is a previous arrest for a crime);

Private School: our own individual mind, body, and soul experience in a particular incarnation; keeping our introspections to ourselves;

Probation: the time lapse between a choice and an action;

Problihood: believing in the extent to which something is likely; envisioning the probability of something happening;

Productive Procrastination: keeping ourselves busy doing things that can be considered accomplishments, while avoiding what we really need to be doing and/or intended to do like meditating or exercising;

Profanity: conversational litter; a denial of our Divinity;

Profit(s): the good experiences from our choices;

Progressive Proofs: every thought we have, each choice we make, every action we take that is compatible with our professed spiritual and/or religious training;

Progressive Realization: refusing to be blinded by religious convention or blind-sided by someone else's definition of our true divine nature; (No action leaves us the same as before. Whether it is heroism or cowardice, restraint or spontaneity, working or playing, watching or participating, growing spiritually or "no-ing" religion - everything we do contributes to the new version of us);

Promissory Note: the Indwelling Christ;

Propaganda: prognostications by fortune tellers, unscrupulous prosperity gurus, and mainstream religious preachers who sell guilt and fear and shame;

Prophet(s): discerning insights that characterize our understanding of the consequences of our thinking, being, and doing so that we can make wiser choices;

Promised Land: Christ Consciousness; a fully illumined consciousness; enlightenment;

Prosecutor(s): the consequences of our poor choices;

Proselytizing, Braggadocic Antics: the over-bearing attempt of religious fundamentalists to convert people to their religious beliefs;

Proselytizing Smog: the defensive uneasiness caused by being subjected to the evangelical persuasiveness of fundamental religious fanatics;

Prosperity: living joyfully, faithfully, confidently, and lovingly at the speed of our Christ Consciousness; a consciousness of giving; realizing that our good doesn't come *to* us it comes *through* us; letting go of your good for your greater good; filling your consciousness with more prayer, meditation, faith, love, positive affirmations, and charity;

Prosperity Affidavit: claiming our health, wealth, and well-being using powerful, positive affirmations;

Prosperity Grimoire: a 'spellbinding' book containing magical denial and positive affirmation statements;

Prosperity Shaping: filling our consciousness with more prayer, meditation, and positive affirmations is prosperity shaping. It gets us past the 'LULL' of attraction so that there is no 'LULL' between manifesting something and waiting for what we want to manifest;

Prosperity Shower: walking between a friendly gauntlet of ten to twenty people who whisper affirmations of prosperity and abundance in your ear;

Prosperity Subtraction: the negative effects of error thoughts, poor choices, and bad habits;

Prostitute-ish: our promiscuous attachment to carnal sense appetites which is contrary to our professed belief in the goodness and sacredness of spiritual principles;

Protagonist: our Divine Self (Christ Self, Buddha Self, etc.);

Prowler(s): repressed emotions; errant thoughts floating into our awareness;

Pseudocode(s): using common everyday language to describe highly esoteric and/or religious jargon so the average person can understand it; (In IT language, a pseudocode uses conventional syntax and basic English phrases that are universally understood instead of specific syntax in writing a program's source code);

Pseudonym: human being for spiritual being; human being for the Christ; the Christ for the Eternal Presence;

Psi-Hitting: significantly better than chance performance on a psi test;

Psi-Missing: significantly worse than mere chance performance on a psi test; (Psi-missing is also evidence *for* psi, because a target can only be missed consistently if the person 'knows' what the target is);

Psyche: our soul; the totality of our conscious, unconscious, subconscious, super-conscious, and quantum [composite] beingness;

Psychic Energy: experiential evidence of an intelligent, powerfully pervasive, invisible force within our physical body that fills us with electrical vitality and a sense of connection with the dynamics of the universe;

Psychic Healing: a form of energetic non-traditional medicine that harnesses placebo power for healing;

Psychic Iridology: (See Third Eye);

Psychic Powers: abilities like – apportation, automatic writing, astral projection, biolocation, clairvoyance, clairaudience, divination, precognition, psychokinesis, pyrokinesis, remote viewing, telepathy, transvection, etc.;

Psychic Scrying: (See Mirror);

Psychoenergetics: parapsychological interaction between consciousness, matter, and energy;

Psychokinesis: moving objects with the energetic power of the mind; anomalous perturbation;

Psychological Shielding: mentally surrounding ourselves with a cocoon of white light to protect ourselves from harm, from things like someone else's cold, or cough, or illness, or injury, or negativity. It works really well when we're surrounded by pessimistic and egocentric people; (In the mid 90's, consciousness researcher William Braud performed experiments to see if we could mentally block or prevent any outside influences that we don't want in our lives. At the end of the experiment the 'shielded' group showed considerably fewer physical effects than the control group. This study, and others like it, have been replicated by other consciousness researchers.); (See White Light Technique);

Psychometry, Psychoscopy, Token-Object Reading, Psychic Reading: a form of extrasensory perception characterized by the self-reported ability to intuit relevant associations from objects of unknown history by making physical contact with that object; (Joseph Buchanan coined the term psychometry because he believed all things give off associative psychic emanations.);

Psychopath(s): a fully entrenched, out-of-control, divinity-denying, worldly ego that feeds on materialism, duality, and separation;

Psychopomps: galvanizing thoughts that 'escort' subconscious material into our waking consciousness;

Psychosynthesis: the belief that spiritual growth can be enhanced by acknowledging the soul's existence and developing the wisdom to connect with the soul; (Roberto Assagioli developed the technique);

Puffy Ooze: vicious gossip; undeserved criticism; narcissistic pontification; obnoxious proselytizing;

Pukio, Pujyu, Pukyu: energy center; (See Chakra);

Pulp Fiction: the rude, crude, lascivious, and tasteless denials of our innate divinity;

Pulpit Theft: the practice, by some clergy, of using canned sermons from the Internet and then passing them off as their own;

Pulpit Yo-Yoing: stream of consciousness sermons where an unprepared message is tossed out to see what sticks;

Punch-Drunk: matriculating through our current skin school experience without paying any attention to how our errant thoughts, choices, attitudes, and actions compromise our spiritual growth, health, wealth, and well-being; (In boxing terms, being punch-drunk refers to a neurological disorder called Dementia Pugilistica which is triggered by repeated blows to the head over an extended period of time. Symptoms include slurred speech, dementia, dazedness, and confusion.);

Punching Bag(s): ourselves – on the receiving end of our poor choices;

Punishment Junkies: ourselves – when we make unnecessary reincarnational stops on our way to enlightenment; (See Punching Bags);

Puñuskiri: keeping ourselves in the dark; (in shamanic terms, puñuskiri means eternally deadened); (Unforgivable Sin);

Puppet-like: mindless conformity to convention;

Puppeteer: our warped ego; being controlled by outside influences or errant beliefs from our embedded theology;

Puppy, Puppies: the playful aspects of our natural instincts;

Puppy Luv, Puppy Love, Infatuation Attraction: the infatuation we have with a literal interpretation of the Bible; (In social relationships, puppy luv is an infatuation or crush felt by young people, usually during their adolescence that is their brand of romance.);

Pure Land: the Land of Bliss, paradise; our Christ Mind (Buddha Mind, Krishna Mind, etc.);

Purgatory: worldly thoughts, held in our subconscious, that are not quite ready to be discarded; : the narrow neural time line between deciding to act and actually acting; (See Bereishafts Potential; Readiness Potential Isthmus); (The Catholic doctrine of purgatory holds that Christian souls who have accepted rites of baptism and have been accepted into the body of the faithful, but who have died unexpectedly with unconfessed sins and/or minor venial faults, will not go to hell necessarily, but will instead spend an indeterminate period of time in a place of temporal punishment. The same 'temporary' suffering is supposed to be the fate of baptized infants who have not reached the age where they can choose to be good Catholics and attend their first confessional. In this limbo environment (purgatory), such souls will suffer for awhile as an act of penance which is supposed to purify them so they can enter the pearly gates in good standing.);

Putty: concepts that are not fully formed;

Pygmies: egotistical, self-absorbed, self-serving, narcissistic thoughts and attitudes;

Pyramid(s): the desire of the many (the pyramid's base) to return to the One, the Eternal Presence, God, represented by the pyramid's summit; its external edifice depicts our ascension, an ascension that brings our human self into perfect alignment with our Christ Self, Buddha Self, Krishna Self, Allah Self; the steps symbolize the many states of elevated awareness we must achieve as we become enlightened; the four sides denote our spiritual, mental, emotional, and physical selves; (Since pyramids mean 'fire in the middle' we could say, without stretching it too far, that the mysterious power associated with pyramids is an apt metaphor for the mysterious, preservative, healing power of the 'fire in the middle' of us – our Christ Nature! It is the Divine Fire in our solar plexus. The Cosmic Flicker at our core, the *Lux Aeterna,* the Eternal Light of our Christ Self);

Pyramidology: moving your awareness to the highest, most elevated level; the study of pyramids and the energy fields that they emanate;

Pyrrhonismic Proneness: the chronic tendency to have totally skeptical ideas;

Qabbalah: Hebrew theosophy; our desire to comprehend the incomprehensible;

Qadric Capacity: using our free will to sustain us in our spiritual work;

Qalam: the 'pen' in which God writes upon our heart; the instrument of spiritual inspiration;

Qi: life force; universal energy; (Also called ch'i, chi, ki);

Qiblihian Stance: facing in a sacred direction during prayer and/or meditation; (In the Bahá'i Faith, the Qiblih is the location where Bahái's face when saying their daily prayers);

Qigong: energy healing using breathing, movement, and meditation;

Quagmire: the repressed self-negating patterns region in our subconsciousness; an ego addicted to itself; bad habits that are *kissing cousins*;

Qualified Circulation: the thoughts and inclinations running around in our heads that are congruent with our professed level of spiritual and/or religious awareness;

Quantum Entanglement: As emanations (expressions) of that Source we are not only in constant communication with That which underwrites our being, we are the One reality expressing Itself in many forms, in many eras, in many dimensions, in many universes, and perhaps, in many Multiverses. The 'Book of Life' the scriptures mention is the quantum registering of every thought, feeling, choice, and action we make (in each of our states of being) in the 'Mind' of the One Reality so that each nano-step of our spiritual unfoldment (return to the Godhead) is recorded. Nothing is lost because our essence is God essence. The unbroken connection, the uninterrupted communication, is built into our spiritual DNA. Whatever we think, whatever direction we take, whatever we feel, whatever we do is instantaneously registered – and recoded – in the memory bank of Cosmic Consciousness. Multiply our individual being, thinking, and doing by everyone else's simultaneous being, thinking, and doing and you begin to appreciate the magnitude, complexity, and organization of Divine Mind; (In 1997, scientists from the University of Geneva in Switzerland split a single photon into two separate particles, essentially creating "quantum identical twins." The quantum pair was placed in a high-tech chamber composed of two fiber-optic pathways (similar to those that transmit phone signals) that extended away from the chamber in opposite directions (seven miles in all). Then they fired the "twins" in opposite directions. By the time each twin reached its termination point, they were separated by a distance of fourteen miles. What makes this experiment so tantalizing is that at the termination point the quantum twins were forced to *choose* between two random routes that were identical in nature? The amazing thing is the twins made precisely the *same* choice and traveled the *same* path each time the experiment was repeated. The twins acted as if they were "communicating" with each other and arriving at the same decision – instantaneously – fourteen miles apart.[i] Einstein called this 'spooky action at a distance.' Today it is referred to as quantum entanglement.);

Quantum Exegesis: The 'Theory of Everything,' the Holy Grail of quantum physics, may always be just a 'TOE' wetting exercise in our attempt to understand the universe in which we live. (I believe our quest to understand the 'nature of things' – both quantum and cosmological – must be a tandem scientifically empirical and spiritually revelatory path); [In *The Elegant Universe*, Brian Green asserts: "Quantum mechanics and the theories of relativity are deep beyond anyone's wildest expectations: wave functions, probabilities, quantum tunneling, the ceaseless roiling energy, fluctuations of the vacuum, the smearing together of space and time, the relative nature of simultaneity, the warping of the space-time fabric, black holes, the big bang. Who could have guessed that the intuitive, mechanical, clockwork Newtonian perspective would turn out to be so thoroughly parochial – that there was a whole new mind-blowing world lying just beneath the surface of things as they are ordinarily experienced.");

Quantum Immortality: From a spiritual perspective there is no death, only transformation. Immortality is assured us because we (the Authentic us) are immortal beings. Our physical bodies (quantum shells) are immortal – although one day we may very well inhabit these 'somatic spacesuits' for hundreds of years. We are suggesting that these quantum (physical) versions of us are temporary containers that help us gather experiences along the way toward our eventual enlightened forms, forms that are more etherealized and transcendent. Once etherealized, we will morph into still other states of being so we can continue to learn, serve, and evolve. We have many assignments ahead of us. This earth experience is just one of many;

Quantum Prosthesis: our next skin school extension (physical body);

Quantum Scroll: incarnated human consciousness;

Quantum Self: The self of us which remembers our past lives and concurrent lives in other dimensions of being; the composite of all of our human and intra-dimensional incarnations and reincarnations; (Our quantum selves [our incarnated selves] are akin to the Theosophist's monad and the Hindu concept of *sutratman*. They are strung like beads on a quantum thread. I believe our dreams, *déjà vu experiences*, and past life regressions are conscious nonlocal recollections of our 'other' selves (beads) on the thread of the interconnectedness of life expressing Itself as us); (Quantum physicists remind us that once we are connected we are always connected. In the mid 1990's, scientists working with the U. S. Army conducted an experiment to determine whether or not our feelings affect DNA, which has been removed from the body. It was reasoned that once tissue [skin, organs] are removed from a human body, our connection with those removed parts ceases to exist. The researchers, under psychologist Julie Motz, collected a swab of tissue [DNA] from the inside of a volunteer's mouth. The DNA sample was isolated and placed in a specially-designed chamber and taken to another room in the same building. Once the experiment began the donor, who was in another room located a good distance away, was shown a series of video images designed to elicit a wide range of emotional responses. While the donor was undergoing the 'treatment' the DNA in the room down the hall was measured for its reaction. An extraordinary thing happened. When the donor's measured responses registered emotional 'peaks' or 'dips,' the donor's DNA showed a simultaneous electrical response that either spiked or dipped. The DNA acted as if it were still connected to its donor at a distance); [In *The Book of Revelation*, Aivanhov assures us that "everything we do is recorded and our actions, sentiments, and thoughts all leave traces, not only on our surroundings, but on us." Pg. 113];

Quantum Septenary: our sevenfold quantum nature; (In Theosophical terms, we possess seven bodies: the physical body, the vital body, the astral body, the mental body, the causal body, the Buddhic body, and the atman);

Quantum Veil: the 'time tunnel' between incarnational experiences;

Quarry, Quarries: the exposed subconscious areas we are consciously working on;

Queen-like: honoring the mature feminine principle;

Queen Anne's Laceness: imaginative; unbridled inspiration;

Quicksand: being pulled down and possibly suffocated by false beliefs; finding ourselves asphyxiated by bogus, fraudulent, and deceptive religious practices; a life-threatening shortcut;

Quicksilver: speedy thinking;

Quid Pro Quo: the inherited guarantee we have when we conscientiously apply truth principles;

Quintessential Machining: mindlessly delivering and/or listening to a spiritual and/or religious message without our heart in it so we merely go through the motions;

Quitetism: believing we can achieve enlightenment solely through mental tranquility;

Quixotic Rhapsody: being guided in and/or self-administering a compelling spiritual visualization that takes us into a high state of hallowed awareness;

~ *Spiritually Speaking* ~

Quokka-like: fearless; dauntless; (In Aboriginal Australian regions quokkas are kangaroo rats that are literally unafraid of humans);

Quoz Creed: putting a great amount of energy around an absurd ideology;

Qutbic Stability: using a central spiritual teaching to bath our consciousness in light; (An Arabic term for axis, pivot, or pole);

Ra: the cosmic Universal Soul in physicality;

Rabbi: religious orthodoxy and piety;

Rabbit-ness: honoring fertility; believing in luck; able to raise our awareness; relishing speed; maintaining proper and acute vigilance;

Raccoon-like: resolutely going after what we want; a tendency to explore every nook and cranny; generous protector; skilled at taking care of ourselves so we can take care of others; (The name *raccoon* is believed to come from the Algonquin Indian word 'arckunem' which means 'hand scratcher.');

Race Karma: our collection of thoughts (race) that have become habitual themes that define our view of the world (our human consciousness); the thoughts, concepts, habits, and activities of the human species (race) that are passed down from incarnation to incarnation, defining the over-all consciousness of the current human species;

Racetrack: undeviated circular thinking;

Racism: the unenlightened ego's prejudice against religious and spiritual thoughts;

Radar: our Third Eye;

Radical Innocence: our innate ability to maintain a child-like sense of wonder, awe, faith, reverence, and belief in the basic goodness of people in spite of being aware of the cruelties, injustices, and violence that seem so prevalent);

Radio: our highly active brain;

Radiesthesic Ability: the extra-sensory ability to detect biological radiations and resonances that surface from our subconscious; (Radiesthesia was borrowed from the French word *radiésthesie* which means 'perception by the senses' or 'the capacity for feeling or sensation' which comes from the Greek word *aisthesis* that means 'a perceiving.');

Raft(s): *wooden rafts* suggest rudderless drifting; *white water rafts* denote an adventuresome spirit;

Ragnarokian Sadism: unfettered and unbridled destructive thoughts that can take over our consciousness once we totally negate our divinity;

Rahmic Mercy: divine compassion and forgiveness;

Railroad(s), Road(s), Highway(s): our nervous system; our circulatory system;

Rain: spiritual influences; spiritual insights, thoughts, inclinations;

Rainbow: uniting heaven and earth; our etherealized spiritual power centers (chakras); astrological centers; the seven known levels of consciousness; the 'many mansions' the Christ as Jesus referred to; our serpentine energies; our bridge in consciousness from temporality to eternity; (According to Homer [Iliad 11:26-8] rainbows represent serpents and appear on the breastplate of Agamemnon in the shape of rainbows. In African religious traditions, especially in Dahomey, the 'celestial serpent' takes the form of a rainbow.

Rainforest: our consciousness, with its mixed variety of worldly, religious, and spiritual thoughts; (According to physicist Bernard d'Espagnat, the doctrine that the world is made up of objects whose existence is independent of human consciousness turns out to be in conflict with quantum mechanics and with facts established by experiment);

Raja Yoga: balancing mental. Emotional, physical, and spiritual energies; one of the oldest systems of developing psychic and spiritual powers and union with our *Higher Self*;

Raka-like: fully expressing our psychic feminine energies in tune with the full moon's influence;

Ram-like Attributes: able to generate potent spiritual thoughts; using the virility of powerful spiritual insights to transform our nature;

Ramp(s): metaphors and analogies;

Rapture: a spiritual thought entering ordinary consciousness which lifts many sense thoughts up to their higher spiritual essences;

Rapture of the Church: the term rapture comes from the Latin word *raptio* (caught up) and refers to our raised awareness (rapture) as spiritual beings in human form (the church) as we discover the Christ (Buddha, Krishna, Allah, etc.) within (the Second Coming); (See Second Coming);

Raqsic Urges: dancing with joy; (*Raqs* sharqi is the classical Egyptian style of belly dancing);

Rasha: evil thoughts; (In Kabbalistic terms, wicked people);

Rasshoo: harnessing the fiery energies of Spirit to turn potential into manifested reality; (Rasshoo is Egyptian for the solar fires formed in and out of the primordial 'waters', or substance, of Space);

Rational Lies: We are all professional rationalizers when you think about it! I mean – we are really good at coming up with explanations to justify our behaviors or beliefs! But think about that word: rationalize. It is actually self-descriptive: Rational Lies! Rational in that they really sound good, and make sense! (But Lies, nevertheless, because they are like a good coat of paint over a flood-damaged car. They create an illusion that keeps us stuck and prevents us from moving forward!);

Rat-ishness: experiencing negatively-charged thoughts and actions that gnaw at us;

Raudive Voices: mysterious, intelligible voices recorded on magnetic tape under conditions of silence or white noise which are heard only when the tape is played; (Konstantīns Raudive, a Latvian intellectual, introduced the electronic voice phenomenon [EVP];

Raven-like: dawning understanding; our shadow side which seeks the light of spiritual understanding; limiting ourselves by using concrete thought which cannot comprehend higher spiritual insights; choosing reductionist thinking;

Razzle Dazzle: Divinely ordering our experience; dutifully applying truth principles;

Readiness Potential Isthmus: the narrow neural time line between deciding to act and actually acting; (See Bereitschafts Potential);

Realignment: taking the opportunity with every thought, word, and action to realign (vibrate in phase) our human self with our Christ Self;

Real Estate: denotes the different levels in our thinking and the different perspectives of our thinking; our physical bodies;

Reality Show(s): our fanciful perceptions of what is real; our earth experience; what is and what isn't; projecting ourselves onto the world and then experiencing the world projecting our projections back onto us; (In *The Nature of Reality, Science and Spirituality*, Makwana asserts: "As early as the Vedic times, the Rishis investigated the nature of reality from two levels of experience, one of which may be called the absolute, acosmic or transcendental level and the other relative, cosmic or phenomenal level. At the phenomenal level one perceives the universe of diversity and is aware of one's own individual ego, whereas at the transcendental level, the differences merge into an inexplicable non dual consciousness. Both of these levels of experience are real from their respective standpoints, though what is perceived at one level may be negated at the other. Reality experienced at the transcendental level is called Brahman. This term denotes the non-dual Pure consciousness which pervades the universe yet remains outside it. [Just as the sun pervades all life on earth yet remains outside it]. Brahman is described as the first principle; from it all things are derived, by it all are supported, and into it all finally disappear.");

Rearview Mirror(s): second guessing ourselves; the past;

Rebel-ish: the non-conformist us; our tendency to reject traditional religious teachings and opt for more spiritual perspectives;

Rebellious Repentance: a pretense of truce and penitence culminating in an uneasy stalemate;

Rebirth: going from an egocentric conscious to a Christed Consciousness; our incarnational and reincarnational experiences;

Recess: a mini sabbatical;

Recidivism, Relapse: learning a new spiritual principle and applying the learning for a while only to revert back to previous behavior;

Reconnaissance: monitoring our own spiritual and/or religious practice and progress;

Recoup, Recouping: recausing our experiences by making better choices;

Rectors of the Spheres: the thoughts that make up our consciousness; angels;

Recycling Rebellion: inner turmoil caused by obtaining higher spiritual knowledge that upsets egocentric apple carts; (See Chemicalization);

Recycling Time: the time it takes to prepare for another incarnation and/or reincarnation; the time between incarnations and/or reincarnations; (In photography language, recycling time is the amount of time for a flash to recharge after it is fired.);

Redemption: We are redeemed every time we replace an error thought, word, choice, or action with a spiritually-charged thought, word, choice, or action;

Red Carpet: our desire to have our ambitions and achievements rewarded; wanting to be publically respected and admired;

Red Cross: our desire for physical healing and recovery;

Red Dragon: our epithumetic (contemptuous, abusive) nature;

Redecorating, Renovating, Remodeling: shifting our perspectives;

Red-ish Impulses: our reddishness implies our propensity for perceiving the world through our physical senses; red is a present-tense impulse, prompting us to live in the now; red denotes sensuality, activity, and our desire to influence the environment around us; enthusiasm and energy; passion and love; intensity; (Red is the color of the base or root chakra. It also stands for the spiritual us, the spiritual expression of our beingness.);

Red Sea: our *oxygenated* blood (sea water); one of the outlets of the Life Force in physical manifestation; our quantum life force expressing as the life flow of the Cosmic Life Force;

Re-Done Tendencies: repeating ourselves or three-peating ourselves; the merry-go-round of circular choices and behaviors that limit our good;

Redundant Self-Condemnation: not being able to recognize the difference between the will to change and the whim to change;

Reef(s): recognizing the need for a sedative (reef) to help control out-of-control emotions;

Reel-ality: All of us have egocentric filters that color our earth experiences. What usually happens is that what most people consider as real is actually a 'reel' experience. That is, most people replay their old self-defeating tapes like 'B' movies. "Reel-ality" trumps any happiness, health, and joy they can gain since they seem to prefer to remain stuck is a deeply ingrained negativity bias);

Reel Time: life review; past life regressions; remembering our past;

Referee(s): our conscience; the power of our discernment; sound judgment; common sense; uncommon sense; the wisdom gained from experience;

Reflash, Rekindle: the reappearance of a bad habit or materialistic belief that we thought we had outgrown; (In firefighting terms, a reflash is a situation in which a fire, thought to be extinguished, reignites.);

Reflexology: using massage and acupressure to focus on specific areas of the foot to heal other areas of the body;

Re-follow: represents having a line of thought, then chasing a 'rabbit,' then returning to the original line of esoteric thought; denotes having followed a particular 'guru' in the past, then re-upping our interest; (In social media, re-follow means starting to follow a person, group, or organization on a social media website again);

Refugee(s): materialistic thoughts that have been raised to their higher spiritual octaves;

Regeneration: elevating our thoughts from worldly patterns to spiritual heights; a sort of spiritual neuroplasticity;

Regurgitation: the status quo; making the same errors over and over again; reincarnating again and again with no appreciable progress toward enlightenment; memorizing scripture just to prove our discipleship without exploring the depth of the scripture;

Rehab, Rehabilitation: each skin school experience;

Reiki: a form of energy healing that uses distant healing as well as healing touch; (A healing touch technique developed in 1922 by a Japanese Buddhist monk as a way to direct the flow of the universal life energy (Chi to Buddhists, reiki in Japanese) and to transfer that energy through the palms of the hands. Reiki practitioners direct chi in order to heal ailments and attune auras. There are three levels of mastery in using Reiki: First Degree is master of self-healing and extending our aura to heal others directly, second degree is distance healing, and third degree is true mastery and ability to teach others to use reiki. Westernized reiki also uses Indian Chakras);

Reincarnation, Resampling: although not a necessary condition for our spiritual growth, it is a skin school experience we choose because we still believe in separation and duality; our descent as spiritual beings into matter; re-entering an earth experience to matriculate through the illusions we have spun; assuming another biological address; repeated physical rebirths that continue until we outgrow our attachments to material bling, flings, and things; reiterations of our not getting it; (Reincarnation is only one of the portals we choose to experience human form. Another choice is incarnation from another dimension of being. When we reincarnate we've more than likely been here before – probably many times before. When we incarnate we come here for the first time from another dimension of being in the multiverse. Whether we're here through reincarnation (re-embodiment) or incarnation (embodiment) the answer is the same: we've chosen physicality and its limitations over universality and its endless foreverness);

Reincarnation's Causa Causarum: forgetting who we really are and choosing another skin school experience to work on our remembering;

Relative(s): all of humankind; our mind, body, and soul; our human self and our Christ Self; worldly thoughts, religious thoughts, and spiritual thoughts; our internal organs; the three levels of our consciousness;

Religion(s): literal-headedness; dogmatic victrolas; thorns on the stems of roses, making the journey toward enlightenment (the flower) more difficult to reach because of their dogmatic snares and judgmental barbs; perspectives that cling white-knuckled to stale theologies; highly exclusive pockets of embedded theology; institutions that feed the amygdala, starve the anterior cingulate, and deflate the frontal lobe, creating an anthropomorphic, vengeful, punitive God 'out there' atmosphere of exclusivism, judgmentalness, intolerance, warped theology, and fear; (What many people call religion may simply be religious faith. Why am I making such a bold statement? Here's my pitch. "Religion" is a word that comes from the Latin word *religare*. What's interesting is *ligare* means "to tie, to bind, to unite." *Religare* means to "re-tie, re-bind, reunite." True religion, then, describes the process of reuniting with our divine nature. It is a conscious reunification because we have never been separated from our divinity. We are indivisibly one with our Core Nature which is divine. To put it another way we are the human form of God expressing at the point of us. We are one with the Source, the Infinite Isness, the Eternal Presence. Are you still with me! Mainstream religious faiths are based on denominational interpretations of scripture (usually literal interpretations) that foster dogmatic, parochial, and exclusive biases that call for a belief in an external, anthropomorphic deity in the sky who favors some and punishes others and/or a devilish satanic presence. They champion duality and separation – we are 'here' and God is 'there' wherever 'there' is. As they are currently practiced mainstream religious faith traditions divide rather than unite. They have taken *religare* out of their practice by denying their innate divinity and the innate divinity in others);

Religious Amnesty: being able to hold beliefs that deviate from those taught by our particular religious denomination, without incurring oppression, expulsion, or being tried for heresy;

Religious Glaucoma: believing in a literal-only interpretation of scripture;

Religious Memes, Memeplexes: canonical habits, gifts of the spirit, songs and hymns, Biblical stories, and any other kind of information that is copied from person to person;

Religious Orthopraxy: demonstrating the 'right' (expected, approved) conduct;

Religious Paralysis: dogma;

Religious Relics: dogma; supposed inerrant scriptural interpretations; close-minded literal translation bias; extreme judgmentalness; prejudicial exclusivity; notion of an external goodie God; (Mainstream religious 'relics' are neurologically wired into the amygdala which produces our 'fight or flight' reactions. This inherited survival mechanism prevents many fundamental religious practitioners from experiencing more transcendent states of awareness which come from the neocortex area in our brain. The neocortex wiring is evolutionarily available too, it's just not the area of neural real estate fundamentalists are as familiar with);

Religious Spam: unsolicited proselytizing by a religious fanatic; (If we find ourselves nodding off during fanatical proselytizing it may be a good thing. Boredom is more than a mere flagging of interest or a precursor to disengagement. Psychologists say that people tune things out for good reasons, and that over time boredom becomes a tool for sorting information — an increasingly sensitive spam filter);

Religious Triumphalism: believing in the superiority of a particular faith tradition;

Religious Victrolas: memorizing and then repeating literal interpretations of scripture without understanding their deeper, more esoteric meanings;

Remedy: our next choice;

Remission of Sins: the disciplined process of liquidating error from our consciousness and our lives through spiritual self-purification practices;

Remote Dowsing: holding a pendulum over a map until it indicates where the person, place, or thing is located;

Remote Control: guilt; fear;

Remote Healing: healing that takes place when the healer is not in direct physical contact with the person being healed; (See Absent Healing);

Remote Viewing: seeing impressions about distant or unseen targets using extra-sensory perception;

Renaissance: moving from one level of awareness to a higher level of awareness; attaining a Christ-centric Consciousness;

Rendezvous: aligning our human self with our Christ Self (Buddha Self, Allah Self, Krishna Self, etc.); putting esoteric truths into practice at the intersection of self and soul;

Renunciation: releasing old thought patterns, negative life scripts, and Self-negating habits so that new thoughts, life scripts, and habits of a spiritual nature will find a place in our consciousness;

Repenting: voluntarily reforming our perspective and value system by turning our materialistically-minded thoughts and actions into spiritually attuned thoughts and actions;

Repercussion Management: realizing that repercussions follow excuses which are the ego's lines-of-least-persistence; (They are a deflated ego's attempt to side-step personal responsibility by manufacturing alibis to camouflage indecision, disinterest, or irresponsibility); limiting the quantity of unfavorable consequences caused by poor choices by making better choices in the first place; (See Remission of Sins);

Repertoire: the pool of spiritual practices at our disposal;

Replacement Theology: esoteric truths, metaphorical truths, spiritual, mystical truths, cabalistic truths, theosophical truths, anthroposophical truths, and metaphysical truths have replaced mainstream dogmatic perspectives as keys to enlightenment;

Report Card: our tendency to evaluate our spiritual progress; the condition of our bodies and our health as a result of our thinking;

Reprieve: our next choice;

Reservoir: our subconscious; our memory;

Reset Buttons: positive affirmations and denials; affirmative prayers; meditation;

Reshimotic Amnesia: our soul's unconscious warehousing of our past incarnations; (According to the Kabbalah, the entire plan of human development is imprinted in us. There is a chain of commands [genes] within in each of us, from the moment we are born to the moment we make our earthly transitions, but it contains not only our current life cycle, but also all the incarnations of our soul. These commands are called reshimot. The plan dictates our attributes, character, fate and every movement. But it also allows us the freedom of choice.);

Residue: the karmic remnants of each skin school experience;

Resilient Reverence: Seeking reverential moments in spite of the fact that reverence is almost unheard of in a firecracker society where celebrity is measured in decibels and individual worth is determined by the size of one's stock market portfolio;

Response-Ability: our positive reaction to life's circumstances; the level of our responsiveness to the challenges we face;

Rest: abstaining from worldly thoughts and intentions; having a spiritual moment; sequestering ourselves from any sense of separation and duality; putting aside error thoughts sense addictions;

Restaurant(s): New Thought bookstores; Spiritual Glossaries like this one;

Restitution Work: aligning our human self with our Christ Self (Allah Self, Buddha Self, Brahma Self, etc.);

Resurrection: a restoration, a revitalization, a reclamation, a re-booting of our Christ potential every time we choose a Christed thought over a worldly thought;

Retooling: repatterning our choices and behaviors; (Our brain has the propensity to reject any belief that is not in accord with our own views. However we also have the biological power to interrupt detrimental and derogatory beliefs. These ideas can alter the neural circuitry that governs how we behave and what we believe);

Retouching: releasing self-defeating habits and behaviors, eliminating error perspectives, and letting go of egocentric whims to improve our spiritual image; (In photography terms, retouching involves air-brushing a photographic image to improve its looks.);

Return On Investment, ROI: the amount of inner peace, joy, love, prosperity, health, wellness, gratitude, compassion, friendship, etc. we receive from applying the truth principles we know; (In business terms, ROI refers to the investment gains received compared to investment costs);

Retweet Forward: repeating something positive that we hear; paying an act of kindness forward; (In social media terms, a retweet is when someone on Twitter sees our message and decides to re-share it with h/her online followers);

Reunion: the complete alignment between our human self and our Christ Self:

Revelation: a disrobing of illusion or unveiling of higher spiritual truths; vortex of higher thought energy;

Revelation, the Book of: a spiritual how-to manual explaining how we can electrify our twelve cranial nerves and open seven major chakras in order to become fully enlightened; a manual of initiation into the higher mysteries; a guide (playbook) disclosing the transcendental process of our spiritual unfoldment into our resurrected, luminous, immortal solar body;

Reverend(s): religious and/or spiritual thoughts;

Revival Hangover: what happens when a religious revival is over and we return to the 'real' world, only to feel out of place and surreal because the effects of the revival haven't worn off;

Revolver(s): angry, frightening, aggressive, protective thoughts and impulses;

Rhabdomancy: a form of divination that uses wands, sticks, rods and pendulums, usually when searching for water, minerals or other valuable items;

Rhapsodomancy: a form of divination that uses a book of poetry opened at random;

Rheumatism: implies our inflexibility and rigidity;

Rhinoceros-like: filling our lives with massive contradictions; acquiring a huge amount of confidence; gaining fiery insightfulness and explosive power; having the ability to rent the veils of illusion and ignorance;

Rhododendron Quality: supportiveness; cooperativeness;

Rib Fib: Eve being produced from Adam's rib is an allegory. Allegorically speaking, it means that all creation occurs when the descending Life Force (Spirit's vertical descent) into matter (the horizontal dimension) forms a right angle. The result of this cosmic penetration is symbolized by the human skeleton which features the spinal column and the ribs that are at right angles to it. Eve, being universal feminine energy is formed out of the horizontal arm (rib) of the allegorical cross (the intersection between Spirit and matter);

Rib-ishness: respecting equality; gaining balance and equilibrium through selfless sacrifice;

Rice-ish: seeing spiritual knowledge as a staple; generating prosperous and pure thoughts;

Rich Text: esoteric (metaphysical, metaphorical, mystical, cabalistic, theosophical, anthroposophical, etc.) interpretations of scripture; (In IT language, rich text refers to bold, italics, underlining, colored text, various font sizes, etc.);

Riddle(s): cryptic thoughts and uncharacteristic feelings;

Rifle(s): the tendency to 'fire' particularly aggressive and hurtful thoughts;

Righteousness: right thinking; Christed thinking; keeping our thoughts, feelings, choices, and actions at spiritual octaves; Feng Shuied thinking;

Right Hand Path: the way of spiritual growth; the enlightened perspective;

Right Side Up: putting spiritual needs and aspirations over material wants and whims;

Ring(s): denote union and a harmonious life outlook; they also stand for eternal and transcendent perspectives; they call for fusion, synthesis, and integration; they remind us of the universality of human emotions, thoughts, and consciousness;

Ringmaster: a healthy ego;

Riot: internal chaos; (See Chemicalization);

Ripcording: holding onto spiritual truths and principles in order to handle any situation confidently and with poise; (In IT lingo, ripcording is a way to download and archive Internet radio broadcasts, digital cable TV radio, and satellite radio);

Rishis: adepts; enlightened ones; illuminated thoughts;

Ritual: traction for spiritual growth;

River of Life: God Essence in Its myriads of forms;

Rivers, Streams: flow of life; the stream of consciousness;

Ro: the cosmic womb; a singularity;

Road Rage: uncontrollable emotions;

Robbery: allowing our poor choices to rob us of our spiritual growth;

Robe: spiritual perspective; the awareness of a sanctified life; a *seamless robe* symbolizes our complete entrainment with our divine nature;

Robin-ish: being constantly poised for blooming and growth; loving and appreciating new beginnings; being mindful of articulation and clarity; joviality;

Robo Delivery: a monotoned, memorized Sunday sermon and/or truth talk that is delivered without feeling or enthusiasm;

Robotic Regimens: being a creature of habit who displays automatic, rigid, mechanical responses as a rule; being seen as emotionless and impersonal; operating more from the head than the heart;

Rock, Paper, Scissors Sabbath: letting pure chance decide if we're going to attend Sunday services;

Rocket(s): male energy; worldly thoughts that take us for a ride;

Rocking Chair(s): suggests comfort; ease; relaxation; retirement;

Rocks, Stones: hard, rigid, material thoughts;

Rod: the spinal cord; *holding a rod* implies mastering the serpentine energies; male generative energy;

Rogue(s): our recalcitrant thoughts and inclinations;

Role Strain: the conflicting expectations we have of ourselves that characterize our struggle to be more spiritual and less material or more material and less spiritual;

Roller Coaster(s): biorhythms; centeredness and off-centeredness;

Roof(s): feeling as sense of being protected and sheltered; an over-arching world view which defines all of our thoughts, emotions, choices, and actions that fall under it; the stratosphere;

Room(s): the three levels of our corporeal consciousness; our mind, body, and soul;

Roommate(s): our human self and our Christ Self;

Rooster-like: being prophetic; acutely aware of wake-up calls; gaining victory over darkness; constantly vigilant; choosing fortuitousness over inertia; being obnoxiously assertive at times;

Root(s): values; basic beliefs; faithfulness; family ties; spiritual principles; religious tenets;

Rootbound: remaining in a particular faith tradition too long so that our spiritual and/or religious growth is stunted; (In gardening terms, being rootbound refers to a condition that exists when a potted plant has outgrown its container. The roots become entangled and matted together, and the growth of the plant becomes stunted.);

Roots of Virtue: spiritually-oriented intentions and choices; good deeds;

Rootstock: universal spiritual laws and metaphysical principles; (In gardening terms, rootstock is the underground part of a plant that contains the roots);

Rope(s): our ability to tie associations, concepts, correlations, and interconnections together;

Rope a Dope: protecting ourselves from the slings and arrows of life by using spiritual practices like meditation, affirmative prayer, visualization, gratitude journals, and dreamscapes so we can weather any storm; (In boxing circles, rope a dope means lying back on the ropes, shielding our face and stomach, and allowing our opponent to throw punches until they tire themselves out so we can exploit their fatigue and defensive flaws.);

Rorschach Context: projected reality; envisioned reckoning;

Rosary: solace; comfort; petitioning;

Rose Garden: enjoying a loving and nurturing environment; satisfying spiritual growth;

Rose-like Qualities: aligning with our Higher Self; becoming our enlightened self; an *opened rose* represents our human nature fully aligned with our Christ Nature; also: wisdom, femininity; sensuality, love, passion, devotion, divine order, perfection, everlasting unity and harmony; intimacy; humanitarian qualities;

Roulette: choosing the physical portals we come through for each reincarnation and incarnation;

Rottenness: wasted potential; neglected and forgotten opportunities;

Rowboat(s): our incarnational and/or reincarnational life's journey;

Royal Priesthood: attaining Christ Consciousness whereby all thoughts, words, and actions are spiritually pure;

Roza: fasting;

Ruach: Spirit; air; holy breath;

Ruah Hakodesh: In Kabbalist terms, the Spirit of God;

Rubber Duck: denotes playfulness;

Rubber Stamp: giving a mindless seal of approval (For example: Constantine I organized the Council of Nicaea in 325 C.E. to establish the Nicene Creed. He outlined the particulars for the 1800 or so bishops he invited to attend and made it clear that anyone who rubber stamped his selections could stay for a three month long party at his expense and anyone who refused to endorse the forced Creed would be excommunicated and exiled); our actions are the rubber stamping of our choices;

Rubik's Cube: the joys and challenges we face when we get serious about crossing out error; (See Cross-like Qualities);

Rubbish: worthless, nonsensical ideas; false teachings;

Ruby-ness: expressing vitality and energy; being loving and considerate; showing courage and bravery; being medicinally helpful in matters of blood loss;

Rudder(s): the choices we make;

Ruins: our capacity to move past ramshackled beliefs, dilapidated and rickety perspectives, run-down assumptions, and broken-down relationships;

Rules: suggestions; guidelines;

Ruling Class: the type of thoughts (spiritual or material) that overwhelmingly fill our consciousness;

Runtime: our soul journey through, and between, incarnational and/or reincarnational experiences; (In software development, runtime refers to the period of time when a program is literally running);

Runtime Error(s): refers to the errors (missteps, sins, disconnects, and misalignments) we make during our incarnational and/or reincarnational experiences;

Rust, Corrosion: being neglectful, lax, indifferent, and inattentive in certain areas of our life; inactivity;

Saabiric Strength: bearing our trials and difficulties with dignity and grace; (A Muslim term for patient and enduring);

Sabbath: sacred rest for divine coupling; taking our focus from the wasteland of hyperactivity to the peace and serenity of the *still small voice*; putting worldly thoughts behind and focusing on spiritual thoughts; (The Sabbath is a portable practice because it isn't restricted to one day of the week. It is a highly spiritual mental practice that takes place in our consciousness);

Sabda Brahmam: the unmanifested Logos; (*Sabda-brahman* is a Vedic term and means transcendental sound vibration);

Sabotage: consistently choosing worldly attitudes over spiritual ones; refusing to accept our innate divinity;

Saccharin Moments: knowing that our day goes the way the corners of our mouth turn;

Sach Khandic Ascent: raising our spiritual awareness to the point that we realize we are one with God; (Sac Khand, the Realm Of Truth, is the Sikh concept of joining with God. It is achieved by the Guru's Grace and through Simran, the act of remembering or calling to mind);

Sackcloth: our lower baser nature

Sacrament: to make sacred through thoughts, words, and actions;

Sacred Cow(s): our penchant for a white-knuckled, tightly held, clinging onto certain religious beliefs that are deemed infallible and irreplaceable;

Sacred Fire: the kundalini, serpentine fire at the base of our spines that rises through our spiritual piety and purity; the white heat of Truth as It burns off the dross of error;

Sacred Geometry: the belief in the geometric unfolding of the universe by divine design; (It is the geometry used in designing religious and spiritual structures and sacred places);

Sacred Language: the manifest and unmanifest universe; God in physicality and ethereality;

Sacred Pipe: According to Native Americans, a pipe that is considered a holy object; (The bowl represents female energy and the stem male energy. It is smoked with tobacco, which is also considered holy, and the smoke carries prayers skyward to the Great Spirit); (See also Incense);

Sacred Ragamuffin: the not so widely held realization that we are the physical expressions of the Eternal Presence in human form; (See also Inconvenient Truth);

Sacred Science: the inner esoteric philosophy and hidden knowledge taught by the mystery schools;

Sacred Torque: not allowing a moment's truce between truth and error, expediency and principle, right and wrong, growth and stagnation, spirituality and materialism;

Sacred Triple Precinct: the degrees of universal existence; three degrees of initiation; states of being; spiritual hierarchies; (The Triple Precinct symbol was first noticed on a Druid stone discovered in 1801 at Suevres. It is also found in Rome in the cloister of san Paolo.);

Sacrifice: choosing our human beingness over our spiritual beingness to experience skin school;

Sacrilege: denying our innate divinity;

Sacrilegious Sarcasm: error thoughts, inclinations, tendencies, words, choices, and actions;

Sacrosanct Congruence: letting go of obsolete values, of non-productive lifestyle habits, and self-nullifying attitudes that sabotage our overall well-being and spiritual growth;

Sadaqa Sanctity: giving charitable contributions; being philanthropic; (Our gut reaction is to give, according to a study published by Harvard scientists who teased apart the workings of people's minds when they're asked to contribute to the greater good at their own expense. People act most generously when they make snap decisions about how much to contribute, or are primed beforehand to recount a time in which their intuitions and emotions had guided them to a good decision);

Sadist: our unenlightened, paranoid, self-aggrandizing, spoiled ego that insists on binging on materiality;

Safari: exploring our basic instincts; seeking out our inner fears;

Safecracker: a materialistic thought that springs from our familiarity with truth principles, but represents our desire to use sacred principles for selfish personal gain at the expense of others; a materialistic motive to 'steal' goodness from Universal Substance with the intent to use what is manifested for selfish gain;

Safe House(s), Safe Haven: truth principles; a Christ-centric Consciousness;

Safekhic Might: the centrifugal strength of the denial of our innate divinity (darkness) to keep us imploded on ourselves and unable to comprehend our divine status;

Safe Mode: applying the truth principles and teachings we know; (In operating systems language, safe mode is a way for the Windows operating system to run with the minimum number of system files necessary);

Safety Belt(s): spiritual laws and principles; positive affirmations;

Safety Net(s): a spiritually-attuned consciousness; a spiritually sound perspective; affirmative prayer and meditation; life-affirming visualizations;

Sage: a highly evolved spiritual idea or insight;

Saha: the world of suffering (our sense-coated consciousness);

Sahajic Bliss: attaining inner peace because of our conscious oneness with God;

Sailboat(s): our ability to 'sail above' negativity;

Saint(s): highly spiritual ideas and thoughts;

Saintly Joviality: letting a little humor, merriment, and tasteful prankstership allow us safe passage through the rigid cracks in our seriousness; (Saintly joviality allows us to feel our way around our somberness, seriousness, and formality long enough to allow humor to soften our rough edges. Our rigidness can become a subconscious straightjacket that protects the raw pieces of our insecurities from being exposed. Unfortunately, this impenetrable veneer steals the joy, glee, and merriment out of our lives unless we get serious about softening our seriousness);

Saint's Life: the *out*picturing of an extremely elevated spiritual thought (saint) that is highly transformative in nature;

Salt-like: able to have persevering spiritual thoughts in spite of trying circumstances;

Salt of the Earth: spiritual thoughts (salt) that form the basis of our worldly consciousness (earth);

Salvation: when spiritual discernment trumps the secular velocity of materialism; the process through which we personally transform our consciousness from a materialistic focus to a spiritual focus – thought by thought, intention by intention, choice by choice, action by action; (We are saved every time we choose a spiritual thought over an error thought. This takes the salvation soteriology of Christianity, *nirvana* of Buddhism, and *moksha* of Hinduism to a change in consciousness within us); [In *Meditations With Meister Eckhart*, Matthew Fox quotes the 14th century mystic regarding the interdependent nature of salvation: "All are sent or no one is sent." Salvation is about God becoming 'all in all,' adds Fox. Pg 114];

Samadhi: the highest state of yoga; a very high state of ecstatic trance; the practice of focusing our attention on a single object while meditating;

Samajnaic Thoughts: extremely enlightened thinking; (A Sanskrit term that means the name of the Buddha);

Samhainian Proclivities: Fiery thoughts and ritualistic tendencies (Also known as La Samhan, All Hallow's Eve, and Halloween);

Sampaku Choices: doing the same thing over and over again and expecting different results;

Samskaraic Tendencies: propensities and inclinations developed in past incarnations that travel with us to subsequent incarnations; (In Hinduism, the impressions left upon our minds by the actions we have taken that literally follow us and must be dealt with on future occasions);

Samurai: duty; honor; protectiveness; (See Knights);

Samvritic Conceptions: beliefs and assumptions based on falsehoods and illusions; (In Hinduism, *samvriti* means holding onto false conceptions that become the origins of *maya*);

Sanat Kumara-like: believing in the attainment of ascended mastership; (According to theosophical writings Sanat Kumara is an advanced being who is the founder of the Great White Brotherhood which is established for the salvation of humankind);

Sanctification: the disciplined process of becoming consciously holy (divine, undefiled, sacrosanct, unprofaned);

Sanctimonious Malnutrition: eating the menu instead of the meal;

Sanctuary: our spiritual and/or religious practice;

Sandbox: a particular area of expertise; playfulness;

Sand Castle(s): false sense of security;

Sand-like Symptoms: depending too much on our sense consciousness to help us master the art of living;

Sandpaper: an evaluative, assessing nature that requires smoothing out the rough edges;

Sandstorm: allowing instability to disorient and confuse us;

Sangam: the confluence of the three holiest rivers in India: the Ganges (Gaṅgā), Yamunā (Jamnā) and the mythical Sarasvati;

Sannyasinic Renunciation: abstaining from overly-consumptive worldly appetites and materialistic cravings in order to advance spiritually; (Sannyasa is a Hindu term for detachment from material life by renouncing worldly thoughts and desires in order to spend the remainder of our lives in spiritual contemplation);

Sapphire-like Poise: establishing harmony; enjoying serenity; seeing calmness as a virtue; having considerable self-discipline and self-control;

Sarcophagus: the dogmatic box we purposefully put ourselves in;

Sargonian Salvation: returning to our spiritual essence by living above the slings and arrows of physical incarnation; (Sargon of Assyria was picked up out of a wicker basket floating in the reeds by a river's brink by the king's daughter long before the same image was repeated by the Hebrews with Moses' rescue);

Sarkic Propensities: our base instincts; (In Gnostic terms, sarkic represents the lowest level of human thought, our fleshy, instinctive urges and desires);

Sasquatch, Big Foot: the presumably unknown parts of us;

Satan, Shaitan: the purely human tendency to consciously forsake the divinity within us through our error thoughts, intentions, choices, and actions; (Satan is not an anthropomorphic celestial being enticing us into a sinful life. Satan is the self-aggrandizing, sense-addicted human nature in all of us, our shadow side. It is the self of us that can tempt us to do things we know are not for our highest good. Satan is the selfish, cunning, devious ego of limitation that motivates us to forsake our innate divinity; (The religious belief that there is an anthropomorphic, evil personage called satan, also referred to as the prince of darkness, that rivals an anthropomorphic God in the sky for our souls, is an absurdity that has been perpetuated for far too long. It has evolved out of an abject denial of our innate divinity and our collective refusal to take responsibility for severing the spiritual ties that reveal our true origin as human expressions of the Eternal Presence in physical form. So, in order to conceal our true nature we have created a convenient scapegoat to blame for our chronic indiscretions); (See Anthropomorphic Satan);

Satellite: a newly introduced thought and/or concept that has not been intellectually processed;

Satellite Dish: our ability to capture and comprehend advanced ideas and concepts;

Satguruishness: attaining the status of a true (trusted, genuine) spiritual teacher instead of a false prophet;

Saturation Index: the amount of cognitive dissonance we can endure before we get the 'deer-in-the-headlights' expression when attempting to grasp complex spiritual teachings; the amount of irritation we endure before we zone out after being over-proselytized by a religious fundamentalist; (In SPA industry terms, saturation index is the numeric value indicating whether water is scale-forming or corrosive.);

Satya: supreme truth;

Satyagrahaic Tolerance: our peaceful, tranquil, non-combative resistance to pesky worldly thoughts that surface in our conscious awareness; (In Sanskrit, *satyagraha* means the same thing as nonviolent resistance);

Saum: taking a sabbatical; ceasing, abstaining from work;

Saw(s): denotes our ability to reduce and divide concepts for use in different ways;

SBNR: an acronym used to describe people who define themselves as Spiritual But Not Religious; (See MSTR: More Spiritual Than Religious. Among the Millennials - Generation Y – people born between the 1980's and early 2,000's, a survey by *Time* magazine found that 72% of this cohort consider themselves to be "spiritual and not religious." According to recent Pew Forum and Barna Group polls there are a growing number of people of all ages worldwide (25-33%) who identify themselves as "more spiritual than religious.");

Scaffolding: brainstormed items; insights and ideas used to construct a line of thought; the outline for a book;

Scales of Justice: the power of discernment; sound judgment;

Scam: keeping the faithful grounded in the amygdala; (See Double-Dealing; Fib(s) and Fiction; Hoodwinked; Cover Ups);

Scar(s): long term consequences for errant actions;

Scarab-like: striving for transformation;

~ *Spiritually Speaking* ~

Scarecrow*ology*: being courageous enough to move beyond the scarecrow power of uncertainties, slim chances, and impossibilities by affirming our oneness with Spirit;

Scareware: the tactics religious fundamentalists use to scare people into following their deluded doctrines; (In IT language, scareware is software (pop up alerts and warnings) that uses false error messaging to lure users into buying a particular software program);

Scavenger Hunt: looking for material solutions to spiritual challenges;

Schemhampheres: an expository on the 72 names of God and God's attending angels;

Schism: the misalignment between our human self and our Christ Self; the spiritual and psycho-emotional gulf between our vertically-challenged ego and our Authentic Self [the extraordinary Us];

Schizophrenia: the warped ego's concern that one of its alter egos is out to get it;

Schlepped Self-Care: taking better care of our automobiles, stock portfolios, fishing rods, plasma TV's, iPads and iPhones, and bling than we take care of ourselves; neglecting the vocabulary of our body, mind, and soul while expecting to gain balance and peace of mind;

School(s): our earth experience as a whole; any particular happenstance;

School Bus: reincarnating in groups;

School of Hard Knocks: our skin school experience;

Schoolroom: our earth experience; (See Skin School);

Science Fiction: the belief in original sin, burning bushes that talk to you, the Sun standing still, the Main Character of the New Testament walking on water, etc.;

Scienta Sacra: the perennial philosophy; the timeless universal gnosis;

Scientist, Researcher: our investigative, evaluative, assessing, experimenting nature;

Scorpion(s): death; rebirth; self-defeating habits; stinging remarks; destructive attitudes;

Scrapbook, Photo Album: life review;

Scribal Corruption, Scribal Bleaching, Scribal Contamination: intentional scribal mistranslations of holy scripture;

Scrimmage(s): each day's experience during each incarnation and/or reincarnation; conflict-riddled thoughts in our temporal consciousness;

Script: ingrained habits;

Scriptural Skedaddledom: the intentional, fear-based practice of fundamental and ultraconservative religious groups to encourage followers to avoid (run from) metaphysical, metaphorical, and theosophical interpretations of sacred scripture;

Scroll Being Eaten: esoteric knowledge being ingested;

Scrooge-ology: is a message of transformation and release. Once we recognize our innate divinity we have the power to release anything that limits or blocks our good. When the Ebenezer Scrooge of us comes out of its attachment to things (its *Amorite* consciousness) and releases its addiction to material and monetary appetites, we can literally be transformed by the renewing of our minds;

Scuba Diving, Deep Sea Diving: exploring our repressed thoughts, emotions, and life patterns through psychoanalysis and psychotherapy;

Scum of the Earth: very impure thoughts (scum) that are the scruff and dross of an unenlightened consciousness (earth);

Sea: a skin school experience;

Seafood: eating seafood suggests dealing with our skin school experiences, including observed and repressed emotions;

Seagulls: psychoanalytic and psychotherapeutic techniques; introspective ideas;

Seagull Revelation(s): insights and ideas that 'fly' in, make a lot of noise, crap on everything, and then leave;

Seahorse-ishness: being highly perceptive and accommodating; having a penchant for safe passage; being patience and protective; having the ability to see both sides of an issue;

Sealing of the Grand Perspective: the imprinting of spiritually-attuned thoughts (the Grand Perspective) in our waking consciousness;

Seamanship: staying above the negativity of the human condition; (See Red Sea; Walking on Water);

Sea Monsters: repressed and highly emotional life patterns (self-defeating habits, outdated beliefs and assumptions) that surface from time to time;

Séance: performing our own introspection and self-examination to see what spirits and phantoms arise in our conscious awareness;

Sea of Glass, Sea of Crystal: the transparency of universal truths; *waves* are truths revealed;

Search Engine Optimization: In spiritual terms, shortening the 'wait time' for our desires and wants to come through us from the unmanifest into the manifest so we can enjoy the fruits of our consciousness; (In social media terms, search engine optimization is the process of improving the volume or quality of traffic to our website);

Sea Serpent(s): tempestuous subconscious impulses and drives;

Sea Sickness: letting our rocky emotions get the best of us, causing disequilibrium and nauseas experiences;

Seasoned Neophyte(s): making a regular practice of going from one religious denomination and/or faith tradition to another without committing ourselves to any of them;

Seasons: levels of spiritual growth and unfoldment;

Seatbelt(s): positive affirmations; affirmative prayers; meditation;

Secondary Listening Area: when we share spiritual truths there is a segment of the listeners who will zone us out because their religious beliefs conflict with the views we are sharing; (In advertising language, the secondary listening area is the outlying area where broadcast transmissions are subject to fading and static.);

Second Coming: when we realize we are divine beings in human form, and then, through disciplined practice, seek to actualize our Christhood; coming into direct conscious alignment with our Christ Self; the point in conscious awareness that we realize we are Christed beings, have been Christed beings, and will be Christed beings; (The Second Coming is not an external cataclysmic future event of the dreaded apocalypse predicted by literally-minded faith traditions);

Second Death: the first death is the abject denial of our innate divinity; the second death is the error-prone words and actions that result from warped thinking; (A second death is the progressive elimination of error thoughts, tendencies, and behaviors, and it occurs on a daily basis until we have purified our consciousness); [In *The Apocalypse Attributed to St. John*, Manly Hall asserts: "The first or natural death is a separation from the world. The second, or philosophical death, is a separation of the soul from worldliness by initiation into the greater mysteries." Pg. 63];

Second World: our waking consciousness;

Secret Doctrine: highly esoteric teachings of antiquity;

Secular Surfing: seeking spiritual growth activities, knowledge, and practices outside of churchianity;

Secular Velocity: speedy error; (When the secular velocity of materialistic choices trumps spiritual discernment, soul growth is usually slowed and blunted. The effects of discordant thinking and acting create incongruences in body, mind, and soul which increase the speed of our inevitable collision with our own shallowness. We must slow our secular velocity enough to speed up our spirituality);

Secure Attachment: error and the consequences of error; the seemingly unbreakable bond between religious fundamentalists and the supposed inerrancy of scripture, dogma, and an anthropomorphic god;

Secured Debt: the karma we generate through our errant thoughts, choices and actions that is attached specifically to us for repayment; (In legal lingo, secured debt is backed by a mortgage, pledge of collateral, or other lien.);

Security Guard: the amygdala;

Seed-like: the promise of potential becoming actualized; the concept forecasting its conception; an inkling announcing the possibility of becoming inked; a thought serving as the foundation for concepts, words, choices, and actions;

Seer-like: clairvoyance; seeing both visible and invisible reality;

See Saw: emotional ups and downs; (See Roller Coaster):

Seismic Self-Abuse: denying our own innate divinity and the divinity in others;

Seismic Sinning: holding onto the "us" that makes the same mistakes over and over again; Xeroxing our errors;

Self: our small 's' self is the human personality, our capital 'S' Self is our Christ individuality;

Self Defense: using denials; (See Denialdom);

Self-Hoodwinking: not realizing that beneath the cut of our clothing and make-up, above the limitations of ego, and besides the politics of our human status and position, the wattage of our true significance is determined by how aligned we are with our Authentic Self;

Selfie: taking a moment to look introspectively at ourselves; seeing ourselves as the spiritual being we really are; (A social media word for self-portrait that is usually on a smartphone or webcam);

Self-ish: thinking, saying, and doing Christ-like (Buddha-like, Allah-like, Krishna-like) things;

Self-Shellacking: being the tin can on our own tail by wasting so much of our valuable time stressing over things of which we have limited personal control or burdening ourselves unnecessarily by getting in our own way;

Self-Storage: the subconscious;

Selling Our Birthright: denying our innate divinity;

Semiotician Awareness, Semiology: being able to understand the symbolic meaning of signs, likenesses, analogies, metaphors, anthropological dimensions, etc.;

Sense Consciousness: our ordinary waking consciousness which uses only the five senses to interpret reality; cosmetic consciousness; self-induced coma consciousness;

__Sensus Divinitatis:__ denotes that when we do not have a 'sense of our divinity' we are liable to error more than we would normally do if we recognized our innate divinity;

Sentencing: the thoughts we have, the choices we make, and the actions we take;

Senzar: referenced in the works of Helena Blavatsky, Senzar is referred to as the mystery speech (sacerdotal language), predating Sanskrit, that was used by all initiated adepts;

Sephiroth: the ten emanations of deity found in the Kabbalah: crown, wisdom, understanding, mercy, power, beauty, victory, splendor, foundation, and kingdom;

Seppuku Meltdown: not having the stomach for upholding (falling on a sword) our religious convictions, being fearless in our principles, fervent in our prayers, firm in our purposes, and faithful in our promises;

Septic Sermonizing: hurtful, venomous, pestilential preaching;

Sequel(s): subsequent incarnations and/or reincarnations;

Seraphim: highly spiritually-charged ideas and concepts; saintly thoughts; (In Kabbalistic terms, a group of angels);

Serer Religion: believing in a universal Supreme Deity called *Roog*;

Serf(s): the intellect, will, and emotions that are controlled by a worldly ego;

Serial Killer: the paranoid ego's habit of killing off spiritual ideas that come into our waking awareness;

Serial Port(s): incarnating and/or reincarnating into the same type of parents because we haven't moved beyond a particular level of consciousness; (In IT language, serial ports are connections on PCs that are used for various peripherals [modems, printers, gaming controllers, etc.];

Sermon Contraband: pulpit chicanery; (See Pulpit Theft):

Serpent Fire: the *sushummic* energies; (see Fire and Kundalini);

Serpents (Snakes): objectivized Universal Energy (the activity of the Holy Spirit) that illuminates human consciousness; symbolizes the fohatic serpentine energies that travel up the spinal cord; represents universal wisdom; the *serpent's tongue* is bi-polar and represents the dual nature of wisdom (egocentric wisdom leads to degradation, spiritual wisdom brings enlightenment); *serpents shedding their skin* means that true wisdom involves growing beyond current knowledge by shedding old concepts which we have outgrown; *venom* can kill or heal, depending on how it is used (egocentric, self-aggrandizing counterfeit wisdom is poisonous – spiritually-oriented wisdom is always an antidote for what ails us); when the *serpent's tail is in its mouth* it symbolizes the timeless universality of the omnipresence, omnipotence, omniscience, and omni-activity of Divine Mind;

Sesame Treat: the inner peace, happiness, and joy we receive when we 'open the doors' to an enlightened spiritual perspective;

Seven Deadly Sins: envy, gluttony, greed, lust, pride, sloth, and wrath;

Sevenfold Path: the quickening of our seven major chakras leading to our enlightenment and liberation from error consciousness; (Helena Blavatsky, in her book, *The Voice of the Silence*, pg. 91, outlines our spiritual journey as the 'Sevenfold Path.' In *Creating Peace by Being Peace: The Essene Sevenfold Path*, Gabriel Cousens writes, "The Sevenfold Path of Peace, based on the ancient teachings of the Essene, takes us beyond narrow definitions of peace to a comprehensive and integrated understanding of the personal, social, and planetary dimensions of peace." The Buddha taught a similar path called the 'Eightfold Path.'); [See Eightfold Path];

Seven Golden Candlesticks: denotes the quickening of all seven major spiritual energy centers (chakras) within us;

Seven Golden Saucers in Revelation: the formative power of the Logos to eradicate all impurities (*pouring the first saucer* upon the earth : destroying psychic illusions; *pouring the second saucer* in the sea: eliminating every vestige of incarnational passion and carnal desire; *pouring the third saucer* on rivers and springs: the egocentrism of our lower mind replaced by Christ-centric wisdom; *pouring the fourth saucer* on the sun: experiencing intense psychic and mystical activity; *pouring the fifth saucer* upon the Throne of the Beast: purifying the sympathetic nervous system of the phrentic mind; *pouring the sixth saucer* on the Euphrates River: expelling all irredeemable elements of our lower, egocentric self; *pouring the seventh saucer* into the air: becoming fully illumined);

Seven Hekhalot Palaces: the seven major chakras;

Seventh Heaven: the fully quickened crown chakra;

Seven Virtues: Charity, chastity, generosity, humility, moderation, meekness, and zeal;

Sexually Transmitted Dis-eases: the unfortunate moral and emotional discomfort we feel about human sexuality being dirty and sinful which expresses itself in disastrous ways, because we think we have to overcompensate for our 'waywardness';

Shabd: the hum of the universe; the sound current vibrating throughout all of the universe; the audible life stream of the cosmos;

Shackles: bad habits; negative thoughts;

Shadow Side: our worldly, egocentric nature that is fixated on materiality which means that our shadow side is our shallow side;

Shaman: Native American holy men and women; pious religious thoughts and emotions;

Shangna Robe: acquiring universal, esoteric wisdom; being initiated into the higher mysteries;

Shareware: access to online spiritual and/or religious content that we can use on a trial basis before we have to pay for it;

Shark Mentality: showing remarkable survival skills; choosing a 'ready, fire, aim' philosophy; being recognized for our forward thinking and fluidity; always being efficiently equipped; having a penchant for predatory thinking and reasoning;

Shear Conformity: constantly pruning ourselves to suit others and then waking up one day realizing we've whittled ourselves away; chipping (shearing) our selfhood away to conform to other people's standards; finding ourselves in a spin cycle of docile conventionality; being railroaded into giving up our individuality;

Sheep: the nonresistant mental and/or emotional surrender to one's divine nature; the *sacrificial lamb* represents Spirit's descent into matter, a spiritual insight that is "killed" when it surfaces in an egocentric consciousness;

Shehinah Quality: our receptive, nurturing nature; (In Kabbalistic terms, the indwelling feminine aspect of the Eternal Presence as us);

Shennanigans: cultivating a life that is constantly engaged in seeking unorthodox material solutions to spiritual ailments;

Sheol Prerogative: choosing a hellish state of consciousness;

Shibbolething: choosing the naked truth before believing in a well-dressed lie; (The term comes from the biblical account that describes how Israelites would ask suspicious foreigners to say the word *shibboleth*. If the foreigner pronounced it *sibboleth*, identifying the foreigner as an enemy, h/she would be killed.);

Shien-Sienic Reverie: complete bliss and happiness; (According to psychologists Lyubomirsky, King, and Diener, the majority of people in the world, across vast continents and cultures, profess that being happy is one of their most cherished goals in life – for themselves, and above all else, their children. What's more, happiness offers myriad rewards, not just for the happy people but for their families, workplace, community, nation, and society. Working on how to become happier, their research suggests, will not only make people feel better but will also boost their energy, creativity, and immune system, foster better relationships, fuel higher productivity at work, and even lead to a longer life.);

Significant Other: our Divine Nature;

Ship: our physical body; our ordinary consciousness; positive mental attitude;

Shipwreck: the inability to remain emotionally stable enough to stay above negativity and pessimistic outlooks;

Shoe(s), Footwear: setting limitations on our understanding; the different kinds of knowledge we have accumulated so far which is limited by the best of our thinking; *taking our shoes off* represents our willingness to open our mind to greater understandings;

Shooting Star: spiritual aspirations; being born again;

Shoplifting: a warped sense of entitlement;

Shouldology: the ability to by-pass any *shoulds* we toss at ourselves and allow the real us proper expression;

Shrapnel: hurtful words used to intentionally maim people's emotional security, cut lesions into someone's self-esteem, or destroy anyone's health and well-being;

Shrine: a favorite religious or spiritual tenet;

Shroud of Turin: The Shroud of Turin is revered by many as the actual burial shroud of Jesus Christ. The cloth appears to have the image of a crucified man on it, complete with blood and markings on the body. (There are, however, a number of problems which make it very difficult to identify this piece of cloth with anything that might have been a real burial shroud of anyone. For example, Radiocarbon dating performed in 1988 by three different labs all agree that the cloth dates to between 1260 - 1390, around the time when the cloth was 'discovered.');

Shruti: revealed scripture; *smriti* is memorized scripture;

Siblings: worldly thoughts, religious thoughts, and spiritual thoughts;

Sibling Rivalry: when siblings contradict each other; (See Siblings);

Sibylline Tendencies: our impulse to prophesy and become seer-like;

Sick Soul: the unenlightened ego;

Sickle: karma; the cutting consequences of error thoughts and actions;

Siddhas Attainment: the perfection of our enlightenment; phenomenal psychic powers and abilities; (Siddhas were wandering adepts in India who were extremely knowledgeable in science, technology, astronomy, literature, fine arts, music, drama, and dance); [People often turn to a higher power for reassurance in times of stress, but new research says that a belief in science may help more spiritual than religious people handle adversity in just the same way];

Sidewalk(s): our preference for taking the road most traveled; our inclination toward convention and tradition;

Sigalions Decision: the choice to quietly pursue our spiritual unfoldment without fanfare, pridefulness or boastfulness;

Signal-To-Noise-Ratio: usually occurs during conversations between religious fundamentalists and New Thought people when the ratio between information relevant to an amicable conversation and argumentative information which is intended to detract from an open, honest and nonjudgmental exchange destroy any good that can come out of it;

Silence, the: disciplined meditation; [We cannot eliminate error thinking merely because we have a basic knowledge of spiritual truths and feel we are tapping into our spiritual powers (disciples). Erasing error requires a disciplined habit of going into the Silence (prayer/meditation)];

Silent Watcher: our accumulated karma that records our ethereal, mental, emotional, physical, and spiritual progress and adds it to our composite genealogy which will constitute our makeup in the next incarnated version of us;

Silver Cord, Psychic Cord: the spinal marrow; the *sutratma* or life thread of the *antahkarana* that links the higher self (*atma*) with our physical body; (See Antahkarana; Sutratma; Umbilical Cord);

Silver Cord and the Golden Bowl: the silver cord is our spinal marrow and the golden bowl is our head which houses our brain; (A more detailed description follows: A beautiful description of the body of humankind suffering under the infirmities of old age is recorded in the 12th chapter of Ecclesiastes. It says, *"or ever the silver cord be loosed, or the golden bowl be broken, or the pitcher be broken at the fountain, or the wheel broken at the cistern: then shall the dust return to the earth as it was, and the spirit shall return to God who gave it."* The silver Cord is our spinal marrow; its loosening is the cessation of all nervous sensation; the golden bowl is our head, the pitcher represents the large vein which carries the blood to the right ventricle of the heart [fountain]; the wheel symbolizes the great artery which receives the blood from the left ventricle of the heart [cistern]);

Silver-like: achieving an awakened spiritual will; enjoying an intellectual sharpness that is considerably above average; speaking eloquence; preserving precious memories; seeing good in the midst of setbacks and disappointments;

Similimum Reasoning: error thoughts that affect everyone in the same way; (In homeopathy, similimum represents the remedy called for in a certain case because the same drug, when given to a healthy person, will produce symptoms similar to the disease in question.);

Sin: choosing error thoughts over spiritual thoughts; missing the point of human existence; the 'siGn' of our unenlightened awareness that fails to see the God in us; the boogie woogie appeal of the senses; error thinking; the kinds of things that have no nutritional value like: resentment, worry, greed, bearing false witness, and guilt;

Sin Avalanche: what happens when we engage in so many missteps that we feel over-whelmed by an avalanche of our mistakes;

Sin Ceiling: the point at which we finally come to grips with our missteps and completely turn our lives around;

Sinnami: having a huge preponderance of error thoughts, error choices, and error actions that overwhelm us with their disastrous negativity; (See Errornami);

Sinsophagus: the large hole we dig for ourselves every time we settle for an error thought over a spiritual one;

Siren: the manipulative unenlightened ego;

Sirric Knowledge: concealed, hidden knowledge;

Sister(s): compatible emotions;

Sister(s)-in-Law: worldly feelings, religious feelings, and spiritual feelings;

Sit-Com(s): our incarnational experience;

Sixth Sense: superior perception; ESP;

Skeleton(s): watered down religious and spiritual teachings and practices;

Skeleton Key(s): ancient religious, spiritual, esoteric teachings;

Skin: our auric envelope;

Skin School: our biological address; human incarnational and reincarnational experiences; filigreed Spirit in human form; a cosmic ego in a bag of skin;

Skinny Dipping: reincarnational and incarnational experiences;

Skread: reading literal-only interpretations of sacred scripture is skimming over the deeper truths; (In urban slang, skread means skim reading);

Skunks: bad habits; false teachings;

Skydiving: bringing elevated spiritual teachings down to earth so they can be understood;

Skylight(s): making an enlightened perspective part of our everyday experience;

Skype-ing: psychic remote viewing;

Skyscrapers, Towers: male energy; the need for an elevated perspective; evolutionary desire to return to our spiritual roots;

Skywriting: capturing esoteric thoughts on paper;

Slackivism, Slackologist: denotes meeting the minimum requirements to join a particular church or study group without subsequent interest shown or meaningful contributions made; learning a new metaphysical concept and then not applying it; (In IT parlance, slackivism refers to actions performed on the Internet in support of a political or social cause but regarded as requiring little time, effort, or involvement [signing an online petition, liking a Facebook post but not commenting on the post, or joining an online campaign on a social media website without true interest shown]);

Slashdotting: telling someone about a certain spiritual and/or religious practice or upcoming event and then telling others we told them so that the person is bombarded with so many solicitors and well-wishers that h/she has a temporary melt down; (In IT language, slashdotting refers to press releases that trigger so much traffic to a particular a website that the website crashes);

Sleeping Pill: a divinity-denying thought;

Sleepover, Slumber Party: each reincarnational/incarnational experience;

Sleepwalking: being, doing, and having from a materialistic consciousness;

Slogging: mentally plodding slowly and laboriously through complex religious exegesis, cumbersome church membership requirements, and/or tedious dogmatic do's and don'ts;

Slot Machine(s): our susceptibility for 'chance' encounters;

Sludge: accumulated karma; a residue of poor choices and actions; (In gardening terms, sludge refers to solid sediment left over from industrial wastewater treatment plants.);

Slums: negative thoughts;

Smart Money: tithes; philanthropic funds;

Smart Phone: electronic knowing, being, and doing; (See iPhone);

Smog: shortsighted, negative outlook;

Smorgasbord: our earth experience; the delights offered in our other extra-dimensional experiences throughout the Multiverse;

Smoke Detector: our discernment when it becomes obvious someone is 'blowing smoke';

Snapdragon Qualities: impulsiveness; impatience; incorrigibleness;

Sniper(s): hurtful thoughts we don't see coming;

Soap Opera: repeating the same mistakes; having the same error thoughts time and time again;

Sofa Sunday: similar to a couch potato experience where we spend an inordinate amount of time on the sofa watching TV instead of going to church;

Soft Launch: represents sharing metaphysical truths with a knowledgeable audience as a test run before sharing the same information with an audience not familiar with the teachings; (In marketing, a soft launch is the release of a new product or service to a restricted audience or market in advance of a full-scale launch);

Solar Eclipse: giving our ego temporary dominance over our divine nature;

Solar Fires: the opening of our chakras;

Solar Logos: the Eternal Presence expressing Itself as our solar system;

Solar Plexus: the abdominal brain;

Soldier(s): militaristic, analytical, rational thoughts;

Somatic Space Suit: our physical bodies;

Somatic Vendetta: the 'blood feud' between our poor eating habits and our physical health;

Son: maturing thoughts;

Sonam: good karma;

Sonday: many churches are accustomed to the term 'Sunday' which references both the day of the week and the day set aside for worship services. Sun or Sol represents the solar deity and for Christians is considered a pagan perspective. So, perhaps the day set aside for Christian worship services should be called Sonday for the Son of God and not Sunday for sun god Sol – I'm just saying ☺

Song of No Words: From the Navajo/Dineh spiritual lens, the 'song' is the air that makes the sound of the perfect love and peace that radiates to the physical sun, to the holy plant 'people'(plants) as we exchange oxygen and carbon dioxide with the plants producing the symbiosis of photosynthesis;

Son of God: the Christ;

Son of Man: the human personality which must be lifted up to its Christ nature;

Soot: the consequences of getting 'burned' by bad behavior;

Sophia: the Holy Spirit; (In the Gnostic tradition Sophia is a feminine figure identical with our soul but also one with the feminine aspect of God. She is the syzygy (Bride) of the Christ as Jesus and the Holy Spirit of the Trinity); Sophia animates all of us as the Divine Spark;

Sophia, Achamoth, Chokhmah, Wisdom: the personification of the Holy Spirit (Sophia) in physicality; (Sophia Achamoth, "Lower Wisdom," the daughter of "Higher Wisdom," becomes the mother of the Demiurge [the one responsible for the fashioning and maintenance of the physical universe], identified with the God of the Old Testament.);

Sophia Perennis: the essence of all expressions of wisdom; eternal wisdom;

Sorcerer: our manipulative, unhealthy ego;

Sores: the negative after effects of error choices;

Sore Throat: the inability to confidently express ourselves or feel that we have anything valuable to share;

Sortilege: a form of divination by means of sticks, coins, bones, dice, lots, beans, yarrow stalks, stones or other small objects;

Soul: capital 'S' Soul is our Christ Self, our immortal divine nature; our small 's' soul refers to our human personality (Quantum Self);

Soul Calligraphy: recording the day's blessings in a gratitude journal with a flair for writing joyfully;

Soul Decay: settling for a materialistic, error-ridden consciousness;

Soul Murder: denying our innate divinity by our thoughts, words, and actions; (In *Thou Shalt Not Be Aware*, Alice Miller writes that " soul murder occurs when an individual is denied access to h/her true self, and in a culture that denies the mystical, soul murder is a regular event." Pg. 191);

Soul Signature: our Quantum Self (the incarnational and/or reincarnational composite of all of our physical beingness);

Soul Sleeping: a person who is totally unaware of h/her innate divinity;

Sound Asleep: being totally unaware of our Divine Nature;

Soup: sensory experience;

Spaceship-like Qualities: astral travel; out-of-body experiences;

Space and Time: holding onto the illusion that things operate and interact outside of us;

Space Tourism: represents attending a session on highly advanced spiritual teachings out of vicarious interest just to report that we attended such a session; (the practice of travelling into space for recreational purposes);

Spamming Gluttony: wrestling with the politics of excess; starving excessive material appetites;

Sparrow-like Outlook: being perpetually energetic; believing in safety in numbers; mastering the art of camouflage; having confidence in the constant availability and accessibility of divine substance;

Spasms: the various and sundry consequences of error;

Speaking in Tongues, Glossolilia: symbolizes our ability to communicate deeper meanings of hidden truths. That means we can communicate esoteric truths, metaphorical truths, mystical truths, cabalistic truths, theosophical truths, anthroposophical truths, and spiritual truths in such a way that people can understand them; (In fundamental religious circles, people who "speak in tongues" do so in an incomprehensible language that seems to have great personal meaning. This mysterious *"glassolalia experience"* has been well-documented and continues to be practiced today in fundamental faith traditions. However, researchers who have studied glossolalia extensively have not found linguistic evidence that any form of language is being spoken. Rather, people loosely string together and repeat familiar phonetic sounds);

Spear-like Tendency: expressing generative male energy; an extremely poignant, forceful thought and/or point of view;

Spear of Destiny: the spear believed to have been thrust into the side of Jesus on the cross by Roman centurion Gaius Cassius Longinus; (It is also known as the Lance of Longinus and the Holy Spear. The Spear of Destiny is said to possess great powers especially the power to grant great success in battles);

Spears Into Pruning-Hooks: sharp, penetrating angry thoughts transformed into helpful, nurturing sentiments and actions;

Speed Bump(s): reality checks;

Speedometer: steps in the initiation process;

Spider-like Attributes: craftly designing our lives based on our resourcefulness and ability to make good decisions; weaving our thoughts and actions in such as way as to benefit greatly from our efforts;

Spiffy Matchmaking: the ability to connect two or more spiritual truths to enhance our hallowed journey;

Spin Doctor(s): the materialistic ego; worldly thoughts and desires; (See False Prophets);

Spinning: the Sufi meditational practice of literally spinning around on our vertical axis, with arms out-stretched. The direction, speed, and number of rotations depend on what is to be achieved – and on our experience with spinning and balance;

Spinning Wheel: traipsing through the Zodiac; making the same mistakes;

Spin Telemetry: Not being fooled by certain evangelists, cultists, astrologers, medical doctors, hucksters, healers, teachers, counselors, consultants, motivational speakers, and new age gurus whose hidden agenda is manipulation, control, and financial gain;

Spirit: the divine essence of the One Presence; the omni-activity of the One Presence called the Holy Spirit;

Spiritual Anorexia: failure to fill ourselves (eat enough) with and digest esoteric knowledge because we believe we are already bulimic with an adequate diet of Biblical exegesis;

Spiritual Anthropology: A person's spiritual growth evolves over time. It is filled with 'artifacts of awakening.' For example, the journey is initially characterized with basic socio-cultural behaviors like feeling part of an 'in group,' fixation on the literal interpretation of scripture, and adopting dogmatic religion as the 'narrow path.' This pre-enlightened path is covered with chards of intolerance and disrespect for other faith traditions, the sub-fields of ceremonial exclusivity and the strongly established bond of 'born again' kinship, fossilized adherence to the inerrancy of Biblical scripture, and the remains of an anthropomorphic deity that has long been shown to be the adornment of preliterate religious groups. (Once we get away from the superficial 'digs' of pediatric religious studies, our excavations into our evolving spiritual consciousness become more mature and expansive, propelling us toward a new era of spiritual, not religious, growth);

Spiritual Apps: meditation; affirmative prayer; positive affirmations; centering breaths; denials (denying the power of outer appearances); centering visualizations; mantric vocalizations; forgiveness; acts of kindness; yoga;

Spiritual Arrhythmias: the consequences of error thoughts and practices;

Spiritual Cataracts: seeing the world through a purely materialistic, egocentric lens; a blurred inner vision;

Spiritual Dehydration: being disconnected from the flow of living water that is our awareness of our Oneness with the Universal flow of Divine Substance;

Spiritual *Echo*nomics: what we send out comes back to us multiplied;

Spiritual Gifts: the higher consciousness thoughts, words, and actions we offer that help others grow spiritually; the *out*picturings of our illumined consciousness;

Spiritual Hydration: having a regular habit of consuming spiritual thoughts, meditating, connecting with our center of Oneness – so we are always filled with the living water - the Indwelling Christ Presence;

Spirituality: the search for the sacred in everyday experience through the awareness of our oneness with our Divine Nature; another way of saying it's about *'Spirit-you-all'*;

Spiritual Lobotomy: dogma; a literal only interpretation of sacred scripture;

Spiritual Metaphysics: Spiritual metaphysics is concerned with the distinction between Absolute and Relative beingness, cosmic consciousness, an individual's spiritual origins, and the fundamental Truths which underlie and transcend all physical manifestation. It uncovers the hidden wisdom beyond literal translations of scripture;

Spiritual Obstetrics: becoming born again, repotted, made new, more enlightened each day; (See Born Again);

Spiritual Orthopedics: walking the spiritual path on practical feet;

Spiritual Pilates: spiritual tone, posture, alignment, and conditioning;

Spiritual Practice: using prayer, meditation, denials and affirmations, visualization, sacred rituals, a giving consciousness, and service to others as spiritual guardrails;

Spiritual Purpose: recognizing, developing, fulfilling, and actualizing our innate divinity;

Spiritual Synesthesia: seeing, feeling, and hearing the incredible nuances and transformational insights of hidden truths; (In *The Heart of Buddhist Meditation*, Nyanaponika Thera tells us: "It is the intrinsic nature of insight that produces a growing detachment and an increasing freedom from craving, culminating in the final deliverance of the mind from all that causes its enslavement to the world of suffering." Pg. 44);

Spiritual URL: our spiritual address which is the Christ Presence within us; (In social media, URL is the technical term for a web address, ie:www.YourSpiritualPractice.com/ URL stands for Uniform Resource Locator);

Spiro-methodology: how our adherence to spiritual teachings and practices helps us make sense of everyday situations;

Spittle: In its positive aspects spittle is seen as healing words; In its negative connotations spittle can be contemptuous, angry, spiteful, disrespectful attitudes;

Spoice: thanksliving; being grateful for the good things in life; (Derived from snowboarding culture spoice means giving gratitude for all of the positivity in our lives); (See Thanksliving; Gratitude);

Spontaneous Admission: thinking, being, and doing something out-of-sync with our professed spiritual and/or religious beliefs and immediately catching ourselves and reminding ourselves of the infraction; an epiphany; the Second Coming; (See Second Coming);

Spontaneous Generation: cosmic vitality in its manifest and unmanifest forms;

Spontaneous Human Combustion: refers to incredibly bizarre cases in which a badly burned human body is discovered in mysterious circumstances suggesting that the fire originated spontaneously in or on the body of the incinerated victim;

Spontaneous Recovery: seeing any alphabet of troubles as the symphony of our spiritual unfoldment;

Spotlight: an illumined perspective;

Spractice(s): spiritual practice(s);

Spring: our 'dark night of the soul' struggle to release ourselves from the bondage of the unenlightened ego and embrace the light and radiance of our divine nature as human expressions of the Eternal Presence;

Spyware: anti-Christed thoughts; (In IT language, spyware is software that actually 'spies' on our computer by capturing private information like Web browsing habits and preferences, email messages, user names, passwords, credit card numbers, etc.);

~ *Spiritually Speaking* ~

Squaring the Circle: liberating our egocentric consciousness from its incarnational limitations to its universal, cosmic status;

Squeegee: clarity, unencumbered line of sight;

Sramaology: disciplined mental and physical effort to increase our esoteric knowledge;

Stable: human consciousness; the physical body;

Stage(s): our earth experience; incarnational and reincarnational experiences as a whole; every choice we make;

Stained Glass: a religious outlook; religious devotion;

Stains: error thoughts, choices, and actions;

Staircase, Stairs: ascending stairs denotes moving upward toward a higher level of awareness and understanding; descending stairs suggests going into our subconscious realm; (See Jacob's Ladder); involution and evolution;

Stardust: Each of us is an atomic pastiche: the iron atoms in our blood carrying oxygen at this moment to our cells came largely from exploding white dwarf stars, while the oxygen itself came mainly from exploding supernovas that ended the lives of massive stars, and most of the carbon in the carbon dioxide we exhale on every breath came from planetary nebulas, the death clouds of middle-sized stars a little bigger than our sun. (We are made of material created and ejected into the Galaxy by the violence of earlier stars. Human beings are made of the rarest material in the universe: stardust. Except for hydrogen, which makes up about a tenth of our weight, the rest of our body is stardust. Our bodies literally had the entire history of the universe, witnessed and enacted by our atoms);

Stargate: the still point in mindfulness meditative practice;

Star People Conviction, Starseed Conclusion: believing that evolved beings from another planet, star system or galaxy have come to Earth to assist us to achieve a higher level of being;

Stars: spiritual ideas; *star light* is the long-lasting, beneficial effect of highly illumined spiritual ideas;

Starvation Diet: a literal only interpretation of religious scripture;

Static: error thoughts, words, choices, and actions;

Statue-like: a fixed thoughts anchored in tradition and/or convention; a well-rooted belief and/or established concept; emotional immobility;

Statue Of Liberty: independence; freedom; patriotism; refuge;

Status Check: all of the thoughts we have, choices we make, and actions we take at a given time;

Status Offence, Status Inconsistency: lowering our standards; misrepresenting ourselves;

Statute of Limitations: the time it takes us to expiate any karma we have incurred; (In legal circles, the statute of limitations refers to the time within which a lawsuit must be filed or a criminal prosecution begun.);

Staycation(s): spending time in our own consciousness (home) by meditating, visualizing, and praying about spiritual subjects instead of physically traveling around the world;

Stepping Into the Breach: the act of putting ourselves into the 0.35 of a second neural timeline it takes to consciously decide to act and actually act a thousand tines each day (See Bereitschafts Potential);

Sterility: an adamantly materialistic consciousness;

Stigmata: severe ecstatic mental stress and strain that produces open wounds on the physical body;

Still Small Voice: the super-psychic vibration (hum) of our conscious connection with Spirit that tells us our ordinary consciousness is completely aligned with our Christ Consciousness;

Stir-Fried Theology: simultaneously enjoying the best practices of many faith traditions;

Stomach: our ability to handle what life has to offer;

Stomach Ulcers: worrying too much about what will happen if we take some time off and rest;

Stones, Rocks: authoritative life force; rigid ideas and/or concepts; spiritual integrity; highly stable spiritual attainment; emotional hardness; *rolling away a stone* symbolizes the beginning of a new level of awareness, a distinct advance in consciousness; the *'stone which the builders ejected'* symbolizes our spiritual growth's rejection (sabotage, rebuff, betrayal) by a recalcitrant and narcissistic ego; See also White Stone);

Stop-Over: an incarnational and/or reincarnational experience on our way to enlightenment; (In airline industry terms, a stop-over is usually an overnight stay (or possibly longer) at a location en-route to our final destination.);

Storage Facilities: long-term memory;

Stork-ness: having the compunction for new beginnings; enjoying new birth; respecting motherhood and fertility; embracing newness and novelty; transforming the old with the new;

Storm(s): anger; emotional upheaval; outrage; indignation; tantrum; ill temper;

Storyteller: our Quantum Self;

Stowaway(s): our repressed psychological and psychic material;

Straightjacket(s): any literal-only interpretation of sacred scripture; dogma;

Strangler(s): divinity-denying thoughts and emotions;

Stray(s): worldly, materialistic, impure, carnal thoughts;

Stream of Conscience: being our own imaginary witness;

Street Corner Busking: proselytizing on city streets to 'save sinners'; (In magic terms, busking refers to providing entertainment on the streets in urban areas and being paid by tips donated by audiences.);

Street Food: standing on a street corner proselytizing a religious message; sharing basic esoteric teachings instead of advanced principles; (prepared or cooked food sold by vendors on a street or other public location for immediate consumption);

Street of Gold: In its literal interpretation Revelation 21:21b says: *"The great street of the city was of pure gold, like transparent glass."* Let's take a look at this verse from a metaphysical perspective: The 'great street' of the city is our spinal column where the Serpentine Energy (Holy Spirit, the Kundalini Fire) flows when we are awakened. The 'city' is our Christ Consciousness. The 'gold' represents the enlightenment which comes from our elevated spiritual understanding. The 'transparent glass' symbolizes the knowledge that there is no separation between us and Spirit; (See Yellow Brick Road);

Street Sweeper(s): denials that clear-up our waking thoughts and stream of consciousness;

Strobe Light Effect: the unenlightened ego's fractured view of reality; (Heisenberg speaks of what is real "Some physicists would prefer to come back to the idea of an objective real world whose smallest parts exist objectively in the same sense as stones or trees exist independently of whether we observe them. This, however, is impossible." Werner Heisenberg, quoted in *The Non-Local Universe: The New Physics and Matters of the Mind*);

Stuffed Animal(s): warmth; comfort;

Stumbling Blocks: dogmatic beliefs; failure to apply spiritual principles; unforgiveness; (See Twelve Poisons);

Subconscious Mind (Depot): the place where all of our human experiences, patterns of behavior, life scripts, faulty coping patterns, and egocentric defense mechanisms are warehoused – our subconscious; subliminally absorbed events;

Subconscious Gnomes: old, self-defeating life patterns, beliefs, and guiding principles;

Sublime Timing: knowing that patience produces immediate results;

Submarine(s): psychoanalysis; psychotherapy; personal introspection; autobiographical journaling; past lives regression therapy; hypnosis;

Subpoena(s): our next thought, word, choice or action that is subject to the influence of natural and spiritual laws; (In legal language, a subpoena is a command, issued under a court's authority, to a witness to appear and give testimony.);

Substandard Deviation: what happens when we're not our spiritual selves;

Suburbia: our physical bodies with the brain being the inner city;

Subway: the subconscious;

Sucker Punch: a purposefully malicious criticism leveled at someone to intentionally undermine h/her credibility; deliberate and hurtful denominational sparring; (In boxing terms, a sucker punch is an unexpected punch that catches an opponent completely off guard.);

Suffering: misalignment with our spiritual nature; human spiritual unfoldment calibrated to its lowest possible setting; the consequences of our incarceration in human form; denying our oneness with Spirit; (Why do we suffer? Here's my answer. Are you ready? We suffer because we believe we are separate from God. And because we believe we are separate from God, we believe we are separate from one another. And because we deny our oneness with one another, we cultivate our spiritual unfoldment calibrated to its lowest possible setting which gives power to outer appearances that reinforce our belief in our separateness from God. That sequence of warped mind action is the cause of all suffering); (One of the major tenets in Buddhism is that "life is suffering." For Buddhists, *dukkha* (suffering) is caused by three poisons: greed, hatred, and delusion. Hinduism holds that suffering follows naturally from personal negative actions (karma). In Christianity, the *Book of Job* is a treatise on suffering. The suffering Job thought would befall him was the suffering he experienced. Whatever form suffering takes, and no matter how it is defined by the world's religions, it comes down to this realization: suffering is the purification we undergo to realign ourselves with Spirit.);

Sufficiency of Truth Principles: studying truth principles equips us with the intellectual knowledge of truth principles, but not the benefits received from their application;

Suffocation: the denial of our innate divinity;

Sufi Whirling: a very brisk twirling meditation that requires focus and balance;

Sugar Shack: a highly enjoyable, euphoric, and blissful spiritual concept that sends us to the heights of esoteric rapture; spiritual insights, theories, and concepts that are mind candy;

Suicide: negating, extinguishing, and/or nullifying a thought – spiritual or material – before it becomes an inclination or intention;

Suicide Wrap: wrapping ourselves around false teachings, false assumptions, and false beliefs that can 'kill' our chances to achieve enlightenment; (In cowboy terms, a suicide wrap is a particular rope wrap bull riders take when wrapping the bull rope around their hand. It is very difficult to get out of a suicide wrap if the cowboy falls off the animal. The wrap is against the rules in most modern rodeos for obvious reasons.);

Suitcase: short-term memory;

Sulfur: soul; animus, existence itself; sacred fire;

Sulukian Path: to enter upon a spiritual journey; (Suluk is a Sufi spiritual training program on the essential perspectives, teachings, and practices of esoteric Sufism);

Summer: symbolizes not only the awareness of our innate divinity but the conscious and disciplined fulfillment of our actualized divinity so that the entrainment of our human self with our Christ Self is complete;

Summit: a high state of consciousness;

Summum Bonum: our belief in the highest good for all;

Sun: the Indwelling Christ (Buddha, Vishnu, Krishna, Allah, Great White Spirit); our Authentic Self, True Self, our Extraordinary Nature; the *sun standing still* symbolizes the centrality of the Indwelling Christ (Buddha, Vishnu, Krishna, Allah, etc.), bringing our highest spiritual aspirations to their position of maximum influence so its light (our innate divinity) shines on the mind (moon) and bathes everything in spiritual understanding;

Sunburn: taking the mind-altering, hallucinogenic route to seek oneness with the Indwelling Christ (Buddha, Vishnu, Krishna, Allah, Great White Spirit); our Authentic Self, True Self, our Extraordinary Nature;

Sunday Filibuster: an extremely long Sunday Sermon that lasts two to two-and-a-half hours or more;

Sunday Service Frostbite: not receiving a warm welcome or even a greeting at a Sunday church service we are attending for the first time;

Sunday Supplement: a Sunday truth talk and/or sermon that waters down the spiritual/religious content in order to reduce the amount of cognitive dissonance that could be felt by guests who may be hearing that particular theology for the first time;

Sunflower-like: our aptitude for aligning our human self with our Christ Self; focusing on the light (spiritual aspirations) instead of darkness (egocentric ambitions); courage; risk savvy;

Sunrise: awakening; renewal and rebirth; illumination; intellectual comprehension; creative impulses;

Sunset: the beginning of a contemplative, introspective, evaluative mindset;

Sunscreen: our egocentrism and the detours it causes;

Super-Abled: being consciously aware and connected with our Divine Nature; living at the speed of our Christ Consciousness;

Super-Conscious Mind: the totality of our spiritual essence;

Supererogatory: going considerably beyond the call of duty;

Super Heroes: externalizations of the Christ Presence within us; (See also, God);

Supernatural: purely divine natural occurrences that take place on lower dimensions of being which make them seem contrary to the natural laws of that particular plane;

Supplementary Dioceses: a collection of spiritually-related concepts and suppositions associated with a compelling theory;

Supreme Architect: the Cosmic Christ;

Surface Map: a literal interpretation of sacred scripture;

Surfer's Remorse, Internet: similar to buyer's remorse, when we realize we've been clicking on the Internet for hours searching for religious and/or spiritual material and end up having nothing to show for it;

Surfing, Water: being able to handle powerful, volatile, turbulent, fierce emotions by staying cool, calm, and collected;

Surge Protector(s): meditation, affirmative prayers, positive affirmations and denials protect us against surges of material appetites and addictions;

Surrender: the kenosis of error thoughts and habits;

Sustaining Period: using different stories, illustrations, and examples to remind a congregation what you told them days, weeks, months, and even years before to drive home a spiritual and/or religious teaching; (In advertising language, a sustaining period is a period of time during the close of an ad campaign that uses fewer advertising spots to remind audiences of the product or service);

Sutratma: an epithet of the Cosmic Soul conceived of as the thread that holds together all creatures and the universe; same as Hiranyagarbha, Prana and Vayu;

Svapnaian Perch: coma consciousness; our skin school experiences; (In Sanskrit, means literally 'a dream state.');

Swaddling Clothes: confining limitations associated with our human form;

Swamp: a collection of bad habits;

Swan-like: having peerless grace and elegance, purity of thoughts, and intentions; cultivating loving and vibrant relationships; establishing lasting harmony between spirit and matter; ability to stay calm and poised in the midst of turbulence; *white swans* denote purity and sacredness; *black swans* represent underlying talents and abilities that need surfacing;

S.W.A.T. Team: our antibodies that fight infections and disease;

Swearing: a form of idolatry;

Sweatshop: an egocentric consciousness;

Sword-like: attaining divine wisdom; having above average fortitude; constantly seeking truth and justice; honoring the word of God; having unquestionable authority; using male generative energy to expand our influence;

Swords Into Plowshares: transforming penetratingly destructive thoughts and hurtful tendencies into spiritual aspirations that 'till the terrain' of our ordinary consciousness, preparing it for its higher receptivity to spiritual ideals;

Sycamore Tree-like: building a false foundation on temporal things; being mindlessly dependent on the ego's illusions;

Sylphs: connectivity; cellular repair; alchemical breath; (According to biologists, cellular membranes were once called 'walls' and considered to be solid barriers that passively confined an undifferentiated blob of protoplasm. But the 'wall' is actually a living system, and is a dynamic, thoroughly porous communications center in constant contact with the cell it serves); [In *The Biology of Belief,* Bruce Lipton says that "each neuron has a mind of its own, governed by its own beliefs and directives inferred by certain genes. Individual cells have the molecular capacity to hold beliefs. If a cell perceives stress, it can actually "rewrite" the genetic directive in order to overcome the stressful situation."];

Sympathy Saved: giving into peer pressure by pretending we are saved because those around us are proudly announcing they are saved;

Symphonic Bliss: feelings of inner peace, joy, love, reverence, prosperity, safety, security, compassion, happiness, fulfillment, etc.;

Synagogue of Satan: a belief system based on divinity-denying thoughts, inclinations, and intentions;

Synthetic Happiness: When we accept something we get, even when it is not what we initially wanted, we still feel satisfied and content with the choice. Synthetic happiness can be as enduring as "natural happiness" that occurs when we get what we wanted in the first place. (I often think about the impact of synthetic happiness when I consider our choice as spiritual beings to experience a human incarnation. Although we want to experience what the oneness and transcendence feels like in our relationship with the One Presence we choose the duality and illusions that characterize our incarnation into matter, and feel satisfied with the synthetic happiness that comes with it);

Synthetic Spirituality: having spiritual knowledge but failing to apply spiritual principles;

Systematic Theology: studying, comparing, cataloging, and then defending parochial perspectives of angelology, anthropology, Bibliology, Christology, ecclesiology, eschatology, pneumatology, etc.;

Syzygic Sabbatical(s): aligning our mind, body, and soul in divine order so we eliminate the following things from our lives: absurdity, aggrandizement, agitation, alcoholism, anger, bitterness, blind ambition, callousness, corruption, cruelty, demeaning comments, drug addiction, envy, excess, excuses, fear, filth, gluttony, greed, hatred, harshness, hostility, hypocrisy, idiocy, immorality, incompetence, indecency, insincerity, jealousy, laziness, litigation, littering, maliciousness, manipulation, materialism, narcissism, negativism, neglect, nit-picking, over-indulgence, paranoia, passivity, pessimism, prejudice, profanity, quarrelsomeness, resentment, redundancy, repugnancy, rhetoric, rudeness, scuzziness, self-centeredness, self-doubt, shortsightedness, snobbishness, substance abuse, thoughtlessness, tokenism, toxic behavior, underhandedness, unfounded suspicions, unsportsmanlike conduct, unnecessary pain, violence, wastefulness, wolfishness, workaholism, and spiteful yakkity-yak; (Syzygy implies synergistic alignment);

Tabernacle: running from one religious belief to another without growing in one's spirituality; knothole spiritual perspective; pick-up-sticks theology;

Table Bomb: a religious pamphlet that is left on a table by the previous occupant to proselytize h/her faith tradition;

Table-like: life, in general, with its personal, professional, and spiritual dimensions; a round table represents the world and/or our zodiacal journey;

Tablets, Posting the Ten Commandments: Resolute adherence to divine laws; *breaking the tablets* means our spiritual light fragmented by strong sense appetites;

Taboo(s): idolatry; unforgiveness; the seven deadly sins; (See Afflictions; Detours);

Tad-aikya: oneness; being aligned with the Absolute;

Tail Bonk: as an after thought, intentionally upsetting a religious fundamentalist by inserting a controversial comment at the end of a conversation about religious beliefs; (In snowboarding terms, intentionally hitting and bouncing off objects, either natural or manmade, with the tail of the snowboard.);

Talent Show, Variety Show: our earth experience;

Talismanic Protection: positive affirmations; resolute denials (See Denialdom);

Talismanic Teachings: spiritual principles that are regarded as especially magical in their prospering power;

Tamala Pattra: being sage-like; pure spiritual thinking; (In Sanskrit, tamala pattras are leaves from the dark-barked tamala tree which symbolizes pure, stainless living);

Tamariskic-like: having supernatural powers; (Tamarisks are evergreen scrubs and trees that symbolize psychic and supernatural powers);

Tamasic Demeanor: the unfortunate quality of denying our innate divinity; keeping ourselves in darkness; (In Sanskrit, *tamas* stands for darkness or indifference and is one of three qualities, the other two being *rajas* [passion] and *sattva* [purity]);

Tanhaic Self-Abuse: clinging to materialism; strong attachment to physical incarnation; the thirst for sense consciousness; (Tanha is a Buddhist term that means 'thirst' and is translated as craving or desire, especially as they apply to pleasurable sensory experiences);

Tao: the path; the way; personal renovation using spiritual means;

Tao Te Chinging: reading and studying Lao Tzu's book by the same name as a spiritual guide;

Tapasic Focus: contemplativeness; meditation; (In Vedic Hinduism, tapas means deep meditation, hermetic asceticism); [Neuroscientists Andrew Newberg and Mark Waldman have found that brain-scan research shows that concentrating and meditating on positive thoughts, feelings, and outcomes can be more powerful than any drug in the world, especially when it comes to changing old habits, behaviors, and beliefs];

Tapestry: our life experiences;

Taproot: our innate divinity; (In gardening terms, a taproot is the main, thick root growing straight down from a plant.);

Tariqahic Devotion: adhering to a religious creed; (Tariquah is an Arabic term that a school of thought that aims at seeking ultimate truth by esoteric means instead of exoteric interference);

Tartarology: studying the significance of the underworld (hell);

Tasawwufic Perfection: mystical devotion; (the Sufi way of life);

Tasawwuric Practice: focusing attention upon a certain ideal (such as oneness, unconditional love, forgiveness), visualizing the nature of that ideal, mentally and emotionally embodying that essence, and then allowing the essence of that ideal to flow freely through our own lives); In Sufi practice, means concentration exercises that one uses to experience ultimate truths);

Taser(s): unexpected dis-eases; sudden illnesses and accidents;

Task of the Masters: spreading the light and gathering what is scattered; (The Masonic formula, *T'ien Ti Huei*, asserts that the 'task of the masters is to "destroy the darkness, and restore the light."); [It is from the fragmenting of the body of *Adam Kadmon* that the universe was formed, including all of the beings that the universe contains. The reintegration of these scattered beings leads to the reconstitution of *Adam Kadmon*, the Universal Man]; (See *Adam Kadmon*);

Tasseography: also known as kypomancy, a form of divination accomplished by reading tea leaves, coffee grounds, or wine sediments to obtain hidden wisdom;

Taste Aversion: trying on different faith traditions for size and finding that we do not prefer certain ones at all;

Tattoos: our willingness to publically retail our wants, needs, preferences, allegiances, wishes, and fantasies; branding our human experience; the mark of the Beast which represents our desire for sentient existence that generally leads to repeated incarnations;

Tat Tvan Asi: means "*Thou art That*" which denotes that we are the universe expressing itself at the point of us;

Tavern: one of the entrances to oblivion;

Tawajjuhic Piety: reverently turning toward spiritual pursuits; (Tawajjuh, as Sufis claim, is the miraculous power of a Sufi Shaikh to grant tremendous knowledge or completely transform someone, by just gazing intently at that person);

Tawhidic Unity: experiencing oneness with the Eternal Presence; (Tawhid is the Arabic doctrine of our oneness with God);

Taxes: error thoughts, words, choices, and actions;

Taxidermy: turning error thoughts, words, choices, and actions into a habit;

Taxing Tariffs: the mental, emotional, physical, financial and spiritual price we pay for the ego's enthronement in our human personality;

Taxi(s), Limousine(s): each of our incarnated physical bodies (vehicles) that we inhabit on our way toward enlightenment (the price we pay is another skin school experience);

Taxing Thoughts: *Taxing thoughts* are any thoughts we have that deny our oneness with Spirit and block our spiritual growth. They are thoughts of lack and limitation which affect our capital gains and complicate our cost of living. They are thoughts that increase our tax liability and erode our tax shelters. These kinds of thoughts are withholding statements. They withhold our good and negatively affect our charitable contributions. Each negative, self-defeating thought becomes an itemized deduction. The kind of deduction that reduces our prosperity;

Tea-ishness: seeking tranquility, inner peace, and comfort; enjoying a self-disciplined route to enlightenment;

Tea Kettle Temperament: our ability to let off a little steam;

Tears: soulful tithes to Spirit;

Techni-Colored Coat: our rainbow body; (See Chakras; Holy Ghost; Kundalini, Speirema, Bhujangini; Rainbow); [Essentially we are rainbow bodies. We are prisms that filter cosmic light energies which are unmanifest in the form of cosmic consciousness. However, as consciousness passes through the medium called 'us' it splits into seven spiritual energy centers (chakras) which each have a particular vibration which corresponds to a color of the rainbow];

Techscuse: using a spiritual term or referring to a spiritual practice just to let others know we have dabbled in metaphysics; (In IT language, techscuse is an excuse to use an electronic device for a useless or unnecessary purpose);

Te'e'i: spiritual impoverishment; spiritual poverty;

Teenager(s): maturing spiritual ideas;

Teeth: logical and pragmatic thoughts that help us digest our human experience; *teeth grinding* denotes difficulty in understanding new information; hesitation in accepting novel information; a *toothache* denotes upsetting information that has been allowed to languish for far too long without doing something about it; a *tooth falling out* suggests the loss of a key piece of information that could have helped us understand something essential for solving our dilemma; *toothlessness* implies the inability to understand or digest information critical for our continued growth and well-being; *rotten or decayed teeth* represent our neglecting to comprehend fully and/or apply what we've learned;

Telekinetic Energy: mind moving matter without the mediation of any known physical energy source;

Telepathic Communication: transmitting information from one person's consciousness to another's without the use of any known sensory channels or physical interaction like speech, iPhones, etc.;

Teleportation: the seemingly instantaneous movement of a person or other being from one location in space-time to another, apparently without going through the restrictions of the normal space-time geography in between;

Teleprompter: reading our inner thoughts out loud;

Telescope: our third eye; highly defined spiritual clarity and discernment;

Tempering Tantrums: turning short fuses into long recluses by walking off anger so we can resolve whatever we need to resolve amicably and sanely;

Temple(s): the universe; the cosmos; our quickened consciousness; our unfolding spiritually-oriented human personality; the *veil in temples* symbolizes the perceptual filter between the intellect and the heart that implies separation and duality, it also represents the 'veil' of human incarnation itself which clouds our being able to see our true nature – spiritual beings having a human experience, the veil could also symbolize dogma which blocks our being able to see beyond a literal interpretation sacred scripture, veils could also represent the human ego which refuses to give up its rulership over the human personality; the *renting of the veil* represents the renunciation of our egocentric perspective which is tied to the illusion of duality and separation; *temples being destroyed* symbolize our being liberated from the belief that the spiritual *us* is separated from the human *us*;

Temple of Medicine: our self-healing oriented physical bodies;

Tempter, Charmer, Enticer: a sense-soaked ego;

Ten Commandments: the "thou shall not" (denial) phase of divinely ordering our enlightenment; [The Ten Commandments came from Chapter 125 in the *Egyptian Book of the Dead*); (See Denialdom);

Tenet Traffic: letting spiritual thoughts, meditation, prayers, and affirmations of peace, love, and joy set the cadence for the pace of our day;

Ten Levels of Initiation: a Theosophical concept denoting our movement toward enlightenment; (The 10 levels are: 1. Birth: attaining individualized "I am" consciousness by mastering the human experience; 2. Baptism: gaining full mastery of our Astral Body; 3. Transfiguration: mastering clairvoyance and clairaudience; 4. Crucifixion: remembering all of our past incarnations (*samma sambuddha*); 5. Resurrection: mastering teleportation, bilocation, and levitation abilities; 6. Ascension: ability to teleport, bilocate, or levitate to anyplace on Earth; 7. Christhood (Bodhisattva, Avatar): the ability to teleport anywhere in the solar system; 8. Buddhahood: the ability to freely roam both in interplanetary and interstellar space while fully consciousness, physically remaining in our celestialized bodies, and carrying on normal activities such as communicating with other beings; 9. Godhood: the ability to materialize and materialize objects, locally and cosmically, and influence events in nearby planetary systems; 10. Planetary Logos: the ability to influence and telepathically communicate with beings anywhere in the universe; (There are believed to be thousands of initiatory levels above and beyond these ten levels, according to Theosophists, such as a Solar Logos, Galactic Logos, Cosmic Logos, Universal Logos, Multiverse Logos, and the Christ.);

Tensegrity, Tensional Integrity, Floating Compression: the transcendental 'webbing' of our consciousness which holds all of the interdimensional and intradimensional parts of us together as a conscious entity; (Tensegrity is a term developed by Buckminster Fuller and Kenneth Snelson and modified by Donald Ingber to describe any structure that stabilizes and supports itself by balancing opposing forces of tension and contraction);

Tent(s): mobile sanctuaries; sanctuaries on the run;

Tepid Turf: the state of mind where we're excited but frustrated, fulfilled yet troubled, and satisfied but agitated that one of the most difficult things to do in life is to truly *know our human selves* let alone our higher, more spiritual Self;

Teratological Thinking: malformed, monstrous material thoughts;

Termite(s): error propensities and dispositions;

Terrorist(s), Extremist(s), Fanatic(s): exceedingly malevolent thoughts, words, beliefs, and actions that deny our innate divinity;

Test(s), Exam(s): feeling that our talents, skills, and/or knowledge is being assessed or evaluated by others or determined by our own resolve and inner strength;

Test Tube: our earth experience;

Tethered Gems: bringing lofty spiritual truths down to earth in a way they can be understood and applied; keeping our over-head down;

Tetragrammaton: refers to the four letters that make up the religious nominative 'JHWH,' translated as Jehovah or Yahweh; (Used by Qabbalists to designate the four Hebrew characters ה ו ה י — that form the present day word for Yehovah);

Textbook, Workbook, Required Reading: the lessons we encounter in our skin school sojourn;

Text Messaging: letting our fingers do the 'talking' electronically; electronic telepathy using our fingers;

Text Purgatory: metaphorically, alludes to the Catholic doctrine of purgatory; (See Purgatory); (In IT language, the time it takes for a response to the text message we just sent);

Textuary: someone who has extensive Biblical knowledge;

Textversation: our penchant for mindlessly quoting scriptural passages to make a point; (In tech language, a conversation via text messages);

Thanatism: believing that our souls die with the body;

~ Spiritually Speaking ~

Thangka: a painted or embroidered banner or tapestry hung in a monastery or a family altar and carried by lamas in ceremonial processions;

Thanksliving: Cultivating a consistent consciousness of thanksgiving by becoming aware of the myriad opportunities to express your gratitude and praise is the essence of *thanksliving*. (See Spoice);

Thatness: the nature of all that is and all that isn't, of the manifest and the unmanifest; a spiritually-attuned consciousness and an egocentric consciousness;

Thaumaturgy: being able to perform miracles; wonder-working spiritual power;

Theandric Existence: being animated by the union of divine and human qualities;

Theanthropic Qualities: being simultaneously the product of two natures: human and divine;

Theatre of the Absurd: our mental, emotional, and behavioral theatrics when dealing with spiritual, religious, and moral matters;

Theme Parks: our penchant for fun, happiness, joviality, and amusement; also denotes major conceptual mindsets relating to merriment;

Themis: divine order and universal harmony:

Theocentrism: believing that God is the central truth of all existence;

Theodidaktosic Attentiveness: listening to the 'still small voice' (our divine guidance); (In Greek mystery schools, *theodidaktosis* means that every initiate is taught from within by h/her own inner god in strict proportion to the degree with which the person has made alliance with h/her spiritual self.);

Theogony: the genealogy of all gods, planets, and zodiacal signs;

Theological Somnambulism: sleepwalking our way past spiritual truths, moral responsibilities, and humanitarian endeavors;

Theomachy: fighting against all gods, divine ideas, and spiritual insights;

Theopantism: believing God is the only reality;

Theopathy: religious fanaticism;

Theophilanthropism: a deep abiding love of both God and humankind;

Theopneustic Actions: divinely inspired acts of kindness, writings and songs, conversations, giving, etc.; (In Greek mystery schools, means divine inspiration or inbreathing during a particular stage of initiation);

Theopsychism: believing our soul is divine;

Theosophia: Divine Wisdom; wisdom religion;

Theotherapy: a religious approach to treating health issues; faith healing;

Therianthropic Thoughts: monstrous thoughts and attitudes that amplify our animal instincts; (Therianthropy comes from the Greek words *theríon* [wild animal] and *anthrōpos* [human body]. It refers to the metamorphosis of humans into animals);

Thermometer, Thermostat: gauging the level of our commitment to spiritual growth – are we cold, lukewarm, or hot?;

Thief in the Night: a selfish worldly thought (thief) that comes to us in a consciousness characterized by the unawareness, refusal, or repression of (night) our innate divinity;

Thieves on the Crosses: lingering duality in spite of our spiritual growth; our elevated consciousness and egocentric consciousness; pure materialism (on the left cross), our Christ-centric awareness on the center cross, and our unfolding yet unquickened spiritual awareness (on the right cross); [In the *Gospel of Nicodemus* the thief named Dismas, the penitent thief, was crucified on a cross on the right side of Jesus, and asked Jesus to remember him in paradise. The unrepentant thief who was crucified on a cross on the left side of Jesus was called Gestas, or Gesmas, and taunted Jesus. An apocryphal Arabic gospel refers to Dismas as Dumachus and describes him as one of a band of robbers who attacked the Holy Family during their flight into Egypt]; (In the Arabic tradition Dismas was called Titus; in the *Codex Colbertinus* he was named Zoatham; in the Russian Orthodox tradition he was named Rach);

Third Coming: when people all over the world actualize their own divinity and witness the fulfillment of the divinity in others. (We will experience the

Third Coming when the entire world is Christ-filled, Buddha-filled, Vishnu-filled, Allah-filled, Krishna-filled, Great Spirit-filled, etc.);

Third Eye: laser-like spiritual perception; superior inner vision; clairvoyance; psychic iridology; the pineal gland's transformative power to heighten our rate of vibration to discern Universal Wisdom and Knowledge so we can comprehend the greater truths; the true "I" of our soul; (See Eye of the Purified Soul; Tickling of the Ant);

Third World: our subconscious;

Thistle(s), Thorns: error impulses, preferences, and susceptibilities; testing; trials; severity;

Thorn-ishness: having error thoughts and emotions, self-defeating habits and choices, anti-Christed actions; *pricks of the thorns* are the karmic consequences of our errant thoughts, words, and actions;

Thorn in the Flesh: our Prometheusian decision as spiritual beings to incarnate and/or reincarnate which brought with it the *out*picturing of our spiritual malaise in the form of physical ailments; the illusion of our self-separateness from the Eternal Presence; (Our apparent separateness, asserts physicist Amit Goswami, results from the camouflage called a simple hierarchy that conceals our self-reference. Once this separateness arises and obscures the unity, however, it defines our perspective. We become solipsistic, a collection of individual island universes with little or no awareness of our common bedrock, and we define our world in terms of our individual, separate selves: our families, our cultures, our countries);

Thought Disorder: a literal-only comprehension of sacred scripture;

Thoughtography: the documented paranormal ability to produce images on photographic film by concentrating on a mental image;

Three Degrees of Initiation: Every nation had its exoteric and esoteric tradition, the one for the uninitiated (exoteric), the other for the learned and more enlightened. For example, the Hindus had three degrees with several sub-degrees. The Egyptians had three preliminary degrees, personified under the "three guardians of the fire." The Chinese had the *Triad* Society. The Tibetans have their "triple step" which is symbolized in the *Vedas* by the three strides of Vishnu. The Triad and Triangle symbology abound. The Babylonians had their three stages of initiation into the priesthood. The Jews, the Kabbalists, and mystics borrowed them from the Chaldees, and

Christians followed the Jewish lead. The Masons have three degrees. There were the three grades of Isis.); (See Ten Levels of Initiation);

Threefold Cord: the strands of Divine Order (Mind, Idea, and Expression);

Threefold Death: diddlysquat order that is characterized by an error-prone mind that has an error-ridden idea that produces an error-riddled expression which leads to the denial of our innate divinity;

Three Saviors: Mind, Idea, Expression (the three phases of Divine Order); (See Divine Order);

Threesome: mind, body, and soul; God, Son, Holy Spirit; Universal Christ, Cosmic Christ, Planetary Christ;

Three Traitors: mind, idea, expression (the three phases of diddlysquat order); (See Diddlysquat Order);

Three Worlds: the Native American belief in an Upper World, Lower World, and the Waking World. (The Upper World was considered perfect and pure. The Lower World was dark and chaotic. In between the two was the Waking World where we live on a day-to-day basis); spiritually, the three worlds are the super-conscious, subconscious, and conscious;

Threshold, Brink, Gateway, Entrance: the veil between Spirit and matter;

Throne of the Beast: epithumetic (derogatory, abusive, contemptuous) state of coma consciousness which springs from our phrenic (lower) mind; (When the 'beast' comes to life after being slain, it represents our desire for sentient existence which generally leads to repeated incarnations. It is our clinging to sensuousness and physicality. A beast with two horns like a lamb denotes false seership and the anthropomorphic devil of pediatric religions);

Throng, Multitude of People: a collection of thoughts;

Thug(s): materialistic thoughts and choices that rob us of our joy, inner peace, and happiness; (See Hooligan(s), Mob);

Thummim: perfection; (In Hebrew mythology, Thummim is the angel of illumination and perfection);

Thunder: our proclivity for emotional outbursts;

Thunderbird: transformation; triumph over trials; regality that prefers solitude; a powerful and indomitable spirit, especially in the face of adversity;

Tickling of the Ant: The most often quoted 'ant verse' from the *Hebrew Testament* is Proverbs 6:6. "Be like the ant," says Solomon, "consider her ways, and be wise." The King James Bible is a little more in your face. It refers to us a sluggards. It says, "Go to the ant, thou sluggard, consider her ways, and be wise." I don't recommend calling people sluggards; however, the derogatory language makes an important point. Most people are a bit sluggish when it comes to applying Truth principles. Solomon was well versed in the wisdom traditions of the East and what we call the Mid-East. He was well aware of what the Egyptians called the *arat* and the Hindus called the *ajna*. Taoists call it the Third Eye. It's located slightly above the eyebrows in the middle of the forehead. It is sometimes called the 'clear sight' or guru chakra. Hindus place a colored dot on their foreheads. Christians place ashes there on Ash Wednesday. Unity prefers to anoint our foreheads with oil. The ancient Egyptians wore a tiara with a small serpent protruding over the Third Eye to honor its influence. Muslims place their faces on prayer mats to achieve a prostration mark that represents piety. In the *Book of Revelation* the third eye is the sixth chakra (pineal gland) and is identified with the 6th church, the Church of Philadelphia. Here's the connection with the *ant*. When the Third Eye becomes active, one feels a tingling behind the skin of the forehead. Some esoteric traditions call that sensation "the tickling of the ant." So, in the Bible, when Solomon advises people to learn the ways of the ant and become wise, the ant's "wisdom" is a play on the esoteric 'tickling of the ant' when the 'clear sight' chakra becomes active. What Solomon is really saying is 'go inside.' If you want to be wise "listen to the ant's speech" – that is, we must listen to our inner guidance. (If you still think Solomon lowered his ear to an anthill to listen to ants we need to talk after you read this glossary. In the wisdom traditions, the Third Eye is the gateway to higher consciousness, and thus enlightenment. The Third Eye is often associated with clairvoyance, precognition, astral visions, out-of-body experiences, and astral travel. (See Third Eye);

Tidal Wave(s): monumental, uncontrollable and destructive emotional outbursts;

Tightrope: trying to be spiritual and material at the same time;

***Tikkun Olam* Obligation:** doing good works; promoting peace and good will; helping the hungry, homeless, and oppressed; (*Tikkun Olam* is Hebrew for 'repairing the world' or 'healing the world.');

Time Capsule(s): each of our reincarnational and incarnational 'bodies';

Time Travel: what we sign up for in each skin school experience; (Because we are indivisibly and eternally connected to the Godhead, we (humankind) have the wherewithal to bypass the constraints of physicality and enter any dimension of being as a matter of will and volition. There is nothing keeping us in this limited particulate existence (skin school experience) except the self-imposed parameters of our consciousness. Space and time are constructs we have created. The interplay between these constructs is also up to us.); (In quantum physics terms, using quantum entanglement to replicate a quantum state in space that previously existed at another point in space, quantum physicists argue that you can theoretically teleport a particle back in time. The idea of moving back in time without bending the fabric of the universe – which may create a few unpleasant snafus – is one concept that quantum physicists are very much interested in these days. They believe that given certain geometries of space-time, time travel into either the past or the future just might be possible.);

Tin-ish: our auric energies;

Tip of the Tongue Quandary: refers to the experience when we feel we know a particular spiritual and/or religious term or concept, yet are unable to retrieve it;

Titans: spiritual truths; spiritual principles and laws;

Tithes: spiritual thoughts, words, choices, and actions; neuroplasticity; (Tithing is really an acronym. It means '*the indwelling truth harmoniously increases never-ending good*);

Tithing: means 'the indwelling truth harmoniously increases never-ending good.';

Toga Monachorum: exoterically, a congregation of monks; esoterically, a collection of religious thoughts;

Toho-Bohuic Thoughts: chaotic thoughts that come from our subconscious negativity, causing confusion and helplessness; (*Toho-Bohu* is Hebrew for 'waste and void,' 'formless and empty,' or 'chaos and desolation' which describe the condition of the earth before God said "Let there be light.");

~ *Spiritually Speaking* ~

Toilet: respectable compost; appropriate release;

Tomb: a high state of consciousness where we integrate and assimilate all previous higher consciousness material in order to unfold fully into our Cosmic Christ status as an Ascended Illuminary;

Tomb of the Soul: our physical body which envelops our I Am-ness;

Tombstone(s): the labels we put on past beliefs, attitudes, and habits that we've put to rest; denotes the collective belief in death instead of transition;

Tongue: aggressive and/or defensive thoughts, words, and actions; *forked tongue* implies hypocrisy and deceit; *tongues of fire* denote illumined conversation, speaking the highest truths;

Tongue Depressor: thinking before we speak; tact and diplomacy;

Tongue-Tied: speaking from a dogmatic religious orientation only and refusing to see the merits of expanded metaphysical perspectives;

Toolbox: our repertoire of spiritual and religious teachings;

Toothbrush, Floss: conscientiously protecting and preserving the fundamental knowledge and subsequent understanding necessary to fully master the human experience;

Tooth Fairy: our belief in an anthropomorphic, goodie god extended to include a feminine influence;

Toothlessness: unwillingness to learn and digest esoteric truth principles;

Toothpaste: denotes preparatory work for rigorous spiritual and/or religious study;

Toothpick(s): represent our propensity for closure when it comes to 'cleaning up' any residual thoughts (assumptions, clarifications, conjectures, hunches) about what we have just learned;

Top Hat: male elegance and flamboyancy; superior intellect; wealth and status;

Topomancy: divining that interprets the contours of landscapes;

Top-of-Mind Awareness, TOMA: when faced with a particular life challenge we tend to have go-to spiritual and/or religious practices, scriptural passages, and/or people we think of immediately; (In marketing terms, top-of-mind awareness is a way to measure how well brands rank in the minds of customers when they think of a certain product category);

Top Soil: basic truths; literal interpretations of scripture;

Torah: the five books of Moses;

Torch: discernment; seeking clarity;

Torch-like Attributes: symbolizes the kundalini force (fiery serpentine energies of the Holy Spirit) rising in our spinal cord to purify our spiritual energy centers (chakras);

Tornado(s): Tornadoes: highly destructive temper tantrums; chaotic, destructive thoughts and unchecked, tumultuous emotions spirally out of control and usually leading to calamitous ends; the destructive vortex of calamitous emotions that contribute to our lives spinning out of control;

Torpedo: a highly destructive memory that surfaces;

Tort(s): errant thoughts, words, choices and actions: (In legal circles, torts are civil, not criminal, wrongs);

Total Depravity: not being able to give up the false for the true; (See Unforgiveness);

Totem Pole(s): genealogical perspectives; incarnational history;

Touchdown: Christhood (Buddhahood, Krishnahood, Allahhood, Great Spirithood); the realization that we are the human expressions of the Christ expressing as us;

Touchscreen: taking an active role in what we want to accomplish;

Toupee: a false positive;

Tourist(s): each of us in our skin school experiences;

Touring: experiencing our waking consciousness, dreams, nightmares, astral travel, and other dimensional travel;

Tourniquet(s): belief in original sin instead of original blessing; belief in an anthropomorphic god and/or satan; strict adherence to encrusted dogma which cuts off our spiritual growth; the denial of our innate divinity;

chronic negative thinking; allowing a warped, paranoid ego rulership of our human personality; unforgiveness; what we believe to be true that isn't true; the seven deadly sins;

Tower of Babel: our incomplete evolutionary ascent in consciousness from a willful, hurried, narcissistic, egocentric desire to attain illumination (characterized by confusion and metaphysical malpractice) to a more natural, centered, enlightened spiritual approach to enlightenment; chaos; the *confusion of tongues* that takes place symbolizes the intellect's inability to comprehend deeper spiritual truths; (See Speaking in Tongues); [Also, in Sumerian texts, Enki creates a *man-shub* which is an incantation thought to have magical powers. Enki's *nam-shub* causes others to lose the ability to speak and may be the source for the Jewish legend of the Tower of Babel]; (Birs Nimrud, in Babylon Province, Iraq, is believed to be the site of the Biblical Tower of Babel); [The implications of neuroplasticity combined with quantum physics, say researchers Begley and Schwartz, cast new light on the question of humankind's place, aspirations, and evolutionary role. The new physics combined with neuroscience suggests that the natural world evolves through an interplay between two causal processes. The first includes the physical processes we are all familiar with – electricity streaming, gravity pulling. The second includes the contents of our consciousness, including volition. The importance of this second process cannot be overstated, for it allows human thoughts to make a difference in the evolution of the phenomenal World.);

Toy(s): playful thoughts and novel ideas that can lead to our letting our inner child out;

Trademarked Abstinence: knowing ourselves before we "no" ourselves;

Traditores: traitorous thoughts; self-preservation antics; (Traditores is the name given to early Christians who purchased exemption from persecution and martyrdom by giving up – or pretending to give up – their faith and holy scriptures to be burned);

Traducianistic Theology: believing the human soul is transmitted through human procreation;

Traffic Light(s): intuitive choices; steps in initiation; decision points on our way to enlightenment;

Tragic Flaw(s): the belief in original sin, an anthropomorphic god, an anthropomorphic devil, the denial of our innate divinity, and incurable diseases;

Train(s): a particular line of thought; a train derailment suggests our thoughts being 'derailed' by another thought or train of thoughts; a train crash implies the collision between two competing lines of thought;

Traitor(s): underhanded, covetous, self-aggrandizing thoughts that cause us to betray our true nature;

Trampolining: the process of entering (birth) and leaving (transition) our skin school experiences;

Trance: a materialistic orientation that causes us to miss out on the spiritual side of life;

Tranquilizer(s): a false sense of security created by upping our consumption of material appetites; religious fundamentalist's dogmatic biases and literalism;

Transfiguration: the complete alignment of our ordinary self with our Christ Self so that our countenance shines;

Transfusion: hearing beautiful music; listening to an inspiring message; coming across a life-changing spiritual truth; having a good belly laugh; playing with children; spending time in a hot tub; enjoying the beauty of a natural setting; rest; an uninterrupted nap; enjoying an intimate moment with someone we care about; hearing a positive prognosis after surviving a life-threatening illness;

Transgression(s): error thought, words, choices, and actions;

Transition Angel(s): spiritual ideas and insights, special people, particular events that are absolutely new to us, but have such an effect on us that we are transformed and empowered as we leave the old us behind and discover the new us;

Transitus Mundi: believing that because life is so ephemeral and transient we should concentrate on our spirituality and forsake everyday life so we can better prepare ourselves for the afterlife; (This term comes from the Latin phrase, *Sic transit gloria mundi* [Thus the glory of the world passes away]);

Transmigration: passing from one dimension, state of being, to another whether it's in a visible realm or an invisible realm;

Transubstantiation, *Metousiosis*: substance [spirit materialized] becomes re-ordained [transmuted, converted] into its original spiritual essence; (The belief that the bread and wine used in the Eucharist become, in reality, the body and blood of the Christ as Jesus. In the Catholic religious tradition, at the moment Jesus said, "This is my body… This is my blood…" the *underlying reality* (the substance) of the bread was changed (converted) into his actual body. In other words, the bread and drink *actually were* his physical body, despite appearances to the contrary or to scientific investigation that called the elements simply bread and wine); (The question that begs to be asked is: Are the scattered parts of a bicycle a bicycle or do they become a bicycle only when they are assembled into a bicycle? Is a shoe itself (the substance) the sum of its parts or distinct from them?); [In *The Coming of the Cosmic Christ*, Matthew Fox states that the "promise of Eucharist was essentially this: Eat me – the Divine Son – and drink me – the Divine Blood – instead of allowing ourselves to be eaten and devoured by parental traditions and start being food for a divinely blessed universe." Pg. 31];

Trap(s), Snare(s), Ploy(s): materialistic urges and addictions; money-making schemes that seem too good to be true; monotony and the status quo; material possessions; literal interpretations of scripture;

Trapdoor(s): blind obedience; trust without verification; dogmatism in the absence of common sense and sound judgment;

Trapezing: not realizing we'll never be comfortable without our own consent;

Trash Compactor: false teachings all rolled up into one counterfeit guru:

Treadmill: repeating the same mistakes and monotonous routines;

Treason: giving up the spiritual life for the material life;

Treasure: our innate divinity with its incredible power to transform us into the extraordinary beings that we are;

Treasure Chest: the Kingdom of Heaven;

Tree-like: dynamic energy and evolutionary growth; the spinal column and nervous system; the cognitive bridge between our subconscious and super-conscious;

Tree House: constantly living, moving, and having our being in a high state of spiritual awareness;

Tree of the Knowledge of Good and Error (Evil), *Arasa Maram*, *Aswattha*, **Bo Tree:** This tree, like other 'world trees' is a spiritual motif of the unfoldment of our human form and/or our earthy consciousness; it represents our belief in dualities and polarities; it denotes the dynamic aspects of physicality by bringing together the temporal worlds of space, time, and consciousness; (Exoterically, it was a tree planted by God in the Garden of Eden. Adam and Eve were commanded and warned not to eat from it, but the first couple are tricked by a crafty serpent who promised they would become as wise as God, that they will know universal knowledge and timeless wisdom (consciousness of duality), and never die if they eat. According to the literal account they indulged in its fruit, were caught by God, and were banished from the garden. The prophet Enoch describes the tree as bearing fruit like grapes with a beautiful fragrance. Talmudic scripture suggests that Eve made wine from the fruit. It is this same tree that Christ is said to have been crucified upon. That fits spiritually, because the Tree of the Knowledge of Good and Error is humankind in physical form);

Tree of Life, World Tree, Etz Haim: our mind and its evolution in consciousness; our chakra system; [The Kabbalah Tree of Life is a representation of the thirty-two paths (spinal vertebrae) comprised of the ten sefirot and the twenty-two paths through which they run.]; (The Tree of Life represents the descent of the divine into the manifest world, and methods by which the divine union can be attained in any of our incarnations. It can be viewed as a map of the human psyche and the matrix of the Godhead's consciousness in space time.); the cosmic energies that animate our fully actualized serpentine energies that electrify (spiritualize) our spinal column and nervous system to prepare us for and sustain our enlightenment; (Our spinal column is the trunk and the nervous system is the branches and leaves. It bears 12 manner of fruits [Revelation 22:2] that are explained in the next sentence. Everyday a life-sustaining transmutation takes place that carries the living 'waters' of Spirit to every one of our 12 major orifices, 12 cranial nerves [olfactory, optic, motor oculi, trochlear, trifacial, abducent, facial, auditory, glosso pharyngeal, pnumogastric, spinal accessor, and hypoglossal], 12 major body systems (integumentary system, skeletal system, muscular system, immune system, lymphatic system, cardiovascular system, urinary system, digestive system, respiratory system, nervous system, endocrine system, and reproductive system), 12 major organs [the twelve fruits], 12 senses [the five (5) physical senses plus the seven (7) awakened chakras (churches)]; 12 *Adityas* of the Hindu tradition; (Sacred trees are found in Shamanic, Hindu, Egyptian, Sumerian, Toltec, Norse and Christian esoteric traditions. The *Gogard Tree* [Gokard Tree] is described in mystical literature as the reflection of the Tree of Life and keeps away forms of deformed decrepitude so that the full perfection of the world can arise. The Tree of Life is described in *The Upanishads* as "a tree eternally existing, its roots aloft, its branches spreading below."); [Nevill Drury, in his *Dictionary of Mysticism and the Occult*, offers an explanation of what the occult Tree of Life represents in its relationship to the *Kabbalah*. The Tree consists of ten spheres, or sephiroth, through which—according to mystical tradition— the creation of the world came about. The sephiroth are aligned in three columns headed by the supernals and together symbolize the process by which the Infinite Light...becomes manifest in the universe. The Tree of Life is also a symbol of the archetypal man Adam Kadmon, and the sephiroth have a role resembling that of the charkas in yoga]; the tree of life is about the evolution of subjective consciousness from the lower planes to the higher planes—the world of physical matter to the world of energetic spirit; (The fruit of the tree of life is the higher emotions and faculties of the our Christ [Buddhic] Nature laid up for the soul when we are perfected. And the fruit of the Tree of Knowledge of Good and Evil is the experience we acquire through the activities of our lower nature and from the development of our moral nature); [Joshua Tilghman, in *The Spirit of the Scriptures*, expresses an esoteric view that is compelling: Sometimes the tree of life is inverted in Kabbalah. The inverted tree of life has its roots firmly established in heaven (spiritual planes) and the rest of the tree emanates into the physical world. Likewise, humankind originated in Eden, a spiritual plane, and ended up in the physical world, earth. The inverted tree depicts this process. Now it is up to us to climb back up the spiritual worlds. I like to picture the inverted tree as the tree of life and the right-side up tree as the tree of knowledge of good and evil. It makes sense for me to picture the two in this way because remember that the true *world tree* contains both the tree of life and the tree of knowledge of good and evil];

Trench Talk: sharing our "story of redemption" with someone who also shares h/her "story of redemption" in order to seal the mutual bond of overcoming life's hardships and challenges;

Trespassing: taking our material interests and ambitions into a spiritual environment;

Tribe(s): a collection of associated thoughts that comprise a religious and/or spiritual tenet;

Tribulation: the confusion, suffering, and chaos we go through everyday as a result of choosing an egocentric nature over a Christed Nature;

Trickster: the deceitful, manipulative, self-serving unillumined ego;

Trigger-Happy Misfires: burning our fingers in our haste to strike while the iron is hot; knee-jerk errors;

Trijnana: triple knowledge (knowledge based on faith, knowledge based on theoretical understanding, and knowledge based on personal experience); (A Sanskrit term for threefold knowledge);

Trinitas, Unitas, Deitas: Trinity, Unity, Deity;

Tripadaic Sickness: fever personified as having three feet or stages of development (cold, heat and sweat); (A Sanskrit term for fever);

Triple Crown: the Holy Trinity (God, Christ, Holy Spirit); Divine Order (Mind, Idea, Expression);

Triple Play: the Holy Trinity; Divine Order (Mind, Idea, Expression); mind, body, soul; our subconscious, waking conscious, and super-conscious;

Triskaidekaphobia: unrealistic fears that cause us to avoid the higher truths; literally, the fear of the number 13; (See Paraskevidekatriaphobia);

Trochomancy: reviewing our past actions to make wiser choices; literally, divining that interprets the psychic significance of wheel tracks;

Trojan Horse(s): highly materialistic thoughts and attitudes masquerading as spiritual aspirations; a spiritual and/or religious cult that appears to be one thing, but is in reality quite another, and usually a self-aggrandizing, malicious nature; (In IT security terminology, a Trojan Horse is a computer program that appears to have a useful function, but has a nasty hidden and potentially malicious function that evades security protocols.); [In Greek mythology, the Trojan Horse was a huge wooden horse that held a select commando unit of Greek soldiers inside. It was placed inside the gates of Troy as a 'gift' to the people of Troy. The Greek commandos crept out of the horse at night and opened the gates for the rest of the Greek army to enter the city of Troy and destroy it.);

Troll-ishness: having error thoughts;

Troubadour(s): thoughts about love, adventure, and creativity;

Troupe: a collection of spiritual and/or religious thoughts, beliefs, and biases;

Truce of God: truces between feuding parties were called by the church on the threat of excommunication to allow members of both feuding parties to go to church without fear of being injured or killed;

Truimphalismic Prejudice: believing in the superiority of our own particular religious creed;

Trumpet-like: bringing the power of the unmanifested aspect of the Eternal Presence into manifestation as a directing force; attaining the compressed, laser-like omnipotence of the Eternal Presence within us that serves as a call to action; the *sound of the trumpet* is our conscious intention to apply the dynamic spiritual knowledge and gifts we have either developed or allowed to lie dormant, it is also the divine vibration (the eternal cosmic hum) that brings potential universes into physical reality - it is this same dynamic energy that allows us to formulate our thoughts in our own consciousness); the *notes on the trumpet* designate the particular direction of our energies, they are also expressions of our own 'will to create and perpetuate wholeness' in our body, mind, and soul; the *loudness of the trumpet's sound* denotes our willfulness and purposefulness to create the life we want;

Truth: what is and what isn't;

Truth Walk: conscious entrainment toward our Christ Nature (Buddha Nature, Krishna Nature);

T-Shirt(s): portable personal interest billboards; snapshot beliefs;

Tsunami(s): episodes of volatile outbursts of anger that cause immense emotional upheavals;

Tsurezuregusaian Thinking: writing anything down that comes into our conscious awareness related to spiritual and/or religious subjects; (In antiquity, was a collection of medieval Japanese essays written by the monk Yoshida Kenko between 1330 and 1332);

Tug of War: pulling against ourselves; working toward two mutually exclusive goals; pursuing two mutually satisfying interests;

Tulip-like: represents our quest for harmony and unity; also denotes our longing for the perfect love of a soulmate; additionally it suggests our infatuation with royalty and nobility; non-judgmentalness; hopefulness;

Tunnel(s): our ability to make laser-like connections (safe passage) with the Domain of the Divine (Heaven) within us as we travel through rocky 'dark night of the soul' experiences with ease, grace, and poise;

Tunnel Vision: when we are so focused on 'proving' a truth principle works that we totally miss its spiritual essence and are unable to experience it at its highest, most elevated level;

Turkey-ness: being able to sacrifice now to reap the benefits tomorrow; honoring fertility;

Turquoise-like: becoming purified; being protective; attaining chakra alignment;

Turtle-ness: being cool, calm, collected; employing an orderly, measured movement; achieving longevity; being patient; undergoing steadiness;

Turtle Theology: carrying our spiritual home (the Kingdom of God) with us wherever we go;

TV: remote viewing;

TV Remote Control: As spiritual beings we have an internal 'remote control' system that is activated by our state of consciousness. (We can change channels (thoughts and emotions), adjust the volume of voice and our thinking, select Christed intentions over worldly thoughts, look ahead (fast forward) to the future and recollect (rewind) memories of the past. We can change 'channels,' raise or lower our volume, fast-forward, and rewind as often as we choose. The channels we turn to can be spiritual thoughts and emotions or egocentric thoughts and emotions.);

Tweeps: represent a guru's followers; the actions that follow choices and/or the choices that follow thoughts; (In IT language, tweeps are a person's followers on Twitter);

Tweetup: our penchant for sharing religious and/or spiritual buzz words in public gatherings in order to attract conversations with people who have similar interests as us; (In social media terms, tweetups are synonymous with 'meetups' that are generated from Twitter connections. They involve informal gatherings that let Twitter followers meet in real life. The gatherings take the form of a mini-Twitterverse.);

Tweezers: a discerning eye; (Positive psychologists tell us that eye contact stimulates the social-network circuits in our brain. It decreases the stress chemical cortisol, and it increases oxytocin, a neurochemical that enhances empathy, social cooperation, and positive communication);

Twelve Deadly Poisons: anger, avarice, cheating, deceit, doubt, gluttony, greed, laziness, murder, phoniness, self-aggrandizement, selfishness;

Twelve-Gated City: the human body with its *12 major orifices*: 2 eyes, 2 nostrils; 2 ears, 2 nipples, 1 mouth, 1 anus, 1 urethra, 1 vagina; *12 major body systems*: cardiovascular system (the blood circulation with heart, arteries and veins), digestive system (processing food with mouth, esophagus, stomach and intestines), endocrine system (communicating within the body using hormones), excretory system (eliminating wastes from the body), immune system (defending against disease-causing agents), integumentary system (skin, hair and nails), lymphatic system, muscular system (moving the body with muscles), nervous system (collecting, transferring and processing information with brain and nerves), reproductive system (the sex organs), respiratory system (the organs used for breathing, the lungs), skeletal system (structural support and protection through bones), sensory system (eyes, ears, nose, tongue, skin); *12 main body organs*: brain, lungs, heart, stomach, large intestine, small intestine, liver, gall bladder, pancreas, spleen, kidney, urinary bladder); *12 senses*: the five (5) physical senses plus the seven (7) awakened chakras [churches];

Twenty Four Elders: our twelve cranial nerves and their higher spiritual attributes which are quickened when we are enlightened; the upper 24 segments of the spinal column; (The 24 elders are mentioned in the Fourth Chapter of the *Book of Unveiling* [*Revelation*]); The twenty-four elders have the same significance as the priests gathered around the statue of Ceres in the Greater Eleusinian Rites and also the Persian Genii, or gods of the hours of the day who cast away their crowns and glorify the Holy One. (They are generally represented as symbolic of the divisions of time);

Twilight: the maturation or near mastery of one level of esoteric knowing and the obvious naïveté of the next higher level of knowledge to be learned;

Twin(s): our Divine Self and our human self when they are fully aligned;

Twitter: electronic handshakes, back rubs, greetings, announcements, high fives, sound bytes, etc.;

Two Crucifixions: our descent into matter [when our physical body becomes our 'cross' and the five physical senses become its five wounds] and our ascent out of the limitations of materiality when we are 'crucified in Golgotha' when we cross out error from our consciousness;

Twonk(s): foolish, asinine thoughts;

Two Witnesses: our two cerebral brain hemispheres; the higher mind (which acts as a receiver and transceiver of cosmic consciousness) and the lower mind; the cerebrum and cerebellum;

Tyagaian Release: relinquishing anything that no longer contributes to our highest good; (A term from the *Bhagavad Gita* that literally means 'abandonment' from anything that hinders our enlightenment);

Tychismic Peculiarity: believing in the role of pure chance to explain everything;

Tympaniaionic Susceptibility: suffering from a life-draining error thought characterized by its abject denial of our spiritual worth; (In folklore, tympaniaion literally means a body possessed by a vampire);

Typhlocomium: exoterically, the infirmary for the blind; esoterically, sense consciousness (coma consciousness); (See Coma Consciousness);

Tyromancy: divining that interprets cheese as it coagulate;

Tzaddik Righteousness: calling for absolute conformity to an impossible standard of religious conduct and purity; (A term from rabbinic orthodoxy that means 'justice and righteousness' as they apply to matters of faith);

Tzaila Ribbing: literally means a *rib*; (See the Book of Genesis for the myth of the creation of the first woman from a rib of the first man, Adam. It is amazing that no other myth describes a "ribbing" process, except Hebrew scripture. Other similar Hebrew words are *Tzela* (fall), and Tzelem (image of God). Could it be that Adam *fell* on his *side* on account of a *woman* (Eve), whom God made in his *image?*);

Tzim-tzum Effect: expansion and contraction, or, as Kabbalists explain it "the centrifugal and centripetal energy of super-conscious spiritual thoughts."

Tzouizaic Choice(s): our choice (ordeal) as spiritual beings to incarnate into human form; (In Greek hierology, refers to an ordeal);

Tzyphonic Knowledge: esoteric, metaphysical, allegorical knowledge;

Ubiquitarianism: believing that Christ is everywhere all the time;

Uchnicha: (See Unicorn-Like);

UFOs: highly-charged spiritual ideas (metaphysical, esoteric, theosophical, anthroposophical, allegorical, and metaphorical ideas) that are totally unfamiliar to us and seem to come out of nowhere because we have not studied and/or heard about them before;

Ugg Thinking: error thinking; self-defeating and self-demeaning thoughts;

Ultimate Attribution Error: coined by psychologist Thomas Pettigrew in 1979 to explain why members of an in-group (us) tend to judge members of an out-group (them) rudely and harshly. Pettigrew suggested that when out-group members behave negatively or undesirably, in-group members attribute their behavior to things like genetic predispositions, poor character, or lack of proper upbringing. However, when out-group members behave positively, in-group members attribute their behavior to luck, special privileges being conferred, unusually extraordinary effort, or some other exception to the rule.

Ultracrepidate Judgmentalness: criticism that goes beyond the sphere of our particular knowledge about the subject we're criticizing;

Umbilical Cord: an ethereal, silver-colored, elastic cord connecting our physical body to its astral body; also denotes the higher consciousness filament that passes from the super-conscious to the physical body; (See Silver Cord);

Umbrella: shelter; category;

Umop-apisdn: an upside-down view of the world characterized by putting material interests and sense attachments first and spiritual growth last;

Umpire: our internal locus of control; our power of discernment;

Unbeliever(s): materialistic, error-coated thoughts, words, choices, and actions;

Unblinking Moocher(s): indigent thoughts that stem from a down-and-out personal philosophy rooted in a self-perpetuated martyr complex;

Unbridled Zelotypia: expressing excessive religious zeal;

Unchurched: materialistic, worldly thoughts;

Unconscionable Vocalizations: taking the name of God in vain; cursing God; any words used to attempt to deny someone's innate divinity;

Uncorked Erasure: Letting an unwanted, materialistic part of us 'die.' (The obsolete part I'm referring to is a bad habit, a debilitating worry or concern, lack of confidence in a certain area of our life, a regret, anger, prejudice, hatred);

Undefiled Parthenogenesis: the stain-free purity of a newly formed spiritual idea; (See Virgin Birth);

Undercooked Repentance: voicing our regret for a misstep and then purposefully repeating the same misstep;

Underemployed: attempting to master our skin school experience by depending only on a literal interpretation of sacred scripture;

Undergraduate(s): the unenlightened us; *graduate(s)*, the enlightened us; *postgraduate(s)*, the adept us;

Understudy: our human self trying to emulate the extraordinary Us (our Authentic Self, Divine Self;

Underthinking: reading and studying a literal-only interpretation of sacred scripture;

Undertow: our karmic baggage;

Underwater, Underworld: our subconscious;

Undocumented Alien(s): bizarre, out-of-context thoughts that enter our waking consciousness that seem to come from nowhere;

Undue Hardship: the reincarnation experience;

Unfollow: deciding not to continue following a certain guru, religious and/or spiritual teacher; (In social media language, unfollowing someone means no longer receiving their updates in our own online timeline.);

Unforgivable Sin: From a human point of view there are many irreconcilable differences. From a spiritual perspective there's only one. The irreconcilable difference is so important I want you to know about it because it's an *unforgivable irreconcilable 'sin.'* This unforgivable irreconcilable sin is not about working on the Sabbath. Nor is it coveting our neighbor's stock portfolio. It's not about lying, or bearing false witness, or stealing. Nor is it about cheating on our income taxes. It's not even secretly replacing the golf ball we couldn't find with another one and not adding strokes to our score. The irreconcilable sin that is alluded to in the Bible is called the unforgivable sin. What is the unforgivable sin? Read Matthew 12:31-32 in your favorite Bible interpretation. There are two important words you need to remember: *unforgivable* and *blasphemy*. They are central for understanding what this passage means. Unforgiveness means failing to give up the false for the true. If you repeat error time and time again and continue repeating it, you're likely to, well, keep repeating it. It's the repetition that makes it unforgivable. *Blasphemy* is the second important word in the Matthew account. Blasphemy is a powder keg word. It refers to blasphemy against the Holy Spirit. And blasphemy against the Holy Spirit is denying your divinity. If you blaspheme (deny your divinity) repeatedly you'll never be able to reconcile the difference between Truth and error, between our spiritual self and our material self, between being enlightened and being clueless.

Unforgiveness: choosing falsehood over truth;

Ungodly Vexations: the depraved and corrupt discomfiture we feel when we know we have violated our professed religious principles;

Unholy Vandalism: the purposeful and demented destruction of religious shrines; the dogmatic treatment of sacred scripture;

Unicorn-like: represents our fully aroused, but controlled, serpent fire energies; the unicorn's helical (spiral) horn represents the tip of the Sushumna which runs along our spinal cord and through the seven major energy centers called chakras; a conical or flame-shaped hair tuft on the crown of a Buddha that later became simply a fleshy protuberance that disappeared, becoming the concealed Third Eye; the horn could also represent the pineal eye (third eye) cyclopean psychic vision; the horn also implies our extra sensory perceptive abilities (ESP); unicorns are white which denotes purity of psychic vision;

Unified Field, Christ Mind: Cosmic Consciousness (Christ Consciousness, the Kingdom of God); the universal *indivisibleness* of God expressing Itself in space time and out of the space time continuum; (The 'glue' that holds the *field* together is Love.); (In quantum physics language, Unified Field Theory was first suggested by Albert Einstein who wanted to unify the general theory of relativity with electromagnetism which is one of the four forces of the natural world (strong nuclear interaction, weak nucleus interaction, and gravity being the other three). This evolving theory holds that forces between objects are not carried directly between objects because they travel through "fields." The attempt is to bring the four mentioned fields together into a single (unified) field theory. Unified Field Theory remains an open field of study.); [In *Light For Our Age*, Robert Sikking posits, "It was necessary for (humankind) to evolve (its) awareness of deity in order that (we) might consciously, as an act of will, demonstrate that deity. It is through this process that (humankind) moves from a state of bliss in coexistence *with** deity to an understanding awareness of (ourselves) *as** deity." Pg.13];

Uninterrupted Path: living joyfully, lovingly, consistently, and confidently at the speed of our Christ Consciousness;

Unio Mystica: unity, full entrainment with the Supreme Being (the Eternal Presence, the One, etc.);

Unipersonality: believing our personality is both human and divine;

United Nations: complete harmony between our three nations (mind, body, and soul; subconscious, conscious, super-conscious);

Universal Cathedral: the totality of humankind's completely Christed (Buddhic, Allahic, Krishnic, etc.) consciousness (cathedral);

Universal Church; an individual's completely Christed (Buddhic, Allahic, Krishnic,etc.) consciousness (church); [In *Unity of All Life*, Eric Butterworth reminds us that " It is paradoxical that the church (is) the staunch defender of the mystical concept of life against the influence of humanistic materialism of science. Today, there is a new thrust in the sciences toward a nonmaterial explanation of life, of particles, and of the universe. There are times when the scientist seems to reflect more religion than religionists themselves." Pg.12);

Universal Magnet: the Truth;

Universal Priesthood: the totality of humankind's illumined thoughts, words, and actions being altruistically demonstrated in service to humankind; (In *Dialogues with Scientists and Sages*, Renēe Weber tells us: "Science seeks the boundaries of nature, in mysticism it's unboundedness; science is the droplet of the ocean, mysticism is the wave. Science works to explain the mystery of being, mysticism to experience it. They share the search for reality because, in their own way, both science and mysticism look for the basic truth about matter and the source of matter. A parallel principle drives both science and mysticism – the assumption that unity lies at the heart of our world and that it can be discovered and experienced by (humankind)" pg. 13);

Universal Substance: the undifferentiated essence of the Eternal Presence; (The omnipresent spiritual substance from which comes all visible wealth is never depleted. It is with us all the time and responds to our faith in it and our demands on it. It is not affected by talk of hard times, though we are affected because our thoughts and words govern our demonstrations. The unfailing resource is always ready to give. Supply is not something that comes to us. It comes through us. Supply is not something that comes to us. It comes through us. Supply is not something that comes to us. It comes through us. It is an inside-out process);

Universality: multiple multiplicity in harmonious cosmic complicity;

~ *Spiritually Speaking* ~

Universe: the intergalactic expression of the One Presence; one of the trillions of quantum atoms; the purposeful inhalation and exhalation of Universal Substance breathing life into a cosmic idea; the *Liber Mundi* of the Rosicrucians; the *Liber Vitae* of the Apocalypse; (Our bodies literally hold the entire history of the universe in our cells, atoms, and molecules. The helium and hydrogen atoms in us are the Adam and Eve atoms, the parent atoms of all other atoms which came out of our little Big Bang. The iron atoms in our blood carrying oxygen to our cells came from exploding white dwarf stars. The oxygen we breathe came from exploding supernovas. Most of the carbon in the carbon dioxide we exhale came from planetary nebulas. We are truly made of star stuff); our collective consciousness; (Quantum theologist Dairmuid O'Murchu says, "In modern physics, the image of the universe as a machine has been transcended by the alternative perception of an indivisible, dynamic whole whose parts are essentially interrelated and can be understood only as patterns of the cosmic process." And Steven Hawking reminds us that the "universe does not have just a single existence or history, but rather every possible version of the universe exists simultaneously in what is called a quantum superposition.");

University, College: every human incarnation;

Unlimited Atonement: the constant and readily available maturation and expansiveness of our illumined consciousness to receive even higher levels of spiritual insights and unfoldment as we become more Christed;

Unpardonable Sin: the repeated, mindless rejection in thoughts, words, and actions of our innate divinity;

Unpolluted: a Christ-centric Consciousness;

Unreliable Narrator: the egocentric us; our warped ego;

Upping Our Consciousness: eliminating self-defeating subconscious and conscious patterns that block our good and raising our awareness to a Christed level;

Uppity Nincompoop: a high-falutin' error thought or intention;

Unquiet City: All of the violence, conflict, cynicism and desperation we find today occur in the *unquiet city*. The *unquiet city* is human consciousness. It is a consciousness of separation perpetuated by well-meaning religious organizations and governmental institutions who, by their very natures, produce violent, conflicting, cynical and desperate "thought communities" within the human personality. These "communities" or "cities" are belief systems that keep us off balance emotionally and spiritually. The *unquiet city* is a consciousness without the awareness of its oneness with Spirit;

Unrecognized Suffering: continuing to believe in a limited, dogmatic, literal only view of sacred scripture and not know that it is a limited perspective (It is one of the most debilitating forms of mainstream religious practice);

Unscheduled Debt(s): spur of the moment errant actions that lead to karmic consequences;

Unschooling: unlearning the embedded theology we grew up with in order to embrace New Thought teachings;

Unvarnished Masquerading: purposefully pretending to be more spiritual than material;

Uparatic Discipline: being completely detached from material appetites; (In Buddhism means restraining ourselves from distractions that interfere with our spiritual development);

Upper Frequency: our super-conscious mental processes;

Upper Room: high spiritual state of consciousness; the Crown Chakra;

Up-Selling Pong: people trying to up-stage one another by sharing a "come to Jesus" story that is more unbelievable than the last one told;

Upside Down: putting material wants and whims over spiritual needs and aspirations;

Upskilling: teaching more advanced spiritual practices;

Upsweep: intellectual vitality and readiness; (In the hair dressing industry, upsweep refers to loosely gathering hair on top of the head.);

Uranomancy: divining that interprets movements in the heavens;

Uranophobia: the fear of heaven;

Urbi et Orbi **Ministry:** seeing our personal spiritual ministry as not only local, but global;

Urgemeter: a desire (urgemeter) that activates when we sense something we want, whether it be spiritual or material;

Urim: light; awareness; (In Hebrew mythology, Urim is the angel of light);

Urn-like: expressing femininity and receptivity; represents womb-like state;

Urujic Conviction: being open and receptive to higher spiritual teachings;

Urvasic Bliss: a beautifully-woven intuition that sets our entire conscious awareness ablaze with indescribable joy; (In the Rig-Veda was a beautiful divine nymph who descended on earth and married Pururavas and became the source of intellectual beauty and joy);

Usufruct Utility: adopting the best practices of another faith tradition as your own;

U-Turn(s), One-Eighty, U-ey(s): changing our mind; becoming more spiritual than religious; becoming more spiritual than material;

Uzzaic Tendencies: depending on our physical strength and sense consciousness instead of our connection to our innate divinity; (In the *Zohar*, Uzza was one of the angels [Azza'el was the other] who told the Holy One that humankind had sinned and were told that, had they been in man's place, they would probably have done worse. The two were thrown from their high status in heaven and changed into men upon earth. This implies that the 'angels,' doomed to incarnation, are in the chains of flesh and matter, and under the darkness of ignorance until they are saved on the 'great day.');

Vaccination(s): affirmative prayers, meditation sessions, positive affirmations, sacred rituals; spiritual visualizations;

~ *Spiritually Speaking* ~

Vain Repetitions: narcissistic trumpery; egotistical posturing; conceited campaigning;

Vain Snow Job: consistently living beneath our talents, over our head, or beside ourselves;

Vairagyaian Disposition: being indifferent to worldliness and material appetites; (Vairagya is a Sanskrit term that means detachment and/or renunciation from the pains and pleasures of the material world. It refers to an internal state of mind and not necessarily our lifestyle);

Valedictory Imperative: saying goodbye to material addictions and self-defeating habits;

Valet Parking: the practice of entering a human form, 'parking' it in a human experience, which is different from the last time we valeted ourselves using a different body to house our soul;

Valium: meditation; affirmative prayer; spiritual visualization; rest; a Sabbath experience;

Valley(s): our subconscious; living at the level of our basic instincts;

Valley of Struggle: the physical world; the repressed region within our subconscious;

Vampire(s): divinity-denying thoughts that suck the life out of our spiritual practice;

Vandalism: hurtful criticism to tear down someone's self-esteem; skewing research;

Vaporware: announcing that certain affirmations, prayers and meditation experiences, and rituals have transformed our lives on the one hand and then by our subsequent choices and actions it becomes apparent that we are not the product of the product; (In IT language, vaporware is hardware and/or software that has been aggressively advertised, but has missed its release date);

Varicose Outreach: over-inflated, puffed-up proselytizing;

Vases: receptivity; femininity; wombs; acceptance;

Vaudeville, Freeriding: the process of trying out many different faith traditions before settling on one and/or combining a few of the best spiritual teachings of several faith traditions as our own spiritual practice; temporary and/or permanent eclectic shopping for just the right faith tradition; (In snowboarding terms, freeriding means snowboarding on all types of terrain);

Vegan: one who practices extreme vegetarianism by refusing to eat or use any animal products whatsoever;

Vegetarian: one who prefers beans and greens over fried and dyed;

Vegi-Vegan Curious: the dilemma we find ourselves in when we are considering either a vegetarian or vegan lifestyle, but haven't committed to either;

Vehmic Theology: the practice of inspiring dread in gullible believers who fall for the absurd claims of manipulative religious officials who frighten people into submission through hell fire and brimstone tactics;

Veil, the: the neural curtain between existence and reality; the quantum film between spirit and matter; the illusion of subject and object; the shroud of physicality; *absence of the veil* means no illusion of separation;

Veil of Lack: belief in our separation from our good;

Vending Machines: portable store counters; consumption depots;

Venial Sin(s): traditionally, denotes forgivable sins, sins that do not result in complete separation from God and consequently eternal damnation; spiritually, implies materialistic thoughts that do not become choices and/or overt actions that dampen our spiritual growth;

Venom, Toxin, Poison: false teachings; error thoughts and destructive emotions;

Ventriloquist Vicars: a scam artist's deceptive practice of vocalizing his/her supposed 'messianic appointment' as the 'chosen one' for a designated purpose which no one else can provide because he/she is the "voice" of God ; (The amazing thing is these ventriloqui-liers actually get followers);

Verbigerating Error: the all too common quirk of repeating indecent (foul, obscene) words or phrases, in speaking or in writing, without meaning to do so in spite of efforts to refrain from slipping into old habits;

~ Spiritually Speaking ~

Verey Pistol: a truth principle that 'fires off' a spiritual insight which lights up our waking awareness like a flare gun lights up the sky; (A verey pistol is a small handgun for firing very light flares);

Veridical Dreaming: having psychic experiences during sleep that later become real events;

Veritophobia: cultivating an irrational or extreme fear of the truth; believing in the inerrancy of written scripture;

Vermin: lower thoughts and base instincts;

Vertical Farming: seeking highly advanced spiritual teachings; (In an agricultural context, vertical farming is the practice of cultivating crops in skyscrapers);

Vertical Stabilizer: the rise of the Kundalini energies; (See Kundalini; Fire);

Vertigo: the fear, or at the least, considerable discomfort in pursuing the heights of spiritual, metaphysical, esoteric, theosophical, anthroposophical, allegorical, and metaphorical thought:

Vesuvian Vexation(s): sudden outbursts of aggravation, agitation, or irritation whenever religious conversations slip into comparing New Thought perspectives with mainstream dogmatic perspectives;

Veteran(s): those who have had many skin school experiences;

Vetoed Prosperity: the consequence of the denial of our divine status through our thoughts, words, and actions;

Vetoist: any thought, belief, word, choice, habit, or action that sabotages our spiritual growth;

Vexxed Vagrant(s): volatile base instincts that spring from our anger, fear, and doubt, especially when we feel alone and isolated (homeless);

Via Dolorosa: Historically, it is the winding route Jesus took when he carried his crucifixion cross; esoterically, it is each of our human incarnations as we 'suffer' our way toward enlightenment;

Via Negativa: a chronic negativity bias; (Researchers have known for a long time that our brains have a built-in negativity bias that primes us for the fight-or-flight response. Our brain typically detects negative information much faster than it detects positive information. Our brain, says Rick Hanson, author of *Buddha's Brain*, "is like Velcro for negative experiences and Teflon for positive ones.");

Via Positiva: a well-defined positivity philosophy; the way of positivity; (Having a positivity bias helps us to sustain hope, and the part of the brain most activated is the anterior cingulate, a key center for generating optimism. Positive emotions, says positive psychologist Barbara Fredrickson, flood our brains with dopamine and serotonin, chemicals that not only make us feel good, but dial up the learning centers of our brains to higher levels. They help us organize new information, keep that information in the brain longer, and retrieve it faster later on);

Vibroturgy: our ability to detect the physical and mental qualities (psychic impressions) of someone else from the inanimate physical objects in their possession and/or objects h/she has touched;

Vicarious Doctrinal Reinforcement: learning doctrinal peculiarities by seeing others being rewarded for their doctrinal obedience;

Vicarious Vacationer: anyone who is not fully engaged in h/her spiritual growth;

Vichy Shower: 'showering our waking consciousness with truth principles; (In SPA industry terms a Vichy shower is a metal arm with 5-7 shower heads that runs parallel to a cushioned treatment table, so we can get a shower while lying down. It is usually associated as part of a body treatment like a salt scrub or body wrap.);

Victimology: the misguided belief that the universe is not wired in our behalf; perpetuating a chronic negativity bias that is rooted in the belief that we will always be helpless sufferers; adhering to a literal-only interpretation of sacred scripture; the belief in original sin;

Video Camera: capturing the good, bad, and ugly;

Videogames: visualizations (guided or self-directed) depicting the attainment of our greater good and the greater good of others;

Video Recording(s): life reviews that surface when we are preparing for the end of life and/or think we are approaching imminent death; mentally reminiscing important events in our lives;

Vijaic Expression: our mystical prompting or sacred urge to express ourselves in physical form through incarnational and/or reincarnational experiences;

Vijnanavadic Thinking: believing that consciousness creates reality; (Vijnanavada is subjective idealism taught by the Yogacara school of Buddhism);

Village: a collection of thoughts;

Villanous Vagabonds: fly-by-night, aimless, prodigal thoughts that derail us from our spiritual growth;

Vineyard: realm of Universal Divine Substance which is constantly and readily available to us;

Vinnana: perfect perception based on perfect knowledge;

Violet-like, Purple: conscious identification with our Divine Nature; oneness and unity; superior wisdom; seeks the peace that passes all misunderstanding; has a deep sense of wonder and awe for the transcendent and cosmic; loves harmony and integration; reverence for all life; self-sacrificing; idealistic; absolutist in theology; (crown chakra); humility;

Viragaic Propensity: the absence of heartfelt desire; indifference; disinterest;

Virgin Birth: the incarnated Christ Presence into physicality; (Actually, at the human level, a virgin birth occurs every time a new truth dawns on us, while we are in a high spiritual state of consciousness. The virginity represents the undefiled and purified stillness of mind in us that gives birth (becomes consciously aware of) to the Christ Pattern within us;

Viricidal Tweaking: the removal of viruses (error thoughts) from our consciousness through disciplined spiritual practice;

Virtual Vagabondage: wandering aimlessly through life without a spiritual rudder;

Viryaian Potency: inner strength; dauntless fortitude and courage; (Virya is a Buddhist term that means dauntless energy and enthusiasm); (According to positive psychologists, enthusiasm really is contagious – there are very few people who, once in contact with somebody truly enthused, can remain unmoved. The powerful enthusiastic energy we give out inspires those around us to become more dynamic and animated);

Visa: commercially, visas (from the Latin *charta visa* "paper that has been seen") is a document validating a person's right to enter and/or leave the territory in which the visa was issued; spiritually, a visa represents our comprehension (document) of a fundamental metaphysical truth (territory) which allows us to enter into an elevated level of awareness in order to understand an even higher esoteric truth;

Vision Quest: making contact with the Higher Power by exposure to the elements and fasting; vision quests are rites of passage, in Native American cultures, to find spiritual guidance and purpose; seeking conscious alignment with our extraordinary spiritual nature;

Visitor(s), Guest(s): pedestrian thoughts and emotions that show up every once in a while;

Visual Bombing: unwelcome thoughts that interfere with our concentration in a guided visualization;

Vitaminizing Vigor: enthusiastically adding as many spiritual principles and practices (vitamins) as we can to our truth walks;

Vitamins: spiritual thoughts and ideas; positive affirmations and denials; affirmative prayers; meditational techniques; spiritual visualizations; spiritual rituals and ceremonies;

Vlogging: our ability to produce thought processes that involve both visual images and mental texting; (In IT language, vlogging is a type of blogging that is embedded with both video and text, and/or other metadata);

Vocal Acupuncture: positive affirmations; affirmative prayer;

Voice Jail: saying and repeating self-negating things about yourself;

Voice Mail: talking to ourselves;

Voiceprint Vyce: represents the vise-like effects of the karma we incur through the use of our spoken words; the biological effects (clamping down) of our spoken words on our physical bodies;

Void, the: unseen Universal Substance; the super-ethereal beingness of the Eternal Presence; (What quantum physicists have described as the *void*,

Kabbalists call *ayin*. From the Kabbalist perspective this vacuum, or void, is characterized by a light that flows from the Absolute (*Ein-Sof*) through it, permeating the 'nothingness.' Actually there is no nothing! The esoteric wisdom traditions teach that the relative realm (physicality) does not manifest until it "passes through" this nothingness realm out of a spiritual (non-physical) realm. The polarities we call 'something and nothing' are essentially two forms of the Universal Spiritual Essence we call God. What we call polarity is spirituality expressing as physicality and ether (the Void); (In quantum physics terms, the 'void' really isn't a 'nothing' but a 'something.' It is a mass of 'virtual' particles that fleetingly appear and then disappear from the observable universe. The 'physical vacuum,' as the void is called in quantum field theory, is far from empty nothingness because it contains an infinite number of particles *in potentia*. This also indirectly means that the 'void' contains *all material objects in potentia* as well. If it were not for this living, moving, vibrant void that is filled with an endless number of quantum fluctuations, there would be no physical universe.);

Volcanic Ash: the fallout (hard feelings, confusion, reciprocal anger, fear) caused by a volatile temper;

Volcano-like: experiencing the rise of the serpent fire that reaches the crown of our head which results in our illumination and enlightenment;

Volundric Escape: freeing ourselves from having our creativity and craftsmanship used for selfish and/or demonic ends;

Voodoo: the abuse of spiritual knowledge and abilities with the intent of harming others; confusing voodoo pins with religious acupuncture; incriminating ourselves;

Vox Humana Vindico: for the purposes of this glossary, means "the human voice liberated" (one voice – the over-all intention of humankind to align our collective consciousness with our innate divinity so we can liberate ourselves from the illusion of duality and separation that have divided us from our True Selves and from each other);

Vows: strong heart resolutions, not lip gloss; vocal witnesses that confirm that the outer you is becoming aligned with the spiritual you; (Vows, like oaths and handshakes are contracts in miniature, binding agreements in a thimble);

Vulture-like Tendencies: being patient and tolerant; persevering; wanting to use obsolete resources; navigating through unconventional territory;

Vuvuzelaian Torture: the 'sound of conscience' that goes off in your head after you know you've done something wrong; (A vuvuzela is a plastic horn which produces a loud monotone note. It is used in South Africa to announce community gatherings);

W

Wabi-Sabic Appreciation: a world view centered on the beauty involved in the acceptance of transience and imperfection; (*Wabi-sabi* represents a comprehensive Japanese world view centered on the acceptance of transience and imperfection.);

Wackadoodle(s): wacky ideas or choices; a fossilized dogmatic beliefs; strange habits; peculiar behaviors;

Wacky Wizardry: using unconventional, but highly effective counseling guidance to help a troubled congregant;

Wadjet Power: opening ourselves to the serpentine energies; (In Egyptian mythology Wadjet is the great cobra serpent [kundalini] that opens our chakras and purifies us. She is one of the oldest of the Egyptian goddesses and sister of Nekhbet-Mother-Mut, the most revered of the Egyptian gods.);

Wahdat al-Wujud: God is the ground of all being; (Wahdat al-Wujud is a major Sufi concept that means the 'unity of existence.');

Wait Lifting: a prosperity consciousness;

Wait on the Lord: entraining our human stature to come into alignment with our Christ Stature;

Waiting Room(s): the space between thoughts; (See Bereitschafts Potential);

Wakan-Tanka: the Native American Great Spirit translated as "all that is holy." The Wankan Tanka has always existed and not only created the universe but is the universe);

Waking Consciousness: our ordinary consciousness when we perceive the physical world; (In *Mind Before Matter*, Seyyed Hossein Nasr asserts that "when we turn to the sacred scriptures of various religions, we discover that in every case the origin of the cosmos and of humankind is identified as a Reality which is conscious and constitutes consciousness understood on the highest level as Absolute Consciousness, which is transcendent and yet the Source of all consciousness in the cosmic realm including ours.");

Walhalla: paradise for slain warriors; super-conscious pool (heaven) for spiritual thoughts that have been sacrificed when they fell victim to strongly entrenched materialistic thoughts and addictions;

Walkie Talkie(s): the inner dialogue we have between our human self and our Christ Self);

Walking the Plank: our decision to plunge into another reincarnation and/or incarnation;

Walking on Water: rising above the negative emotions associated with our human experience;

Walls: limitations in awareness; rigid beliefs and biases; spiritual myopia;

Wampum: beads made from shells; money-making ideas;

Wand: spinal cord; involution and evolution; masculine energy;

Wanderjahric Exploits: our intuitive decision to sequester ourselves from our normal routines in order to engage in deep thought, travel, and the search for novelty as we seek to deepen our self-definition; (*Wanderjahr* is a German term for 'year of wandering.');

War(s), Battle(s): the inner conflict between spiritual thoughts and grossly material thoughts; the collision between our professed beliefs and our actions;

Warden-like: our bossy, militaristic, authoritarian ego;

Warm Boot: sharing highly esoteric information with someone who was once familiar with the content, but sees the current conversation as a welcome reminder; (See Cold Boot, Hard Boot);

Washing Machine(s): cleaning our soiled perspectives so we can brighten them;

Washing of the Feet: clarifying our understanding of sacred literature and spiritual teachings;

Washing of the Hands: symbolizes the purity of conscience and intentions as we prepare to do the work that is ours to do;

Wasp-ness: our impulse toward becoming angry and upset; *being stung by a wasp* denotes suffering the consequences of our volatile nature;

Waste: error thoughts, words, and actions and their anti-Christed consequences;

Wasteland: a consciousness filled with highly materialistic thoughts that spring from a ruling illusion that denies our innate divinity;

Water: the conscious mind that changes and varies at the next stimulus which presents itself; thoughts and emotions that conform to the external world; cleansing ordinary thoughts and soothing customary emotions; refreshment; spiritual life force; formless thoughts; femininity; space; adaptability; fluidity;

Waterboarding: pushing dogma and false teachings down people's throats;

Waterfall(s): renewal; revitalization; the descent of Spirit into matter;

Water Footprint: the ability to control our emotions (water); (In conservation of resources language, the amount of fresh water used in the production or supply of goods and services used by people or groups such as supermarkets, carwashes, and landscapers);

Water Lily-like: developing spiritually from our ordinary awareness to our elevated Christed awareness; peaceful;

Waterlogged: being in a highly negative emotional state for a long time;

Water Poverty: being cognitively superior and emotionally challenged; leading from the head and not from the heart; (In ecological circles, water poverty is the condition of not having access to, or sufficient quality of, water to meet our basic needs);

Water Turning Into Blood: spirit descending into matter by incarnating in a physical container as us (turning water into blood); (See Red Sea);

Wato: the meditational practice of mentally positing an unanswerable question, continually, without any intention of engaging the intellect, and while maintaining a sincere interest in answering the question. (Meditation works in two ways, by taking away and reducing damage that can occur from anger, stress, depression and anxiety, but also by promoting happiness, joy, compassion and other forms of positive emotions. Recent research by Californian university UCLA has added to existing evidence that shows meditation over a number of years thickens the brain and strengthens the connections between brain cells);

Wax Museum: the attachment to old concepts, beliefs, and values;

Way of the Fool: materialism;

Wazifaian Aptitude: concentrating on certain divine attributes and/or qualities in order to more effectively express those qualities in our daily lives; (*Wazifa* is the Sufi practice of reciting and meditating on some or all of the 99 names of Allah);

Weapon(s): defense mechanisms; excuses and rationalizations; beliefs;

Weapons of Mass Corruption: divinity-denying thoughts, beliefs, and actions; (See Weapons);

Weather Vane: flexibility; unpredictability; going with the flow;

Web Glow: represents the radiance (glow) that comes over us when we pray and/or meditate; (In social media terms, it's what happens when we look better in online photos that we do in person);

Webinar: belief in instantaneous global learning;

Webisode(s): represent original visualizations turned into guided visualizations for the benefit of others; (In IT parlance, webisodes are original TV episodes converted for online viewing);

Weeds: negative thoughts and actions; intrusiveness;

Weeping Statues: denote our pining for our reunion with Spirit; (Statues all over the world that inexplicably – and literally - weep tears and/or blood;

Weeping Virgin: a loving thought that has not coupled with a highly intuitive and wise thought;

Weight of the Choice: the fulcrum of decisions whereby we choose the spiritual over the material or the material over the spiritual;

Weikza: Burmese term for people with occult power;

Well: our Christ (Buddha, Vishnu, Allah, Krishna) Self; deep spiritual truths; *digging a well* represents preparatory creative thought; *drawing from a well* symbolizes formative thought which produces material things; *filling in a well* represents our resistance to higher truths;

Well-Bred Now*ology*: realizing that our happiness, peace of mind, and salvation are present tense attitudes and not dependent on a future perfect condition;

Well-Built Weltanschauung: a world view built on esoteric knowledge and the consistent application of that higher knowing;

Weltschmerzic Woe(s): the sense of disillusionment and discontent we feel by allowing ourselves to be the product of a worldly ego instead of the product of our Divine Nature; (*Weltschmerz* is a term coined by the German author Jean Paul Richter and denotes the kind of feeling experienced by someone who understands that physical reality can never satisfy the demands of the mind);

West: our sense-oriented consciousness;

Whales: deep sensitivity; ability to navigate the depths of our subconscious urges, patterns, and desires; despite being plunged into the emotional depths of the unknown and swallowed up by the mammoth nature of overwhelming circumstances we trust our resilience and personal power to pull us out;

Wheel, Wheel of Life, Wheel of Things, Cosmic Wheel: seeing cycles and circular movements and their relationship to us; denotes the physical world; the spokes remind us of the sun's rays and our connection to our Indwelling Sun (our Extraordinary Christ Nature); wheels also denote totality and the steady movement toward new dimensions (ceaseless cycles) of being; the axle is the 'still point' in a world of constant motion; wheels are the symbols of the world with their circumferences denoting manifestation as a whole;

Wheelbarrow(s): a collection of intentions; labor intensive work;

Wheelhouse: an area of spiritual expertise in which we feel very comfortable sharing: (In baseball lingo, the wheelhouse is the part of an batter's swinging range where he can make the best contact with the ball. If a pitch is right in the wheelhouse it is right where we want it, in the spot where we have the best chance of hitting it well.);

When Hell Freezes Over, A Cold Day in Hell: conventionally, usually denotes an event that will never happen - given that 'hell' is an very hot place and would melt the ice (It has a stubbornness tone to it); Spiritually, this metaphorical phrase represents a much repeated error perspective that assigns too much power and majesty to the concept of 'hell.' (Hell is a damnable, nefarious, diabolical state of consciousness. It is no match for the super-heated 'white heat' of truth which makes the heat of 'hell' more like an ice cube which could very well melt under the intense het of Spirit);

Whetherproof: being extremely decisive and not prone to wondering 'whether' we're going to do this or do that;

Whineology: chronic complaining; (See Negative Thinking);

Whiplash: what happens when our poor choices catch up to us;

Whirled View: an egocentric world perspective characterized by circular reasoning, twisted outlooks, convoluted frames of reference, and curved standpoints;

Whirlpool(s): emotions that send us into a spiral; depression and melancholy; (According to positive psychologists, we can beat depression when we: recognize automatic thoughts and negative dialogue at the times when we feel defeated; dispute automatic negative thoughts by marshaling contrary evidence; come up with different, more objective, explanations of what has happened to us; distract ourselves from depressing thoughts; and recognize and question the depression-sowing assumptions governing so much of what we do); (In *For Your Own Good*, Alice Miller says that "depression is the result of being separated from our true self." pg. 108);

Whirlwind: the motion (force) of the Holy Spirit;

White Hair: the wisdom that comes from mature and introspective aging;

White Light Technique: mentally surrounding ourselves, those we love, our property, and things we care about with an orb of white light for protection; (Parapsychologist William Braud demonstrated that it is possible to block or prevent any outside influences we do not want. He calls the process 'psychological shielding.' In his experiment, he instructed subjects to visualize a protective shield or screen around them which would prevent 'influences' from raising their EDA levels. A second group was told not to try to block outside 'influences.' "Influencers" were not aware of who was shielding/blocking their attempts and who wasn't. The findings showed that the "shielded" group showed considerably fewer physical effects than the "unprotected" group); (See Psychological Shielding);

White-ness: denotes illumination and high-level knowing (wisdom), purity, perfection, expansive thinking; having a sense of peace and purposefulness; being protected by our identification with the Eternal Presence; (See the White Light Technique); reverence; humility;

White Rainment, White Robe: divine wisdom and incarnational purity;

White Stone: our new, pure, psychological nature (self) that is established when we have mastered our egocentric nature by becoming more spiritual; (Alba Petra was the sign of initiation mentioned in the *Book of Revelation*. The word *prize* was engraved on it, and it symbolized the word given to neophytes who successfully passed all the trials in the mysteries. It is the potent white cornelian of the Rosicrucians, who borrowed it from the Gnostics. 'To him that over-cometh will I give to eat of the *hidden* manna (occult knowledge which descends as *divine wisdom* from heaven), and will give him a *white stone*, and in the stone a new name written (the 'mystery name' of the inner man or the EGO of the new Initiate), which no man knoweth saving him that receiveth it." (*Revelation*, ii. 17.);

Whodunnit-itis: the frame of mind we put ourselves in when we attempt to sidestep our own cupability for our error-prone thoughts and behavior by implying that there must have been an outside influence that caused our deviant behavior and not us;

Widow, Widower: half of something; (Widowhood is love without commitment, intellect without intuition, head without heart, ambition without wisdom, knowledge without faith, literal Bible translation without spiritual interpretation);

~ *Spiritually Speaking* ~

Widow's Son: (The title applies to Hiram Abiff [the widow's son], who was a worker in brass, not the architect of Solomon's Temple. He made the brass pillars, the brass lavers, shovels and basins of Solomon's Temple. In the first Book of King she is said to have been 'a widow's son of the tribe of Naphtali.' Freemasons call themselves widow's sons. He was the central character in the building of the Temple and one of three leading characters along with King Solomon and Hiram, King of Tyre. Hiram Abiff was the only one on Earth who knew 'the secrets of a Master Mason,' including the most important secret of all, the 'Grand Masonic Word,' the name of God (the 'ineffable name). Since, in occult lore, knowing the name of a spirit is a key to having its power, there was a very great power in knowing the word.);

Wife: the intuitive, wise, nurturing half of intellect (husband);

Wild Boar(s): spiritual authority; a *white wild boar* represents an entire cycle of manifestation; (In antiquity the boar represented the constellation known as the Great Bear, Ursa Major);

Wilderness: a perplexed and/or puzzled state of awareness; an unenlightened perspective;

Wilderness Wooziness: the condition we find ourselves in when we allow our sense appetites to form permanent outposts in our mind;

Wildflowers: individuality; independence; freedom;

Willow-ness: developing our psychic abilities; attaining superior intuition; achieving incredible flexibility and adaptability;

Willow Sunday: is another name for Palm Sunday;

Will to Believe: having more willpower than won't power when it comes to holding onto our spiritual and/or religious beliefs;

Willy-Nilly Infidelity: our mindless tendency to slip in and out of having positive, optimistic, spiritual thoughts;

Wimpy White Lie: telling a trivial half-truth as a way to get someone excited about joining a particular faith tradition; itsy-bitsy misdirections; acting like we believe in a more traditional faith practice in order to be respectful, conforming, or kind;

Wind: disturbed emotions, strong emotions; a *breeze* represents heightened emotions; a *rushing mighty wind* represents the fiery energies of the Holy Spirit;

Wind Chimes: harmony; peace; tranquility;

Wind Mill(s): transformation; spiritual unfoldment;

Window Dressing: mainstream religious sermons that lack doctrinal and metaphysical depth;

Window of Convenience: we all have a 'soul choice' moment where we decide to enter a skin school experience and/or exit a skin school experience; (In airline industry terms, a window of convenience refers to a traveler's ideal departure or arrival time – plus or minus a couple of hours. ☺);

Wine: spiritual wisdom and advanced knowledge; superior comprehension;

Winged Globe: an idea divinely ordered; a human personality transitioning toward its Christedness; a soul being lifted by Spirit; humankind experiencing the Third Coming; bitterness morphing into forgiveness; coma consciousness being raised to Christ Consciousness; selfishness amped-up to generosity; the soaring power of the human spirit; the world egg;

Wings: freedom from material limitations; grander perspective;

Winter: denotes the birth of our awareness that the Christ Presence is expressing Itself as us, that our Core Essence is divine;

Wintering: hibernating from our spiritual practice by pursuing material appetites and addictions;

Wireless Network: our brain's neural pathways; from a quantum physics perspective is called non-locality;

***Wirklichkeitic* Perspective:** being in touch with reality instead of illusion; (*Wirklichkeitic* is the German term for reality); [In *The Demon-Haunted World: Science as a Candle in the Dark*, Carl Sagan asserts that "Science is not only compatible with spirituality; it is a profound source of spirituality. When we recognize our place in an immensity of light-years and in the passage of ages, when we grasp the intricacy, beauty, and subtlety of life, then that soaring feeling, that sense of elation and humility combined, is surely spiritual. So are our emotions in the presence of great art or music or literature, or acts of exemplary selfless courage such as those of Mohandas Gandhi or Martin Luther King, Jr. The notion that science and spirituality are somehow mutually exclusive does a disservice to both");

Wisdom: logic in a hurry;

Wisdom Teeth: superior comprehension and deep understanding; uncommon sense; the power of discernment and sound judgment;

Wishcraft: wanting or hoping something to become true instead of knowing it is true in spirit;

Wishy-Washy Outreach: making outrageous claims and insincere promises to entice prospects to attend church services;

Wisteria-like: attaining immortality; achieving longevity, endurance and staying power; mastering patient waiting;

Witsun-Day (Pfingsten): the fiftieth day after Easter;

Witz Work: the desire to enter a high state of consciousness through disciplined meditation for the first time; (Witz is the first mountain in the Mayan creation story);

Wizard-like: our idiosyncratic tendency to pursue highly esoteric concepts and ideas that take us to the limits of human thought;

Wizard of Oz: our Christ Nature; (See Christ; God);

Wobbegong(s): emotions that are hidden under a façade of calmness, but can erupt later; (In Aboriginal Australian terms, wobbegongs are docile carpet sharks unless they are provoked)

Woebegone Parachute: the first moment we realize that we are the Christ expressing at the point of us which results in our catching our 'Fall' so we can begin our flight back home, but at the same time comes with the realization that we have chosen another unnecessary reincarnation;

Wolf: speaking eloquence; superior intellect; cunning; consummate esoteric knowledge;

Womb: reproductive principle; motherhood; moon energy; container of the seeds of life; the Holy Grail;

Women: emotions; intuition; intuitive wisdom; maternal tendencies; feminine propensities;

Wooden Vizor: represents the mindless rigidity that unyieldingly defends certain conventional religious teachings by refusing to allow an enlightened perspective to 'shine its light' on a darkened face;

Woodpecker-ness: being able to open doors no one else sees; attaining hardiness; hammering out solutions; insuring safety and security; being known for our sturdiness and resilience;

Wood Pile: preparation; diligence; thinking ahead; labor; anticipatory warmth;

Word of God: Word, or *Logos* is the potentializing aspect of God; the Christ; the cosmic beingness which underwrites all manifestation; the Eternal Isness which forms Itself into light, sound, vibration, and energy; the manifested Absolute in the world of form; the entire manifested and unmanifested universe(s); (In *The Coming of the Cosmic Christ*, Matthew Fox quotes Meister Eckhart: "If every creature is a word of God, then the suffering of every creature is the suffering of the word of God);

Work: Some human souls experience a cacophony of jobs and occupations. Others graft themselves onto one line of work. Both routes are spiritual practices. Growth comes when there is congruence between who we are and what we do for a living. For some, work itself becomes a sort of morphine. For many, the asphyxia of suffocating work strangles their creativity and steals their health and happiness. Both routes mirror our spiritual unfoldment. Both hint at our alignment with Spirit. However, our chief occupation is burning off the dross of error and becoming consciously one with our Christ Nature;

Workshop Coosie: a spiritual teacher who 'cooks up' and then 'serves up' a menu of spiritual teachings to fill a student's higher consciousness pallet; (In cowboy terminology, a coosie is literally a cook which is an Americanization of the Spanish word for cook, cocinero.);

World: our Adamic (sense) consciousness; our collective, sense-addicted, whirled consciousness spun on the axis of our imaginations;

World Axis: the spinal cord, the plumb line of enlightenment; a spear; an obelisk;

World Egg, Golden Embryo, Center of the World, Brahmanda, Kernal of Immortality, Seed of Being: the entire manifested universe; the Multiverse that births universes; our consciousness which births thoughts; (The World Egg represents not so much the manifested cosmos, but the potentiality of a cosmos in the making.);

Worldliness: habitually choosing mammon over manna;

World Pain: the consequences caused by our collective coma consciousness: (See Coma Consciousness);

World Peace: our individual and collective consciousness harmoniously at rest; (My hope is that the horrors of war, and hunger, and disease will be replaced by the sounds of laughter, and the warmth of handshakes and hugs, and the reciprocity of goodwill. That will happen when the 'world' (our human consciousness) finds the peace (conscious alignment with the Christ Presence within) which passes all misunderstanding).

World Soul: humankind's collective personality (egocentric consciousness);

World Tree: The World Tree is a collective, analogous symbol common to many of the world's mythologies and religions. It is described as the buffer [our waking consciousness] having thick, tough roots that reach down into the dark, shadowy, deep recesses of the earth into the belly [subconscious regions] of the underworld. Its branches reach robustly into the skies (our super-conscious] so that it is ultimately a tree of union connecting the three worlds [states of consciousness]. It is an anchor, grounding us with its roots.); (Buddhism tells of Sakyamuni's birth and a flash of light that traveled around the world that sparked the first growth of the Tree of Perfection [World Tree] – a sacred Fig Tree that it is believed to have been 400 feet high and bloomed with flowers and fruit that glowed. It is said that the Buddha was born, received his enlightenment, preached his first truth talk, and died all under the Bo Tree [Bodhi Tree]); (Christianity and Judaism have their Tree of Life – see the Tree of the Knowledge of Good and Error and the Tree of Life. In Norse mythology Yaggdrasil is the holy Ash World Tree surrounded by nine worlds – see Yaggdrasil World tree. It is said to connect the Underworld [our repressed subconscious patterns] to Heaven with its branches and roots. The Egyptian Holy Sycamore stands on the threshold of life and death. The *Arbor Philsophica* is another tree that is said to bear alchemical symbols representing seven planets and the processes of alchemy. Other world trees include the Oak Tree in Finnish and Slavic mythology, the Irminsul Tree [Yggdrasil] in Germanic and Norse mythology, the Ashvattha Fig Tree in Hindu mythology, the Vilagfa Tree in Hungarian mythology, the Ceiba Tree in Mayan mythology, the Izapa Stela 5 identifies a world tree in Mesoamericam mythology, the Kalpavriksha Tree in Southern Asian mythology, the Haoma Tree in the Avestic tradition, and the Agac Ana Tree in Turkic mythology, to name a few.);

Worried Well: our proclivity for being perfectly well but worrying about getting sick; concern about displeasing an anthropomorphic god 'out there' who can send us to hell in a hand basket;

Worryologist, Worrywart: negativity hypochondriacs who worry about everything; worrywarts have a Ph.D. in worryology; (If worrywarts find themselves in an uncharacteristic moment when they don't have anything to worry about, they worry about the fact that they aren't worrying. The word 'worry' comes from an Anglo-Saxon word which means to *strangle or to choke*. The Greek word for worry in the *New Testament* means 'to divide, rip, or tear apart.' Worry, it seems, 'chokes' the joy out of life. It rips and tears at the fabric of living full out);

Worshipping the Fire: turning our pious attention on our inner Christ Light (Buddha Light, Krishna Light, etc.);

Wounded Convictions: valuing creature comforts over soul fulfillment; settling for suffocating jobs, lingering health problems, disintegrating relationships, self-nullifying habits, and paralyzing addictions;

Written Covenant: sacred affidavit;

Wu-Chang: the five principle virtues of Confucianism: empathy, propriety, rights and customs, wisdom, and trust;

Wusband(s): past thoughts (wusbands, men, grooms, male energy) that are no longer used or referred to; (In social media, wusbands are ex-husbands);

Wu-Wei Essence: seeing non-activity as the essential nature of the Tao;

Xanthippean Spirit: our tendency to launch into an argumentative, nagging disposition; difficulty in aligning our human self with our Divine Nature; (*Xanthippe* was the nagging wife of Socrates and mother of their three sons);

Xebec Uppitiness: the tendency to judge people solely on outer appearances; our proneness to interpret scripture at face value instead of looking a little deeper at a passage's esoteric implications;

Xeno-Christed Consciousness: anti-Christed thoughts and intentions;

Xenoglossy: being able to speak and/or write in a language never learned before and one that is totally foreign to the speaker;

Xenography: writing in languages unknown to the writer;

Xenomancy: divining that interprets the past, present, and future by studying the appearance and actions of the first stranger who appears;

Xenophanic Play: our natural capacity for satire and witticisms;

Xibalbaian Patterns: subconsciousness patterns and life scripts; (Mayan term for the underworld);

X-ing: being the best Christ we can be; ('X' comes from the Greek letter Chi, which is the first letter of the Greek word *Χριστός* which in English means 'Christ.' There are references to 'Xp' and 'Xt' as far back as 1021 CE in the Anglo-Saxon Chronicle. And the terms 'Xtian' and 'Xpian' have been used for 'Christian' as early as the 1500's, with 'Xtianity' for 'Christianity' as early as 1634.);

Xisuthrus Tendency: refraining from the errors of our youth by disciplining ourselves to follow the inner guidance of our divine nature so we can establish a higher state of awareness (Google the Chaldean Xisuthrus and Jewish Noah flood stories);

Xochipilling: seeing the value in using flowers, music, singing, poetry, and dance as part of the architecture for spiritual growth; (*Xochipilli* was the god of art, games, beauty, dance, flowers, and song in Aztec mythology.);

Xochitlic Chakra: a chakra that is opening (flowering) to send its serpentine energies upward through the spinal column; (Xochitl is an Aztec word meaning 'water flower.');

Xolochauic Dilemma: being 'deformed' (compromised) by our misdeeds; (In Aztec mythology, xolochaui means 'to wrinkle or double over.');

Xoxo Embrace: a hugs and kisses greeting and/or parting to show friendship and camaraderie;

X-Ray: a high degree of inner clarity; inner vision; superior discernment;

X-Syncing: aligning our human self with our Christ Self; (See X-ing);

Xuan Weirdness: a sterile dogmatic thought (eunuch) that cuts off any chance of allowing a spiritual interpretation being drawn from it for further discussion; (Xuan is a god in Chinese mythology);

Xylolic Emotions: volatile, erratic emotional outbursts characterized by their fickleness and frivolity; (xylol is a colorless flammable volatile liquid hydrocarbon used as a solvent);

Xylomancy : divining by observing the position of twigs lying on the ground;

Xylyly Quackery: signifies our penchant for believing in false doctrines (molten calves) and making them part of our religious practices and prejudices;

Xystical Veering: represents our catching ourselves being overcome by materiality and then side-stepping our downward spiral so that we are not consumed by the fruits of materiality;

Xystus-like Genealogy, Sixtus-like Genealogy: being well-born, well-bred, and by implication, we are well-born in our spiritual genealogy since we all come from the same Source;

Y2K: the absolutely misunderstood, highly speculative, grossly over-exaggerated external cyber event referred to as a sort of Armageddon-like happening that never occurred; (See Armageddon); our penchant for believing in catastrophe;

Yacht(s): our inclination toward wealth, luxury, and pleasurable experiences;

Yagouaroundic Temperament: our disposition to be gregariously reclusive and shy when our religious beliefs are different from mainstream religious beliefs; (Yagouaroundis are small, shy, reclusive cats native to Central and South America, coastal Mexico, and southern Texas);

Yahoo, Google: cyber juggernauts; electronic Akashic Records;

Yajdic Bliss: through contemplative meditative practice finding spiritual ecstasy and oneness in God realization;

Yakin and Boaz: a Kabbalistic and Masonic symbol that denotes the two pillars of bronze (Yakin, male and white; Boaz, female and red), cast by Hiram Abif of Tyre; Yakin represents wisdom and Boaz, intelligence;

Yakity Yakitis: the obnoxious, nonstop diatribes of pushy proselytizers intent on selling their brand of religious practice;

Yakootic Itches: migratory habits that stem from our wanting to experience different faith traditions, causing us to wander from one religious organization to another; (Yakoots refers to a nomadic Mongolian tribe native to Southern Siberia);

Yakshan Thoughts: demonic thoughts and inclinations;

Yamaboosheean Thoughts: highly mystical and intuitive insights; superb healing thoughts; (*Yamabooshee* are a sect in Japan of very ancient and revered mystics);

Yama Volition: self-control and self-restraint based on an internal locus of control;

Yang: masculinity; that which is invisible;

Yaqian Cosmology: the belief in five separate worlds: the desert wilderness world, the mystical world, the flower world, the dream world, and the night world. Much of the spiritual work is centered upon perfecting these worlds and eliminating the harm that has been done to them, especially by people;

Yard Sale: recycling past wants and needs; recirculating and downsizing material whims;

Yardstick: feeling a need to gauge our progress; an inclination to measure up;

Yatobyoic Susceptibility: impure, diseased, filthy thoughts and/or inclinations that infect our consciousness and contribute to our complete disregard for anything spiritual; (*Yatobyo* is a highly infectious disease of rodents [especially rabbits and squirrels] that can be transmitted to humans by ticks or flies);

Yatus Inclinations: base instincts and passions; (Yatus or Yatudhanas is a Sanskrit term for a kind of spirit corresponding to the Greek daimon);

Yawnogenic Sermons: boring Sunday sermons that lack substance and credibility;

Yearbook: taking a retrospective glance at our youth; reflecting on the basic truth principles that have gotten us where we are;

Yeasty Fallout: experiencing an uneasy restless energy whenever we intentionally violate spiritual and/or moral principles;

Yeheedahic Union: the total alignment of our higher (Christ, Buddhic, Krishnic) and lower (human ego) selves; (In the Kabbalah, *yeheedah* means oneness); (In *Women and the Mystical Experience in the Middle Ages*, F. Beer quotes Julian of Norwich: "I saw a great oneing between Christ and us.");

Yeksuic Focus: disciplined concentration;

Yellow-ness: denotes our intellectual, deductive, and analytical prowess; concerning ourselves with validating knowledge; thinking in terms of a linear sequence; having a strong self-sense that is in partnership with the personal ego; idealism; intellect; imagination; philosophy; (Yellow is the color of the Solar Plexus Chakra);

Yellular Sermon: a minister raising the decibel level of h/her sermon to a prolonged shouting pitch;

Yeserdoodling: the mindless parroting of a religious leader's tenets without investigating their legitimacy, truthfulness, or reliability;

Yesterday: the present's recoil;

Yeuic Beingness: substance giving substance to itself; (In Chinese mysticism, yeu means the primordial substance of the universe from which all proceeds as a fountain or source, and into which all will ultimately return when the great cosmic world period or *manvantara* reaches its end);

Yeukish Inebriation: our enthusiastic itchiness to explore higher truths once we've been intrigued by the depth of knowledge we're being exposed to; (Yeuk is a middle English word for itch);

Yew-like: enjoying uncanny longevity; being able to divine guidance; having power and strength; employing deceptive qualities;

Yezdegerdian Thoughts: anti-Christian sentiments;

Yezidic Beliefs: our eclectic proclivity to integrate the best practices of Christianity, Gnosticism, Zoroastrianism, Islam, and Judaism into our religious world view; (From Arabic roots, its meaning is 'he will increase');

Yggdrasil, World Tree: the Tree of the Multiverse; (On Earth, it represents the human body and its eventual wearing out as a physical form. In other dimensions it represents whatever physical and/or ethereal forms we inhabit);

Yin: femininity; visibility;

Ylemic Outpicturing: our ability to expand the essence and substance of our thoughts once we 'give birth' to a primordial idea; (In quantum physics, ylem refers to the primordial matter of the universe, originally conceived as composed of neutrons at high temperature and density.);

Ymir: the cosmic monster (dark matter) becoming matter in the form of worlds; quantum waves becoming particles (creating matter); (In Norse mythology, the primeval giant slain by Odin and his brothers and from whose body they created the world: the sea from his blood, the earth from his flesh, the mountains from his bones; and the sky from his skull);

Yogacharya: a mystical school; our super-consciousness; mastering ecstatic meditation; (*Yogacharya* is a Sanskrit term for a mystical school);

Yoga Initiative: attaining conscious union with our innate divinity using the physical body as the 'tuning fork'; neuro-musculoskeletal massage;

Yogibogeybox: not withstanding the tools spiritualists use in their trade, yogibogeyboxes are metaphors for *us* – our talents, skills, abilities, and knowledge that determine the quality of our spiritual path;

Yogis, priests, priestesses, shamans, lamas, popes, ministers, cardinals, rabbis, imams, gurus, monks, mullahs, nuns, curates, bishops, chaplains, clerics, etc.: higher religious thoughts, tendencies, and inclinations; pious, saintly, ecclesiastical thinking;

Yoke: The more we discipline ourselves to follow Truth principles (take up the yoke), the more freedom from error and from the consequences of error we will have in actualizing our good; responsibility; sacrifice; the burden of our human incarnation;

Yong-Grub: the state of absolute rest (Paranirvanic freedom); (In Tibetan mysticism, yong-grub means nirvana, or in its largest sense the still more sublime condition of paranirvana);

Yonic Receptivity: the feminine principle; womb; universal receptacle;

You*ology*: proudly wearing our narcissism; living from an 'all about me' philosophy;

Yourodevoy Yoke: the propensity for using only worldly thoughts to interpret reality instead of amplifying those sensory perceptions with higher, more spiritually-oriented insights; suffering from mental deficiencies like racism, sexism, same sex prejudice, unforgiveness, religious intolerance, bigotry, etc.; (*Yourodevoy* is Russian for a person who suffers from mental deficiencies);

YouTube(s): examples of remote viewing; putting our spiritual beliefs on display for others to see; acting a491-iving our Truth;

Yoyo-ness: creatively playing with spiritual insights and perspectives to see how they resonate with the ups and downs of our current world view;

Ystextlic: our susceptibility for misquoting scripture; (In tech parlance, the tendency to have difficulty texting);

Yttrium Dusting: used metaphorically, suggests flammability, ignitability, incendiariness; (*Yttrium* is a chemical element with symbol Y and atomic number 39. It is a silvery-metallic transition metal chemically similar to the lanthanides);

Yuanfenic Alignment: entraining our human self with our divine nature: (Yuanfen is a Chinese term that means a binding force or relational bond, usually between lovers and friends);

Yunx Perspective: the ability to obtain a 360° perspective on a religious issue; (Yunx are birds that are able to turn their heads almost 360 degrees. When disturbed at the nest, they use snake-like head twisting and hissing as a threat display.);

Y'war' Reticence: wariness of lunatic fringe religious doctrines;

Zabernistic Heckling: parochial religious bullying that shows absolute distain and disrespect for the beliefs and values of faith traditions outside of religious fundamentalism; (A German term that originated from an incident in 1913 involving an overzealous soldier who wounded a cobbler for laughing at him, ultimately triggering the army's take-over of the town from local authorities.);

Zadkielic Orientation: right-thinking; righteousness; (Zadkiel is believed to be the name of the angel who stayed Abraham's hand to keep him from sacrificing his son on the altar);

Zammarran Tendencies: timid, sheepish, thoughts;

Zampun: the sacredness; (The Tibetan mystical tree of life);

~ *Spiritually Speaking* ~

Zamzummim Action: meditation; the act of pondering and/or reflecting on something expansive and huge; astute planning; (In Hebrew terms, zamzummims were giants);

Zandaqahic Beliefs: heretical beliefs; unconventional religious beliefs; (In Islam, holding religious views contradictory to the teachings of Islam.);

Zantay Zap: making esoteric truths understandable; bringing spiritual truths 'down to earth'; sharing esoteric truths exoterically;

Zany Zingers: the frustration we feel when we're about to make ends meet and then someone or something moves the ends;

Zappy Televangelizing: entertaining religious burlesque that borders on blasphemy;

Zazen: Zen meditation;

Zazzy Zanyism: stylish ecclesiastical buffoonery; lively sanctimonious horseplay;

Zealous Faithfulness: never yielding to the growl of a dog, the tears of a crocodile, the cravings of a vulture, or the howling of a hyena;

Zebra-like Qualities: experiencing the cosmic life force; having considerable mental power; being able to balance esoteric (white) and common everyday (black) knowledge;

Zeitgeist, die: the spirit of an age; the thinking characteristic of the thought leaders of an age; our current state of consciousness (age) characterized by its material thoughts and/or spiritually-attuned thinking;

Yellow Brick Road: our spinal column that is the royal pathway (golden route) to enlightenment; (The yellow brick road is introduced in *The Wonderful Wizard of Oz* by L. Frank Baum as a guideline for Dorothy to follow. It leads to the Emerald City [Christ Consciousness] where the Wizard [our Higher Self] is. Baum's novel also mentions a red brick road which is the sister road to the yellow brick road, and leads south to the Country of the Quadlings [the world of sensory experience, our skin school experience]; (See Street of Gold);

Zelophobic Sermons: irrational Sunday talks designed to frighten congregants into believing in a jealous God;

~ *Spiritually Speaking* ~

Zen: a school of Mahayana Buddhism that emphasizes the attainment of enlightenment using meditation and superior intuition as the chief higher consciousness routes;

Zendikian Maxims: heretical religious platitudes meant to mislead, frighten, and confuse faithful followers; (A zendikian is an atheist or unbeliever);

Zenful: being well-practiced in Zen techniques;

Zenzizenzizenzic Proportions: symbolizes the human genome of over 3 billion base pairs taken to its eighth power of magical probabilities, denoting the universality of humankind's physical expressions of Spirit;

Zero: nothing and everything; the marriage of the infinitesimal and the infinitely endless; veiled neutrality;

Zero Day Exploit, Day Zero: the belief in and proselytizing of original sin by religious fundamentalists who tell us we were born as sinners *after* we get here; (In IT language, a zero day exploit is a malicious computer attack that takes advantage of a security breach before the breach is known. In other words a software developer has zero days to prepare for the breach);

Zeroing: crossing out all error; (See Crucifixion);

Zero Point Field: Christ Consciousness at the speed of light (the vast, limitless, quantum sea of energy which connects everything in the universe with everything else in the universe and beyond. The Zero Point Field, or vacuum, or void, or *ether* are all quantum synonyms for the spatial dimension of Cosmic Consciousness. They are merely effects. Cosmic Consciousness is the inviolate mechanism that guarantees the orderly beingness that permeates and connects everything. It is the 'hum' of the activity of God Mind.); (The concept of the Zero-Point Field was developed in by Albert Einstein and Otto Stern in 1913, using a formula developed by Max Planck in 1900. The term *Zero-Point Energy* (now called Zero Point Field) originates from the German concept *Nullpunktsenergie,* which means 'vacuum energy.' Zero-point energy is the lowest possible energy that any quantum mechanical physical system can have. It is the energy of its ground state. All quantum mechanical systems undergo fluctuations even in their ground state. The Zero Point Field (ZPF) is an ocean of cosmic vibrations in the space between things. It is referred to by many physicists as the 'vacuum' because all matter is thought to be removed so there is nothing left to, well, remove. The 'Field' is called 'zero' because fluctuations in the field are detectable at temperatures of absolute zero (believed to be the lowest possible energy state). It is the energy present in the emptiest state of space at the lowest conceivable energy state, which is believed to be the closest that subatomic motion ever gets to absolute zero. According to Zero Point Field theorists, our universe is underwritten by a vast, limitless, quantum sea of energy, which may connect everything in the universe with everything else in the universe. It has been calculated that the total energy of the 'Field' exceeds all energy in matter by a factor of 10^{40}, or 1 followed by 40 zeros.);

Zervana Akarna: the Ain Soph of the Zoroastrians; (See Eyn Soph); (The Pali notion of the boundless or limitlessness of the One Universal Abstract Space out of which emanates Ahura Mazda, the eternal Light);

Zhen Jiu, Needle Fire, Moxibustion: acupuncture;

Zicu: primordial matter; universal spirit-substance;

Ziggurats: ascension into a higher state of being (consciousness) and anticipating the favor of the Eternal Presence; (See Skyscrapers and Towers);

Zigsaw Puzzle(s), (alternate name for Jigsaw Puzzle): our intellectual, rational penchant for wanting to contribute to and see the big picture;

Zigzagginess: our tendency to run back and forth, from side-to-side, up and down, and around in circles in pursuit of worldly appetites;

Zikric Devotion: maintaining a sacred awareness of our relationship with God by using devotional acts like the repetition of divine names, supplications, and aphorisms; (In Arabic means remembrance of God);

Zingaro-like Curiosity: gypsy-like wandering from one faith tradition to another in order to find a spiritual home; (In Greek, *zingaros* were gypsies);

Zinnia-like: our capacity for laughter and joyfulness;

Zip Code(s): esoterically, represents our states of consciousness (subconscious, waking conscious, super-conscious, altered state of consciousness);

Zip Line: an accelerated stream of confidence;

Ziploc Bag(s): imply stored energy;

Ziraleet Elucidation: expressing joy; (Arabic for expressing joy among women);

Zivug Coupling: the conscious integration of our human self with our divine nature; (In Kabbalistic terms, *zivug* means coupling and is an idiom for marital relations);

Znaharka Discernment: feminine intuition; wisdom of the heart;

Zodiac: soul resume;

Zohak: a three-headed serpent which personifies our satanic, divinity-denying thinking;

Zohar: the seminal work of the Kabbalah, written by Rabbi Shimon bar Yochai (2nd century) and his students. It is one of the basic texts of the oral Torah and Kabbalah;

Zoinks Response: expressing fear, panic or trepidation at referring to ourselves as the human expression of the Christ; (The word zoinks originated from the cartoon character Shaggy on the TV show Scooby Doo when he was frightened or scared);

Zoism: believing life originates from a singular vital cosmic principle;

Zombie(s): regurgitated, hollow, soulless, lifeless materialistic thoughts;

Zone of Proximal Development: the spectrum of a truth seeker's current esoteric understanding (when seeking truths independently) and h/her potential abilities that can be actualized under the guidance of a guru and/or gurus;

Zone Therapy, Reflexology: a health practice, invented by William Fitzgerald, that is based on the belief that every organ in our body is connected to a different spot on the bottom of our feet, the roof of our mouth, and our hands; (See Reflexology);

Zoo-like: cultivating an egocentric perspective; succumbing to old, caged-up subconscious patterns and perspectives;

Zooform: (See Cryptozoology);

Zoolatry: being stuck in our base instincts;

~ Spiritually Speaking ~

Zoomancy: divining that interprets the movements of animals;

Zoosemiotician Awareness: being able to study the behaviors, and interpret animal signs that are not communicative in the traditional sense, such as camouflage, spiritual tendencies, courtship behavior, mimicry, etc.;

Zooty Materialism: flashiness; a consciousness of bling and extravagance;

Zorinology: the tendency to employ "stinking thinking" in our relationships with others; (Zorino is a euphemism for skunk fur);

Zsa Zsa Zsu Teaching: a spiritual teaching that strikes you as such a phenomenal teaching that you want to adopt it immediately to enhance your life and well-being; (Zsa Zsa Zsu is a term that comes from the TV show Sex and the City and it refers to the feeling you get when you meet someone that you like immediately and want to be around all of the time);

Ztrqlouyszxkqdpldbbg: this describes what happens when you say something you wish you hadn't said and wish you could take the words back;

Zugzwang Footing: putting ourselves at a disadvantage because our previous choices have put us in a position to do something we'd prefer not to do; (Zugzwang is a chess term for chess blockade);

Zwischenzuging: the impulse to think, say, or do something to buy more time to get out of the mess we're in so we can contemplate our next move; (Zwischenzug is a chess move made to play for more time);

Zynga'd Outlook: a religious and/or spiritual world view that is completely off the mark, hopelessly lunatic fringe, and so far out that it will be difficult to reel the zynga'd believer back from oblivion;

Zyzzyvas Philosophy: the belief in surrendering to inevitable change; not underestimating the strength in numbers; (A zyzzyva is a yellowish South American weevil);

* * * * * * * *

About the Authors

Rev. Dr. Bil Holton and Rev. Dr. Cher Holton are metaphysicians, ordained ministers, and prolific authors, who have a solid reputation for their strength of character, engaging personalities, and creative yet practical application of combining neuroscience, Positive Psychology, and neurotheology to their metaphysical teachings. Their ability to bring spiritual Truth into such clarity that people are able to walk the spiritual path with practical feet put them in high demand as teachers, speakers, and spiritual coaches.

The Holtons work with both corporate and spiritual clients, with a mission of helping people connect to the "Extraordinary You" within — in business and in life. They are co-founders of the online ministry, Your Spiritual Practice, and have an impressive list of clients around the world. Check out their Blog for lots of free articles!

On a personal note, Bil and Cher like to push the envelope and maintain their zest for life by taking what they call "Indiana Jones Adventures" such as white-water rafting, sky diving, and fire walking. American-style ballroom dancing is also in their DNA, and although they have retired their competitive dance shoes, Bil and Cher love to perform ballroom showcases and exhibitions. Their two sons, beautiful daughters-in-law, and incredible grandchildren all live nearby, and bring great joy!

To order books or invite the Holtons to speak at your organization, spiritual center, or association, contact their office through their websites:

www.TheMetaphysicalWebsite.com

www.YourSpiritualPractice.com